LONDON ASSOCIATION OF CLASSICAL TEACHERS

LACTOR 15

DIO: THE JULIO-CLAUDIANS

Selections from Books 58–63
of the *Roman History* of Cassius Dio

TRANSLATED AND
WITH HISTORICAL COMMENTARY BY
Jonathan Edmondson

DIO: THE JULIO-CLAUDIANS

First Published August 1992

© The London Association of Classical Teachers, 1992

ISBN: 0 903625 21 0

CONTENTS

C. CLAUDIUS (Book 60) A.D. 41 – 46

PREFACE

This LACTOR is something of a departure from previous volumes in the series, in that it is more ambitious in scope. Its aim is threefold: (a) to provide a new translation of selected passages from Cassius Dio's *Roman History* on the Julio–Claudian period; (b) to provide a full historical commentary on these selected passages; and (c) to help the reader evaluate critically the qualities and defects of Dio as a historical source for the Julio–Claudian period.

The two main continuous narrative sources for the Julio–Claudian period (A.D. 14 – 68) are Tacitus, *Annals* and Cassius Dio, *Roman History*, Books 57 – 63. (Suetonius' lives of Tiberius, Gaius, Claudius and Nero are less useful as narrative, since their purpose was to provide not a history of the period, but rather a mixture of political and personal details about the individual emperors.) Tacitus was writing about a hundred years before Dio and so was much closer to the events of the Julio–Claudian period. He also wrote at much greater length than Dio. As a result he is on balance a more valuable source. However, there are several gaps in all the manuscripts of Tacitus, which means that we lack crucial parts of his account of the Julio–Claudians: viz., the years A.D. 29 – 31, the entire reign of Gaius (Caligula), the first years of Claudius' reign and the final part of Nero's. As a result these years have not received the same attention from those studying the period as those for which Tacitus' narrative survives. Thus the major aim of this book is to make more widely available those parts of Dio that fill the gaps in the narrative of Tacitus, *Annals*, so that students can have in accessible form a complete coverage of the Julio–Claudian period as follows:

A. TIBERIUS	A.D. 14 – 29	Tac. *Ann.* 1.1 – 5.5
	29 – 31	Dio 58.2.7 – 58.12.8 [= selections **A.1 – A.7**]
	31 – 37	Tac. *Ann.* 6.6–50
B. GAIUS (CALIGULA)	37 – 41	Dio 59 [= selections **B.1 – B.23**]
C. CLAUDIUS	41 – 46	Dio 60.1–28 [= selections **C.1 – C.14**]
	47 – 54	Tac. *Ann.* 11–12
D. NERO	54 – 66	Tac. *Ann.* 13–16
	66 – 68	Dio 63.1–29 [= selections **D.1 – D.8**]

It has not been possible to include the whole of Dio's text for those years where Tacitus is missing; about one–quarter has been omitted. Any act of selection is subjective, but it is hoped that nothing of major importance has been left out. Most of Dio's account of Sejanus' rise and fall in 30 – 31 is included [selections **A.1 – A.7**], since this is one of the most important events of Tiberius' reign. In his account of Gaius, Claudius and Nero Dio tends to stress somewhat repeatedly certain themes: Gaius' unjustified condemnation of members of the propertied classes, Claudius' domination at the hands of his wife Messallina and his imperial freedmen, Nero's addiction to lyre–playing and chariot–racing. Some of this repetitive detail has been omitted in the interests of economy.

One of the problems in trying to reconstruct any period of Roman history is the patchy, problematic and often unsatisfactory nature of the surviving source material. The purpose of the Introduction is to help readers assess critically Dio's value as a source for the Julio–Claudian period. For this one needs to have some understanding of Dio's family background and career, and of the political and cultural context in which he was writing his *Roman History*. For all these factors will have shaped his views and treatment of the past. Furthermore, it is important to ascertain the nature and quality of his source material: how much reliable evidence was available to him on the Julio–Claudian period? How well researched was his history? In what ways did Dio use his source material? Finally, we need to establish Dio's general aims and preoccupations in writing his history: to what extent does its underlying purpose affect its quality as a source? The Introduction does not attempt to provide a summary of the Julio–Claudian period: for this the reader should consult some of the works listed in the Suggestions for Further Reading.

This LACTOR is the first to provide extensive historical commentary. The purpose of the commentary is threefold: (a) to help readers understand what Dio actually says on individual historical issues where his meaning is not immediately clear; (b) to help readers evaluate the quality (or otherwise) of the information that he provides; to this end, references are given to relevant ancient sources (literary texts, inscriptions, papyri, coins, art and architecture) and discussions by modern scholars that can help to confirm or call into question Dio's version of the historical point at issue; and (c) to demonstrate how any ancient historical narrative can be used to throw light on a wide range of issues far beyond the immediate historical events that are being described.

Dio provides valuable information, if read critically, on the historical events of the reigns of Tiberius, Gaius Caligula, Claudius and Nero. But, more generally, he also throws light on many aspects of Roman society, institutions, economy and culture (usually of relevance for periods both before and after the Julio–Claudians). Since much of this information is provided incidentally, it does not suffer from the problems of bias or slant that affect some parts of his historical narrative. Readers can learn much from Dio about procedures at meetings of the senate, the problems of providing grain for the city of Rome or methods used for executing Roman criminals, not to mention the nature of Roman wills, the varieties of dress worn in public by emperors and senators, or even the use of sun–hats and cushions at the amphitheatre. To find the information that Dio provides on such matters, and further discussion of them in the historical commentary, readers will need to use the detailed indices.

It should be stressed that it is not necessary for all readers to follow up all of the references to ancient and modern works found in the commentary. It is hoped that there is sufficient material provided in the commentary itself to explain most of the items in Dio's narrative that readers might find puzzling. The references to further discussions are there to provide guidance for those wanting to pursue further a particular event or aspect of Roman society. As for modern discussions, references are provided just to the more accessible works in English, wherever possible. Those approaching the subject for the first time should not be put off by these references. A–level students may wish to follow up a few of them, as resources permit; undergraduates will have the time and experience to use them more fully. But the fundamental aim has been to provide a translation and commentary both complete and comprehensible in themselves.

ACKNOWLEDGEMENTS

I should like to thank most warmly various friends and scholars who have helped to bring this volume to fruition. Of course they are not to be held liable for any of its shortcomings. Richard Smail has been very supportive in encouraging the wider scope of this volume, as also has Stephen Spurr, General Editor of the LACTOR series. Michael Crawford, Virginia Hunter, John Rich, Stephen Spurr and, especially, Barbara Levick provided many useful comments on the introduction and the historical commentary. I should also like to thank Carolyn King of the Cartographic Drafting Office at York University for her skill and patience in preparing the maps. But, most of all, I am heavily indebted to John Crook, who first set me thinking about Dio and then read the entire manuscript in various versions over an extended period. It is much the better for his wise, sensitive and incisive comments. I am again indebted to my parents for all their encouragement over many years and to my parents–in–law, who have taken an active interest in the completion of this book. And finally, as a small token for all her support, this book is dedicated to my wife, Kathryn, who has had to live with Dio for far longer than we all expected.

York University, Toronto   October 1991

LIST OF ABBREVIATIONS

1. ROMAN EMPERORS AND OTHER HISTORICAL FIGURES

Aug.	=	Augustus
Cl.	=	Claudius
D.	=	Cassius Dio
G.	=	Gaius (Caligula)
N.	=	Nero
Sej.	=	Sejanus
Tib.	=	Tiberius

2. GREEK AND LATIN AUTHORS

Translations of all authors listed are available in the Loeb Classical Library series; those marked with an asterisk are also available in Penguin Classics.

References to Dio's *Roman History* are made by giving just the book, chapter and section number, without the author's name; if the passage is included in this selection, the selection number is given in square brackets: e.g. 59.1.1 [= **B.1**].

Digest	*Digest of Roman Law*
Dion. Hal.	Dionysius of Halicarnassus, *Roman Antiquities*
Cic. *ad Fam.*	(*) Cicero, *Letters to his Friends*
Cic. *Phil.*	(*) Cicero, *Philippics*
Hdt.	*Herodotus, *Histories*
Jos. *AJ*	Josephus, *Antiquities of the Jews*
Jos. *BJ*	*Josephus, *Jewish War*
Juv. *Sat.*	*Juvenal, *Satires*
Petr. *Sat.*	*Petronius, *Satyricon*
Philo, *Embassy*	Philo, *Embassy to Gaius*
Philo, *Flaccus*	Philo, *Against Flaccus*
Plin. *Letters*	*Pliny the Younger, *Letters*
Plin. *NH*	(*)Pliny the Elder, *Natural History*
Plut. *Alex.* (etc.)	(*)Plutarch, *Life of Alexander* (etc.)
RG	*Res Gestae Divi Augusti*
Sall. *Cat.*	*Sallust, *Catiline*
Sen. *Contr.*	Elder Seneca, *Controversiae*
Suet. *DJ, Aug., T., G., Cl., N.*	*Suetonius, *Lives of the Deified Julius (= Caesar), Augustus, Tiberius, Gaius, Claudius, Nero* (etc.)
Tac. *A.*	*Tacitus, *Annals*
Tac. *Agr.*	*Tacitus, *Agricola*
Tac. *Germ.*	*Tacitus, *Germania*

Tac. *H.*	*Tacitus, Histories
Thuc.	*Thucydides, *History of the Peloponnesian War*
Vell. Pat.	Velleius Paterculus, *Compendium of Roman History*
Xiph.	Xiphilinus

3. COLLECTIONS OF SOURCES (INCLUDING INSCRIPTIONS)

References are given to the following by selection number, not by page.

AE	*L'Année Épigraphique* (1888–)
Braund	D.C. Braund, *Augustus to Nero: a sourcebook on Roman History, 31 B.C. – A.D. 68* (1985)
CIL	*Corpus Inscriptionum Latinarum*
EJ	V. Ehrenberg and A.H.M. Jones, *Documents Illustrating the Reigns of Augustus and Tiberius* (2nd ed., 1955)
IGRR	*Inscriptiones Graecae ad Res Romanas pertinentes* (ed. R. Cagnat, 1906–27)
ILS	*Inscriptiones Latinae Selectae* (ed. H. Dessau, 1892–1916)
LACTOR 8	*Inscriptions of the Roman Empire A.D. 14 – 117* (ed. B.H. Warmington, 1971)
LR I, II	N. Lewis and M. Reinhold, *Roman Civilization. Selected Readings. I. The Republic and Augustan Age*; *II. The Empire* (3rd ed., 1990)
McCrum & Woodhead	M. McCrum and A.G. Woodhead, *Select Documents of the Principates of the Flavian Emperors* (1961)
RIC	H. Mattingly, A.E. Sydenham et al., *Roman Imperial Coinage* (1923–)
Sherk	R.K. Sherk, *The Roman Empire: Augustus to Hadrian* (Translated Documents of Greece & Rome, 6) (1988)
Sherk, *RGE*	R.K. Sherk, *Rome and the Greek East to the death of Augustus* (Translated Documents of Greece & Rome, 4) (1984)
Smallwood	E.M. Smallwood, *Documents Illustrating the Principates of Gaius, Claudius and Nero* (1967)

4. MODERN WORKS

ANRW	*Aufstieg und Niedergang der römischen Welt* (ed. H. Temporini and W. Haase, 1970–)

Balsdon, *Gaius*	J.P.V.D. Balsdon, *The Emperor Gaius (Caligula)* (1934)
Balsdon, *Life & Leisure*	J.P.V.D. Balsdon, *Life and Leisure in Ancient Rome* (1969)
Barnes, 'Dio'	T.D. Barnes, 'The composition of Cassius Dio's *Roman History*', *Phoenix* 38 (1984), 240–55
Barrett	A.A. Barrett, *Caligula: the corruption of power* (1989)
Bieber, *Theater*	M. Bieber, *A History of the Greek and Roman Theater* (1961)
Birley, *African Emperor*	A.R. Birley, *The African Emperor: Septimius Severus* (rev. ed., 1988)
Birley, *Fasti*	A.R. Birley, *The Fasti of Roman Britain* (1981)
Bowersock, *Sophists*	G.W. Bowersock, *Greek Sophists in the Roman Empire* (1969)
Bradley, *Nero*	K.R. Bradley, *Suetonius' Life of Nero: an historical commentary* (1978)
Braund, *RFK*	D.C. Braund, *Rome and the Friendly King* (1984)
Brunt, *RIT*	P.A. Brunt, *Roman Imperial Themes* (1990)
CAH	*Cambridge Ancient History*
Campbell, *Emperor & Army*	J.B. Campbell, *The Emperor and the Roman Army 31 B.C. – A.D. 235* (1984)
Coarelli, *Guida arch. di Roma*	F. Coarelli, *Guida archeologica di Roma* (3rd. ed., 1980)
Crook, *CP*	J.A. Crook, *Consilium Principis* (1955)
Crook, *Law & Life*	J.A. Crook, *Law and Life of Rome, 90 B.C. – A.D. 212* (1967)
Dudley and Webster, *Conquest*	D.R. Dudley and G. Webster, *The Roman Conquest of Britain, A.D. 43–57* (1965)
Frere, *Britannia*	S. Frere, *Britannia* (3rd ed., 1987)
Friedländer	L. Friedländer, *Roman Life and Manners* (7th ed., Engl. tr., 1908)
Gardner, *Women*	J.F. Gardner, *Women in Roman Law and Society* (1986)
Garnsey, *Famine*	P.D.A. Garnsey, *Famine and Food–Supply in the Graeco–Roman World* (1988)
Garnsey, *SSLP*	P.D.A. Garnsey, *Social Status and Legal Privilege in the Roman Empire* (1970)
Garnsey and Saller, *RE*	P. Garnsey and R.P. Saller, *The Roman Empire: Economy, Society, Culture* (1987)
Griffin, *Nero*	M.T. Griffin, *Nero: the end of a dynasty* (1984)
Hopkins, *Conquerors*	K. Hopkins, *Conquerors and Slaves* (1978)
Hopkins, *Death*	K. Hopkins and G. Burton, *Death and Renewal* (1983)

Humphrey, *Circuses*	J.H. Humphrey, *Roman Circuses: arenas for chariot racing* (1986)
Jones, *Dio Chrysostom*	C.P. Jones, *The Roman World of Dio Chrysostom* (1978)
Levick, *Cl.*	B. Levick, *Claudius* (1990)
Levick, *Tib.*	B. Levick, *Tiberius the Politician* (1976)
Liebeschuetz, *CCRR*	J.H.W.G. Liebeschuetz, *Continuity and Change in Roman Religion* (1979)
Magie, *RRAM*	D. Magie, *Roman Rule in Asia Minor* (2 vols., 1950)
Millar, *Dio*	F. Millar, *A Study of Cassius Dio* (1964)
Millar, *ERW*	F. Millar, *The Emperor in the Roman World* (1977)
Millar, *REN*	F. Millar, *The Roman Empire and its Neighbours* (2nd ed., 1981)
Momigliano	A. Momigliano, *Claudius: the emperor and his achievement* (rev. ed., 1961)
Nash	E. Nash, *Pictorial Dictionary of Ancient Rome* (2 vols., 1968)
Ogilvie, *Romans & Gods*	R.M. Ogilvie, *The Romans and their Gods in the age of Augustus* (1969)
PIR	*Prosopographia Imperii Romani*
Peddie, *Invasion*	J. Peddie, *Invasion: the Roman invasion of Britain in the year A.D. 43* (1987)
Price, *Rituals*	S.R.F. Price, *Rituals and Power: the Roman Imperial Cult in Asia Minor* (1984)
RE	*Real–Encyclopädie der klassischen Altertums–wissenschaft* (ed. A. Pauly, G. Wissowa, W. Kroll, 1894–)
Rickman, *Corn Supply*	G.E. Rickman, *The Corn Supply of Ancient Rome* (1980)
Saller, *Patronage*	R.P. Saller, *Personal Patronage under the early Empire* (1982)
Salway, *Britain*	P. Salway, *Roman Britain* (1981)
Scramuzza	V. Scramuzza, *The Emperor Claudius* (1940)
Seager	R. Seager, *Tiberius* (1972)
Sear, *Architecture*	F. Sear, *Roman Architecture* (1982)
Smallwood, *Jews*	E.M. Smallwood, *The Jews under Roman Rule* (1976)
Sutherland, *RHC*	C.H.V. Sutherland, *Roman History and Coinage 44 B.C. – A.D. 69* (1987)
Syme, *AA*	R. Syme, *The Augustan Aristocracy* (1986)
Syme, *RP*	R. Syme, *Roman Papers*, I – II (ed. E. Badian, 1979); III – V (ed. A.R. Birley, 1984–88)
Syme, *RR*	R. Syme, *The Roman Revolution* (1939)
Syme, *Tac.*	R. Syme, *Tacitus* (2 vols., 1958)
Talbert, *Senate*	R.J.A. Talbert, *The Senate of Imperial Rome* (1984)

Versnel, *Triumphus*	H. Versnel, *Triumphus* (1970)
Veyne, *Bread*	P. Veyne, *Bread and Circuses* (Engl. tr., 1990)
Wallace–Hadrill, *Suet.*	A. Wallace–Hadrill, *Suetonius: the Scholar and his Caesars* (1983)
Warmington	B.H. Warmington, *Nero: reality and legend* (1969)
Webster, *Army*	G. Webster, *The Roman Imperial Army* (3rd. ed., 1985)
Webster, *Invasion*	G. Webster, *The Roman Invasion of Britain* (1980)
Wirszubski, *Libertas*	C. Wirszubski, *Libertas as a Political Idea at Rome during the late Republic and early Empire* (1950)
Yavetz, *Plebs*	Z. Yavetz, *Plebs and Princeps* (1969)
Zanker, *Power of Images*	P. Zanker, *The Power of Images in the age of Augustus* (1988)

ABBREVIATIONS FOR SCHOLARLY JOURNALS

AJAH	*American Journal of Ancient History*
AJP	*American Journal of Philology*
BICS	*Bulletin of the Institute of Classical Studies*
CPh	*Classical Philology*
CQ	*Classical Quarterly*
G&R	*Greece & Rome*
HSCPh	*Harvard Studies in Classical Philology*
JHS	*Journal of Hellenic Studies*
JRA	*Journal of Roman Archaeology*
JRS	*Journal of Roman Studies*
LCM	*Liverpool Classical Monthly*
Num.Chron.	*Numismatic Chronicle*
PBSR	*Papers of the British School at Rome*
PCPhS	*Proceedings of the Cambridge Philological Society*
TAPA	*Transactions of the American Philological Association*
ZPE	*Zeitschrift für Papyrologie und Epigraphik*

INTRODUCTION

Dio's *Roman History* was a massive enterprise: it took at least twenty-two years to prepare and compose, and in eighty books it narrated the history of Rome from 753 B.C. right down to A.D. 229. For much of the imperial period Dio provides our sole surviving extensive narrative. Dio's *Roman History* is thus of major importance as a historical source. But before any ancient historian can be safely used as a source, his quality (or otherwise) has to be assessed. How reliable a witness is Dio on the Julio-Claudian period? Can everything that he reports be accepted at face value?

The purpose, therefore, of this Introduction is to explore some of the factors that affected the way in which Dio conceived of the Roman past and wrote Roman history. His social origins and education, his personal experiences as a leading Roman political figure, and the general literary conventions of his age all influenced, if often subconsciously, Dio's view of the Roman past (Sections 1 and 2). The quality of his history was also affected by the quality of the sources available to him, and by the way in which he interpreted and used them: in short, by the manner in which he wrote his history (Section 3). Finally, his general aims as a historian were more ambitious than just to narrate past events in chronological sequence; these underlying purposes further shaped his interpretation and reporting of the Roman past (Section 4). An awareness of such factors will allow a more critical assessment of the quality of Dio's *Roman History* as a source for the Julio-Claudian period.

1. DIO: GREEK ARISTOCRAT AND ROMAN POLITICIAN

1.1 Dio's Social Background

Reconstructing the life and social background of any Greek or Roman author is a difficult task. Usually only a tiny amount of reliable information survives; as a result, many insecure hypotheses have to be developed to fill out the few known facts. Sometimes these hypotheses (which are often nothing more than half-truths or guesses), by being constantly repeated, have taken on the status of "facts". Therefore, in reading any modern biography of an ancient author, we need to distinguish carefully between proven fact and plausible hypothesis. Dio, however, provides a fair amount of autobiographical detail in the course of his *Roman History*, although there are still some gaps in our knowledge which continue to fuel controversy among scholars. But the main details of his life and career can be reconstructed with reasonable certainty.[1]

---

[1] For a full account see F. Millar, *A Study of Cassius Dio* (1964), 5-27 [= Millar, *Dio*]; T.D. Barnes, 'The composition of Cassius Dio's *Roman History*', *Phoenix* 38 (1984), 240-55 [= Barnes, 'Dio'].

1.1.1   Dio's birth (c. 163 – 165) and family

Dio was born in Nicaea (modern Iznik) in the Roman province of Bithynia
and Pontus (75.15.3; 80.5.3). This Greek-speaking province stretched across the
north-west corner of modern Turkey along the southern shore of the Black Sea.
Nicaea was one of its two main towns and maintained a fierce rivalry with its
neighbour, Nicomedia, a newer foundation, but the capital (or metropolis) of
the Roman province.[2] Dio does not reveal the exact date of his birth, but it
probably occurred between 163 and 165. This can be inferred with a reasonable
degree of certainty from two known facts: that Dio was praetor at Rome in 194
(Section 1.2.2) and that in this period politicians usually held the praetorship
when they were about thirty years of age.[3]

Dio's family was one of the most prominent of Bithynia. His father, (?) M.
[i.e., Marcus] Cassius Apronianus, had a distinguished career as a Roman
senator.[4] After a praetorship, he was appointed governor first of Lycia and
Pamphylia in southern Turkey (attested on an inscription: *IGRR* 3.654) and
then of the neighbouring province of Cilicia (69.1.3; 72.7.2). He must have
returned to Rome to hold a suffect consulship before being appointed governor
of Dalmatia (modern Yugoslavia) (49.36.4), since this last post was always held
by an ex-consul. Being a Roman senator, Dio's father was obliged to own land
in Italy in addition to his ancestral estates in his native Bithynia.[5] Various
brickstamps survive from Ostia, the port city of Rome, stamped with the name
M. Cassius Apronianus (*CIL* XIV 4089, 26 = XV 2164). They suggest that
Dio's father owned brickworks here, and hence possibly an estate as well. Dio
himself owned an estate near Capua in Campania, where he resided when he
was not actively engaged in public business at Rome (76.2.1; cf. 80.1.3). Not
surprisingly, he shows a detailed local knowledge of the Bay of Naples region
(48.50-51). The family must also have owned a house in Rome, just as Cassius
Dio, possibly Dio's grandson or great-grandson, did in the tenth region of the
city at the end of the third century (*PIR*[2] C 491). The family was thus based very
much in two areas: their native Nicaea and their adopted homeland, Italy.[6]
They not only owned land, but would also have built up considerable social
contacts and obligations in these two distinct areas.

Dio is given a variety of names in the surviving manuscripts and Byzantine
summaries of his *Roman History*: Dio Cassius, Dio Cocceianus, Cassius Dio,
Dio Cassius Cocceianus.[7] Various inscriptions recording Dio's second consulship in 229 provide further details: three refer to him simply as Dio (*CIL* XIII

---

[2] For a vivid picture of life in Bithynia in the late first/ early second century A.D. see
Pliny, *Letters*, Book 10 and the speeches of Dio Chrysostom of Prusa, a Bithynian orator
and sophist (especially speeches 38-41); C.P. Jones, *The Roman World of Dio Chrysostom*
(1978), esp. 83-103; W. Ameling, 'Cassius Dio und Bithynien', *Epigraphica Anatolica* 4
(1984), 123-38.

[3] Millar, *Dio*, 13; Barnes, 'Dio', 242.

[4] *PIR*[2] C 485; his *praenomen* Marcus is uncertain.

[5] In theory at least one-third of one's total landholdings, reduced by M. Aurelius to one-
quarter: R.J.A. Talbert, *The Senate of Imperial Rome* (1984), 55-56.

[6] Dio clearly associated himself with Italy and the Romans: at the very start of his
Roman History he describes Italy as "this land we inhabit" (fr. 1.2).

[7] The evidence is well summarized in A.M. Gowing, 'Dio's name', *CPh* 85 (1990), 49-54.

6752, 7337, 7502), while three give his name as Cassius Dio (*CIL* III 3511, 5587; VI 2998 = *ILS* 2177). Two more recently discovered inscriptions introduce further elements, and complexities: one records his name as Cl. (= Claudius) Cassius Dio (*AE* 1971, 430), the other as L. Cassius Dio (*Roman Military Diplomas*, II (1985), no. 133). Combining the evidence from manuscripts and inscriptions, we can reconstruct Dio's full name as "L. Claudius Cassius Dio Cocceianus".[8]

Dio's full name provides further clues as to his social milieu. First, the fact that Dio was polyonymous (i.e., had a string of names) reveals that he was of high social status. In the second century it had become common for members of the Roman élite to parade their lineage in this way.[9] Secondly, it reveals a distinct mix of Greek and Roman elements. "Dio" (a common Greek name derived from the god's name "Zeus") emphasizes his Greek roots, while his other (Roman) names suggest that his family on both his father's and mother's side had been awarded Roman citizenship: on his father's side by a Cassius, on his mother's by a Claudius (possibly the emperor).[10] The element "Cocceianus" suggests a tie of kinship with another family of Roman citizens, the Cocceii, and may connect Dio the historian with Cocceianus Dio, the orator from the neighbouring Bithynian city of Prusa.[11]

However, it is not completely certain that his full name was L. Claudius Cassius Dio Cocceianus. First, a strong case has been made that the element "Cocceianus" was assigned to him only in Byzantine times as a result of confusing him with Dio Cocceianus, the orator from Prusa.[12] Secondly, the "Cl." on the inscription from Beroea, Macedonia (*AE* 1971, 480) might be a stone-cutter's error for "L.", in which case his name would have to be reduced to L. Cassius Dio. Parallels, however, while uncommon, can be found for such a combination of the first-name (*praenomen*) Lucius and the family name (*nomen*) Claudius: e.g. L. Claudius Proculus Cornelianus (*ILS* 1013) or L. Claudius Bibullius Regillus Herodes (*ILS* 8824).[13] His full name may, therefore, have been L. Claudius Cassius Dio. But despite these uncertainties, Dio was clearly from one of the growing number of élite families from the Greek East who gained admission to the Roman senatorial order in the second century.[14]

1.1.2   Dio's education (c. 170 – 180)

Dio reveals nothing about his early years or his education. But as a member of an élite family in a Greek-speaking province, he will have received training in grammar, literature, mathematics, geometry, music, but most of all rhetoric (the

[8] As accepted by P.M.M. Leunissen, *Konsuln und Konsulare in der Zeit von Commodus bis Severus Alexander* (1989).
[9] R. Syme, 'Clues to testamentary adoption', *RP* IV, 159-73; 'The paternity of polyonymous consuls', *RP* V, 639-47.
[10] Cassii are prominent in inscriptions from Nicaea: Millar, *Dio*, 8-9.
[11] Jones, *Dio Chrysostom*, 7 and nn. 62-63.
[12] Gowing (above, n. 7).
[13] For other examples cf. *PIR²* C 790, 891, 938, 980.
[14] R. Syme, 'Greeks invading the Roman government', *RP* IV, 1-20; K. Hopkins, *Death and Renewal* (1983), 200; the fullest study is H. Halfmann, *Die Senatoren aus dem östlichen Teil des Imperium Romanum* (1979).

art of public speaking).[15] Dio reports that he had read many Greek authors, especially those who wrote in the Attic dialect, to improve his style (55.12.5). After initial studies in Nicaea, Dio probably went for further training in rhetoric to one of the flourishing intellectual centres of Asia: Ephesus, Smyrna or (the less prestigious) Pergamum. He was fortunate that his lifetime coincided with one of the great ages of Greek rhetoric.[16] His concern for rhetoric is evident throughout his history, and it had an important effect on the way Dio formulated his thought and historical narrative (Section 3.4.2).

1.1.3   Dio's engagement and marriage

Dio provides no direct information about his marriage and any children that may have resulted from it. However, he gives a faint hint when he reports that Commodus forced "us senators, our wives and our children" to present him with two gold coins every year on his birthday (72.16.3) or that "we senators and our wives" took part in the funeral of Pertinax (74.4.4; 74.4.6). Furthermore, Cassius Dio, consul in 291, was possibly a grandson, or great-grandson, of the historian (*PIR*[2] C 491). Recent work on the Roman family has shown that men of the competitive office-holding élite tended to marry in their early twenties, while men of lower social status put this off until their late twenties or early thirties.[17] Thus Dio is likely to have married in the mid- to late-180s. Given his prominent social position both in Bithynia and also at Rome, he would have married a wife of good family to enhance his social status. Senators from the Greek East might marry into another prominent family from their own province; but if they were ambitious, they would seek a connexion with a family from another province of the Greek East, or, better still, an Italian senatorial family, as, for example, did Herodes Atticus, the famous sophist and Roman senator from Athens (consul in 143), when he married Appia Annia Regilla.[18]

1.1.4   The significance of Dio's social background for evaluating Dio as a historian of Rome

Thus Dio was from a wealthy, propertied family of high social status in Bithynia. His father's admission to the Roman senate considerably enhanced the family's prestige, not least in their home area. Such wealth and social status gave Dio some important opportunities: it allowed him to gain a full education in the liberal arts (especially rhetoric) and gave him the leisure time to engage in politics, and to write history. For both of these activities his rhetorical skills would have been considerably advantageous. But his social origins also helped to determine his general mind-set or outlook; not surprisingly, his social and political views were distinctly conservative, which sometimes slants his reporting of the past (Section 3.4.3). Finally, being a Bithynian aristocrat who pursued a senatorial career at Rome, Dio represented very much a blend of the two main

---

[15] For details see H.I. Marrou, *A History of Education in Antiquity* (Engl. transl., 1956), 325-90.
[16] G.W. Bowersock, *Greek Sophists in the Roman Empire* (1969).
[17] R.P. Saller, 'Men's age at marriage and its consequences in the Roman family', *CPh* 82 (1987), 21-34; B.D. Shaw, 'The age of Roman girls at marriage', *JRS* 77 (1987), 30-46.
[18] A.R. Birley, *Marcus Aurelius: a biography* (2nd ed., 1987), 63-64.

cultures of the Roman Empire: he was at once both a Greek and a Roman.[19] His experience as a public figure at Rome gave him special qualifications to write a *Roman History*, but his enduring Greekness and his continuing contact with his Greek roots meant that he analysed and described the Roman past very much in Greek terms. As we shall see, he owed a considerable debt to the Greek historiographical tradition.

1.2 Dio's Political Career

1.2.1 *Dio in Rome; the start of his public career (180 – 190)*

By the time that he had reached his late teens Dio had joined his father in Rome, since from the year 180 onwards he reports events there as an eyewitness (72.4.2; 72.7.1). Once in Rome he could easily have received further instruction in rhetoric from one of the many Greek sophists encouraged to reside there by the emperor and the imperial family.[20] During this period he may well have watched the proceedings of the senate along with other sons of senators, ideal training for one looking forward to a senatorial career. In the 180s Dio began his public career. Like Tacitus, Pliny and many other Roman politicians, he established his public reputation by acting as an advocate in the lawcourts (73.12.2). This experience doubtless proved useful when he was summoned to the emperor's advisory council (Section 1.2.4). He also gained administrative experience by accompanying his father to his province of Cilicia (72.7.2) – probably during 182-183.[21] It was traditional for a Roman provincial governor to take with him to his province a group of family and friends to form his entourage (*comites*, "companions").[22]

Dio gives no details of his early political career, but he probably began in the standard way by holding at the age of about twenty (i.e., in c. 184) one of the minor magistracies (*XX viri*), the first step for anyone wanting to enter the senate.[23] Three were in charge of the mint (*III viri monetales*), ten held judicial posts (*X viri stlitibus iudicandis*), four were road commissioners (*IV viri viarum curandarum*) and three oversaw arrests and executions (*III viri capitales*).[24] At some time late in the decade Dio must have been appointed to a quaestorship, perhaps in 188 or 189, when he would have been of roughly the appropriate age (25 years old), but again we have no direct evidence of this. The twenty quaestors were all broadly concerned with finance: two assisted the emperor, four were attached to the consuls, two to the public treasury of Saturn, while twelve served as financial officials in Italy or the provinces.[25] Given Dio's Greek background, he may have served in a Greek province, perhaps Asia; but again

[19] Millar, *Dio*, 174-92.
[20] Bowersock, *Sophists*, 43-117.
[21] Barnes, 'Dio', 242.
[22] F. Millar, *The Roman Empire and its Neighbours* (2nd ed., 1981), 62.
[23] On senatorial careers see Talbert, *Senate*, 9-27; A.R. Birley, *The Fasti of Roman Britain* (1981), 4-35.
[24] Birley, *Fasti*, 4-8; Talbert, *Senate*, 9-16.
[25] Birley, *Fasti*, 12-14; Talbert, *Senate*, 17-18.

there is no evidence to confirm or deny this.[26] Election to a quaestorship brought admittance into the senate, but it is only under the year 192 that Dio refers to himself explicitly as a senator (72.16.3; 72.18.2; 72.20.1). This apparent gap can probably be explained by the fact that Dio's account of the years 188-192 are extremely brief (72.13-15). It is possible that he held another magistracy (the tribunate or the aedileship) in 191 or 192, but again there is no evidence for it. The vividness of Dio's narrative for the years 189-192 strongly suggests that he was in Rome and very much involved in public affairs.[27]

1.2.2   Dio's praetorship (194); his first provincial governorship? (c. 197 – 202)

Dio was nominated to the praetorship by the emperor Pertinax during his brief reign from 1 January to 28 March 193 (73.12.2). This would mean that Dio held office as one of the eighteen praetors in 194.[28] A praetorship involved substantial judicial and administrative duties in Rome, as well as financial outlay, since praetors had to organize, and provide funds for, various sets of public games.[29] After his praetorship Dio remained in Rome during 195–197, taking part in meetings of the senate and other public events (75.4.2-6; 75.7.4; 75.8.1-5). Dio is silent about his activities between 197 and 202. This was the normal stage in a career for an ex-praetor to hold a provincial governorship. Being from the Greek East, Dio probably governed a Greek-speaking province: Cilicia, Lycia and Pamphylia, Galatia, Thrace, Macedonia, Achaea, Cyprus or Cyrenaica and Crete (probably not Bithynia and Pontus, since it was unusual to govern one's native province). A rescript of the emperor Septimius Severus addressed to a provincial governor "Dio" (*Digest* 50.12.7) might just relate to Dio the historian. Dio was certainly back in Rome by 202 (76.1).

1.2.3   Dio's first consulship (c. 205)

On a number of occasions Dio mentions that he had held a consulship (43.46.5-6; 60.2.3 [= **C.1**]; 76.16.4), but does not reveal when. This has led to intense controversy among modern scholars: most scholars argue that Dio held a first consulship under Septimius Severus in 205 or 206, while a few prefer a date as late as 222-223, i.e., under the emperor Severus Alexander. On balance, the arguments for the early date are much stronger than those for the later one.[30] What is not in doubt is that Dio held a *suffect* consulship: i.e., he was one of the substitute consuls who replaced the ordinary consuls (*consules ordinarii*), the main pair of the year, after they had held office usually for the first two months (cf. 43.46.5-6).

1.2.4   Dio as friend and adviser of the emperor

Dio had been a "friend of the emperor" (*amicus Caesaris*) probably at least since his elevation to the praetorship in 194 (Section 1.2.2). "Friends of the

---

[26] Millar, *Dio*, 15.
[27] Millar, *Dio*, 15, 131-34.
[28] For some rather forced arguments that he in fact held it in 195 see Barnes, 'Dio', 242.
[29] Birley, *Fasti*, 14-15; Talbert, *Senate*, 20, 59-64.
[30] For clear summaries of the evidence and arguments see Millar, *Dio*, 204-07; Barnes, 'Dio', 243.

emperor" can broadly be defined as those who were admitted to the emperor's morning reception (*salutatio*), but three types need to be distinguished. The largest group consisted of those who attended the imperial court with greater or lesser regularity: members of the senatorial and equestrian orders, foreign dignitaries temporarily in Rome, literary figures, and sometimes even actors and charioteers; most of these did not come into close, regular contact with the emperor. Secondly, there were those who accompanied the emperor when he travelled outside Rome: his "companions" (*comites*). Finally, there were those who were summoned by the emperor to act as his advisers on judicial and administrative matters (i.e., the body referred to by modern scholars as the *consilium principis*). None of these three groups had a fixed membership nor a rigid institutional framework. The emperor admitted to his entourage whomsoever he wished in one or more of the three capacities.[31] Dio had won Septimius Severus' favour by sending him on his accession in 193 a copy of his work on dreams and portents foretelling Severus' rise to power (72.23, quoted below, p. 26). By the time of his first consulship he was serving as an adviser to the emperor at trials (75.16.2-4; 76.17.1).[32] Furthermore, he describes Severus' daily routine in sufficient detail to suggest a considerable familiarity (76.17.1-2). The fact that Dio does not go on to relate Severus' routine when on campaign may confirm the suspicion that Dio did not accompany Severus on his frequent overseas expeditions.[33]

1.2.5   Dio under Caracalla, Macrinus and Elagabalus (211–222)

Dio was in Rome when Caracalla succeeded Septimius Severus as emperor in February 211 (77.1.4–6). His account of Caracalla is extremely vivid and hostile, stressing his cruelty and licentiousness. Dio mentions himself only once during the reign: in the winter of 214–215 he was in Bithynia with the imperial court, which was spending the winter at Nicomedia. He was thus acting as one of the travelling companions (*comites*) of the emperor.[34] Dio was also required to act as an adviser of the emperor during his stay in Bithynia, and became exasperated at Caracalla's flippant disregard for the conduct of public business (77.17.3-4; 78.8.4). Being a local aristocrat, he was well placed to persuade his fellow Bithynians to provide the substantial food supplies and other resources needed to entertain the imperial court on tour. As always, the burden of hospitality fell very much on the local aristocracy (77.18.3-4). After Caracalla left Nicomedia early in 215, Dio seems to have returned to Rome; for he reports in detail two letters that Caracalla sent to the senate in 215 (77.20.1-2; 78.1.5). He was certainly in Rome in April 217, when he describes in vivid terms how the senate received letters from Macrinus announcing his proclamation as emperor by the troops after Caracalla's assassination in Mesopotamia (78.16.2-17.4; cf. 78.20). It was during this period when he was not holding public office that Dio was hard at work composing his history (Section 2.2).

[31] J.A. Crook, *Consilium Principis* (1955); F. Millar, *The Emperor in the Roman World* (1977), 110-22.
[32] For the date see Barnes, 'Dio', 243.
[33] For a full account see A.R. Birley, *The African Emperor: Septimius Severus* (revised ed., 1988).
[34] On these see T.D. Barnes, 'Emperors on the move', *JRA* 2 (1989), 247-61, esp. 259-60.

Dio remained in Rome for almost all of Macrinus' brief reign (8 April 217 – 8 June 218) and attended the senate (78.36.1; 78.38.1-2). Just before the end of the reign he was appointed by Macrinus to his next important administrative post – as *curator* (financial overseer) of Pergamum and Smyrna, two major (and fiercely competitive) cities in Asia (79.7.4). A *curator* was appointed from among the ex-praetors or, occasionally, the ex-consuls, and was responsible for overseeing all aspects of the financial well-being of the city or cities to which he was appointed. It was never a regular position in all cities of the Empire, but a special posting when and where conditions required.[35] Dio held his position in Pergamum and Smyrna from 218 until perhaps 221.[36] As it turned out, from 218 onwards he was to spend little time in Rome and Italy.

1.2.6 Dio under Severus Alexander: governor of Africa, Dalmatia and Upper Pannonia (222 – 228)

At the start of Book 80 Dio gives a somewhat breathless account of his later political career:

> I have described events so far [i.e., up until 222] with as much accuracy as I could manage. As for the rest I have not been able to go into accurate detail since I did not spend much time in Rome. For from Asia I went to Bithynia, I fell ill and from there I hurried to my command in Africa. I returned to Italy and almost immediately was sent as governor to Dalmatia and then to Upper Pannonia. After this I returned to Rome and to Campania and then immediately set off for home.
>
> (80.1.2-3)

From such a bare summary it is not easy to reconstruct precisely when Dio held these important posts in various parts of the Empire. It is usually assumed that he held all three under Severus Alexander, who at the age of only fourteen succeeded Elagabalus as emperor on 12 February 222. On this view Dio was proconsul of Africa in 222-223, then spent three years as legate of Dalmatia in 223-226 and then three years as legate of Upper Pannonia in 226-229. However, we know that Dio was back in Italy to hold his second consulship at the very start of 229 (Section 1.2.7). Therefore, either Dio began this series of provincial posts slightly earlier than assumed (i.e., in 221 still during the reign of Elagabalus) or he did not remain in Dalmatia and/or Pannonia for his full three-year term as governor.[37]

Dio's appointment to these three senior provincial positions well illustrates his high standing among the Roman political élite. The proconsulship of Africa was second only to that of Asia in terms of prestige for a senator. Dio may well have been appointed to the post in Dalmatia because of links that his father had made with the local aristocracy during his time there as Roman governor (49.36.4). The appointment in Upper Pannonia (on the Danube frontier and bordering on Dalmatia) was a senior military position, involving command of

---

[35] See further G.P. Burton, 'The *curator rei publicae*: towards a re-appraisal', *Chiron* 9 (1979), 465-87.
[36] Millar, *Dio*, 23.
[37] Dio may well have wanted to suppress the fact that he held office under Elagabalus, one of the emperors he detested most. On these provincial posts and their date see Millar, *Dio*, 23-24; Barnes, 'Dio', 244-45; R. Syme, *Emperors and Biography* (1971), 144-45.

two legions, and was one not often held by senators from the Greek East.[38] Dio arrived in Pannonia with strong views on the general deterioration of the Roman legions and so immediately embarked on a rigorous, and unpopular, programme of training and instilling of discipline. The Praetorian Guard back in Rome, fearful that they might also receive the same sort of sharpening up, strongly disapproved and demanded that the emperor remove Dio from his post. But Severus Alexander refused and confirmed Dio in his position as governor (80.4.2). Dio also paints a bleak picture of the local environment (49.36.2-3). Dio's military experience and his strong views on the deterioration of Rome's forces in his own day should be taken into account when we are assessing his picture of the Roman army in earlier parts of his history.

1.2.7   Dio's second consulship in 229; his retirement from Roman public life

Dio returned to Italy to take up a second consulship: he was appointed ordinary consul with the emperor Severus Alexander for the year 229, a distinct privilege.[39] The emperor showed Dio additional favour by meeting the not inconsiderable costs of holding the consulship (80.5.1).[40] The Praetorian Guard continued to display intense hostility towards Dio, especially when Alexander agreed to pay his costs as consul. The emperor was afraid that they might kill Dio if he came to Rome to take up his office, and so allowed him to spend his consulship in Italy out of the reach of the Praetorian Guard (80.5.1). Dio presumably stayed on his country estate near Capua (76.2.1).

After laying down his consulship in March 229, Dio remained in Italy and occasionally joined the imperial court both in Rome and, when the emperor was residing at one of his country villas, in Campania (80.5.2). But it was not long before Dio asked permission (possibly in 230) to be excused further service as a member of the emperor's entourage since he was suffering from a medical problem with his feet. Once excused, he set out for his home province of Bithynia, where, now over sixty-five years old, he settled down to spend the rest of his life in retirement at Nicaea (80.5.2-3). Dio closes his *Roman History* at this point and so we do not know how much longer he lived after his return home.[41]

1.2.8   The significance of Dio's political career for evaluating Dio as a historian

Dio finished his *Roman History* with a quotation from Homer's *Iliad*:

> "Hector was led out of the range of the missiles by Zeus and out of the dust,
> Away from the slaying of men and the blood and the uproar."
>
> (80.5.3, quoting Hom. *Il.* 11.163-64)

[38] Millar, *Dio*, 25-26.
[39] He also held the consulship with another leading political figure and biographer of the emperors, Marius Maximus, in 223: Birley, *African Emperor*, 205.
[40] A number of inscriptions on which the names of the ordinary consuls appear as a dating mechanism confirm Dio's consulship: *CIL* III 3511, 5587, 11773; VI 2998 = *ILS* 2177; *Archäologische Anzeiger* 1915, 245, 18; *AE* 1960, 348; *AE* 1971, 430; M. Roxan, *Roman Military Diplomas* II (1985), no. 133; note also a papyrus from Dura Europus: *Dura Final Report* V.I, no. 69. For consuls' expenses see Talbert, *Senate*, 59-66.
[41] For the suggestion that Dio outlived Severus Alexander see M. Eisman, 'Dio and Josephus: parallel analyses', *Latomus* 36 (1977), 657-73.

This was aptly chosen; for Dio had indeed seen much slaying of men, blood and uproar during his forty years at the very centre of power in Rome (from c. 190 to c. 230). His personal experience (often very close to the emperor) was crucial in allowing him to report in Books 72–80 of his *Roman History*, often as an eyewitness, on the tumultuous events of his own lifetime. But it also qualified him to reflect authoritatively upon the governing system of the Principate as a whole (see Section 4.3).

However, we cannot overlook a simple chronological fact that detracts from his value as a source for the Julio-Claudian period. Dio was at the centre of power, and was researching and composing his *Roman History*, between c. 190 and c. 230: that is, 160–200 years after the events that he describes in Books 58 – 63. As we shall see, he relied heavily on historical sources from nearer the period (Section 3.2.1). But this long gap between himself and the events naturally led to some errors of fact and anachronisms, and, more generally, a partially faulty perspective on the Julio-Claudian period. Some of these errors he simply took over from his sources; but at other times he misunderstood what his sources meant and so unwittingly introduced errors of his own. He misidentifies individuals: for example, he attributes the nickname "the Golden Sheep" to the wrong M. Iunius Silanus (59.8.5; cf. 60.27.1n. [= **C.13**]) and confuses two consular brothers, and compounds his error by putting one of their consulships in the wrong year (59.6.2 + n. [= **B.4**]). He also makes mistakes about foreign kings: thus Polemo was not the son, but the grandson of Polemo (59.12.1 [= **B.10**]), and he confuses Mithridates king of the Iberians with Mithridates king of Bosporus (60.28.7 [= **C.14**]). As for anachronisms, he reports that in 39 Gaius divided the province of Africa into two parts (59.20.7 [= **B.15**]). In fact, a separate province of Numidia was created only under Septimius Severus.[42] What Dio should have said is that Gaius stripped the proconsular governor of Africa of the Roman legionary force that he had commanded and appointed a separate commander to take charge of these troops who were based in the region of Numidia. He also consistently talks about the "governor" of Upper or of Lower Germany (59.22.5 [= **B.17**]; 63.17.3 [= **D.4**]; 63.24.1 [= **D.6**]) well before these areas were constituted as provinces in the 80s.[43]

On a more general level, Dio is guilty of assuming that some central features of his own age were just as important in the Julio-Claudian period. Thus he overplays the rôle of the Praetorian Guard during the Julio-Claudian period in establishing new emperors and maintaining them in power (especially in his account of Claudius: 60.1-2 [= **C.1**]). This was certainly true in his own day, but much less so in the early Principate.[44] Furthermore, writing from the perspective of an age in which the senate was struggling to retain its importance, he underestimates the influence of the senate under the Julio-Claudians. But more seriously he presents the Principate from the very start as a fully developed system of government; in this he simply describes the system familiar to him from his own age. He fails to convey the crucial point that it was only gradually

[42] Birley, *African Emperor*, 147.
[43] For the date see A.C. King, *Roman Gaul and Germany* (1990), 167-68.
[44] On the growing power of the praetorians and the army in the Severan age see Birley, *African Emperor*, 196-97.

that the Julio-Claudian emperors built up what came to be their traditional privileges and powers.[45]

Furthermore, Dio lived through a period of intense political upheaval at Rome: an age in which the army came to play a much more dominant role in the running of the state, when the "tranquil majesty of the Roman peace" (Gibbon) of the second century was giving way to the violent anarchy of the third century. Of all the emperors under whom Dio lived, not one died peacefully in his bed in Italy: all either died overseas on campaign against foreign enemies or were assassinated at home or abroad (see Appendix 1). He described his era as one of "iron and rust", a marked decline from what he saw as the golden age of Marcus Aurelius (71.36.4). He witnessed the violent overthrow of the Antonine dynasty. He lived through the series of civil wars that Septimius Severus had to fight to legitimate his claim to power. He observed, sometimes at uncomfortably close quarters, the undignified conduct of such erratic emperors as Commodus, Caracalla and Elagabalus – especially towards the senatorial order. And after his retirement from politics in 230, he probably witnessed the growing pressures on the Empire from outside the frontiers, which gave rise to fifty years of anarchy after the assassination of Severus Alexander in 235.[46]

Such events cannot have failed to make an impact on the way Dio looked at the past: so many conspiracies and civil wars, for instance, helped to convince him that civil strife had to be avoided at all costs.[47] And his personal experiences of the emperors and leading figures of his own age helped to suggest to him ways of reporting the Julio-Claudian past (Section 4.3). In short, the present had a distinct influence on the way that he reconstructed and recounted the past. Thus, we have to be careful of taking everything that he says at face value; it was often coloured by his own social prejudices and political experiences.

2. DIO AND THE WRITING OF HISTORY

2.1 The Nature of History in the later second century A.D.

The second century saw an impressive renaissance of Greek literary culture: the speeches of Aelius Aristides; the satirical essays of Lucian; Galen's scientific and medical works; Pausanias' antiquarian researches on the important sites of Greece; the philosophical works of Favorinus and Maximus of Tyre; the novels of Chariton and Achilles Tatius; most of all, Philostratus' biographies of the most famous sophists of the period vividly attest the intellectual climate of the age.[48] Much of this work sought to recapture and advertise the glory of the classical Greek past, in part to cover up the unpalatable reality that all Greeks

---

[45] For further discussion (and explanation of why Dio did this) see Millar, *Dio*, 93-102.
[46] On this period see A.R. Birley, *Marcus Aurelius: a biography* (revised ed., 1987); Birley, *African Emperor*; Millar, *Dio*, 122-73; R. MacMullen, *Roman Government's Response to Crisis* (1976).
[47] Millar, *Dio*, 74-76.
[48] The fullest study of the literary culture of the age is B.P. Reardon, *Courants littéraires grecs des IIe. et IIIe. siècles après J.-C.* (1971). More briefly, C.P. Jones, *Culture and Society in Lucian* (1986), 149-59.

were now firmly subjects of a Roman Empire.[49] The period is often known as the Second Sophistic, since many Greek rhetoricians (known as "rhetors" or "sophists") flourished in the important intellectual centres of Athens, Ephesus, Smyrna and Rome. Their activities gave a new impetus to the development of Greek rhetoric, especially the skills required to deliver an extempore speech on an imaginary or historical theme. Many of these sophists were also active at Rome as official advocates or ambassadors for their native cities of the Greek East.[50]

History also flourished during the second century. The classical Greek historians of the fifth century B.C. (Herodotus, Thucydides and Xenophon) were consciously imitated by a number of historians. Appian, a Greek from Alexandria who acted as an advocate in Rome, wrote a history of Rome (*Rhomaika*), arranged geographically (in imitation of Herodotus) in accordance with the areas of the known world successively conquered by Rome.[51] Arrian from Nicomedia in Bithynia wrote some of his historical works according to a Herodotean, geographical plan (*Parthian Affairs, Indian Affairs, Bithynian Affairs*), others in imitation of Xenophon (*The Anabasis of Alexander*).[52] On a less dignified level, the Parthian campaigns of the emperor Lucius Verus in the early 160s gave rise to a whole host of sycophantic histories of the war by Greek authors, roundly criticized by Lucian in his essay, *How to Write History*.[53]

Throughout classical antiquity history was always considered a branch of literature; most of all, it was closely associated with rhetoric.[54] Its purpose was not just to retell past events, but also to entertain. This had a profound effect on its nature and style. Not only did histories include speeches, composed by the historian to show off his rhetorical skill, but narrative sections were also highly rhetorical in flavour. Precise historical accuracy was not necessarily the prime objective. Some details may have been embellished, or even invented, to enhance the artistic style of the narrative. In short, the ancient historian's view of what constituted "historical truth" was very different from a modern historian's. It is important to bear this in mind when evaluating Dio's *Roman History*.

2.2   Dio's Literary Career

For Dio, as for many other leading public figures at Rome (e.g. Sallust, the elder Pliny, Tacitus), the writing of history was an appropriate and congenial activity to be pursued in periods of leisure during and/or after a political career. According to the *Suda* (a Byzantine encyclopaedia of the late tenth century) Dio

---

[49] E.L. Bowie, 'The Greeks and their past in the Second Sophistic' in *Studies in Ancient Society* (ed. M.I. Finley, 1974), 166-209.
[50] Bowersock, *Sophists* (*passim*).
[51] Bowersock, *Greek Sophists*, 112-13; E. Champlin, *Fronto and Antonine Rome* (1980), 98-100.
[52] P.A. Stadter, *Arrian of Nicomedia* (1980).
[53] Cf. Jones, *Culture and Society in Lucian*, 59-67.
[54] T.P. Wiseman, *Clio's Cosmetics* (1979), ch. 3; id., 'Practice and theory in ancient historiography', *History* 66 (1981), 375-93; A.J. Woodman, *Rhetoric in Classical Historiography* (1988).

wrote eight separate historical works: *Dreams and Portents foreshadowing the rise to power of Septimius Severus*, *Wars and Civil Wars of Septimius Severus*, *The Roman History*, a biography of Arrian of Nicomedia, *Events during the Life of Trajan*, *Journeys* (*Enhodia*), *Persian Affairs* (*Persika*) and *Getic Affairs* (*Getika*: i.e., affairs in Dacia). The last two works are certainly not by Dio: the *Persian Affairs* was by Dinon of Colophon, the *Getic Affairs* by Dio Chrysostom of Prusa.[55] The work on journeys remains a complete mystery. The *Events during the life of Trajan*, if by Dio, was doubtless incorporated into his full-scale *Roman History*. Scholars are divided as to whether Dio wrote a biography of Arrian, a fellow Bithynian.[56] Thus the only works that can be securely attributed to Dio are the first three in the list, since he himself mentions them all in a revealing passage in his only surviving work, the *Roman History*:

1   After this [sc. the murder of Commodus in December 192] very serious wars and civil wars broke out. I composed the history of these for the following reason. I had written and published a booklet about the dreams and portents which gave
2   Severus reason to hope for the imperial power. I also sent him a copy of the work; he read it and then sent me back a long, complimentary note. I received this letter in the evening and then went to sleep. As I was sleeping, the divine power commanded me to write history. And so this then is how I came to write about the
3   events with which I am now occupied. And since this work won very much approval from Severus himself and others besides, it was indeed then that I conceived a desire to compose a history of everything else that concerned the Romans. As a result, I decided not to leave this first history as an independent work any longer, but to incorporate it into this present history. My intention is to write about, and leave behind for posterity, in a single project all events from the
4   beginning up to whatever point may seem best to Fortune. This goddess gives me confidence to continue my history when I become hesitant and procrastinate over it; when I am struggling and refusing to go on, she wins me back by sending me dreams; and she bestows on me fine hopes that the future will allow my history to survive and in no way diminish its lustre. She has been allotted to me, so it seems, as an overseer to guide me through my life and as a result, I am devoted to
5   her. I collected all the achievements of the Romans from the beginning down to the death of Severus within the space of ten years, and I wrote them up in another twelve years. As for subsequent events, they shall be recorded, as far as it shall prove possible. (72.23.1-5)

From this passage something of Dio's development as a historian can be traced. His first work was a booklet recounting the dreams and portents which foretold Septimius Severus' rise to power. That it won Severus' immediate favour is not surprising, since he needed all the propaganda and support that he could muster after marching on Rome to seize power from Didius Julianus. The date of this work is uncertain, but 193, the year of Severus' accession, seems highly plausible.[57] Severus' favourable response encouraged Dio to embark on a more ambitious work of contemporary history. It started out as an account

[55] C.P. Jones, *Dio Chrysostom*, 122-23, 139-40.
[56] In favour: Bowie (above, n. 49), 182 and note 46; against: Millar, *Dio*, 10, 70. For Dio's use of Arrian's *Parthica* see Stadter, *Arrian of Nicomedia*, 140-41.
[57] Millar, *Dio*, 29; cf. Barnes, 'Dio', 246, who casts a mild doubt in favour of 195.

describing the civil strife following the assassination of Commodus in 192, during which Severus came to power; but it was eventually expanded to include the civil wars against Pescennius Niger (193-94) and Clodius Albinus (probably 196-197), as well as his two wars against the Parthians (194-195 and 197-98). Dio explicitly states that this work included more than one foreign war. It must, therefore, have included the Second Parthian War of 197-98, which makes a completion date of c. 202 plausible, although once again not certain.[58]

This second work was also well-received by Severus. As a result, Dio decided to start work on a full-scale *Roman History*, into which he would incorporate his second work. In the surviving parts of the *Roman History*, Dio provides some valuable information for tracing its genesis; but unfortunately he is not precise enough for us to do this with absolute certainty. Thus a whole range of suggestions have been made on exactly when Dio wrote his *Roman History*.[59] However, a careful reconsideration of the four key passages (72.23; 78.10.1-2; 80.1.2; 80.5.3) allows, in my view, the following reconstruction.

1. At the outset Dio made three decisions about his *Roman History*: it would start with the foundation of Rome (i.e., in 753 B.C.), incorporate his earlier work on the wars and civil wars of Severus and continue "up to whatever point may seem best to Fortune" (72.23.3).

2. He spent ten years collecting evidence on events down to the death of Severus (72.23.5). If we are right in assuming that he started work in 202, this research would have been complete by 211.

3. His slow progress and frequent procrastination (72.23.4), and possibly also Severus' death in February 211, led him in the spring of 211 to decide to end his history with Severus' death (72.23.5). In spring 211, therefore, he started composing his history, now set to cover the years 753 B.C. to A.D. 211. The composition of it took twelve years (72.23.5) and was, therefore, complete soon after the accession of Severus Alexander in February 222. Dio tells us that he wrote his history for the most part when residing on his estate near Capua when he had time off "from the affairs of the city" (76.2.1). Dio was in Italy for most of this decade, and took part in meetings of the senate and other rituals in the city of Rome (Section 1.2.5). This period is the most fitting time for Dio to have been composing his history.

4. However, in 211 soon after the accession of Caracalla and Geta as joint-emperors on 4 February, but before Geta's assassination on 26 December, Dio had a dream in which Septimius Severus encouraged him also to write up the events of Caracalla's reign (78.10.1-2). Dio thus decided to extend his history beyond the death of Severus, but again without fixing a terminal point; hence his remark that he would record events subsequent to the death of Severus "as far as it shall prove possible" (72.23.5).

5. His prolonged absence from Rome during the 220s on provincial service (Section 1.2.6) restricted Dio's access to source material for his history of the years subsequent to 211 (80.1.2). He, therefore, decided to close his detailed

---

[58] On these civil wars and wars, the exact chronology of which remains uncertain, see Birley, *African Emperor*, 108-135. For the date of Dio's work Barnes, 'Dio', 247; *contra* Millar, *Dio*, 29.

[59] For a clear summary of the arguments see Barnes, 'Dio'.

history with the death of Elagabalus in 221 and merely to add a brief coda on events as far as his own second consulship, i.e., 229 (80.2.1).

6. His history of the years 211 to 229 was complete by 230, when he retired from public life in Rome and returned to Bithynia. Once back in Bithynia Dio was commanded by a divine vision to append a quotation from Homer, *Iliad* 11 at the very end of the *Roman History* (80.5.3). This confirms that the work was complete before he returned to Bithynia in 230.

Thus, on this reconstruction Dio was researching the Julio-Claudian part of his history at some stage in the latter half of Septimius Severus' reign and composing it under Caracalla, Macrinus or Elagabalus. Although he moderately approved of Septimius Severus as an emperor, he had no respect for Caracalla or Elagabalus. Macrinus' conduct as emperor was acceptable, but Dio could not come to terms with the fact that a mere equestrian had for the first time been appointed emperor (78.41).[60] The excesses of these emperors, and especially their high-handed treatment of senators, would not have encouraged Dio to represent their Julio-Claudian predecessors in a very favourable light.

3. THE NATURE OF DIO'S HISTORY OF THE JULIO-CLAUDIAN PERIOD

3.1 Problems of Dio's Text

A major problem confronting any study of Dio on the Julio-Claudian period, and a major reason for the neglect of this part of the *Roman History*, is the fragmentary survival of Dio's text. Eleven manuscripts of Dio survive, but only two are of importance for his account of this period. A manuscript of the eleventh century (Marcianus 395 = M) contains the text of 44.35.4 – 60.28.3, but with several missing leaves (57.17.8 – 58.7.2; 59.25.1 – 60.2.1; 60.17.7 – 60.20.2; 60.22.3 – 60.26.2) and some smaller gaps or lacunae (at 58.7.3, 8.3; 59.11.2, 13.9; 60.15.3, 23.2). Two of the missing sections (60.17.7 – 60.20.2; 60.22.3 - 60.26.2) can be restored from a fifteenth century copy of this manuscript (Laurentianus 70,10 = L'). Thus only about half of Dio's original account of Tiberius survives, about three-quarters of that of Gaius, about half of that of Claudius, but absolutely nothing for the reign of Nero. The other gaps can to a certain extent be filled from various excerpts from, and epitomes (or summaries) of, Dio's *Roman History* made in the Byzantine period.[61]

TABLE 1. STATE OF DIO'S TEXT FOR BOOKS 57 - 63

refs.	years	state of text
A. TIBERIUS		
57.1 - 57.17.8	14-17	manuscript (M)
57.17.8 - 58.7.2	17-31	epitomes/excerpts
58.7.2 - 58.28.5	31-37	manuscript (M)

[60] See Millar, *Dio*, 138-50 (Severus), 150-60 (Caracalla), 160-68 (Macrinus), 168-70 (Elagabalus).
[61] Dio's text was painstakingly reconstructed from the epitomes and excerpts by Boissevain for his magisterial edition of 1895-1901.

B. GAIUS

59.1 - 59.25.1	37-40	manuscript (M)
59.25.1 - 59.30.3	40-41	epitomes/excerpts

C. CLAUDIUS

60.1 - 60.2.1	41	epitomes/excerpts
60.2.1 - 60.17.7	41-43	manuscript (M)
60.17.7 - 60.20.2	43	manuscript (L')
60.20.2 - 60.22.2	43	manuscript (M)
60.22.3 - 60.26.2	43-45	manuscript (L')
60.26.2 - 60.28.3	45-46	manuscript (M)
60.28.3 - 60.35.4	46-54	epitomes/excerpts

D. NERO

61.1 - 63.29.6	54-68	epitomes/excerpts

Excerpts were made from Dio (and many other authors) in the tenth century for various compilations prepared under the Byzantine emperor Constantine VII Porphyrogenitus: especially for the collections of examples of virtue and vice, pithy remarks and embassies. Since these were direct excerpts, they are good indicators of what Dio actually wrote; but they are usually brief, and so it is sometimes difficult to pinpoint exactly where they originally stood in Dio's narrative.[62] Much fuller are two epitomes of Dio's *Roman History*. In the 1070s the monk John Xiphilinus of Trapezus composed "Epitomes of Dio of Nicaea's *Roman History* .... embracing the reigns of twenty-five Caesars from Pompeius Magnus to Alexander son of Mamaea": i.e., he summarized Books 36 to 80 of Dio's *Roman History*, covering the years 69 B.C. to A.D. 229.[63] In 1118 for his *Epitome of World History* Zonaras used Dio as his main source for two periods of Roman history: from Aeneas to 146 B.C. and from the death of Caesar to the reign of Nerva (44 B.C. to A.D. 96). However, even in the eleventh century Dio's text did not survive in full. For Xiphilinus comments that his account of Antoninus Pius was no longer preserved in any surviving manuscript (cf. 70.1.1). Zonaras' abandonment of Dio between 146 and 44 B.C. may indicate that this part also did not survive in full.

Of these two works Xiphilinus' is the fuller summary (especially for Books 57 – 63) at about one-quarter of Dio's original in length. By comparing Xiphilinus with the original text of Dio in sections which survive, we can see that Xiphilinus was inconsistent in the way that he summarized: sometimes he quoted long sections almost verbatim, while elsewhere he passed over in silence some important incidents (e.g. Claudius' invasion of Britain in A.D. 43–44). He also tends to omit some of Dio's attempts to explain the causes of events, a distinctive feature of the *Roman History* (below, Section 4.1). It is, therefore, difficult to build up a completely balanced impression of Dio's original text from Xiphilinus.[64] Zonaras seems to have summarized more evenly, but

---

[62] Millar, *Dio*, 1-2; P.A. Brunt, 'On historical fragments and epitomes', *CQ* 24 (1980), 477-494, esp. 483.
[63] Millar, *Dio*, 2-4; 195-203; cf. Brunt (above, n. 62), 488-92.
[64] Brunt (above, n. 62), 490-91; Millar, *Dio*, 195-203.

paraphrased Dio rather than quoting him verbatim. He is, therefore, not even as useful a guide as Xiphilinus for reconstructing exactly how Dio reported a particular incident. In addition, various other Byzantine authors occasionally used Dio as a source and sometimes preserve material not found in Xiphilinus or Zonaras: notably Petrus Patricius (e.g. 59.25.9 [= **B.19**]; 60.28.7 [= **C.14**]) and John of Antioch (e.g. 59.29.1a; 59.30.1a; 59.30.3 [= **B.23**]), historians of the sixth and seventh centuries respectively, or John of Damascus, a church historian of the eighth century.

Passages that derive from the Constantinian Excerpts, Xiphilinus, Zonaras and the other Byzantine authors are marked with an asterisk in the translation below, to differentiate them from genuine Dio. When assessing Dio as a historian, we need constantly to bear in mind whether we are dealing with Dio's authentic text or with Byzantine summaries of it. The latter, though useful, are not a completely reliable guide as to how Dio described and/or analysed a particular historical event.

3.2   Dio and his Sources

3.2.1   Dio's sources of information

Dio spent ten years collecting evidence for his history of Rome from its foundation to the death of Severus (72.23.5, quoted above, p. 26; cf. frag. 1.2, quoted below, p. 34). He relied on three types of source material: written sources, oral testimony and autopsy (53.19.6, quoted below, p. 33). For his account of the Julio-Claudian period oral sources were obviously not available, while autopsy was useful only for confirming geographical or ethnographic details (59.17.1 [= **B.13**]; cf. 48.50-51; 49.36.4).[65] In addition to formal written sources, Dio also drew material from the general traditions that still circulated about individual emperors (58.11.7 [= **A.7**], 59.1.1 [= **B.1**]).[66] The quality of Dio's *Roman History* depends to a large degree on the nature of the source material that he was using. During his years of research Dio was for the most part in Rome or at his country estate at Capua, and so had good access to earlier histories and written records. He never names any of his sources; so it is pointless trying to pinpoint which author has provided him with a particular piece of information.[67] But to assess the reliability of his history, it is important to ascertain the general nature of the written sources at his disposal, and the ways in which Dio used them.

First, there are sufficient parallels in Dio's account of the Julio-Claudian period to Tacitus, *Annals* and Suetonius, *Lives* (both composed in the early

---

[65] The earliest oral report concerns the death of Trajan: 69.1.3.
[66] He often signals this by saying, "I have heard that ....": see Millar, *Dio*, 36 (with references); for a different, but less persuasive, interpretation cf. R. Syme, *RP* III, 1035, n. 65. By contrast, Tacitus claims to have rejected this type of evidence: Tac. *A*. 4.10-11.
[67] See the comments of Millar, *Dio*, 34 against such traditional, but futile, attempts to trace the exact sources of Dio's information.

second century) to suggest that he had access to both these works. However, there are also sufficient divergences to prove that he was not using these sources alone.[68] Other surviving historical works were available to him: Josephus, *Antiquities of the Jews* and *The Jewish War* (composed in the later first century) and Plutarch's imperial lives (composed in the early second century, of which only those of Galba and Otho now survive).[69] There is little trace that he used Velleius Paterculus, the historian writing under Tiberius. However, other annalistic accounts of the Julio-Claudian period (now lost) were available to Dio: for the reign of Tiberius the works of Aufidius Bassus (the *German War*, and, especially, the *Histories*) and M. Servilius Nonianus; for the reigns of Gaius, Claudius and Nero the histories of Pliny the Elder, Fabius Rusticus and Cluvius Rufus.[70] All these works were written by Roman senators or high-ranking equestrians who lived through the periods that they described.

Dio explicitly mentions two of Seneca's works, the *Apocolocyntosis* and *Consolation to Polybius* (60.35.3-4; 61.10.2), and so probably used them and others as sources.[71] He may also have consulted the autobiographies of Tiberius and Claudius, as did Suetonius (Suet. *Tib.* 61.1; *Cl.* 41.3), and the memoirs (*commentarii*) of such major figures as the younger Agrippina, used by Tacitus and the elder Pliny (Tac. *Annals* 4.53; Plin. *NH* 7.8.46), or of such prominent generals as Cn. Domitius Corbulo and C. Suetonius Paullinus.[72] Thus for his account of the Julio-Claudians Dio had at his disposal plenty of material written during, or very soon after, the period. This is obviously of benefit for the quality of his history, as long as he was aware of the possible biases and slants that such contemporary authors may have introduced into their accounts. Cluvius Rufus, for example, was forced to act as a herald on Nero's tour of Greece, an undignified rôle for an ex-consul (63.14.3); such personal indignities may have coloured his presentation of Nero.

Dio also used the written records of proceedings of the senate (the *acta senatus*) and the records of daily events of public interest (the *acta diurna*).[73] The former included the names of the annual magistrates, accounts of trials and summaries of emperors' speeches in the senate, the latter news of the imperial family, details of public spectacles and new public buildings. Dio provides much more abundant detail about public spectacles and public buildings than does Tacitus, who tartly observed that they were beneath the dignity of history (e.g.

---

[68] On Dio and Tacitus see R. Syme, 'The year 33 in Tacitus and Dio', *Athenaeum* 61 (1983), 3-23 [= *RP* IV, 223-44]; on Dio and Suetonius G.B. Townend, 'The sources of the Greek in Suetonius', *Hermes* 88 (1960), 98-120.

[69] On Dio and Josephus see Eisman (above, n.41).

[70] See further J.J. Wilkes, 'Julio-Claudian historians', *Classical World* 65 (1972), 177-92, 196-203; G.B. Townend, 'Traces in Dio Cassius of Cluvius, Aufidius and Pliny', *Hermes* 89 (1961), 227-48. See also the index entries for the individual authors in R. Syme, *Tacitus* (2 vols., 1958).

[71] Millar, *Dio*, 78.

[72] Wilkes (above, n. 70), 181-82, 185-90.

[73] On the *acta senatus* see P.M. Swan, 'Cassius Dio on Augustus', *Phoenix* 41 (1987), 272-91, esp. 285; on the *acta diurna* B. Baldwin, 'The *acta diurna*', *Chiron* 9 (1979), 189-203, esp. 196.

59.7.1-8 [= **B.5**]; 60.33.3-4; 61.9.1; 63.3.1 [= **D.1**]; cf. Tac. *Ann.* 13.31). Such details most likely derive from the *acta diurna*. Whether Dio had himself consulted these records, or whether he picked up such details at second-hand from the works of earlier historians is not clear.

Thus Dio had many different types of written information at his disposal: some of it authoritative, but much that was sensationalist and owed more to fiction than to fact. This variety in the nature and quality of his sources often shows through and gives the *Roman History* an unevenness of texture. It contains much detailed, well-researched and credible information, but also many anecdotes, which provide more insight into contemporary and posthumous invective against the emperors than reliable historical fact. Thus, before accepting everything that Dio reports, we need to evaluate it critically and assess its credibility.

3.2.2   *Dio's method of collecting evidence*

Dio gives no indication as to how he collected his source material. The normal method was for the historian, often assisted by a literate slave or freedman, to make extensive notes and even some verbatim extracts as he was reading his sources (or more often, as they were being read aloud to him).[74] It was such notes and extracts that then formed Dio's basic raw material when he came to compose his history. However, any act of reading involves interpretation. Thus Dio's own prejudices and prejudgements on the past influenced what he chose to annotate and what he chose to omit. The process of historical selection and interpretation began as soon as he commenced research. The manner in which he consciously or subconsciously interpreted his source material again affects Dio's quality as a historical source.

3.3   Dio's Method of Composition

Dio took twelve years to compose his history of events from the foundation of Rome to the death of Severus in 211 (Section 2.2). Much of this composition took place at his country villa near Capua,

> where I live whenever I am residing in Italy. I chose this place for a number of reasons, but especially because of its peace and quiet, so that when I have time off from the affairs of the city I can compose this history.
>
> (76.2.1)

It has often been assumed that Dio composed his history in chronological order, starting with the foundation of Rome and gradually proceeding towards the events of his own lifetime. This assumption has then led to attempts to date individual sections of the history.[75] This is a dangerous methodology based on a dangerous assumption. Not only does Dio not provide any information on

---

[74] For Pliny the Elder's working methods as a historian see Plin. *Letters* 3.5.10-11: works were read to him (presumably by a slave), while he took notes and made extracts; cf. Lucian, *How to Write History* 48. For Plutarch's working methods as a biographer see C.B.R. Pelling, *JHS* 99 (1979), 74-96, esp. 83ff; *JHS* 100 (1980), 127-40.

[75] Millar, *Dio*, 30-32, 38-39, 193-94; cf. Barnes, 'Dio', 251-52.

this matter, but other historians (e.g. Thucydides) clearly wrote their history in sections and did not necessarily progress in linear fashion from start to finish.[76] As we have seen, Dio incorporated his earlier work on the civil wars and wars of Septimius Severus into his *Roman History* (Section 2.2). Here is one section, therefore, that at least in its initial form was written before his account, for example, of the Julio-Claudian period. And so, although it would be useful to know when he was writing his account of the Julio-Claudian Principate, it is impossible to do so.

Dio, like all other ancient historians, considered his history a literary work; it had to be carefully structured and artistically expressed. Thus composition involved a second stage of selection and arrangement of material, and interpretation. Dio's task during this stage of composition was to select from his notes and extracts what he considered the most important material and then to mould this into his own narrative and framework of analysis (cf. Lucian, *How to Write History*, 48-51). He would not have composed with his written sources in front of him, copying or combining material directly from them. It may be that he first produced a rough draft before making revisions and final polishing, but again he provides no explicit evidence for this.[77] Most importantly, this method of composition ensured that the picture he drew of the past, though in part derived from previous accounts, was very much one of his own literary creation.

At the start of his account of Augustus Dio outlines his general method of presenting imperial, as opposed to Republican, history. He explains how it was much more difficult to verify events that took place under the emperors than those of the free Republic. Government was now carried on behind closed doors and so was much less accountable and hence verifiable. He then reveals how he coped with this problem:

> Therefore, from this point on [sc. 27 B.C.] I shall relate all those events which it is necessary to relate just as they have been reported by some source, whether they really occurred like this or in a different fashion. However, there shall be added to these accounts something of my own judgement, as far as possible, on those points on which I have been able to form an opinion that is different from the common view, taking account of all the material that I have collected from my reading, from oral reports and by autopsy. (53.19.6)

Three important points emerge from this passage about Dio's methods of composition. First, he was selective in his reporting of the past. Secondly, for factual details he relied on existing written sources, backed up (where relevant) by oral reports and autopsy. Thirdly, he supplemented the existing sources by including "something of his own judgement". In all this he followed the historiographical principles of his most important model as a historian, Thucydides (cf. Thuc. 1.20-22).

First, Dio's principle of selectivity. Given the massive scale of his history, he could not afford to report the past in the same detail as his sources; he had to select the most important material. He is explicit on this point in a surviving fragment from the (mostly lost) Preface:

[76] For Thucydides see V.J. Hunter, *Thucydides the Artful Reporter* (1973); S. Hornblower, *Thucydides* (1987), ch. 6.
[77] Despite Barnes, 'Dio', 251-52.

> I have read almost everything that has been written by anybody about them [sc. the Romans]; but I have not written up everything, but included only what I judged most important. (fr. 1.2)

Hence, for example, he includes just one or two items of a package of reforms or gives just one or two examples of a particular characteristic of the emperor. He frequently reminds his readers of this principle of selectivity: e.g. 59.22.5 [= **B.17**]; 60.11.6; 63.17.2 [= **D.4**]; 63.18.3. He does not want to burden his readers with too much detail (59.18.3 [= **B.14**]; cf. 72.7.3), and so knowingly omitted some historical incidents from his history. Thus when using Dio as a source, one must never assume that we have all the details of an emperor's reign; his history was never meant to be comprehensive.

To keep the length of his history under control, Dio restricted himself to writing a history of the Romans, not a world history:

> I shall recount the affairs of the Romans in full to the best of my ability; as for the affairs of other peoples these shall only be written up if they have a bearing on my subject. (fr. 2.4)

Thus, he refuses to go into unnecessary details about the Etruscans (fr. 2.4), Egyptians (58.27.1; 75.13.3) or Jews (37.17.4). His excuse for not writing much about the latter was that the history of the Jews had been related in great detail by other writers, and it had no particular relevance to his history (37.17.4). His concentration on the Romans was also perhaps in part a reaction against the genre of world history, which had once again become very popular during the second century A.D. (Lucian, *How to Write History* 18). Thus just as Thucydides had reacted vehemently against Herodotus' type of history in the fifth century B.C., so Dio, who modelled himself on Thucydides, distanced himself from those numerous contemporary historians who modelled themselves on Herodotus.

Along with his selection of what was most important, he also had to decide what was appropriate for inclusion in his history. History had always been considered a dignified genre of literature; sensationalist details were unfit for inclusion, being appropriate only for biography (Lucian, *How to Write History* 20, 27-28; Tac. *A.* 13.31; 14.32-33; cf. Plut. *Alexander* 1). Just occasionally Dio felt that he had to break this rule, and so had to apologize for including what some might consider an undignified detail (e.g. 63.20.6 [= **D.5**]; 66.9.4; 72.18.3).

Secondly, Dio was for the most part content to rely on existing accounts of earlier Roman history and accept the traditional versions of events. He did not attempt to write a completely new or original history of Rome. Not only was that impractical given the massive chronological scope of his work, but complete originality was never expected of the historian in classical antiquity.

Thirdly, however, this did not stop Dio including "something of his own judgement". By this Dio means that he used his historical judgement to criticize his sources when necessary. Sometimes he showed scepticism towards the traditional version of an event, even if he could not suggest a more credible alternative (59.17.3 [= **B.13**]; 59.28.2 [= **B.22**]; 63.3.2 [= **D.1**]; 63.17.5 [= **D.4**]). At other times he just reported variant accounts of the same event, but without adjudicating between them (58.11.6-7 [= **A.7**]); 59.2.6 [= **B.2**]); 63.25.3 [= **D.6**]). But occasionally he was openly critical of his sources and attempted to give what he saw as the correct version (59.24.2; 63.24.4 [= **D.6**]). But Dio also used his historical judgement in other ways: for example, in interpreting the past as he researched and composed his history, but most of all in explaining historical events. For, as we shall see (Section 4.1), one of the hallmarks of Dio's history is its constant concern to explain causes of events and motivations for particular actions.

Dio did not just slavishly reproduce what he found in his sources; his task as a historian involved considerable remoulding of his material. He did not always discuss events in the same chronological order as his source: thus he often reports the same events as Tacitus, but sometimes under different years.[78] He also combined events from different years into a cluster to illustrate a particular characteristic of the emperor (Section 3.4.1). And finally, he often included the later stages, or ramifications, of a story at the same time as it is introduced, usually signposting these "flash-forwards" with the remark "but this happened later" (57.2.6-7, cf. 58.3.1 [= **A.1**]; 58.11.7 [= **A.7**]; 59.15.5 [= **B.11**], cf. 60.17.2 [= **C.9**]). In short, he relied heavily for his evidence on previous accounts, but significantly recast this evidence to suit the underlying themes and purpose of his history.

3.4 Dio's *Roman History*

Dio's work covered the history of Rome from the foundation of the city right down to his own day, a span of about a thousand years. Going back as far as the foundation was one of the hallmarks of earlier histories of Rome (e.g. Fabius Pictor, Livy, Dionysius of Halicarnassus), but Livy's monumental work written under Augustus had accomplished the task so successfully that later historians were forced to adopt different approaches: they covered much briefer periods or concentrated on a war or series of wars. Dio was the first historian since Livy to start once again with the foundation of Rome. Both Dio and Livy wrote under emperors who had won power after violent civil wars and were seeking to legitimate their position by respecting the traditions of the Roman past. Their histories helped to set Septimius Severus and Augustus firmly into a historical sequence that connected them right back to the foundation of the city.

3.4.1 Structure

By starting with the foundation of Rome, Dio declared himself firmly part of the annalistic tradition; but to emphasize the point, he also structured his material within an annalistic framework, the traditional and most appropriate medium for recounting Roman history.[79] Thus he divided his narrative clearly between events in Rome and events overseas, sometimes signposting the transition from one to the other (58.25.1; 58.26.1; 59.12.2 [= **B.10**]; 60.19.1 [= **C.11**]; 73.14.3; 79.3.1). Events at Rome are narrated year by year, but external

---

[78] e.g. 57.19.4 (on the prediction that Galba would become emperor, reported under the year 20; cf. Tac. *A*. 6.20, but reported under the year 33); 58.27.1 (on the appearance of a phoenix in Egypt, reported by Dio under the year 36 as an omen of Tiberius' death; cf. Tac. *A*. 6.28 under the year 34).

[79] T.P. Wiseman, *Clio's Cosmetics* (1979), 9-26; C.W. Fornara, *The Nature of History in Ancient Greece and Rome* (1983), 52-75.

events over several years are sometimes combined into a single narrative cluster (60.9 [partly = **C.6**]; 60.19-23 [= **C.11**]; 62.19-23), very much a technique used by Tacitus (cf. Tac. *A*. 12.31-40; 15.1-17). To mark the transition from one year to the next, Dio usually mentions by name the new pair of ordinary consuls (58.17.1; 58.20.5; 58.25.2; 58.26.5; 58.27.1; 59.9.1; 59.13.1-2; 60.10.1; 60.23.1 [= **C.11**]; 60.25.1; 60.27.1 [= **C.13**]; 60.29.1; 63.1.1 [= **D.1**]).[80]

However, Dio did not write exactly in the manner of the earlier Roman annalists. He was more flexible in the way that he marked the transitions between years: for example, he introduces the year 34 as "the twentieth of Tiberius' reign" and then only names the new consuls in the context of their supervision of decennial celebrations (58.24.1); similarly, he reports the change from 39 to 40 incidentally in a passage focusing upon Gaius' increasing cruelty and licentiousness (59.24.2). More drastically, he put the personality and actions of the emperor very much at the centre of his picture to an even greater degree than Tacitus had done (cf. Tac. *A*. 1.1-14 on Augustus; id. 6.51 on Tiberius).

Dio arranged his material in a distinctive and more or less regular pattern (see Table 2). Each reign opens with an account of the emperor's accession, followed by a brief survey of the emperor's character and the main features of his rule. Dio here emphasizes those aspects of the emperor's character that will later receive the most attention. He then clearly signposts the transition from the biographical opening to the annalistic narrative: "such was Nero's character; I shall now relate each event in succession" (61.6.1). He closes each reign with a list of omens presaging the emperor's death, a brief summary of the character of the dead emperor and finally a bald chronological calculation of the length of his life and reign. To illustrate this in more detail, the structure of Dio's accounts of the reigns of Tiberius and Claudius is analysed in Table 3.

TABLE 2. THE MAIN STRUCTURAL FEATURES OF DIO'S ACCOUNT OF AUGUSTUS TO NERO

1.   ACCESSION AND BRIEF SURVEY OF THE CHARACTER OF THE EMPEROR AND THE EMPEROR'S RULE:

Augustus	53.12-21		Tiberius	57.1-13
Gaius	59.1-5		Claudius	60.1-3.1
Nero	61.1-5			

cf. Vitellius (65.1-7); Vespasian (66.1.1, 10.3-11.3); Titus (66.18-19); Domitian (67.1.1-3.4); Trajan (68.6.3-7.5); Hadrian (69.3-7); Commodus (72.1); Pertinax (73.1-4); Macrinus (78.11.1-3)

---

[80] When the emperor holds the consulship, Dio sometimes fails to give his colleague's name: e.g. 59.24.2; 60.17.1 [= **C.9**]. In the latter case Dio eventually mentions Claudius' consular colleague of the year 43 at 60.21.2 [= **C.11**]. Dio's epitomators are not so punctilious in this matter: no consuls are reported at the start of 31, 41, 48-65 and 67-68.

2. TRANSITION TO ANNALS:

Augustus	53.22.1	Tiberius	57.13.6-14.1
Gaius	59.6.1	Claudius	60.3.1
Nero	61.6.1		

cf. Hadrian (69.8.1); Caracalla (77.12.1); Macrinus (78.11.4).

3. OMENS OF EMPEROR'S DEATH:

Augustus	56.29	Tiberius	58.26.5-27.1
Gaius	59.29.3-4	Claudius	60.35.1
Nero	63.28.1 (only one of Dio's original list preserved?)		

cf. Otho (64.7.1-2); Vitellius (65.8.1-2, 16.1); Vespasian (66.17.2); Domitian (67.16); Commodus (72.24.1-3); Caracalla (78.7-8); Macrinus (78.25-26.1, 30.1)

4. SUMMARY OF REIGN INCLUDING PITHY REMARK(S):

Augustus	56.43-45	Tiberius	58.28.5
Gaius	59.30.1a	Claudius	60.35.2-4
Nero	63.29.3		

cf. Hadrian (69.23.2-3); M. Aurelius (71.34.2-36.4); Pertinax (74.5.6-7); Septimius Severus (76.16-17); Caracalla (78.10); Macrinus (78.40.3-41.4)

5. CALCULATION OF LIFE AND REIGN OF EMPEROR:

Augustus	56.30.5	Tiberius	58.28.5
Gaius	59.30.1 (reign only)	Claudius	60.34.3
Nero	63.29.3		

cf. Galba (64.6.5); Otho (64.15.2); Vitellius (65.22.1); Vespasian (66.17.3-5); Titus (66.18.4, 26.4); Domitian (67.18.2); Trajan (68.33.3: reign only); Hadrian (69.23.1); Antoninus Pius (71.1.1: reign only); M. Aurelius (71.34.5); Pertinax (73.10.3); Didius Julianus (73.17.5); Septimius Severus (76.17.4); Caracalla (78.6.5); Macrinus (78.41.4)

TABLE 3. THE STRUCTURE OF DIO'S ACCOUNT OF TIBERIUS AND CLAUDIUS

A. TIBERIUS

57.1-13	Accession of Tiberius and brief survey of his character and the nature of his rule (includes material on the revolts of the Pannonian and German legions):
7.2-9.3	his initial moderation (his "democratic", i.e., Republican, behaviour);
10	his filial piety towards Augustus
11-12	his approachability
13.1-5	his increasing harshness
57.13.6-14.1	Transition from biography to annals: "Such was the conduct of Tiberius, at least as long as Germanicus was alive." (57.13.6) His change of character after the death of Germanicus.

"I shall now relate in order the various events of his reign, at least those worthy of record." (57.14.1)

58.26.5-27.1	Omens foreshadowing the death of Tiberius
58.28.5	Death of Tiberius; brief closing remark: "Tiberius possessed a great many virtues and a great many vices and displayed each set as if he did not possess the other." Date of his death (incorrect); length of his life and reign (also, therefore, incorrect).

B. CLAUDIUS

60.1.1-3.1	Accession of Claudius and brief survey of his character and the nature of his rule:
2.1	Claudius' healthy mind, but sickly body
2.4	Claudius influenced by women and freedmen
2.5	his enjoyment of alcohol and sex, which made him malleable to the designs of women and freedmen; his cowardice, which also overpowered his reason and allowed him to be forced into things by others
3.1	despite all this, when free from freedmen and women, he did many things in a proper fashion
60.3.1	Transition from biography to annals signposted: "he was of such a nature.... I shall now relate in succession the things that he did."
60.34.2-3	Death of Claudius; date of death; length of life and reign (Xiphilinus)
60.35.1	Omens foreshadowing Claudius' death (Xiphilinus)
60.35.2-4	Claudius' burial and some pithy remarks sum up his reign (Xiphilinus)

In his biographical introductions to each emperor Dio often clusters together events drawn from different periods of the reign. We have to be aware, therefore, that some events have been displaced chronologically in his narrative, to fit in with Dio's style of writing history. Furthermore, even in his annalistic sections Dio developed his biographical portraits of the emperor. To illustrate a particular character trait (e.g. Tiberius' duplicity, Gaius' contrariness, Claudius' conscientiousness or Nero's flippancy), he used anecdotal evidence. Thus when he relates how Domitian used to impale flies on the end of his stylus, he feels it necessary to defend his inclusion of anecdotes:

> Although this incident is unworthy of the dignity of history, I have, nevertheless, included it because it is very revealing of his character and because he continued to do this even after he became emperor. (66.9.4: Xiphilinus)

Dio often brings such anecdotes to a climax with a witty remark, or punch-line, which adds touches of humour to his narrative, and enhances the impact of the anecdote (59.19.1-7 [= **B.14**]; 59.26.8-9; 60.17.6 [= **C.9**]; 63.26.4 [= **D.7**]). He drew many of them from the rich collection of traditional stories (especially about evil rulers) which circulated widely in the Roman period and which any writer or orator could adapt to fit whatever historical context was required.[81]

Many of the anecdotes that Dio tells of Gaius are also found in Suetonius' life, but in completely different geographical and/or chronological settings.[82] Such anecdotes, therefore, are worthless as evidence for precise historical events, but may still reveal much about general Roman attitudes and prejudices.

Dio includes omens not just of the impending death of the emperor, but also of other important events throughout his narrative. Omens were a traditional feature of Roman annalistic history (Livy 43.13.1; Tac. *A.* 14.12; *H.* 2.50), and so were quite appropriate in a work of Dio's type. They enhanced the dignity of history and also served a literary purpose, providing variety in narrative sections.[83] They had also become prominent in biographies of the emperors (Suet. *Aug.* 97; *Tib.* 74; *G.* 57; *Cl.* 46; *N.* 46). Dio showed a keener interest in them than many ancient historians: his first literary work, after all, had been a booklet outlining the dreams and omens that had foretold Septimius Severus' rise to power (Section 2.2). But this interest should not be interpreted to mean that Dio believed in them; for in an excerpt from his narrative of the Second Punic War he is openly sceptical about their meaning (fr. 57.22). Finally, the calculation of the length of emperors' lives and reigns is a feature that Dio took over from the biographical tradition (cf. Suet. *Aug.* 100.1, *Tib.* 73.1; *G.* 59, *Cl.* 45, *N.* 57.1). In general, such precise computations were considered beneath the dignity of history.[84]

Dio thus used a historiographical structure appropriate to the changed political realities of the imperial age. For just as the traditional Republican constitution remained in place, but was now considerably overshadowed by the activities of the emperor, so Dio retained a traditional annalistic structure, but introduced some of the techniques of biography to help analyse, and emphasize, the character of each emperor.

3.4.2 Literary Style

Because history was considered very much a branch of literature, a central part of the historian's task was to embellish his account in an appropriate literary style and to fill out his narrative in a plausible fashion (Lucian, *How to Write History* 43-46).[85] Dio clearly followed this principle:

> I have used a finely-wrought style, as was appropriate for the subject matter. Let no-one, however, for this reason suspect the truth of what I have written – a thing that has happened with some other writers. For I have been anxious to be accurate in both these respects, as far I have been able. (fr. 1.2)

To improve his style of writing, he read widely in those authors who wrote in the Attic dialect of Greek (55.12.4-5). Indeed he writes in a style reminiscent of the

---

[81] See R.P. Saller, 'Anecdotes as historical evidence', *G&R* 27 (1980), 69-83.
[82] The stories told of Gaius at 59.13.6 and 59.22.3-4 [= **B.16**] are also found at Suet. *G.* 30.2, 27.1, and 41.2; cf. the anecdote told of Tiberius at 57.21.7 is also found at Petr. *Sat.* 51 and Plin. *NH* 36.26.66.
[83] Millar, *Dio*, 16, 29; Syme, *Tacitus*, 521-23.
[84] W.F. Snyder, 'On chronology in the imperial books of Cassius Dio's Roman History', *Klio* 33 (1940), 39-56.
[85] Fornara (above, n. 79), 134-37.

classical writers of Attic Greek: the orators Aeschines, Lysias, Isocrates, Demosthenes, the philosopher Plato, but most of all the historian Thucydides.[86]

One of the most distinctive features of Dio's *Roman History* is its consistently rhetorical style. Dio was thoroughly steeped in rhetorical techniques as a result of his education, his reading of classical Greek authors, and his experience at Rome as an advocate in the law-courts, as a senator and Roman magistrate, and as an imperial counsellor. Not surprisingly, his narrative is punctuated by highly rhetorical set speeches, although from the reign of Tiberius onwards they are markedly less frequent that they had been in his narrative of the free Republic and the reign of Augustus (Table 4).[87]

TABLE 4. SPEECHES IN DIO'S ACCOUNT OF TIBERIUS – NERO

59.16.1-7 Speech of Gaius in the senate announcing his change in attitude towards Tiberius: a mixture of direct and reported speech [= **B.12**]

61.15.3-4 Brief extract from speech of Thrasea Paetus, reacting to the adulation of his fellow-senators towards Nero (Xiphilinus)

62.3-5 1st. speech of British leader Boudica: on the evils of the Romans and Roman imperialism (Xiphilinus)

62.6.2-5 2nd. speech of Boudica: full-blown invective against the Romans and their effeminate leader Nero (Xiphilinus)

62.9-11 3 short speeches of the Roman general, Suetonius Paullinus, each to a separate division of the Roman army on the eve of battle with Boudica: standard hortatory speeches with invective against barbaric Britons (Xiphilinus)

63.5.2-3 Brief speeches of Tiridates and Nero at Tiridates' coronation in the Forum at Rome in 66 [= **D.1**] (Xiphilinus)

63.22.3-6 Speech of Vindex, justifying his revolt against Nero [= **D.6**] (Xiphilinus)

Set speeches had always been a feature of Greek and Roman historiography, not least because they gave the historian the chance to show off his rhetorical skills (Lucian, *How to Write History* 58). Dio, like other historians, felt free to invent these speeches more or less from his own imagination; they did not have to correspond to the actual words of speeches delivered at the time in question, as long as they were appropriate to the occasion. Dio's speeches for the most part contain fairly standard rhetorical commonplaces and trite moralizing, but occasionally demonstrate a marked rhetorical power. Most dramatic in the Julio-Claudian section are the balanced sets of speeches given to Boudica and Suetonius Paullinus, full of sensationalist, if traditional, invective against the effeminate, luxurious Romans and the barbaric Britons respectively (62.3-4; 62.6.2-5; 62.9-11). Dio uses a mixture of reported and direct speech for a speech

---

[86] On the popularity of Attic style in the later second century cf. Lucian, *How to Write History* 21; C.P. Jones, *Culture and Society in Lucian* (1986), 149-59. For historians keen to imitate Thucydides cf. Lucian, *How to Write History* 15, 25-26, 42.

[87] See further Millar, *Dio*, 49-55, 78-83, 100-118. In those parts of Dio's history now lost there may have been a few more speeches which the later epitomators chose to omit.

delivered by Gaius in the senate, but in the central emphatic section he introduces a familiar rhetorical device: he has Gaius assume the personality of Tiberius, who then advises Gaius how to deal with a recalcitrant senate (59.16.1-7 [= **B.12**]). Dio also includes a number of famous remarks (many no doubt apocryphal) made by the emperor or other leading figures. They often serve as punch-lines for the anecdotes which Dio uses to illustrate the character of a particular emperor (59.6.3 [= **B.4**]; 59.22.3-4 [= **B.16**]; 59.26.9 [= **B.20**]; 59.27.6 [= **B.21**]; 60.17.6 [= **C.9**]; 63.29.2 [= **D.8**]).

Dio's rhetorical skills are prominent throughout his history. At climactic moments of his narrative, or when he wishes to stress particularly strong moral disapproval, he launches into high-flown rhetoric for special emphasis. Thus he celebrates Sejanus' condemnation and Gaius' assassination with long series of melodramatic rhetorical contrasts (58.11.1-2 [= **A.7**]; 59.30.1a [= **B.23**]). Similarly, Gaius' dressing up as various divinities (59.26.5-8 [= **B.20**]), Nero's forcing members of the most distinguished Roman families to compete in the circus, theatre and amphitheatre (61.17.3-5) or his frequent appearances as lyre-player, tragic actor and charioteer (63.8.2-4, 9.1-6 [= **D.2**]) elicit from Dio fully-blown rhetorical tirades of moral indignation. Much of this emphatic rhetoric echoes themes found in the formal speeches: for example, the speech that Dio gives to Vindex (63.22.3-6 [= **D.6**]) reproduces language already used in a purple passage of fierce invective against Nero's artistic appearances in Greece (63.9.1-6 [= **D.2**]).

But for Dio rhetoric also had a formative influence on his whole cast of thought and his mode of presenting the past. A central, structural feature of Greek rhetoric was antithesis: i.e., the elaborate, sometimes forced, drawing of contrasts between events, types of behaviour or even causes of events: "while doing this, he still did that"; "sometimes he would act ...., at other times ....."; "something happened allegedly because ....., but really because ......". Such formulations occur throughout Dio's speeches and narrative. His fondness for antithesis led him to emphasize, and sometimes over-emphasize, contradictions in people's character: thus, in Dio's view Tiberius was naturally duplicitous, always appearing to want one thing when in fact he wanted the complete opposite (58.6.2-4 [= **A.5**]), while Gaius' character was marked by a whole series of contradictions (59.3-4 [= **B.3**]). Furthermore, this antithetical mind-set led Dio to analyse emperors very much in comparative terms (Section 4.3).

Dio's antithetical style also substantially affected his view of human nature and the nature of government, and hence his historical interpretation. He frequently reports the alleged reasons for a particular action, but then tries to establish, as a contrast, the real reason (59.10.7 [= **B.8**]; 59.21.2 [= **B.15**]; 60.24.5 [= **C.12**]). Thus the actions of individuals and especially those in power are interpreted and presented in a realistic or even cynical way. It allows him, in exactly the same manner as Thucydides, to expose the true nature of power.[88] Although emperors made a show of moderation and civility, they were fully aware that their power allowed them to justify virtually any course of action (59.16.7 [= **B.12**]; cf. 61.1.1-2; 61.11.1).

Dio shows a keen eye for the paradoxical and uses antithesis to bring this out

---

[88] On this see J. de Romilly, *Thucydides and Athenian Imperialism* (1963).

with good ironical effect.[89] Thus he wryly reports that Tiberius on the same day entertained Asinius Gallus on Capri and condemned him by letter in the senate at Rome (58.3.3 [= **A.1**]) or that Gaius was libidinous, but came to hate all those after whom he had lusted (59.3.3 [= **B.3**]) or that Claudius, although the ruler of Romans and Roman subjects, was a slave to his wives and freedmen (60.2.5 [= **C.2**]) or that Nero, the descendant of Augustus, sought to emulate lyre-players, while Helius, an imperial freedman, emulated Caesars (63.12.2 [= **D.3**]).

In his narrative Dio often adopts a mildly ironical tone, which he heightens with touches of wit and humour. This comes out clearest in his treatment of Gaius, when, for example, he relates how Gaius summoned some senators in the middle of the night and danced for them (59.5.5 [= **B.3**]), or how on his farcical British campaign he gave the order to collect sea-shells ("he needed booty, of course, for his triumphal procession"), and proudly claimed that he had enslaved the Ocean (59.25.2-3 [= **B.18**]). He underscores the ridicule of Gaius masquerading as various divinities by reporting two sardonically witty remarks, one made by a humble Gallic cobbler (59.26.9 [= **B.20**]), the other by a sycophantic senator (59.27.6 [= **B.21**]). But most of all he retells the story of Gaius' triumphal procession at the bridge at Baiae with amused scepticism and tired irony (59.17 [= **B.13**]. Dio quietly scoffs at Gaius' military pretensions: he put on the breastplate of Alexander, "so it is claimed" (59.17.3); "he charged right into Puteoli as if he was attacking some enemy" (59.17.4); "a whole collection of things followed in his wake, as though they were booty" (59.17.5); "of course he had to deliver an address, since he was on such a campaign and had won such a great victory" (59.17.6). Such ironic humour and sardonic wit enhance the literary quality of the work and help to make his history more entertaining to read.[90]

All this serves to emphasize the essentially literary nature of Dio's work; he is at all stages keen to produce a polished account of the past. Although he makes the traditional claim that his concern for literary embellishment in no way reduces the accuracy of his history (fr. 1.2), Dio clearly felt no compunction in rearranging some of his material for stylistic purposes. He was often keener to produce a striking rhetorical effect than establish the fundamental veracity of some piece of historical information. We would be wrong to criticize him for this; for historians in antiquity had a markedly different view of what constituted historical truth than that of modern historians. But nonetheless, Dio's concern for style had a distinct impact on his analysis of the past and led him to emphasize, subordinate or suppress certain pieces of evidence, depending on how they fitted into his overall stylistic framework.

3.4.3   Dio's interests and viewpoints

There are certain recurrent features in Dio's narrative which suggest themselves as special interests. First, he gives quite some prominence to Roman

---

[89] This love of paradox was a feature of other literary works of the period: see Reardon (above, n. 48), 237-74.
[90] For the often neglected place of wit in history see P. Plass, *Wit and the Writing of History* (1988).

political institutions and customs. He is interested in minor constitutional details: for example, that it was the praetors' duty to carry out the duties of the consuls when they were out of Rome (59.24.3), or that a tribune rather than a consul would summon the senate to appoint a suffect (i.e., replacement) tribune (60.16.8). He dutifully reported changes in the number of magistrates appointed and the length of their period in office (59.20.5 [= **B.15**]; 60.21.2 [= **C.11**]; cf. 43.46.5-6), as well as the many minor changes made in the oath sworn annually by the magistrates to uphold the acts of the present emperor and certain of his predecessors (47.18.3; 57.8.4; 59.9.1; 59.13.1; 60.4.6; 60.10.1). Furthermore, he regularly points out when various social and political customs were instituted, and distinguishes between customs still in force in his own day and those that had become defunct (see Appendix 2).[91] His long career as Roman senator, magistrate and provincial governor helps to explain this interest. Much of this material is concerned with procedures in the senate or customs of the senatorial order, and so reflect and emphasize his pride in being of senatorial status. But some of it is of such minor historical importance as to suggest that Dio had a strong antiquarian streak as a historian.

Dio shows more interest in financial matters than many other Greek and Roman historians, possibly the result of his having to deal with finance during his quaestorship and (especially) when he was curator of Pergamum and Smyrna (Section 1.2).[92] Thus he notes the first striking of silver coins at Rome (8.7.2), gives precise details on the value of the *aureus* (55.12.4) and often mentions the images on coins (44.4.4; 47.25.3; 60.22.3; 77.12.6; 77.16.5). He takes particular interest in the public treasury and the various changes in its administrative structure (cf. 43.48.3; 53.2.1; 53.16.1; 53.22.3; 53.32.2; 60.4.4; 60.10.3-4; 60.24.1-3 [= **C.12**]). He gives precise figures for treasury reserves at the start of Gaius' reign (59.2.6 [= **B.2**]). Not surprisingly, in Maecenas' speech advising Augustus how to run the Empire finance receives a good deal of attention (52.25, 28-30).[93]

He also shows interest in scientific issues. He has a long digression explaining the causes of solar and lunar eclipses (60.26). He is at pains to explain why at Hierapolis in Asia certain vapours killed all living things except eunuchs; he had clearly gone to the area to make enquiries, but was unable to explain this puzzling phenomenon (68.27.3). Finally, he includes a digression on the sources of the Nile, justifying it on the grounds that he had "accurately investigated it in many quarters" (75.13.3-4). Thus, although Thucydides was clearly his model as a historian, Dio did not totally exclude Herodotean features from his history.[94]

Despite these scientific interests, Dio still displays a traditional belief in the importance of the supernatural, especially for explaining otherwise inexplicable events. In his view the world was governed by two forces: divine power (*daimonion*) and fortune (*tychê*).[95] He prefers to use the rather vague concept

[91] The table in Millar, *Dio*, Appendix IV is far from complete.
[92] I owe this point to Michael Crawford.
[93] He discusses the treasury further at 41.17.2; 46.31.4; 53.2.1; 55.31.4; 56.33.2; 58.4.8; 58.18.3; 59.9.4; 59.15.4-5; 59.30.3; 66.2.5; 69.8.1; 71.32.2.
[94] On Herodotus' interest in science see Hdt. 2.19-27. On interest in Herodotus in Dio's own day cf. Lucian, *How to Write History* 2, 18; C.P. Jones, *Culture and Society in Lucian*, 152.

of "divine power" rather than attribute acts to individual deities. This divine power was most often revealed to him personally through dreams: he was commanded by "divine power" in a dream to write his history of the wars and civil wars of Septimius Severus (72.23.2, quoted above, p. 26); Severus himself later appeared to Dio in a dream, encouraging him to extend his *Roman History* beyond Severus' death (78.10.1-2); finally, "divine power" came a third time to Dio in a dream, commanding him to append some lines from Homer's *Iliad* at the end of his history (80.5.3).[96] Dio attributes many of the omens that he reports to divine intervention (59.29.3 [= **B.23**]; 60.33.2c). Similarly, according to Dio Vindex, while leading a major revolt against Nero in 68, committed suicide because he was vexed at the fate which "the divine power" had allotted to him (63.24.4a [= **D.6**]).

Alongside this generalized divine control of human affairs was the more personalized power of fortune. Dio claims that he owed much to the goddess Fortune when he was struggling to make progress on his *Roman History* (72.23.3-4, quoted above, p. 26). And one of the leitmotifs of his history is its interest in reversals of fortune. This was a commonplace of ancient thought and a feature of Greek and Roman historiography right back to Herodotus. The rise and fall of Sejanus gave Dio an excellent opportunity to investigate the theme (58.11.1 [= **A.7**]); Dio uses it as an example of what can happen when men rise to power unexpectedly in comparison to when men of natural worth assume their rightful positions in power (58.5.3-4 [= **A.4**]).[97] He is hostile to the emperor Macrinus for this same reason: he was not a man of natural worth (being merely of equestrian status); and so even though he performed many worthwhile deeds, he did not deserve to become emperor (78.41.2-4). Such traditional beliefs are consistent with the great revival of Greek pagan cult centres (especially oracular shrines) and the considerable interest in dreams and their interpretation during the second century.[98]

Dio's distaste for those who rose to power unexpectedly is a good illustration of his overall socio-political viewpoint. He was staunchly conservative and a firm believer in the maintenance of the traditional hierarchies of Roman society. Having reported in his account of 217 how the Roman people came to agree that their only true ruler at the time was Jupiter, he comments: "This shows very well how it is an innate feature of mankind to respect the better and to despise the worse." (78.20.3). He uses revealing terms (again derived from Thucydides) to describe the various social groups at Rome: the senatorial order are the "men of sense", "the foremost men" or "those of much repute", while the plebs are referred to as "the multitude", "the many", "the rest", or still more pejoratively

---

[95] See Millar, *Dio*, 179-81; J. Puiggali, 'Les démons dans l'Histoire romaine de Dion Cassius', *Latomus* 43 (1984), 876-883.

[96] Other writers were similarly encouraged to write in dreams: e.g. Pliny the Elder (Plin. *Letters* 3.5.4) and the medical writer Galen (Bowersock, *Sophists*, 73).

[97] Dio elaborates the same themes in his treatment of the rise and fall of the last king of Rome, Tarquin the Proud (cf. fr. 12.9), and the Romans' unexpected defeat by the Samnites at the battle of the Caudine Forks in 321 B.C. (cf. fr. 36.10).

[98] R. Lane Fox, *Pagans and Christians* (1986), 150-67; S. Price, 'The future of dreams: from Freud to Artemidorus', *Past and Present* 113 (1986), 3-37; J.J. Winkler, *The Constraints of Desire* (1990), 17-45.

as "the rabble" or "the crowd" (58.11.5 [= **A.7**]; 59.9.7 [= **B.7**]).[99] He censures the plebs for encouraging unworthy conduct by emperors (59.27.2 [= **B.21**]; 59.28.10; 61.5.2) and for their sudden changes in allegiance: they supported Sejanus throughout his lifetime, but were quick to blame all their misfortunes on him after his death; in short, they showed little courage in blaming a dead man rather than the true cause of their misfortunes, the emperor Tiberius (58.12.4). He is also highly critical of the increasing indiscipline of the Roman army during his own lifetime (73.16.3; 74.2.4-6; 80.4.2) and the growing influence of the Praetorian Guard on political events (73.10.2; 73.11.3). He himself tried to instil discipline in the legions under his command when he was governor of Pannonia, and in so doing aroused the anger of the Praetorian Guard (80.4.2; Sections 1.2.6-7). It is not surprising, therefore, that he criticizes the Praetorians for causing damage and looting in Rome after Sejanus' fall (58.12.2) and also exaggerates their rôle in establishing Claudius in power (60.1.2-4 [= **C.1**]). In all this he had become completely assimilated to the outlook of the senatorial order.[100] However, he also criticizes the Roman upper classes for undignified behaviour, especially for fawning sycophantically upon the emperor (59.16.9-10 [= **B.12**]; 59.24.5-6; 59.27.2-6 [= **B.21**]; 59.29.5; 60.31.8; 61.15.1-4). He was similarly outraged when an emperor forced members of the senatorial and equestrian orders to perform in the theatre, amphitheatre or circus (61.17.2-5; 61.19.1-2) or when he failed to act in a traditional, dignified and appropriately Roman fashion (59.22.2 [= **B.16**]; 59.28.1-7 [= **B.22**]; 63.9-10 [= **D.3**]).

Dio also reveals a typically senatorial, conservative attitude when he describes the growing political importance of emperors' wives and imperial freedmen. This comes out most strongly in his treatment of Claudius, whom he censured for being dominated by his wives Messallina and then Agrippina and by his imperial freedmen (60.2.4-5 [= **C.2**]; 60.8.4-6 [= **C.6**]; 60.14.1-4 [= **C.8**]; 60.15.5-16.3 [= **C.8**]; 60.17.5-18.4 [partly = **C.10**]; 60.27.4 [= **C.13**]; 60.28.2-5; 60.30.6b; 60.31; 60.32.1-2; 60.33.3a-b; 60.33.6). This was a theme taken over from the traditional picture of Claudius (cf. Tac. *A.* 11-12; Suet. *Cl.* 29; Seneca, *Apocolocyntosis*), but one very much emphasized by Dio.[101] Like many of the senatorial class, Dio found it difficult to accept that people of lower rank should have greater influence than themselves with the emperor. Not surprisingly he has Maecenas advise Augustus that emperors should consult most of all "the foremost men" (i.e., the leading senators) (52.33.3). But as often in monarchies, those with greatest access to the ruler had the greatest influence.[102] Occasionally Dio also lets fire a general, hostile remark against women or particular freedmen: thus Boudica, the leader of the revolt in Britain against Rome in 61-62, possessed "a greater intelligence than often belongs to women" (62.2.2), while Pallas, Claudius' freedman, was "altogether vulgar and objectionable" (61.3.3).

---

[99] For Thucydides on the crowd see V. Hunter, 'Thucydides and the sociology of the crowd', *Classical Journal* 84 (1988) 17-30.
[100] Millar, *Dio*, 73-118; J.W. Rich, 'Dio on Augustus' in *History as Text* (ed. Averil Cameron, 1989), 86-110.
[101] cf. the influence of Helius under Nero (63.12.2 [= **D.3**])
[102] See M.I. Finley, *Aspects of Antiquity* (1968), 128-42; F. Millar, *The Emperor in Roman World* (1977), 69-83; K. Hopkins, *Conquerors and Slaves* (1978), ch. 4.

Dio's conservative viewpoint and his reflections on the Roman past led him to fear most of all a return to "democracy" at Rome (i.e., the Republican system of government). Democracy led to unstable government and, at worst, civil strife, an idea again taken over from Thucydides (cf. Thuc. 3.70-85). Dio preferred stability, as he reveals in his account of the change from monarchy to Republic in 509 B.C.:

> All changes are very dangerous, and most of all changes in types of government cause the most and greatest harm to states and to individuals alike. Therefore, sensible men judge it best to remain always under the same form of government, even if it is not the best form, rather than to be continually shifting, at one moment changing to one form of government, now to another. (fr. 12.3a).

Thus, in referring to the civil strife of 68-69, he talks about the "confusion and uproar of civil war" (59.12.3 [= **B.10**]), while he attacks Gaius' attempts to give the plebs once again a say in the election of magistrates on the grounds that chaos would ensue if there was any return to "democracy" (59.9.6-7 [= **B.7**]). He later remarks with cynical relief on the failure of this experiment: the Roman plebs had so forgotten how to behave like free men that they could not carry out their responsibilities (59.20.4 [= **B.15**]). Stable government was for him best achieved under an oligarchy or moderate monarchy (44.1-2; 47.39.4-5; 53.19.1; 56.43.4).[103] He expresses this trenchantly in terms again reminiscent of Thucydides in the speech put into the mouth of Maecenas, supposedly advising Augustus in 27 B.C. on the best form of government:

> The supposed freedom of the mob proves in reality to be the harshest form of slavery, under which the better elements suffer at the hands of the worse, until both are eventually destroyed. (52.14.5)

His socio-political views, and especially his conservative outlook, affected the way in which Dio presented the past. They caused him to introduce his own personal slants and to interpret historical events very much from his senatorial viewpoint. Dio is by no means the only Greek or Roman historian to display such subjectivity; but while complete objectivity is impossible to achieve for any historian, such slants and colouring of the past need to be taken into account when we are assessing the quality of the evidence that Dio provides for the Julio-Claudian period.

4. THE PURPOSE OF DIO'S HISTORY

Dio outlined the main purpose of his history in the Preface:

> I am anxious to write a history of all that happened to the Romans while they were at peace or war that is worthy of record, so that no one either Roman or non-Roman shall look in vain for the essential facts. (fr. 1.1)

---

[103] Millar, *Dio*, 74-77. Many of Dio's views on the best form of government are outlined in the speeches that he puts into the mouth of Agrippa (52.2-13) and Maecenas (52.14-40), on which see Millar, *Dio*, 102-118; P. McKechnie, 'Cassius Dio's speech of Agrippa', *G&R* 28 (1981), 150-155.

Thus on the surface at least Dio saw his history as providing the main outlines of Roman history for Roman and non-Roman (i.e., Greek) readers. Most modern scholars have taken Dio at his word and argued that his work rarely rises above the level of jejune narrative.[104] But this view ignores several major underlying features of Dio's history which suggest that his aim was more complex than just to recount past events.

4.1 Explaining the Past: Causation and Motivation

A close reading of Dio's history soon reveals that he, like his model historian Thucydides, was keen to establish the causes of the events that he describes. In a complex passage he argues that historical events and their causes are mutually interrelated and, therefore, have to be analysed in close connexion with one another:[105]

> I shall now go on to describe each event separately as it occurred. For it seems to me to be particularly instructive in doing this if when one is discussing actions, one submits them to rational analyses; for by so doing, one may demonstrate by cross-examination the true nature of the actions from these analyses, and one may prove the validity of the analyses from their consistency with the actions. (46.34.5-35.1)

For such "rational analyses" Dio uses a variety of techniques. Sometimes he reports the reason for the event given at the time: for example, Gaius postponed all lawsuits so that more people could attend the public shows (59.7.5 [= **B.5**]), Claudius invaded Britain in response to an appeal for intervention from a deposed native leader (60.19.1 [= **C.11**]). Occasionally he is not totally happy with the reason given by his source and so adds a personal note of scepticism, but without providing an alternative reason of his own (63.8.5 [= **D.2**]). But much more frequently he discusses causation in a distinctly Thucydidean fashion: he records the alleged reason for a particular event, and then contrasts it with what, in his judgement, was the real reason (59.10.7 [= **B.8**]; 59.21.2 [= **B.15**]; 59.28.1 [= **B.22**]; 60.14.3-4 [= **C.8**]; 60.24.5 [= **C.12**]; 60.27.5 [= **C.13**]; cf. Thuc. 1.23). To examine causation in more detail, he occasionally uses speeches: for example, he discusses the major reasons for the general dissatisfaction with Nero in a speech given to Vindex (63.22.3-6 [= **D.6**]). Many of the reasons highlighted in the speech (for example, Nero's flippant attitude towards the senate, his confiscations of property through unjust condemnations and his undignified conduct as lyre-player, tragic actor and charioteer) have already been introduced in his earlier narrative of the reign, but the speech draws the causal threads together in a clear and effective manner.

Furthermore, Dio uses causation as a way of structuring his narrative. He links historical events if he can find a causal connexion between them: for

---

[104] So Millar, *Dio*, 73-74; A.A. Barrett, *Caligula: the corruption of power* (1989), xxii.
[105] Millar, *Dio*, 45 fails to do justice to the complexity of the passage and is wrong to assert that it was "merely a passing thought, which has no relevance to the actual structure of his history". I hope to discuss this more fully elsewhere.

example, he argues by implication that Gaius' illness in 38 caused not only his general deterioration as ruler, but also his execution of large numbers of senators (59.8 [= **B.6**]). He similarly links Gaius' increasing megalomania with the plot to assassinate him, while also giving some more specific causes of the conspiracy (59.29.1-2 [= **B.23**]). More elaborately, he links the requisitioning of transport ships for Gaius' triumphal procession at the bridge at Baiae with the subsequent grain shortage (59.17.2 [= **B.13**]); the expense of this ceremony then led to a shortage of funds in the treasury; these financial problems in turn engendered further executions of wealthy Romans and then the military expeditions to Gaul and Germany (59.18.1 [= **B.14**]; 59.21.1 [= **B.15**]). Thus his interest in causation often provides a major dynamic behind his narrative.

Parallel to this interest in causation was Dio's keenness to establish the motivations that led historical figures to act as they did. Dio clearly derived some of these motives directly from his sources, but many were the product of his own imagination. Sometimes the motives are presented as clear-cut (58.3.1 [= **A.1**]; 59.2.4 [= **B.2**]; 60.3.2 [= **C.3**]; 60.8.5 [= **C.6**]), even if some of them are rather trivial: for example, Gaius did not depose Ptolemy from his position as allied king of Mauretania just because of his wealth; he had probably led a revolt against Rome (59.25.1 + n. [= **B.18**]). At other times he is less certain and so explores various possibilities, allowing his readers to choose for themselves (59.1.4-5 [= **B.1**]; 63.25.3 [= **D.6**]). He is also careful to distinguish between professed and real motivations (58.24.3; 59.23.7; 60.14.3-4 [= **C.8**]; 60.27.4-5 [= **C.13**]). This interest in motivation contributes in an important way towards his analysis of human nature (Section 3.4.2). Furthermore, the contrasts drawn between real and alleged motives allow him to expose the general self-interestedness of many individuals, another feature inherited from Thucydides (cf. Thuc. 2.53; 3.82-84).

Thus when using Dio as a historical source, we have to be careful to distinguish between proven historical events and Dio's own personal explanations of these events. It is dangerous to take all his historical interpretations as authoritative.

4.2   The Moral Lessons of the Past

One of the underlying purposes of many ancient historical writers was to draw moral lessons from the past.[106] While Dio does not explicitly state this as an aim, the frequency with which he makes moral comments and draws moral lessons from past events suggests that he considered this part of his overall purpose. As we have seen, he incorporates many elements from biography into his history: he is especially keen to establish the personality of each emperor (Section 3.4.1). In so doing, he often makes explicit comments about their virtues and vices, and with the Julio-Claudians Dio has more opportunity to outline vice than virtue. Many of these comments illustrate how an emperor should behave politically as ruler (see Section 4.3), but some also serve as

---

[106] For example, the Roman historians Sallust and Livy and the Greek biographer Plutarch: cf. Sallust, *Catiline* 2, 5, 11; Livy, Preface; Plut. *Pericles* 1.

examples of good or bad moral conduct.[107] Other historical figures are also commended for their moral integrity or censured for their depravity. Dio has considerable praise for Germanicus (57.18), for Corbulo and Verginius Rufus, two senatorial commanders who both refused to lead revolts against Nero (62.19.2-4; 62.23.5; 63.25.2-3 [= **D.6**]) and, more generally, for those senators who died nobly during the reign of Claudius (60.16.7). Those censured include Claudius' wife Messallina for her licentiousness, shameless conduct and pride (60.30.6b-31.2), and Ofonius Tigellinius, Nero's friend and Praetorian Prefect, for his licentiousness, luxury and cruelty (62.13.3). Thus, writing in the tradition of Livy and Plutarch, Dio hoped that his readers would imitate the virtues displayed in his history and avoid the vices.

Historical events provided Dio with suitable material for drawing moral lessons. Thus he uses the rise and fall of Sejanus to illustrate the dangers of being puffed up with pride and the instability of human fortune (57.22.1; 58.5.3-4 [= **A.4**]; 58.11.1 [= **A.7**]). Sex. Marius' sufferings at the hands of Tiberius illustrate the maxim that wealth does not always lead to happiness (58.22.2-3). Gaius' complete disregard for Tiberius' will is used to illustrate how "no command can have any weight against the ingratitude of one's successors" (59.1.3 [= **B.1**]). Agrippina's determination that her son Nero should become emperor shows how people will go to any lengths to gain advantage, even at the cost of personal suffering (61.2.2). Many of these moral lessons are trite and lack originality. Even so, they are still very much part of Dio's historical purpose. They are yet another aspect of his general interest in analysing human nature.

4.3   Dio and the Political Analysis of the Principate

We have already seen that Dio was an active political figure in Rome under the Severans (Section 1.2) and that he shows a particular interest in political and constitutional matters in his *Roman History* (Section 3.4.3). Despite this, most scholars have asserted that he only very rarely used his political experience to provide some political analysis of the Roman past (most notably in his treatment of Augustus).[108] However, a close reading of his narrative of the Julio-Claudian emperors reveals that it was at least in part designed to interpret their divergent approaches to imperial rule. By his presentations of these emperors and by his chosen emphases he further developed his views, those of a Roman senator of Greek origin of the Severan age, on the most effective, and palatable, form of imperial government.

For Dio, Augustus came close to representing his ideal Roman emperor, notwithstanding his revolutionary and unpalatable rise to power (56.43-45).[109] His closing remarks on Augustus' reign well illustrate this:

---

[107] The same is found in Suetonius' imperial lives: see A. Wallace-Hadrill, *Suetonius* (1983), 142-74.
[108] Millar, *Dio*, 73-118.
[109] Rich, (above, n. 100); M. Reinhold and P.M. Swan, 'Cassius Dio's assessment of Augustus' in *Between Republic and Empire* (ed. K.A. Raaflaub and M. Toher, 1990), 155-73.

> They (sc. the Romans) missed him because, mixing monarchy with democracy, he
> preserved both their freedom and gave them order and security as well, so that
> they lived, untroubled either by the licence of democracy or the oppression of a
> tyrant, enjoying freedom and moderation in a monarchy without fear, under
> kingly rule yet not enslaved, governed democratically yet without discord.
> (56.43.4)

The conduct of Augustus' immediate successors, and their shortcomings as
emperors, thus served to emphasize still further the ideal qualities that Dio saw
in Augustus. This is not to say that this was the major purpose of Dio's account,
or that he achieved any very penetrating analysis of the Principate; but it is
impossible to ignore his attempts at political analysis in any balanced assessment of Dio as a historian.

In explicit or implicit terms Dio frequently compares Tiberius, Gaius,
Claudius and Nero as emperors not only with one another, but also with
Augustus. Thus he comments that people did not realize at the time how
fortunate they had been under Augustus until they experienced Tiberius
(56.45.1-3). Later he compares Gaius unfavourably with Tiberius, and hence *a
fortiori* with Augustus. First, he accepted in one day all the honours that
Augustus had taken only with reluctance during his long reign, some of which
Tiberius had refused to accept at all (59.3.2 [= **B.3**]). Secondly, although he
initially censured Tiberius for his licentiousness and cruelty, he eventually came
to emulate and even surpass him in these respects (59.4.1 [= **B.3**]). And then the
comparison is made quite explicit:

> The deeds of Tiberius, although they were thought to have been very harsh, were
> as far superior to those of Gaius as those of Augustus had been to those of
> Tiberius. (59.5.1 [= **B.3**])

Dio does, however, commend Gaius at the start of his reign, but again in
comparative terms: as long as he used Augustus as a model of how to rule,
everything went well (59.7.7 [= **B.5**]; 59.9.4 [= **B.7**]). His speech at Tiberius'
funeral reminded the people of Augustus (59.3.8 [= **B.3**]), and he further
underlined his respect for his great-grandfather by mounting a striking ceremony to dedicate the new shrine for the deified Augustus (59.7.1-2 [= **B.5**]).
Later, however, he turned away from Augustus: he resented the crowd
addressing him as the "young Augustus" (59.13.6) and preferred to pose on
occasion as the descendant of Augustus' rival, M. Antonius (59.20.2 [= **B.15**]).
Most of all, Gaius' deterioration was marked by a dramatic reversal in attitude
towards Tiberius. At the start people thought that Gaius could not be guilty of
any duplicity of thought or speech (59.6.4 [= **B.4**]); that is, he represented the
complete antithesis to Tiberius, whose worst fault was his duplicity (57.1.1-6).
But then Gaius suddenly turned to model himself on Tiberius (59.16.1 [=
B.12]). Dio underlines the significance of this *volte-face* by including a full
speech, in which Gaius outlines his change in attitude towards the senate; by a
familiar rhetorical device, he even has Gaius adopt the persona of Tiberius to
reinforce dramatically this change (59.16.2-7 [= **B.12**]).

In similarly comparative vein, Dio repeatedly stresses how Claudius reversed
many of the changes brought in by Gaius (60.4.1 [= **C.4**]; 60.4.5; 60.5.8-9;
60.6.3 [= **C.5**]; 60.6.8; 60.7.1 [= **C.5**]; 60.8.1 [= **C.6**]; 60.17.2; 60.25.8). This

helped to distance Claudius from his immediate predecessor and enhance his reputation. Finally, Nero is written off almost immediately by an explicitly unfavourable comparison with Gaius:

> Finally he [sc. Nero] lost all shame ..... and tended towards the conduct of Gaius. And once he had conceived a desire to emulate him, he quite surpassed him; for he considered that it was one of the marks of an emperor, in fact that it was an obligation, not to fall behind anyone even in the most disgraceful deeds. (61.5.1: Xiphilinus)

Not only was the conduct of both these emperors marked by licentiousness and bloodthirstiness (59.24.1; 59.25.7; 62.24.1), but both were nurtured in such vices by their attendant "tutors in tyranny" (59.24.1; 61.10.2).

But it is not just by means of such explicit comparisons that Dio weaves his political analysis into his historical narrative. For each of the Julio-Claudian emperors he highlights certain characteristics and modes of conduct, which underline their fitness or unfitness to rule and illustrate still further, if often implicitly, the ideal qualities that Dio saw in Augustus. In short, such emphases represent Dio's attempts at the political analysis of the Principate.

a. Tiberius

Dio characterizes Tiberius as being a mixture of good and bad (57.23.5; 58.28.5). He is praised for his moderation in refusing honours, a familiar Augustan virtue (57.8.1-3; 57.9.1; 58.22.1), but censured for his lack of generosity towards his fellow citizens (57.10.1-2; 57.21.3; 58.1.1a; 58.2.6 [= **A.1**]). He was also extremely suspicious, which made him indecisive as a ruler and over-anxious to investigate comments made about him (57.3.2-6; 57.23.2-3; 58.13.1). This was a particular failing in a ruler, as Dio has Maecenas warn Augustus (52.31.7-8). But the main problem that Dio saw in Tiberius was his ambivalence and duplicity (57.1.1-6; 57.2.3; 57.15.4-7; 57.23.5). He stresses at the very start of his account of the reign how this was a serious drawback to effective and harmonious rule (57.1.3-6). His subjects, and especially the senatorial order, could not handle this dissimulation: it prevented the sort of dignified working relationship between emperor and senate in which Dio firmly believed (52.19-20; 52.31-32). Furthermore, after Tiberius withdrew to Capri, he came to rely heavily on his successive Praetorian Prefects, Sejanus and Macro (58.2.7-8 [= **A.1**]; 58.3.8-4.4 [= **A.2, A.3**]; 58.5.1-4 [= **A.4**]; 58.12.7; 58.21.3; 58.27.2). Dio used this to show how an emperor had to stay at the very centre of power and also select worthy and reliable deputies, in order to prevent the sort of political in-fighting that was so detrimental to good government (52.15.1-4). The careers of Sejanus and Macro also exemplified the danger of having a single Praetorian Prefect: Dio felt that there should be two, so that each could act as a check on the other (52.24.1-2). Dio formed these views from his own experience: for he comments with distaste about those Praetorian Prefects who dominated Roman political life during his own lifetime.[110] In short, Dio highlighted the ways in which Tiberius diverged from the Augustan model of the Principate.

---

[110] For example, Perennis under Commodus (72.9.1), C. Fulvius Plautianus under Septimius Severus (75.14-76.6; 58.14.1), Ulpius Julianus and Julianus Nestor under Macrinus (78.15.1), and Comazon under Elagabalus (79.3.5-4.2).

b. Gaius (Caligula)

With Gaius, Dio gets his first chance to analyse the effects of having an autocratic and idiosyncratic emperor in power. Dio outlines most of his faults as ruler in his opening remarks on the reign: he was profligate in spending public funds (59.2.4 [= **B.2**]), extremely licentious (59.3.3 [= **B.3**]) and highly contrary by nature (59.4.1-6 [= **B.3**]). Gaius' love of luxury and heavy spending allowed Dio to isolate what he saw as one of the main causes of financial ruin under the Principate, and also one of the main political problems that the senatorial class faced under bad emperors: for it quickly led to financial exhaustion, which forced the emperor to attack the landowning classes in Italy and the provinces for their property, mostly through false accusations (59.10.7; 59.14.1-2 [= **B.11**]; 59.15.1-2 [**B.11**]; 59.18.1 [= **B.14**]; 59.21.1 [= **B.15**]). Such conduct again went against the advice that Dio has Maecenas give to Augustus on the importance of careful stewarding of financial resources (52.28-30) and on the specific dangers caused by mounting too many extravagant public spectacles, especially chariot-races (52.30.4-8). But the most problematic aspect of Gaius was his maddening inconsistency as a ruler. Just as with Tiberius' duplicity, Gaius' subjects could not cope with such contrary behaviour: survival became a matter more of luck than judgement (59.4.6 [= **B.3**]; cf. 59.10.3; 59.28.10-11 [= **B.22**]). Most of all, it forced senators into many acts of sycophancy, which pained Dio since it undermined the prestige of the senatorial order (59.24.5-8; 59.25.4-5 [= **B.18**]; 59.27.2-6 [= **B.21**]; 59.29.5 [= **B.23**]). In short, it prevented a dignified relationship either between emperor and plebs or between emperor and senatorial order. Gaius' autocratic style of rule allowed Dio to analyse another model of how an emperor should not behave.

c. Claudius

Dio's portrayal of Claudius is made up of two very separate strands. On the one hand he is berated (as in other senatorial sources) for his failure to control his wives and his imperial freedmen (60.2.4 [= **C.2**]; 60.17.5-8 [= **C.10**]). But he also received much more praise from Dio than from either Tacitus or Suetonius for his appropriate or fitting conduct as emperor (60.6.1 [= **C.5**]; 60.12.1). He was conscientious as an administrator (60.4.4 [= **C.4**]; 60.5.6; 60.10.3-4) and as judge, sitting with judicial advisers, a practice of which Dio had personal experience (Section 1.2.4) and firmly approved (60.4.2-3 [= **C.4**]; 60.5.7; 60.28.6; 52.33.3). Claudius is often shown as participating as an ordinary member in deliberations of the senate (60.6.1 [= **C.5**]; 60.12.3) and is repeatedly praised for not allowing special celebrations that would have reduced the time available for conducting public business (60.5.7; 60.6.4-5 [= **C.5**]; 60.12.5; 60.17.1 [= **C.9**]; 60.25.8; 60.30.6a).

He also showed many of the traditional virtues of a good Roman emperor.[111] He was beneficent towards the Roman plebs (60.11.1-5 [= **C.7**]; 60.13.5), showed considerable moderation, a quality that Dio has Maecenas recommend to Augustus (60.5.3-4; 60.12.5; 60.28.1; cf. 52.31.9; 52.34.7), and

---

[111] On which see A. Wallace-Hadrill, 'The emperor and his virtues', *Historia* 30 (1981), 298-323.

related easily and affably with all sections of Roman society: both the senate (60.11.8-12.3; 60.27.2-3 [= **C.13**]; 60.29.1) and the lower orders (60.6.1 [= **C.5**]; 60.10.1; 60.13.5). Such a mixture of liberality, moderation and affability all contributed to Claudius' obvious civility, the most important virtue for a Roman emperor to possess.[112] And most of all, civility was very much one of the virtues that Dio emphasized in Augustus (53.12.1).

d. Nero

It is more difficult to form a clear impression of Dio's portrayal of Nero, since nothing of his original account of the reign survives; we have to rely on the summaries and excerpts prepared in the Byzantine period (Section 3.1). However, Xiphilinus' epitome is detailed enough to see that a dominant theme was Nero's unfitness to rule. He compared unfavourably even with Gaius (61.5.1, quoted above, p. 51). He represented a disastrous combination of many of the faults that had marred his predecessors as emperor. Like Tiberius he was too willing to abrogate his responsibilities as ruler to others (Agrippina, Seneca and Burrus at the start of the reign, later Tigellinus and the freedman Helius). With Gaius he shared a love of extravagance (especially on spectacles) and a theatrical style as ruler: his profligacy led to financial problems and countless depredations of the propertied classes in Italy and the provinces, just as had occurred under Gaius. Like Claudius he was influenced to a dangerous degree by the women and freedmen of the imperial court.

Throughout Dio stresses Nero's licentiousness, and censures him for it (61.4.3; 61.9.2-4; 61.11.1-2; 62.15.2-6; 62.28.2-3; 63.13.1-3 [= **D.3**]). But more significantly, Nero is roundly criticized for preferring elaborate jokes, lyre-playing and chariot-racing to the serious business of governing the Empire (61.3.2; 61.4.1-2; 62.14.1). Furthermore, by indulging in these pursuits, he brought not only ridicule about himself, but shame upon the whole political office of the emperor (61.20.1-2; 63.6.3-4 [= **D.1**]; 63.9.1-6 [= **D.2**]). He consistently disgusted, and also ridiculed, members of the senatorial and equestrian orders (61.9.1; 61.17.2-5; 61.19.2-4; 62.27.1; 63.26.4 [= **D.7**]). Such undignified conduct was inappropriate for any Roman, let alone an emperor (63.12.2 [= **D.3**]), and Dio argues that it was a major cause of the revolts which occurred during his reign: the Pisonian conspiracy of 65 (62.24.2) and the revolt of Vindex in 68 (63.22.4-6 [= **D.6**]). And most serious of all it led Rome once again into civil wars, a state of affairs that Dio particularly abhorred (52.14.5, quoted above, p. 46; 52.15.5-6).

Towards the end of his account of Nero Dio twice reminds us that Nero was the descendant of Augustus (63.12.2 [= **D.3**]; 63.22.5-6 [= **D.6**]). In his closing remarks he goes further and underlines the fact that Nero was the last survivor of the family of Aeneas and Augustus: it was an omen of the family's demise that just before Nero's death all the laurel trees planted by Augustus' wife Livia and all her sacred chickens suddenly perished (63.29.3 [= **D.8**]; cf. 62.18.4). It symbolized the way in which Nero had destroyed his inheritance. By such an emphasis, Dio invites us, with some sadness, to compare this degenerate and

---

[112] A. Wallace-Hadrill, '*Civilis princeps*: between citizen and king', *JRS* 72 (1982), 32-48 at 44.

flippant ruler with his ideal emperor Augustus. Nero's death marked the end of an era. In short, the Julio-Claudian emperors had departed too far from the ideals of Augustus' Principate; their style of rule had become too unpalatable to too many sectors of Roman society to preserve them in power.

Thus, in relating the contrasting personalities of the Julio-Claudian emperors, and their varied conduct, Dio carried further his political analysis of the imperial system of government at Rome. Much of his material was derived from earlier sources, but Dio moulded it to suit his own historical purposes. Dio himself was deeply involved in public life at Rome for almost forty years. During this time he gained great experience, sometimes at uncomfortably close quarters, of the processes of imperial government. Furthermore, he was writing his history at a time when the Principate was once again being sullied by such eccentric emperors as Commodus, Caracalla and Elagabalus. These personal experiences gave him particular qualifications to analyse the best form of government for Rome. His views on this topic are most explicitly worked out in the speech that he puts into the mouth of Maecenas, supposedly advising Augustus in 27 B.C. (52.14-40). But his political views and his political analysis were further developed throughout his historical narrative.

5. CONCLUSION: DIO'S VALUE AS A HISTORICAL SOURCE

Dio's greatest value is that he alone provides a reasonably complete chronological coverage of the Julio-Claudian period. For some parts of this period (especially those missing from Tacitus' *Annals*) Dio is the only surviving ancient narrative: e.g. for the fall of Sejanus, the entire reign of Gaius, the early part of Claudius' reign and the fall of Nero. Thus without Dio we would simply not know about a number of events during this period.[113] In addition, he also provides a whole host of information on political institutions and social customs at Rome, which enrich our general knowledge and understanding of Roman society. Dio admits that his narrative was not comprehensive; in a work covering almost a thousand years of Roman history this could hardly be expected. Thus his historical detail is not as rich as Tacitus', but is much fuller than that, for example, of Velleius Paterculus. However, Dio was writing serious and dignified history, which gives his account a greater reliability than Suetonius' rather gossipy and sensationalist lives of the Julio-Claudian emperors. Furthermore, Suetonius, as a biographer, felt no need to relate incidents in chronological order.

However, there are limitations to Dio as a historical source. He was writing almost two hundred years after the events of the Julio-Claudian period. He is, therefore, only as reliable as his sources. He also used a great variety of sources of widely varying quality, which gives his narrative a somewhat uneven quality. He sometimes combined elements from more than one source on a particular issue, which led to some inconsistencies. The fact that he was writing so long after the events led him on occasion to misunderstand his sources and hence

---

[113] Note, for example, the number of times the standard modern biographies of the Julio-Claudian emperors (see Suggestions for Further Reading) have recourse to Dio.

introduce factual errors into his narrative. He is also guilty of certain anachronisms, some of which were made unwittingly, but others quite consciously to paper over points that he could not understand in his sources. He was also writing about the early emperors with hindsight, with the knowledge of how later emperors had behaved. But most of all, he could not help writing from the perspective of the Severan age, when the structures of Roman government were very different from those of the Julio-Claudian period.

Tacitus was substantially closer to the events of the Julio-Claudian period than was Dio, which might suggest that his account is to be preferred. Tacitus, in general, provides a more penetrating analysis of the Principate. But Tacitus was also writing with hindsight, and very much from a personal standpoint. He had strong views on the passing of the traditional dignity of the senatorial order and so was deeply hostile to the emperors. As a conscious literary artist, he also moulded his historical material to fit his overall scheme and purpose as a historian. It does not necessarily follow that Tacitus should always be trusted at the expense of Dio just because he was closer to the Julio-Claudian period.

Furthermore, Dio, like all ancient historians, was creating very much a literary work. He embellished his narrative in his own distinctive style, which occasionally led him to alter the sequence of events and give more emphasis to some events than others. His entire work is marked most of all by rhetoric. In his style, historical method and general philosophical outlook, he was influenced by earlier Greek historians, most notably Thucydides. This all helped to determine the way in which Dio wrote history. Finally, his overall aim as a historian was more ambitious than just to retell past events; he was constantly seeking to explain the past, a quality that distinguishes the true historian from the mere antiquarian. He also used the past to edify his readers on moral conduct and to provide some political analysis of the early Principate. Thus his work contains two very different types of historical evidence: a description of events in Roman history and Roman institutions, but also an attempt to explain and interpret the Roman past. When using Dio as evidence, we need to distinguish carefully between these two levels. His description of events and institutions can to a certain degree be controlled against other evidence; his interpretations and explanations need to be treated with greater caution.

Many modern historians have been quick to reject Dio's interpretations of the Julio-Claudian period, but often on insufficient grounds. After all, Dio did have more experience and understanding of Roman imperial politics and society than any historian writing today. Just because Dio can be shown to be in error over certain points, it does not follow that we must reject all his interpretations. Rather we need to take all other surviving evidence (literary, archaeological, inscriptional, numismatic) into account to evaluate critically Dio's version of a particular event. If Dio's version stands up to such critical scrutiny, it can then be used with some confidence for reconstructing Roman politics and society in the Julio-Claudian period.

THE ROMAN HISTORY

TIBERIUS TO NERO

THE REIGN OF TIBERIUS

A.D. 29–31

THE FALL OF SEJANUS

* * * * *

*A.1 HONOURS FOR SEJANUS. ARREST OF ASINIUS GALLUS
A.D. 29–30

(58.2.7–3.6: Xiphilinus)

A.D. 29

2.7   Sejanus was being raised to still greater heights, and it was voted that a public festival should be held to mark his birthday. Indeed the sheer number of statues set up by the senate and the equestrian order, the tribes and the leading citizens anyone would have found difficult to count.

2.8   Envoys were sent both to him and to Tiberius separately by the senate, the equestrians and also the people. The people selected their envoys from the tribunes and plebeian aediles. They offered prayers and sacrifices on behalf of both of them alike, and took oaths by their Fortune.

A.D. 30

3.1   Tiberius now seized the opportunity to attack Gallus. He had married Tiberius' former wife and spoken his mind freely about Tiberius' style of rule. Gallus was now paying court to Sejanus, either genuinely because he believed that Sejanus would become emperor or through fear of Tiberius.

3.2   Or perhaps it was a plot to make Sejanus unpopular with the emperor and so bring about his downfall. Anyway it was Gallus who proposed the greater and more important of the honours voted him, and he was eager to be one of the envoys. So Tiberius sent a letter to the senate about Gallus, declaring among other things that he was envious of the emperor's friendship with Sejanus, in spite of the fact that Gallus himself was a close

3.3   friend of Syriacus. He did not reveal this to Gallus, but instead entertained him very hospitably. So Gallus experienced a quite remarkable thing, something that had never happened to anyone else. For on the very same day that he was banqueted at the house of Tiberius and drank to their friendship, he was also condemned in the senate-house. As a result, a praetor was sent to arrest him and lead him away to be punished.

3.4   And yet after acting as I have described, Tiberius refused to let Gallus die, although he was ready for death as soon as he heard of the decree. Instead, to make him suffer as much as possible, Tiberius told Gallus to be of good cheer and instructed the senate that he should be kept in custody unbound until he himself reached the city. His object, as I said, was to make him suffer as long as possible both from the loss of his civic rights
3.5   and from fear. And so it was; he was kept constantly under guard by the consuls in office, except when Tiberius was consul: he was then held in custody by the praetors; and this was done not to prevent his escape, but to prevent his death. He had neither a companion nor an attendant with him; he neither spoke to anybody, nor saw anyone, except when he was
3.6   forced to take food. And the food was of such a quality and of such an amount that it neither gave him any pleasure or strength, nor did it allow him to die. This was the most terrible part of his ordeal. Tiberius adopted the same approach in several other cases as well.   **[Xiphilinus]**

*A.2 SEJANUS MOVES AGAINST DRUSUS   A.D. 30
(58.3.8–9: Valesian Excerpts; Zonaras)

3.8   Sejanus also brought a slanderous accusation against Drusus by using Drusus' wife. For by seducing the wives of almost all the men of note, he would find out from them what their husbands were saying or even doing. Furthermore, he made them accomplices in his crimes by promising to marry them. When Tiberius simply sent Drusus to Rome, Sejanus, afraid that Tiberius might change his mind, persuaded Cassius to take action against him.   **[Valesian Excerpts]**

3.9   After raising Sejanus to a great peak of glory and making him part of his family by betrothing him to Julia the daughter of Drusus, Tiberius later put him to death.   **[Zonaras]**

*A.3 SEJANUS' POWER INCREASES   A.D. 30
(58.4.1–4: Xiphilinus)

4.1   Now Sejanus was growing more powerful and more formidable all the time; as a result, the senators and all the other sections of Roman society treated him as if he were actually emperor, while they had only contempt for Tiberius. When Tiberius learned this, he neither treated the matter lightly nor avoided the issue; he was afraid that they might declare Sejanus
4.2   emperor outright. As a result, he did nothing openly, to be sure. For Sejanus had completely won over the entire Praetorian Guard and had gained the favour of the senators, partly by benefactions, partly by the hopes that he inspired, and partly by intimidation. In addition, he had won over all Tiberius' close associates so completely to his side that they immediately reported to him absolutely everything the emperor said or did, whereas no-one told Tiberius what Sejanus was up to.

4.3   So Tiberius changed his line of attack: he appointed Sejanus consul, named him 'Sharer of my Cares', kept on calling him 'My Sejanus' and **4.4** used it openly in letters addressed to the senate and to the people. Men were taken in by this behaviour, thinking it to be genuine: they set up pairs of bronze statues of them both everywhere, wrote their names together in inscriptions, and brought gilded chairs into the theatre to honour both of them. Finally, it was voted that they should hold the consulship together every five years and that a delegation of citizens should go out to meet both alike whenever they entered Rome. Eventually they sacrificed to the images of Sejanus just as they did to those of Tiberius.

[Xiphilinus]

*A.4 SEJANUS' POSITION IN A.D. 31   A.D. 31

(58.5.1–7: Xiphilinus)

5.1   Sejanus was now so great a person both in terms of the excessive extent of his pride and the scale of his power that, to put it in a nutshell, it was he who appeared to be emperor and Tiberius a kind of off-shore monarch, **5.2** since he spent his time on the island known as Capri. There was plenty of anxious jostling around Sejanus' doors. People were afraid not only that they would not be seen by him, but also that they might be among the last to appear; for every word and nod was carefully observed, especially those **5.3** of the leading citizens. For those who hold power through their own inherent merit do not go out of their way to seek popularity from others; and if they fail to receive signs of acceptance, they do not keep calling out for them, since they know full well that they are not being scorned. But, on the other hand, those who reach an important position by some unexpected stroke of good fortune certainly seek after all these things, since they think them necessary for their merit to be fully recognized. And if they fail to receive these signs of acceptance, they are then annoyed as if they were being slandered, and grow angry as if they were being humiliated. **5.4** Therefore, one might say that people take more trouble over these sorts of person than over emperors, because it is a virtue for emperors to pardon people, even if they have committed an offence; but these other powerful individuals are convinced that it is a proof of weakness, whereas to go onto the attack and take vengeance is thought to provide confirmation of their great power.

5.5   Now on the first day of the month many people were assembling at the house of Sejanus. The couch in the room in which he was greeting them completely collapsed under the weight of the crowd sitting on it; and as he was leaving the house, a weasel darted through the middle of the crowd. **5.6** And when he had finished sacrificing on the Capitol and was walking down to the Forum, the servants who were acting as his bodyguard turned off along the road leading to the prison, since they were unable to keep up with him because of the crowds. And as they were going down the steps **5.7** down which condemned criminals were thrown, they slipped and fell. And after this as he was taking the auspices, not one bird of good omen appeared, but instead many crows kept circling around him cawing, then flew off in a group towards the prison and perched on top of it.

[Xiphilinus]

*A.5 TIBERIUS PLAYS CAT-AND-MOUSE WITH SEJANUS   A.D. 31

(58.6.1–7.3: Xiphilinus)

6.1   Neither Sejanus nor anyone else took these omens to heart. For in view of the present circumstances not even if a god had clearly prophesied that such a great change was soon to take place, would anyone have believed it.

6.2   They constantly swore by his Fortune and addressed him as Tiberius' colleague in power, not referring to the consulship, but to the supreme power. But now there was nothing that Tiberius did not know about Sejanus, and he was planning how he could put him to death. But since he could not find any way of doing this safely in the open, he treated both Sejanus and the others in a remarkable fashion, so that he could discover

6.3   exactly what was in their minds. He kept sending various kinds of dispatches with news of himself to Sejanus and also to the senate. At one moment he would say that he was in a bad state of health and very close to death; and at another that he was feeling extremely well and would come

6.4   straight to Rome. At one moment he would lavish praise upon Sejanus, and then would utterly denounce him; and while he would honour some of Sejanus' friends on his account, for others he would show no respect. So Sejanus, filled in turn with extreme elation and extreme fear, was in constant suspense; for he had no reason to panic and hence attempt a revolution, since he was still being honoured; nor did he have the confidence to undertake a daring venture, since he was being discredited.

6.5   However, he was not alone; for everyone else was also in a state of uncertainty. They would hear the most contradictory stories one shortly after another, and so could no longer admire Sejanus, but nor could they despise him. As far as Tiberius was concerned, they could only guess whether he was dead or on his way to Rome.

7.1   Sejanus was upset by all this, and so much the more when, first, a large cloud of smoke burst out of one of the statues of him, and then, after they had removed its head to allow them to see what was going on inside, a large snake leapt up. Another head was immediately put back in its place.

7.2   And when Sejanus was about to offer sacrifice to himself because of this omen (for he used to include himself in such sacrifices), a rope was found coiled around the statue's neck. There was also the case of a statue of Fortune, which had belonged, so people claim, to Tullius, who had once been one of the kings of Rome. At this time Sejanus had the statue in his

7.3   home, and took great pleasure from this fact. As he was conducting a sacrifice, he saw it turn away from him.

[Xiphilinus; manuscripts of Dio resume in the middle of 58.7.2]

A.6 RELATIONS BETWEEN TIBERIUS AND GAIUS CALIGULA
A.D. 31
(58.7.3–8.3)

7.3   After these occurences people were suspicious, but as they were unsure
of Tiberius' intentions and also had to take into account his capricious
nature and the instability of human affairs, they steered a middle course.

7.4   In private they took careful thought for their own safety, but in public
they paid court to Sejanus for a number of reasons, but most of all because
Tiberius had appointed both him and his son priests along with Gaius. So
they bestowed on him proconsular power, and also voted that all future
consuls should be told to conduct themselves in office in imitation of him.

7.5   As for Tiberius, though he honoured Sejanus with the priesthoods, he did
not summon him to his presence. Instead, when Sejanus requested
permission to go to Campania on the grounds that his fiancée was ill, the
emperor instructed him to remain where he was, because he himself was
just about to come to Rome.

8.1   It was for these reasons then that Sejanus was again becoming
estranged. Another factor was that Tiberius, after appointing Gaius to a
priesthood, commended him and gave some indications that he wanted to

8.2   make him his successor as emperor. Sejanus would have stirred up a
rebellion, especially as the army was ready to obey him on any matter,
except that he saw that the Roman people were immensely pleased at the
compliments paid to Gaius out of respect for the memory of his father,
Germanicus. He had previously thought that they too were on his side,
but now, realizing that they were keen supporters of Gaius, he lost heart.

8.3   He kept regretting that he had not begun a rebellion when he was consul.

A.7 THE FALL OF SEJANUS
A.D. 31
(58.8.4–12.1)

8.4   In a letter to the senate about the death of Nero Tiberius referred to
Sejanus simply as Sejanus, without adding his usual titles. Furthermore,
because people were carrying out sacrifices to Sejanus, he put a ban on
offerings of this kind being made to any mere mortal. And because
Sejanus was being voted many honours, he refused to allow any measure
that proposed honours for himself. He had also made this prohibition
earlier in his reign, but reiterated it because of Sejanus; for anyone who
did not allow himself to be honoured in any way would not be likely to
allow anybody else to receive honours.

9.1   In this situation Sejanus was held more and more in contempt. People
avoided meeting him or being left alone with him, in a way too obvious
not to be noticed. So when Tiberius was informed of this, he was
encouraged to think that he would have the people and the senate on his

9.2   side, and so launched his attack upon Sejanus. First, to put him as much
off his guard as possible, he circulated a rumour that he was going to give

Sejanus tribunician power. Then he despatched Naevius Sertorius Macro to the senate-house with a letter denouncing Sejanus. He had already secretly appointed Macro to command the bodyguard and had explained

9.3 to him in advance everything that needed to be done. Macro entered Rome by night, pretending to be on some other business, and communicated his instructions to Memmius Regulus, who was consul at the time (his consular colleague took Sejanus' side), and to Graecinius Laco, commander of the Night-Watch.

9.4 At dawn Macro went up to the Palatine – for the session of the senate was to take place in the temple of Apollo. He met Sejanus, who had not yet gone in, and seeing that he was agitated because Tiberius had not sent him any message, he took him aside and encouraged him, telling him in

9.5 confidence that he was bringing him tribunician power. Overjoyed at the news, Sejanus hurried into the senate-chamber. Macro then sent the praetorians who were guarding Sejanus and the senate back to their camp, after revealing his authority to them and stating that he had a letter from

9.6 Tiberius granting them rewards. Then, after stationing the Night-Watch around the temple to replace the praetorians, he entered the temple, delivered the letter to the consuls and left before any of it was read. He ordered Laco to keep watch there, while he himself hurried to the camp, to prevent any revolutionary uprising.

10.1 Meanwhile the letter was read out. It was long and did not contain a wholesale denunciation of Sejanus, but first dealt with some other issue, then made some slight criticism of his conduct, then something else, and after that some further point against him; and it ended by saying that two senators who were among his closest friends had to be punished and that

10.2 Sejanus himself must be kept under guard. Tiberius did not give orders to put him to death on the spot: it was not that he did not wish to do so, but he was afraid that some disturbance might arise if this happened. At any rate, on the grounds that it was impossible for him even to make the journey to Rome in safety, he summoned one of the consuls to him. This was all that the letter disclosed; but it was possible to hear and see the

10.3 many different effects that it had. Before it was read out, the senators had been congratulating Sejanus on his imminent grant of tribunician power. They had kept cheering him, anticipating the honours they hoped would

10.4 be his and making it clear to him that they would support the grant. But when nothing of the sort was found in the letter and they kept on hearing the complete opposite of what they had expected, they were at first confused, then completely dismayed. Some of those who were sitting near Sejanus actually stood up and left him. They no longer wanted to share the same seat with the man whose friendship they had previously

10.5 cherished. After this praetors and tribunes surrounded him, to prevent him from rushing out and causing a riot. And he certainly would have done this, if at the outset he had been startled by hearing a general denunciation. As it turned out, he paid no particular attention to the successive charges as they were read out, thinking each one a trivial matter in its own right, and hoping most of all that no further charge was

contained in the letter, or at any rate none that he could not deal with; so
he let the time slip by, and stayed in his seat.

10.6   At this moment Regulus called him forward, but he took no notice: not
out of contempt (for by now he was humble enough), but because he was
not used to taking orders. When the consul raised his voice and at the
same time pointed to him, calling out for a second and a third time,
"Sejanus, come here", he merely asked, "Do you mean me?" At last,
however, he got to his feet and Laco came back in and stood right
10.7 alongside him. At last when the letter had been completely read out,
everyone with one voice started to denounce and curse Sejanus, some
because they had suffered wrongs at his hands, others through fear, some
to conceal their friendship with him, others out of joy at his change of
10.8 fortune. Regulus did not call for a general vote or ask any individual
senator to bring up the question of the death penalty: he was afraid of
some opposition and consequent disorder, since Sejanus after all had
numerous relatives and friends. He just asked a single senator whether
Sejanus should be imprisoned and on getting an affirmative answer, he led
him out of the senate and took him down to the prison, accompanied by
Laco and the other magistrates.

11.1   On that occasion one could have seen for oneself a perfect proof of
human powerlessness, enough to prevent anyone from ever becoming too
proud. For the man whom at dawn everyone had escorted to the senate-
house, as though he was much more important than they, this same man
they were now dragging off to prison as if he was no better than anyone
else; the man whom they had previously honoured with many garlands,
11.2 they were now encircling with bonds; the man whom they had protected
like a master, they now watched over like a runaway slave, uncovering his
head as he tried to cover it up; the man whom they had honoured with a
purple-bordered toga, this man they were now beating around the head;
the man to whom they had bowed and sacrificed as if to a god, this man
11.3 they were now leading away to his execution. The people also started to
attack him, vilifying him for all the people that he had destroyed and
ridiculing him for all the hopes that he had inspired. As for all the images
of him, they went around hurling them down, cutting them down and
dragging them down, as if they were actually injuring his very body; he
11.4 was becoming a spectator of the things that he was about to suffer. For the
time being, he was thrown into prison.

Not much later, in fact on the same day, the senate met in the temple of
Concord, not far from the prison, when they saw the people's hostility
towards him and that none of the Praetorian Guard were about; they
11.5 passed a decree sentencing him to death. After they had passed judgement
in this way, his body was hurled down the Steps and the mob abused it for
three whole days and then threw it into the Tiber. His children were put to
death by senatorial decree: his daughter, who had been engaged to
Claudius' son, was first raped by the public executioner, since it was not
considered proper for a girl who was still a virgin to be put to death in
11.6 prison. His wife Apicata was not condemned, but when she found out that
her children had been executed and saw their bodies on the Steps, she went

inside and wrote a note about the death of Drusus, in which she denounced Livilla, his wife. Livilla had been the cause of the quarrel between her and her husband Sejanus and their subsequent separation.

11.7 She sent this note to Tiberius and then committed suicide. This was how Tiberius received the note; and once he had read through its contents, he had Livilla and all the others mentioned in it put to death. I have now heard that he pardoned Livilla as a result of the actions of her mother Antonia, and that Antonia herself purposely starved her daughter to

12.1 death. This happened later.

THE REIGN OF GAIUS (CALIGULA)

A.D. 37–41

* * * * *

B.1 TIBERIUS' WILL IS SET ASIDE AND GAIUS MADE EMPEROR
A.D. 37

(59.1.1–5)

1.1   These, then, are the traditional stories about Tiberius. He was succeeded by Gaius, the son of Germanicus and Agrippina; he was also known, as I have said, as Germanicus and Caligula. Tiberius had bequeathed his **1.2** position as emperor also to his grandson Tiberius. But Gaius sent Macro to the senate with Tiberius' will and had it declared null and void by the consuls and the others who had been won over in advance on the grounds that Tiberius had gone insane: he had named as their ruler a mere boy, who **1.3** did not yet even have the right to enter the senate. So Gaius promptly stripped him of power there and then, and later, in spite of having adopted him, put him to death. Yet Tiberius had expressed his intention in his will in a number of different ways, as if that would give it greater force, and all these points had been read out by Macro on that occasion in the senate. But of course no command, however solemn, has any weight with **1.4** ungrateful and powerful successors. So Tiberius suffered the same treatment as he had given his mother, with this difference: whereas he had carried out none of the dispositions of her will in favour of anybody, his own bequests were paid to all the beneficiaries except his grandson. This more than anything made it perfectly plain that the objection to the will **1.5** had been contrived entirely because of the young boy. For Gaius did not have to publish it (for he was certainly not unaware of what was written in it); but since many people also knew its contents and since it was likely that either he or the senate would take the blame for suppressing it, so it seemed, he decided to have it nullified by the senate rather than conceal it.

B.2 GAIUS' EARLY EXTRAVAGANCE   A.D. 37

(59.2.1–6)

2.1   At the same time, by duly paying to everyone else Tiberius' bequests as if they were his own, he gained with ordinary people a reputation for generosity. Accompanied by the senate, he inspected the Praetorian Guard at drill and distributed the money bequeathed to them, 250 *denarii*

a man; and he handed out a supplementary donative of the same amount
2.2 from his own funds. To the people he also paid over the 11,250,000 *denarii*
left to them, and in addition the sixty *denarii* apiece which they had failed
to receive when he assumed the toga of manhood together with the
2.3 interest, which amounted to fifteen *denarii*. The Urban Cohorts and the
Night-Watch, the regular troops on service outside Italy and all the other
citizen forces in the smaller garrisons were all paid their bequests. The
Urban Cohorts received 125 *denarii* a man and all the others seventy-five.
2.4 He acted similarly with regard to Livia's will, carrying out all its
provisions. If only he had spent all his money in a proper manner, he
would have been thought a generous and magnificent ruler. It is true that
it was his fear of the people and of the army that in some instances led him
to make these gifts, but in general they were made on principle. For he
paid the bequests not only of Tiberius but also of his great-grandmother
2.5 Livia both to these various groups and to private individuals as well. But
as it turned out, he lavished huge sums on actors (whom he had recalled
without delay), horses, gladiators and other things of this kind, and so in
the shortest space of time he exhausted the substantial resources that had
accumulated in the treasury. And at the same time he blamed himself for
having made his earlier benefactions, putting it down to his easy-going
2.6 nature and his lack of judgement. At any rate, he had found in the
treasury 575 million *denarii* (or, according to other sources, 850 million),
and yet did not make any part of it last even into the third year of his
reign; but at the very start of his second year in power he found himself in
need of vast additional sums of money.

B.3 GAIUS' CONDUCT AS EMPEROR   A.D. 37

(59.3.1–5.5)

3.1 He showed just the same failing too in practically all other matters. At
first he seemed very democratic: he neither sent any written instructions to
the people or the senate, nor did he assume any of the imperial titles; but in
3.2 time he became very monarchical. Thus in a single day he took all the
honours which Augustus had been slow to accept, and then only one by
one as they had been voted to him during his long reign; and some of these
Tiberius indeed had refused to accept at all. With the exception of the title
'Father of the Fatherland' he deferred none of them, and it was not long
before he assumed that one too.
3.3 He turned out to be the most lustful of men: he even seized one woman as
she was being handed over in marriage to her husband, others he snatched
from their husbands when they were married. But then he came to hate
them all except one, and he would certainly have come to detest her, if he
had lived longer. His mother, his sisters and his grandmother Antonia he
3.4 treated at first with great respect. He immediately gave Antonia the title
'Augusta' and appointed her priestess of Augustus, granting her on the
spot the full privileges of the Vestal Virgins. To his sisters he also granted

these privileges of the Vestal Virgins and in addition the right to watch the games in the circus with him from the same front seats, and the right to have their names included not only in the prayers offered annually by the magistrates and priests for his own welfare and the welfare of the state, but also in the oaths of allegiance that were sworn to his rule.

3.5 He sailed in person overseas and with his own hands collected and brought back the bones of his dead mother and brothers; and wearing a purple-bordered toga and attended by lictors, as if at a triumph, he had

3.6 them laid to rest in the Mausoleum of Augustus. He annulled all the measures that had been passed against them, punished all who had conspired against them and recalled those who had been sent into exile because of some connexion with them. Yet, after doing all this, he acted in a most impious fashion towards both his grandmother and his sisters. He forced his grandmother to commit suicide because she had criticized him for something; and as for his sisters, after taking them all as sexual partners, he banished two of them to an island; the third had already died.

3.7 He even demanded that Tiberius, whom he called his 'grandfather', should be granted the same honours by the senate as Augustus had been. But the senate failed to vote Tiberius these honours immediately. (The senators could not bring themselves either to honour him or to dishonour him, because at this stage of his reign they had no clear idea of the young man's mind, and so were postponing all decisions until his arrival in Rome.) As a result Gaius paid Tiberius no other mark of distinction besides a public funeral. It was night-time when he brought the body into the city,

3.8 and at daybreak he had it laid out. And although he made an oration over his body, he did not so much praise the dead emperor as remind the people of Augustus and Germanicus and commend himself into their hands.

4.1 For indeed Gaius was by nature so contrary in all respects that he not only rivalled, but even surpassed Tiberius' licentiousness and bloodthirstiness, for which he had the nerve to censure him. Conversely, he in no way

4.2 imitated those aspects of Tiberius' conduct that won his praise. He was the first to insult him and the first to castigate him. The result was that others, believing that they would gain his favour by so doing, went in for rather reckless freedom of speech. But later he started both to eulogize and to revere him, so much so that he punished some for what they had said. Those people he hated as enemies of Tiberius for their abusive comments; but he also hated those who had praised Tiberius in any way on the

4.3 grounds that they were his supporters. He put a stop to accusations on the charge of treason, but then destroyed very many people using this very charge. His anger against those who had conspired against his father, mother and brothers had abated, so he claimed, and he had burned the papers about them. But he put many of them to death using that very evidence. For he did genuinely destroy some of these papers, but not, however, the originals which contained detailed proof, but just the copies

4.4 that he had made of them. In addition to this at the start of his reign he forbade the setting up of any images of him, but eventually proceeded to manufacture statues; and having once refused to sanction a vote that sacrifices be conducted to his Fortune, going even so far as to have this recorded on an inscription, he eventually ordered that temples and sacrifices be granted him, as if to a god.

4.5 He rejoiced in turn in large crowds and then solitude. He grew angry if requests were made of him and then if requests were not made of him. He would display great enthusiasm for some projects and then become very uninterested when it came to carrying them out. He would both spend money unsparingly and seek out funds in a most sordid fashion. He was likewise annoyed and delighted both with those who flattered him and

4.6 those who spoke their minds on some matter. He did not punish many who had committed great crimes, but slaughtered many who were not even under suspicion. Some of his entourage he flattered to an excessive degree, while others he utterly insulted. The result of this was that no-one knew either what to say or how to act towards him; but those who managed to survive did so more by luck than judgement.

5.1 To such an emperor were the Romans at this time handed over. The result was that people thought that the deeds of Tiberius, although they seemed very harsh at the time, were as far superior to those of Gaius as

5.2 those of Augustus had been to those of Tiberius. For Tiberius always remained in control and used others as agents to carry out his own plans. Gaius on the other hand was controlled by charioteers and by gladiators, and was the slave of actors and other people connected with the stage. Indeed he constantly kept Apelles, the most famous of the tragic actors, at

5.3 his side – even in public. As a result of this, both he and they on their own initiative used their authority to do everything that men of this type dare whenever they are granted any power. For everything that had to do with their profession, on the slightest excuse he would arrange and organize in a very lavish fashion, and he forced both the praetors and the consuls to do the same. The result was that hardly a day passed when there was not

5.4 some such performance. At first he was merely a spectator and part of the audience at these performances, and he would cheer and take sides as if he was one of the crowd; and on one occasion he was annoyed with those who supported the opposite side and so did not turn up at the spectacle. But as

5.5 time went on, he started to imitate them and compete in many events. For he would drive chariots, fight in gladiatorial combats, indulge in dancing and act in tragedies. And he would do this all the time, but on one particular occasion he summoned the leading senators suddenly in the middle of the night as if on some urgent business and then danced in front of them.

B.4 GAIUS' RELATIONS WITH THE SENATE; HE DENOUNCES TIBERIUS   A.D. 37

(59.6.1–7)

6.1 In the year of Tiberius' death and his own accession, Gaius at first showed great deference to the senators on an occasion when some members of the equestrian order and the Roman plebs were present at a meeting of the senate. He promised to share his power with them and to do whatever they thought best, even calling himself their son and ward.

6.2 He was then five months and four days short of his twenty-fifth birthday. Later he released those who were in prison, including Quintus Pomponius, who had been kept in custody for seven whole years after his consulship and ill-treated. He did away with charges of treason, which he saw were

6.3 the commonest cause of the prisoners' present sufferings. He also piled up all the papers left behind by Tiberius relating to their cases and burnt them (or so he pretended), saying, "I have done this so that, no matter how strongly I may wish some day to recall someone's past injustices towards

6.4 my mother and brothers, I shall be unable to punish him." For these acts he was praised; for people expected him more than anything to tell the truth, since they thought it impossible that he could have any duplicitous thoughts or make any duplicitous statements because of his youth. He increased their hopes by ordering that the Saturnalia be celebrated over a period of five days and by collecting just an obol from each of those who were eligible for the grain dole instead of the *denarius* which they had in the past given the emperor for the manufacture of images.

6.5 It was voted that he should be made consul at once by removing Proculus and Nigrinus, who were then in office, and that from then on he should be consul every year. He did not, however, accept these proposals, but waited instead until those two had completed the six-month term for which they had been appointed; only then did he assume his consulship, taking his

6.6 uncle Claudius as colleague. The latter, who up to this time had been enrolled among the equestrians and had been sent to Gaius after Tiberius' death as an envoy from the equestrian order, now for the first time, although forty-six years of age, became consul and a senator both at the

6.7 same time. In all this then Gaius' conduct seemed reasonable, as was the speech that he made in the senate when he took up his consulship. In it he denounced Tiberius for every single one of the crimes for which he was usually accused; he also made many promises about his own future conduct. The senate, afraid that he might change his mind, decreed that this speech should be read aloud every year.

B.5 GAIUS' CONSULSHIP; THE DEDICATION OF THE TEMPLE OF THE DEIFIED AUGUSTUS; MEASURES CONCERNING PUBLIC SHOWS   A.D. 37

(59.7.1–9)

7.1 After this, Gaius dedicated the shrine of Augustus, wearing triumphal dress for the occasion. Boys drawn from the noblest families and whose parents were both still alive sang the hymn, accompanied by girls chosen according to the same criteria. The senate together with their wives and the people were given a public banquet, and spectacles of all sorts were put

7.2 on. Musical events were staged, as well as horse-races that lasted for two days, with twenty heats on the first day and twenty-four on the second,

7.3 since this coincided with the emperor's birthday. For it was the last day of

August. And he put on the same kind of entertainment on many other occasions as well, whenever he thought it appropriate. Previously there had never been more than ten races held at a time. On this occasion he also arranged for four hundred bears to be slaughtered, along with other wild

7.4 beasts from Libya. In addition, the boys from noble families performed the Trojan Game on horseback, while the chariot which he used for the procession was drawn by six horses, another innovation. However, the emperor himself did not give the charioteers the starting-signal, but watched the races from the front seats alongside his sisters and his fellow-priests of Augustus.

7.5 So that no-one should have an excuse for not attending the spectacles (in fact he grew terribly annoyed if anyone stayed away from a show, or got up to leave in the middle), he postponed all lawsuits and suspended all periods of mourning. As a result, women who had just lost their husbands were allowed to marry even before the customary waiting period had

7.6 elapsed, as long as they were not pregnant. To encourage people to attend the shows without having to worry about greeting him in a formal manner (for up until then anyone who met the emperor in the streets would greet

7.7 him), he abolished the custom altogether. And he permitted those who so desired to come to the shows not wearing shoes, on the grounds that it had been the custom from very early days for people in Rome to try cases in summer barefoot. Furthermore, under Augustus it had often also been the

7.8 rule at the summer festivals, although it had been reversed by Tiberius. It was also at this time that senators were first permitted to sit on cushions rather than on the bare wooden benches and to wear hats at the theatre, as the Thessalians do, so as not to get sunburnt. And if the sun was particularly fierce, the Diribitorium, specially fitted out with wooden

7.9 benches, was used instead of the theatre. Such were Gaius' acts during his consulship. He held it for two months and twelve days; the remainder of the six-month period he handed back to those who had previously been designated for it.

B.6 ILLNESS OF GAIUS; MURDER OF TIBERIUS GEMELLUS A.D. 37

(59.8.1–3)

8.1 After this Gaius fell ill. He himself did not die, but he had Tiberius murdered, even though he had assumed the toga of manhood, been appointed 'Leader of the Youth' and finally been adopted as Gaius' son. The charge against him was that he had prayed for, and looked forward to, Gaius' death. Gaius put many other people to death on the same

8.2 charge. So the man who had bestowed upon Antiochus, son of Antiochus, his father's kingdom, Commagene, and in addition the coastal region of Cilicia, the man who had released Agrippa, grandson of Herod, from captivity (for he had been imprisoned by the emperor Tiberius) and restored him to his grandfather's kingdom now not only stripped his own brother and son of his inheritance, but actually had him put to death. And

he did not even despatch a letter to the senate about this. Later he took
8.3 similar action in a number of other cases. And so Tiberius perished for
allegedly having sought to profit from Gaius' illness.

B.7 FINANCES, ELECTIONS AND THE RECRUITMENT OF NEW EQUESTRIANS   A.D. 38

(59.9.4–7)

9.4 Gaius acted commendably and well in the following matters. As for the
accounts of public funds, he published them in full, following the example
of Augustus: they had not been published during Tiberius' absence from
the city. He helped the troops put out a fire and provided financial aid for
9.5 the victims. Since the roll of the equestrian order was becoming depleted,
he summoned men of distinguished family and great wealth from all over
the Empire, even from outside Italy, and enrolled them in the order. He
even gave some of them permission to wear senatorial dress before they
had held any of the magistracies which entitle us to enter the senate. Gaius
granted this in the hope that they would enter the senate in due course.
Previously, it seems, only those who were from families of senatorial rank
had been allowed to do this.
9.6 These measures caused general satisfaction; but when he put the
elections once more into the hands of the people and the plebs, so
reversing the arrangements of Tiberius, when he abolished the one per
cent tax, and when at a gymnastic contest which he had arranged he threw
tickets at random into the crowd and distributed a great number of gifts
9.7 to those who successfully scrambled for them, he pleased the rabble, it
is true; but he distressed sensible people, who reflected that if the
magistracies should fall once more into the hands of the common people,
and public funds be exhausted, and private resources dry up, many
disasters would occur.

B.8 DEATH OF MACRO   A.D. 38

(59.10.6–8)

10.6 Gaius was also blamed for compelling Macro and Ennia to commit
suicide. He remembered neither Ennia's love nor Macro's services in
helping him, in particular, to win sole power. The fact that he had
appointed Macro to govern Egypt had not the slightest influence. He had
also involved Macro in a scandal, in which he himself was very much
implicated. For he brought many charges against him, including that of
10.7 acting as a pimp. After this many others were also executed, some after
being condemned in court, but others even before conviction. Gaius
claimed that he was punishing them for wrongs committed against his
parents, his brothers or against others who had perished through their

actions. But really it was because of their property. The treasury had
10.8 become exhausted, and Gaius never had sufficient funds. These people
were condemned as a result of witnesses who spoke against them and also
on the basis of those papers which he once claimed to have burned. And
others were destroyed as a result of the illness that he had suffered the
previous year and the death of his sister Drusilla. For among other things
anyone who had entertained or greeted a person or had even taken a bath
during that period was punished.

B.9 DEATH OF DRUSILLA   A.D. 38

(59.11.1–4)

11.1   Drusilla was married to Marcus Lepidus, a man who was both the
emperor's favourite and his lover. She also slept with Gaius. She died at
this time. Her husband delivered the eulogy over her, while her brother
11.2 gave her the honour of a public funeral. The Praetorian Guard under their
commander and the equestrian order [ran round the pyre] in their
respective groups, and boys of noble birth performed the Trojan Game on
horseback around her tomb. She was then voted all the honours that had
been bestowed on Livia. It was also decreed that she should be deified,
that a golden statue of her should be set up in the senate-house, that a cult
statue should be dedicated to her in the temple of Venus in the Forum of
the same size as that of the goddess, and that she should receive the same
11.3 kind of cultic honours as Venus. It was also decreed that a shrine of her
own should be constructed, that she should have twenty priests (not just
men, but women also), that women should swear an oath by her name
whenever they appeared as witnesses, that on her birthday a festival
similar to the Games of Cybele should be celebrated and that the senate
and the equestrian order be banqueted. Accordingly, at this time she
received the title 'Panthea' and was deemed worthy of divine honours in
11.4 all cities. A certain Livius Geminius, a senator, swore that he had seen her
ascending to heaven and consorting with the gods. He invoked destruction
upon himself and his children if he should be lying. He called on Panthea
herself and all the other gods to act as witnesses. For these acts he received
25,000 *denarii*.

B.10 ARRANGEMENTS ABOUT ALLIED KINGS; AEDILESHIP OF VESPASIAN   A.D. 38

(59.12.2–3)

12.2   Meanwhile Gaius granted to Sohaemus the territory of the Ituraean
Arabians, to Cotys Lesser Armenia and, later, parts of Arabia in addition,
to Rhoemetalces the territory which had previously belonged to Cotys,
and to Polemon son of Polemon his ancestral kingdom, all on the vote of

the senate. This all took place in the Forum with Gaius sitting on the Rostra on a chair between the consuls. Some add that awnings of silk were

12.3 used. At a later date he noticed that there was a lot of mud in an alley and ordered that it should be thrown on the toga of Flavius Vespasianus, who was aedile at the time and responsible for keeping the alleys clean. This incident at the time was not viewed as being very important; but later when Vespasian had become emperor and stabilized affairs after the confusion and uproar of civil war, people decided that it had happened not without the intervention of the gods; Gaius had handed over the city specifically to Vespasian for its restoration.

B.11 GAIUS' ATTEMPTS TO RAISE FUNDS; HIS LOVE OF CHARIOT-RACING   A.D. 39

(59.14.1–15.5)

14.1   At the same time as he was bringing about these murders since he was exceedingly short of funds, he found yet another way of raising money. He forced the consuls and praetors and others to buy, whether they wanted to or not, at an excessively high price those gladiators who had survived a

14.2 gladiatorial combat. And he compelled them to put on gladiatorial contests at the Circus Games. In particular he sold these gladiators to those who had been allotted the task of putting on these games; for he gave orders that two praetors be appointed by lot to run the games, as had been the case in the past. During these sales he himself would sit on the

14.3 auctioneer's platform and keep the bidding going. Many people came from outside Rome to bid against them. They were encouraged by the fact that he had lifted the legal restrictions on the number of gladiators allowed at games, since he himself liked to attend gladiatorial shows frequently. The result was that some men were forced to purchase them,

14.4 others thought that it would help keep them in favour with Gaius, but the majority of buyers consisted of those who were thought of as being wealthy and who wanted any excuse to spend their resources, so that they would become poorer and thus save their lives.

14.5   And yet after doing all this, he later poisoned the best and the most famous of these gladiators. He also did the same thing with horses and

14.6 charioteers of rival factions. For he was a keen supporter of The Greens or Leeks (whose name was taken from the frog-green colours that they wore), so much so that the area in which he used to practise driving

14.7 chariots is still to this day called the 'Gaianum'. Moreover, one of the horses, which he called Incitatus, he would even invite to dinner: he would serve him golden barley, pour him wine in golden goblets and even swear oaths by his health and his fortune. He even promised to appoint him consul. He certainly would have carried this out, if he had lived for longer.

15.1   As a means to boost his supply of revenue, it had been voted earlier in the reign that all those who had wanted to leave money to Tiberius and were still alive should bestow the same favour upon Gaius at the time of

their deaths. To make it appear as if he was entitled to receive legacies and
accept such bequests even though it was against the law (since at that time
he had neither a wife nor any children), he had a decree passed to this

15.2 effect. But at this point of his reign he simply took over for his own use
without any semblance of a decree all the property of those ex-centurions
who had bequeathed it to anybody but the emperor after the triumph

15.3 which Gaius' father had celebrated. And when even these measures did
not succeed, he thought up a third method of gaining revenue as follows.
Gnaeus Domitius Corbulo, a senator, had noticed during the reign of
Tiberius what a bad state the roads were in. He, therefore, kept complain-
ing about it to those in charge of looking after the roads and still more

15.4 kept making a nuisance of himself on this subject in the senate. So Gaius
won him over and used him to attack all those who had ever been in
charge of the roads, whether they were alive or dead, and had received
money for their repair. He proceeded to fine them as well as those who had
contracted from them the right to do the work, on the grounds that they

15.5 had spent none of this money. As a reward, Corbulo was then appointed
consul, but later during the reign of Claudius he was accused and brought
to book. For Claudius refused to claim any sum of money still outstand-
ing and even returned to those who had been fined the money which they
had handed over; some of this he drew from the public treasury, the rest he
had to extract from Corbulo himself. This took place later.

B.12 CHANGE IN GAIUS' ATTITUDE TOWARDS TIBERIUS; RE-INTRODUCTION OF THE CHARGE OF TREASON; HONOURS FOR GAIUS   A.D. 39

(59.16.1–11)

16.1   Up to this point in his reign not only had Gaius continually denounced
Tiberius in front of everybody, but rather than taking people to task when
they slandered him either in public or in private, he had actually taken
pleasure in what they had said. But now he entered the senate-house and
made a long speech praising him, in which he also censured at some length
the senate and people on the grounds that they were quite wrong to

16.2 criticize Tiberius. "It is within my power as emperor," he said, "to do such
things. But you are not only committing a crime, but also committing an
act of treason by your attitude towards a man who was once your ruler."
As a result, he re-examined one by one the cases of those who had
perished, and tried to prove, so it seemed to people, that the senators had
been guilty of causing the destruction of most of them: they had laid the
charges against some, given evidence against others, but in short had

16.3 voted to condemn them all. This evidence, supposedly drawn from those
very documents that he had once claimed to have burned, was read out by
the imperial freedmen. He then addressed them.

    "If it is true that Tiberius treated you unjustly, you ought not to have
honoured him during his lifetime, no by Jupiter, nor should you now be

changing your minds on issues on which you have many times made
16.4 declarations and passed resolutions. You not only handled Tiberius in a
devious manner, but also put Sejanus to death after puffing him up with
pride and corrupting him. As a result, I ought not to expect any decent
treatment from you." After making such remarks, he introduced Tiberius
16.5 himself, as it were, into his speech, who addressed him as follows. "All
your remarks have been well-made and are quite truthful. Therefore, show
neither affection nor mercy to any of them. For they all hate you, and they
are all praying for your death. They will murder you, if they can.
Therefore, don't even consider what actions you can take to win their
16.6 favour, and don't worry if they gossip. Rather, take thought only for your
own pleasure and safety; you'd be quite justified in doing this. For if you
act in this way, you will suffer no harm and enjoy all the greatest pleasures.
And yet you will still be honoured by them, whether they are willing or
16.7 unwilling. But if you do show them any affection or mercy, you will derive
no practical benefits, while in theory any good reputation you receive will
be meaningless; for you will gain no further advantage, but rather become
the victim of conspiracies and die an inglorious death. For no man is ruled
by his own free will. As long as a person is afraid, he seeks the protection
of the stronger; but whenever he gains in confidence, he takes it out on the
weaker."

16.8   After making this speech, Gaius reintroduced the charge of treason and
gave orders that this should immediately be inscribed on a bronze plaque.
He hurried out of the senate-house and set out on the same day for the
suburbs. The senate and the people were greatly afraid, remembering the
accusations that they had often made against Tiberius and balancing what
16.9 Gaius had just said against what they had heard in the past. As things
stood, through shock and despondency they were unable to make any
statement or conduct any business. But the next day they reassembled and
made many speeches praising Gaius as a most sincere and pious ruler,
since they were most grateful to him for not having put them to death.
16.10 And for this reason they passed a resolution to offer a sacrifice of oxen to
his clemency every year both on the anniversary of the day on which he
had made his speech and also on the days belonging to the palace. In
addition they voted that a golden image of Gaius should be carried up to
the Capitol and hymns be sung in its honour by boys of the noblest
16.11 families. They also gave him permission to celebrate a lesser triumph, as
if he had defeated some external enemy. And this is what they decided on
this occasion, and later they proposed many additional honours on almost
any excuse.

B.13 GAIUS AND THE BRIDGE AT BAIAE   **A.D. 39**

(59.17)

17.1   Gaius, however, was not impressed with this kind of procession, since
he did not think it particularly noteworthy to ride across dry land on

horseback; but he was keen to ride across the sea, in a manner of speaking, by constructing a bridge between Puteoli and Bauli, a small place about

17.2 three-and-a-half miles across the bay from Puteoli. Boats were collected for the bridge: some were requisitioned from other places, others were constructed specially for the occasion. For an insufficient number of boats could be collected in the very short space of time available, even though all possible efforts were made. This requisitioning of boats caused

17.3 a severe famine both in Italy and especially in Rome. The bridge of boats was constructed to provide not just a way across, but also resting-places and inns, which even had a supply of running water fit for drinking.

When everything was ready, Gaius put on what he alleged was the breastplate of Alexander the Great and over it a cloak of purple silk, embellished with a lot of gold and many precious stones from India. He also strapped on a sword, took hold of a shield and put a garland of oak-

17.4 leaves on his head. Then he sacrificed to Neptune and various other gods, including Envy, to protect himself from any malign act of the evil eye, as he put it. He charged onto the bridge from Bauli at the head of a whole troop of armed cavalry and infantry, and stormed into Puteoli as if he was

17.5 attacking some enemy. And there he remained for the next day, as if resting from battle, and then, dressed in a gold-embroidered tunic, he rode back across the same bridge in a chariot; the chariot was drawn by the most successful prize-winning racehorses. A whole collection of what supposedly were spoils accompanied him, including Darius, a member of the Arsacid dynasty, who was at the time one of the Parthian hostages

17.6 being held in Rome. His friends and companions followed close behind, riding in vehicles, dressed in flowered clothes; then the army and the rest of the crowd, each group dressed in their own distinctive fashion.

Of course he had to deliver an address, since he was on such a campaign and had won such a great victory; so he mounted a platform which had been constructed on some boats somewhere in the middle of the bridge.

17.7 He started by commending himself for undertaking such great deeds, and went on to praise the soldiers for having put up with so many hardships and undergone so many dangers; he singled out especially the fact that

17.8 they had crossed the sea on foot. To reward them for this achievement, he distributed money among them, and after this they were treated to banquets for the rest of the day and the whole of the night, he on the bridge as if he were on some island, they on other boats anchored around it. Light shone down upon them in abundance from the bridge itself and

17.9 from the mountains nearby. As the place was crescent-shaped, fires were lit all around, as if they were in a theatre; as a result, no-one realized that it was dark. For he wanted to make the night day, just as he had made the sea land. After consuming an enormous amount of food and drink, in his drunkenness he hurled many of his companions off the bridge into the sea.

17.10 As for the others, he sailed around them in boats equipped with rams and sank them. As a result, some people perished, but the majority managed to escape, even though they were drunk. The reason for this was that the sea was very smooth and placid, both when the bridge of boats was being

17.11 constructed and when these other events were taking place. Gaius drew great satisfaction from this, declaring that even Neptune was afraid of him. He went on to make all kinds of fun of Darius and Xerxes, claiming that he had bridged a far wider stretch of water than they had.

B.14 GAIUS AND TRIALS: DOMITIUS AFER AND SENECA   A.D. 39

(59.18.1–19.8)

18.1 This was the end of the incident of the bridge, but it also caused the death of many men. For Gaius had exhausted all his funds on this project and so started to plot against many more people for their property. He held some trials himself in private, others he held with the whole senate.

18.2 The senate also held some trials by itself; but its verdicts were not final and binding, since appeals were often made against its decisions to the emperor. The decisions of the senate were made public in the usual way, but the names of all those condemned by Gaius were displayed on lists, as

18.3 if he was afraid that their guilt would escape people's notice. These people were punished: some in prison, others were hurled down from the Capitol, and the rest committed suicide in advance. Even those who had been driven into exile were not safe; for many of them were put to death either on the road or when they were already living in exile. There is no need to bore my readers by going into meaningless details about most of the cases.

18.4 But Calvisius Sabinus, who was one of the leading senators and had at that time just returned from being governor of Pannonia, was indicted with his wife Cornelia. It was alleged that she had gone round visiting guards and had watched soldiers at drill. They did not wait for the verdict,

18.5 but committed suicide. Titius Rufus also did exactly the same thing, when he was accused of having said that the senate thought one way and voted another. One Junius Priscus, a praetor, was accused on a variety of charges, but the real reason for his death was because he was wealthy. In his case Gaius, when he learnt that he possessed nothing worth killing him for, made the amazing statement: "He deceived me and perished for no purpose. He could have lived."

19.1 One of the men on trial at the time was Domitius Afer. He came near to losing his life for an extraordinary reason, and was saved in an even more remarkable fashion. Gaius bore a grudge against him in any case, because in the reign of Tiberius he had brought an accusation against a woman

19.2 who was related to Gaius' mother, Agrippina. Sometime later Agrippina happened to meet Domitius and when she realized that he had stepped out of her way in embarrassment, she called out to him and said, "Don't be afraid, Domitius; it's not you that I hold responsible, but Agamemnon." At this time Afer had set up a image of the emperor, with an inscription to the effect that Gaius was twenty-seven years old and holding the consul-

19.3 ship for the second time. This irritated Gaius, who felt that he was being criticized for his youth and unconstitutional behaviour. So for an action for which Afer had expected to be honoured the emperor immediately brought him before the senate and read out a long speech denouncing him. Gaius always claimed to be the best of all orators, and knowing that Afer himself was an extremely gifted speaker, he made every effort on this

19.4 occasion to excel. And he would certainly have put him to death, if Afer had in the slightest way tried to outdo him. As it was, he made no speech in reply nor even a defence, but pretended to be truly amazed and astounded by Gaius' ability. He repeated the accusation point by point,

19.5 praising it as if he were merely a listener and not himself on trial. And when he was given the chance to speak, he resorted to entreaty and lamentation and finally threw himself on the ground and lay there prostrate, asking for mercy, as though he feared Gaius' powers as an orator more than his powers as Caesar. When he saw and heard this, Gaius relented, believing that he had really overwhelmed him with his

19.6 eloquence. For this reason and because of his freedman Callistus, whom he respected and whom Domitius had won over, Gaius stopped being angry. And when Callistus later criticized him for having accused the man in the first place, Gaius answered, "It would have been wrong of me to keep such a speech to myself."

19.7 So Domitius escaped by allowing himself to be proved a skilful orator no longer. Lucius Annaeus Seneca, on the other hand, who surpassed all his Roman contemporaries and many others as well in wisdom, was nearly destroyed, not because he had committed any crime or was even suspected of having committed one, but merely because he had pleaded a case

19.8 brilliantly in the senate in the presence of the emperor. Gaius ordered his execution, but then let him off. He believed one of his sexual partners when she told him that Seneca was suffering badly from consumption and it would not be long before he died.

B.15 ELECTIONS; AFRICA; GAIUS' EXPEDITION TO GAUL   A.D. 39

(59.20.1–21.4)

20.1 He immediately appointed Domitius consul, after removing those who were then in office on the grounds that they had failed to proclaim a supplication for his birthday, even though the praetors had put on circus games and had slaughtered wild-beasts on that day, something which took place every year, and on the grounds that they had held a festival to commemorate the victories of Augustus over Antonius, as was customary.

20.2 For in order to find some complaint against them, he chose to pose as the descendant of Antonius rather than of Augustus. Indeed he had revealed beforehand to those with whom he consulted that no matter which course of action the consuls took, they would make a serious mistake, whether they sacrificed to celebrate the defeat of Antonius, or whether they chose

20.3 not to sacrifice to celebrate Augustus' victory. It was on these grounds then that he summarily dismissed these consuls from office, after shattering their *fasces*, at which one of them was so distraught that he committed suicide. Domitius then and his colleague were elected in theory by the people, but in fact by Gaius himself. True, Gaius had restored the

20.4 elections to the people. But they had become rather slack in this matter, since for a long time they had not handled on their own initiative any kind of business that was appropriate for them. Furthermore, the number of candidates who were keen to put themselves forward for political office never exceeded the number of posts that had to be filled. But if there ever were more than the number required, the result was arranged among themselves. So the semblance of democracy was maintained, but there was

20.5 no substance to it. This led Gaius himself to abolish free elections once again. Subsequently things went on much as in the reign of Tiberius; but as for praetors, sometimes fifteen were chosen, sometimes one more or one

20.6 less, just as circumstances required. Such was Gaius' practice in the matter of elections.

In general he approached everything, no matter what it was, with envy and suspicion. For example, he sent Carrinas Secundus, an orator, into exile for delivering, as a mere rhetorical exercise, a speech against tyranny.

20.7 Again, when Lucius Piso, son of Plancina and Gnaeus Piso, was chosen by lot to be governor of Africa, Gaius was afraid that arrogance might lead him to start a rebellion, especially as he was to have under his command a large force made up both of citizen legionaries and of non-citizen auxiliaries. So he divided the province into two parts, assigning the military forces and the Numidians in the vicinity to another official, an arrangement that has continued from that time to the present.

21.1 Gaius had by now spent practically all the money that he had acquired in every possible way from every possible source of supply in Rome and the rest of Italy. He could find no other possible way of gaining more revenue from this region, and still his expenses were pressing hard on his

21.2 heels. So he launched an expedition to Gaul, ostensibly because the Celts were hostile and stirring up trouble; but his real purpose was to exploit Gaul and its abundant wealth, and Spain as well. Still, he did not announce his expedition immediately, but first went into one of the suburbs and then suddenly set out, taking with him many actors,

21.3 gladiators, horses, women and all sorts of other luxuries. When he arrived in Gaul, he did no harm to the enemy – in fact, when he had advanced a little way beyond the Rhine, he returned and then set out as if to invade Britain, though at the water's edge he turned back and was considerably irritated by some slight successes won by his subordinate officers – but he inflicted many cruel injuries on subject peoples, allies

21.4 and fellow citizens alike. On the one hand, as for those who owned any property, he used every excuse to strip them of it; on the other hand, both individuals and cities brought him large gifts, quite voluntarily of course. Some men were put to death for alleged rebellion, others for conspiring against him; but the only fault of one and all was that they were wealthy.

B.16 FURTHER EXTRAVAGANCE AND ARROGANCE OF GAIUS IN GAUL   A.D. 39

(59.22.1–4)

22.1   All the same, Gaius saved nothing. He maintained his customary level of expenditure not only on things like some games he put on at Lugdunum, but particularly on the legions. He had mustered 200,000

22.2   troops, or, according to some authorities, 250,000. He was acclaimed *Imperator* by them seven times, whenever he thought it appropriate, though he had not won a single battle or killed a single enemy soldier. He did once capture a few of the enemy by deceit and put them in chains. But he lost a large part of his own troops, some by striking them down one by one, others by slaughtering them in a group as they stood in formation.

22.3   On one occasion he saw a crowd of prisoners or some other people and gave instructions for them all to be butchered, in those famous words, "from one baldhead to the next". On another occasion he was playing dice. When he realized that he had no money left, he demanded the census lists of the Gauls and ordered the wealthiest of them to be put to death.

22.4   When he rejoined his fellow dice-players, he said, "You're playing for a few *denarii*, while I have collected one hundred and fifty million." Men perished like this for no good reason; for example, a man called Julius Sacerdos, who was fairly well off, but not so rich as to be a likely victim, was, nevertheless, slaughtered as a result of mistaken identity.

B.17 THE CONSPIRACY OF GAETULICUS AND LEPIDUS; GAIUS' ATTITUDE TOWARDS CLAUDIUS   A.D. 39

(59.22.5–23.2; 23.4–5)

22.5   As for most of those who perished, there is no need for me to mention them all by name, but I shall report the deaths of those for whom history at least demands a mention. First, Lentulus Gaetulicus, who had an excellent reputation in every way and had been governor of Germany for ten years, was put to death by Gaius on the grounds that he was popular

22.6   among his troops. Another victim was Lepidus, that lover and favourite of Gaius, the husband of Drusilla, the man who together with Gaius had had sexual relations with the emperor's other sisters, Agrippina and Julia, the man whom he had allowed to stand for office five years earlier than was

22.7   customary, and whom he kept saying he would leave as his successor as emperor. To commemorate this, Gaius gave the army a bounty, as if he had defeated an enemy in battle, and sent three daggers to be dedicated to

22.8   Mars the Avenger in Rome. As for his sisters, he deported them to the Pontian islands because of their sexual activities with Lepidus, after accusing them in a letter to the senate of many treasonable and licentious acts. Agrippina was given Lepidus' bones in an urn and told to carry it

22.9   back to Rome, keeping hold of it in her lap the whole way. And as many honours had previously been voted to his sisters clearly on his own account, he forbade the award of any distinction to any of his relatives.

23.1   Gaius then sent a report on this matter to the senate, as though he had escaped from some great conspiracy. For he was always pretending to be **23.2** in danger and leading a miserable life. When they received his report, the senators voted him an ovation, among other things, and sent envoys to inform him of this, some of whom they selected by lot, but they specifically appointed Claudius. This caused Gaius further annoyance, so much so that he again forbade any kind of praise or honour to be bestowed on any member of the imperial family. This was because he believed that the honours that he received were unworthy of him. ....

23.4   .... He was so capricious by nature that no-one could handle him with **23.5** ease. He did not receive all these ambassadors on the grounds that he suspected some of them of being spies; instead he selected a few, and sent the rest away before they had reached Gaul. Those whom he did receive he treated with no respect at all; and he would have killed Claudius, if he had not felt contempt for him, because Claudius, partly by his nature and partly by deliberate intention, gave the impression of great stupidity.

*B.18 GAIUS AND ADDITIONS TO THE ROMAN EMPIRE:
MAURETANIA AND BRITAIN   A.D. 40

(59.25.1–5: Xiphilinus)

25.1   While the senate was passing these measures, Gaius sent for Ptolemy, the son of Juba, and learning that he was rich, had him put to death and .....   **[Manuscript breaks off]**

How the Mauretanias started to be governed by the Romans.

... Gaius reached the Ocean, with the intention apparently of invading **25.2** Britain, and paraded all the troops on the beach. He embarked on a warship, and then after putting out to sea for only a short distance, sailed back into port again. Next he took his seat on a lofty platform and gave the soldiers a signal as for battle, telling the trumpeters to urge them on. **25.3** But suddenly he gave an order to gather up the sea-shells. Having secured these spoils (he needed booty, of course, for his triumphal procession), he proudly claimed that he had even managed to enslave the Ocean itself. And he distributed many rewards among the troops. He took the shells back to Rome, so that he could show off his booty to the people there too. **25.4**   The senate did not know how it could remain silent in the face of these events, since they had learned that Gaius was very proud of his exploits, nor was he sure what sort of honours it could bestow upon him. For if anyone bestows great praise or honours upon somebody for a small exploit or for none at all, he can be suspected of ridiculing and laughing at **25.5** the exploit itself. Nevertheless, when Gaius entered the city of Rome, he came very close to destroying the whole senate, on the grounds that he had been voted honours only fit for a human being. He summoned the people and hurled much silver and gold among them from some high platform. Many died in the scramble to pick these up. Some authors allege that small pieces of iron were mixed in with the silver and gold.

[Xiphilinus]

*B.19 PROTOGENES, IMPERIAL FREEDMAN, AND THE DEATH OF PROCULUS A.D. 40

(59.25.9–26.4: Petrus Patricius; Zonaras; Xiphilinus)

25.9 He summoned a meeting of the senate and apparently granted them amnesty, saying that there were very few people with whom he was still angry. This indeed caused double the anguish for them all, since each senator could now think only about his own safety.

[Petrus Patricius]

26.1 The senate was greatly afraid because it had failed to condemn certain people. **[Zonaras]**

Now there was a certain Protogenes, who assisted the emperor Gaius in all his harshest measures and so always carried two books around with him, one of which he called his 'Sword' and the other his 'Dagger'. One
26.2 day he entered the senate apparently on some other business. Naturally all the members saluted and welcomed him. But Protogenes gave Scribonius Proculus an evil look and said, "What? You greeting me, when you hate the emperor as you do?" On hearing this, all those present surrounded
26.3 Proculus and tore him to pieces. Gaius took great pleasure in this incident and then informed the senate that his anger towards them had abated. They, therefore, voted that various festivals be held in his honour, that he be allowed to sit on a high podium even in the senate-house, so that no-one could get near him, and that even there he be attended by a military
26.4 bodyguard. They also voted that his statues should be guarded. As a result of this Gaius' anger against them abated, and suddenly with youthful eagerness he accomplished a few excellent things. Pomponius, who had been accused of plotting against him, he released, since he had been betrayed by a friend. As for Pomponius' mistress, since she did not make any statement against him even under torture, he refused to harm her and even rewarded her with money. **[Xiphilinus]**

*B.20 GAIUS' DIVINE PRETENSIONS A.D. 40

(59.26.5–27.1: Xiphilinus)

26.5 Gaius was praised for this, partly out of fear, but partly for genuine reasons. But when people started calling him a demi-god and even a god, he went completely out of his mind. Even before this he had been demanding that he be considered something more than a mere human being, and he kept declaring that he was having sex with Luna, the moon-goddess, and being crowned by Victory. Furthermore, he kept pretending that he was Jupiter, and used this as a pretext for having sex with many

26.6 different women, but most of all with his sisters. At other times he claimed to be Neptune, because he had bridged such a large stretch of water. He also played the part of Hercules, Bacchus, Apollo and the other gods, not just the male, but the female deities as well. He often appeared as Juno, Diana or Venus. In addition to this change in names, he would take on all the other appropriate attributes as well, so that he could appear most like

26.7 them. At one moment he would be seen in female form, holding a wine-bowl and a thyrsus; at another he would be wearing a male costume and carrying a club and lionskin or a helmet and shield. Now he would appear clean-shaven and then bearded; at one time he appeared shaking a trident, at another brandishing a thunderbolt. He would resemble a maiden dressed either for hunting or for war, and then shortly afterwards appear

26.8 as a married woman. Thus, by changing his costume, his props and his wigs, he would play a whole variety of rôles quite convincingly. And in every respect he wanted to appear more than just a human being and an emperor.

There was once a man from Gaul, who saw him conducting business

26.9 from a high platform dressed up as Jupiter and burst out laughing. Gaius summoned him and asked, "What do you think of me?" And he replied (and I quote his actual words), "You're just a big joke!" Nevertheless, he did not even suffer any harm; for he was a cobbler. Thus it seems that such people find it easier to stomach the frank, honest remarks of people of low rank than those made by people of some distinction.

26.10 It was these costumes that he used to assume, then, whenever he was pretending to be some god; and in addition supplications, prayers and sacrifices would be offered to him as was thought fit. At other times he

27.1 usually appeared in public wearing silk or triumphal dress. He would kiss only a very small number of people. As far as most senators were concerned, he would just stretch out his hand or his foot for them to prostrate themselves before. As a result those who did receive kisses from him would express their gratitude to him even in the senate, even though he used to kiss dancers every day in full view of everyone.

[Xiphilinus]

*B.21 GAIUS AND LUCIUS VITELLIUS   A.D. 40

(59.27.2–6: Xiphilinus)

27.2 And yet all these honours paid to Gaius as though to a god came not just from the masses, who are accustomed all the time to act in such a sycophantic fashion, but also from people of high social standing. Take the case of Lucius Vitellius. He came from an excellent family and had plenty of common sense. Furthermore, he had made a name for himself as

27.3 governor of Syria. Among other brilliant achievements there was the way that he had dealt with Artabanus, who was planning to attack Syria, since he had suffered no punishment for his invasion of Armenia. Vitellius terrified him by a surprise appearance when Artabanus was already nearing the Euphrates. He induced him to come to a conference, forced him to sacrifice to the images of Augustus and Gaius, and made a peace with him on terms that were to the Romans' advantage. Furthermore, he even took his sons as hostages.

27.4 Well, this Vitellius was summoned by Gaius and it seemed likely that he would be put to death. The complaint against him was the same as the one the Parthians had against their king when they expelled him: namely, that jealousy made him the object of hatred, fear the object of conspiracies. Gaius of course hated all who were more powerful than himself and was suspicious of all who were successful, feeling sure that they were about to

27.5 attack him. Yet Vitellius managed to save his life. Dressed humbly in a style unworthy of his social status, he fell at the emperor's feet, burst into tears and then addressed him many times as a god and prostrated himself before him. And finally he vowed that if he were allowed to live he would

27.6 offer sacrifice to him. As a result he calmed and appeased Gaius to such an extent that he survived and even came to be regarded as one of Gaius' most intimate friends. On one occasion, when Gaius claimed that he was having sexual intercourse with Luna, the moon-goddess, he asked Vitellius if he could see her with him. Vitellius, trembling as if in awe, kept his eyes fixed on the ground and answered in a half whisper, "Only you gods, master, may look upon one another." So, starting from here, Vitellius later came to surpass all others in adulation. **[Xiphilinus]**

*B.22 GAIUS' MEGALOMANIA: IMPERIAL CULT   A.D. 40

(59.28.1–11: Xiphilinus)

28.1 Gaius gave orders that a sacred precinct should be consecrated to him in the province of Asia at Miletus. He said that he had chosen this city because Artemis had already taken over Ephesus, Augustus Pergamum and Tiberius Smyrna. But the real reason was that he wanted to take over all for himself the large and exceedingly beautiful temple that the Milesians were at that time building in honour of Apollo.

28.2 He then went to still greater lengths, and actually set up in Rome itself a temple of his own, granted him by vote of the senate, but built at his own expense on the Palatine. He had already constructed a sort of lodge on the

28.3 Capitoline, so as to share quarters, as he put it, with Jupiter. But he did not approve of being the junior partner in this union of households and blamed the god for having occupied the Capitoline before him. So he pressed on with the erection of another temple on the Palatine, and actually wanted to transfer to it the statue of Olympian Zeus, after

28.4 remodelling it to resemble himself. He found this impossible to achieve.

For the ship built to carry the statue was wrecked by lightning, and loud laughter was heard every time anybody went near the statue to take hold of its base. Gaius uttered terrible threats against the statue and set up another instead.

28.5 The temple of Castor and Pollux which stood in the Roman Forum he cut in two, and in so doing created an entrance to the palace right through the middle of the temple between the two statues, so that, as he used to put it, he could have the Dioscuri as his gate-keepers. He designated himself Jupiter Latiaris and appointed as his priests his wife Caesonia, Claudius and other very rich individuals. He received in return

28.6 two and a half million *denarii* from each of them. He went even further and swore himself in as a priest of himself, and appointed his horse a fellow-priest. All sorts of different kinds of expensive birds were sacrificed to him daily. He even had a machine for answering thunderclaps with thunderclaps, and whenever there was a flash of lightning, he sent a flash in return. Whenever a thunderbolt fell, he would hurl a javelin against a rock, quoting each time the line of Homer: "Either lift me up or I will lift you!"

28.7 When Caesonia gave birth to a baby daughter after only one month of marriage, he claimed this was due to divine intervention, exulting in the fact that he had become both a husband and a father in such a short period of time. He named the girl Drusilla, took her up to the Capitol and placed her solemnly on the knee of Jupiter, as if she was his child. He also put her alongside Minerva to be suckled.

28.8 Now this god, this Jupiter (for he was addressed by these titles so often at the end of the reign that they even appeared in documents) was doing all this at the same time as he was collecting money in a most disgraceful and terrible way. One might pass over the goods-for-sale and the taverns, the prostitutes and the lawcourts, the craftsmen and the wage-earning slaves, and all the other activities from which he did not cease collecting

28.9 every sort of revenue. But how could anyone keep silent about the rooms which were marked out in the palace itself and about the wives of the leading citizens and the children of the most revered whom he dishonoured by setting up as prostitutes in these rooms and by harvesting revenue from all alike for their services? Some of them were happy to do this, but others were quite unwilling, but did it so as not to be thought to

28.10 bear any grudge. The masses, however, were not even in the slightest disturbed by these events, but rather took pleasure together with him in his licentiousness and also in the fact that each time he collected gold and

28.11 silver from them, he would throw himself onto it and roll in it. However, when he introduced some severe measures about taxes and inscribed them on white boards in very small letters and then hung these from a very high position (he did this to ensure that the regulations should be read by as few people as possible, and as a result many would be liable to the penalties, since they would be unaware of what was lawful or unlawful), the masses suddenly rushed into the Circus in a great crowd and uttered a storm of protest.   **[Xiphilinus]**

*B.23 THE ASSASSINATION OF GAIUS AND ITS AFTERMATH

A.D. 41

(59.29.1–30.3: Xiphilinus; John of Antioch)

29.1   Since Gaius continued to play the complete madman in every way, a conspiracy was formed against him by Cassius Chaerea and Cornelius Sabinus, even though they were tribunes in the Praetorian Guard. There were a good many people involved in it, fully aware of what was going on, among whom were Callistus and the prefect of the Praetorian Guard.

[Xiphilinus]

29.1a   Practically all of Gaius' entourage were persuaded to take part in it, both to further their own interests and to benefit the state. Furthermore, those who chose not to join the conspiracy concealed their knowledge of it, since they were glad to see a plot forming against him.

[John of Antioch]

29.2   Those who carried out the assassination were those I have mentioned. Chaerea was in general rather an old-fashioned sort of man and he also had particular grounds for anger; for Gaius kept accusing him of being effeminate, even though he was the most robust of men. Whenever it was his turn to collect the password, Gaius would give him one such as "Lust"
29.3   or "Venus". An oracle had come to Gaius' attention a short time before, warning him to beware of a Cassius. Gaius thought that it referred to Gaius Cassius, who was then governor of Asia, since he was descended from that Cassius who had assassinated Julius Caesar. He, therefore, had him arrested and brought to Rome. But in fact the divine power was
29.4   warning him about this Cassius Chaerea. An Egyptian called Apollonius similarly foretold the whole story in his native land. Because of this he was summoned to Rome and brought before the emperor on the very day on which Gaius was destined to die. Since his punishment was postponed for a little while, he was saved.

The assassination was carried out as follows. Gaius was celebrating a
29.5   festival on the Palatine, in which he was putting on a spectacle. While this spectacle was taking place, he himself was eating and drinking, and providing a banquet for the others. Even Pomponius Secundus, who was consul at the time, was eating his fill, sitting at the emperor's feet and constantly bending over to kiss them. Pained as they were by these disgraceful proceedings, Chaerea and Sabinus, nevertheless, kept them-
29.6   selves under control for five days. But when Gaius himself wanted to dance and act in a tragedy, and proclaimed a three-day extension of the festival for this very purpose, Chaerea and his supporters could endure it no longer. They waited for Gaius to leave the theatre to watch the boys of aristocratic families whom he had summoned from Greece and Ionia to sing the hymn composed in his honour. They intercepted him in a narrow
29.7   alley and murdered him. Once he was down on the ground, none of those

present could restrain themselves. Everybody kept stabbing him savagely,
even though he was dead; some even tasted his flesh. His wife and
daughter were promptly murdered.

30.1   So Gaius, after doing all this within a space of three years, nine months
and twenty-eight days, learnt by experience that he was not a god.

[Xiphilinus]

30.1a   He was now spat upon by those who used to prostrate themselves in his
honour, even when he was not present. He became a sacrificial victim of
those who used to call him 'Jupiter' and 'god' in speeches and in written
texts. Statues and images of him were ripped down, as the people
especially remembered the terrible things that they had suffered at his
30.1b hands. All the soldiers in his Germanic bodyguard rioted and raised such
disturbances that they caused further deaths.   **[John of Antioch]**

30.1c   The crowd remembered what he had once said to the people, "If only you
all had one neck!" They then pointed out that it was he who had one neck,
30.2 while they had many hands. And when the Praetorian Guard started to
break ranks and run around trying to find out who had murdered Gaius,
Valerius Asiaticus, a man of consular rank, brought them to order in a
remarkable way as follows. He climbed up to a place from where he could
easily be seen and shouted, "I wish that I had killed him!" This alarmed
them and they stopped rioting.   **[Xiphilinus]**

30.3   All those who in any way acknowledged the authority of the senate kept
their oaths and remained quiet. While this was going on around the corpse
of Gaius, the consuls, Sentius and Secundus, immediately transferred the
public funds from the treasuries to the Capitol. They then posted the
majority of the senate and a sufficient number of soldiers to guard these
funds, to ensure that there was no looting at the hands of the masses.
These men then held discussions with the prefects of the Guard and the
supporters of Sabinus and Chaerea about what course of action to take.

[John of Antioch]

THE REIGN OF CLAUDIUS

A.D. 41–46:

THE FIRST YEARS IN POWER

★ ★ ★ ★ ★

*C.1 CLAUDIUS BECOMES EMPEROR   A.D. 41

(60.1.1–2.3: Xiphilinus)

1.1   Claudius became emperor in the following way. After the murder of
Gaius the consuls sent guards to every part of the city and called a meeting
of the senate on the Capitol. At this meeting many different views were
expressed: some favoured a democracy, others a monarchy; some sup-
1.2   ported one candidate for emperor and some another. So they spent the
rest of the day and the whole night without coming to any positive
decision.
        Meanwhile some soldiers who had broken into the palace to look for
1.3   plunder found Claudius hiding in a dark corner somewhere. He had been
with Gaius as he left the theatre and then, frightened at the uproar, had
crouched down out of the way. At first the soldiers took him for someone
else, or thought that he might have something valuable, and dragged him
from his hiding-place. Then, recognizing him, they hailed him as emperor
and escorted him to their camp. Afterwards they and their comrades
entrusted him with the supreme power, since he was a member of the
1.3a   imperial family and was considered suitable. He protested and tried
to back out, but it was to no avail. The more he attempted to avoid
the honour and resist, the more firmly the soldiers insisted upon not
accepting an emperor chosen by others but bestowing one themselves on
the world. So Claudius accepted the burden, though with apparent
reluctance.
1.4   For some time the consuls sent tribunes and others forbidding him to
do any such thing, but rather instructing him to submit to the authority of
the people, the senate and the laws. But when the soldiers who had been
supporting the consuls deserted them, they too at last gave way and voted
2.1   Claudius all the remaining prerogatives of imperial power. So it was
that Tiberius Claudius Nero Germanicus, son of Drusus the son of Livia,
came to power as emperor, without having had any previous experience
at all in any position of authority, except that he had been consul.
He was now in his fiftieth year. In mental ability he was by no means
inferior.   **[Xiphilinus]**

[Manuscript resumes]

For his faculties had been in constant training, and he had actually written
some historical treatises; but physically he was in poor shape, and his
2.2 head and his hands shook slightly. Because of this he also had a slight
stammer, and so he himself did not read out all the measures that he
introduced in the senate, but gave them to the quaestor to read, although he,
to start with at least, was present for the most part. As for those measures
that he did read out for himself, he would generally do this seated.
2.3 Furthermore, he was the first of the Romans to use a covered chair. This
started a trend; for since that time right down to the present day not only
emperors, but also we ex-consuls have been carried in such chairs. Of course
before Claudius, both Augustus and Tiberius and others were carried in the
same kind of litters as women are still accustomed to use today.

C.2 CLAUDIUS' WEAKNESSES   A.D. 41
(60.2.4–7)

2.4   It was not so much these physical disabilities, however, that caused the
deterioration in Claudius as the freedmen and women with whom he
associated. For he, more clearly than any other emperor, was dominated
by slaves and by women. Ever since childhood, he had been brought up
amid illness and great terror, and for that reason had feigned a greater
stupidity than was really his, a fact that he himself admitted in the senate.
2.5 Furthermore, he had lived for a long time with his grandmother Livia and
for another long period with his mother Antonia and with the freedmen.
And furthermore he had had many affairs with women. So he had
acquired none of the qualities appropriate for a free man, but, although he
had power over all the Romans and their subject peoples, he had himself
become a slave. They would take especial advantage of him when he had
2.6 been drinking heavily or when he was making love. He had an insatiable
appetite for both these activities and was easily persuaded when he was
indulging one or the other. In addition he was afflicted with cowardice. As
a result, he was often frightened out of his wits, and so could not think out
logically any of the things that ought to have been within his grasp. They
2.7 jumped upon this failing of his and took full advantage of it. By terrifying
him, they would derive full profit. And they also inspired as much fear in
other people. To give a brief example, many people received invitations to
dinner on the same day from Claudius and from them. The guests ignored
him for one reason or other and crowded around the freedmen.

C.3 CLAUDIUS' REACTION TO HIS SUCCESSION   A.D. 41
(60.3.1–7)

3.1   Though in general he was as I have described, he did a number of things
in a proper manner when he was free from the shortcomings that I have

3.2 just mentioned and in control of himself. I shall now recount his acts in detail. He immediately accepted all the honours voted to him except the title of 'Father of the Fatherland', and that he took later on. However, he did not enter the senate at once, but waited until the thirtieth day. For he had seen how Gaius had been assassinated, and realizing that others had been proposed by the senate as better candidates for emperor than himself, he did not feel particularly confident. He exercised great caution

3.3 in everything. He made all who came into his presence, men and women alike, undergo a search to see if they were armed, and at parties he always had some soldiers present. This last practice, which he introduced, is still in force to this day; but the indiscriminate searching of everybody ceased during the reign of Vespasian.

3.4 Claudius put Chaerea and some of his associates to death, even though he was very pleased at Gaius' murder. Instead of feeling grateful to the man by whose actions he had become emperor, he was angry with him for having dared to murder an emperor. For he was looking far ahead to ensure his own safety. In this he acted not so much as the avenger of Gaius, but rather as if he had caught Chaerea plotting against himself.

3.5 Chaerea's death was followed by the suicide of Sabinus, who did not think it right to live on after his comrade's execution. As for the others who had openly canvassed for a return to democracy or who had been thought of as worthy candidates for emperor, far from bearing them a grudge, he even bestowed honours and offices upon them. In clearer terms than all previous rulers he not only promised them immunity, as he put it, in

3.6 imitation of the Athenians, but actually carried out his promise. He abolished the charge of *maiestas*, not just for treasonous writings, but also for treasonous acts. And he did not punish anyone on this charge for

3.7 offences committed in the past or in the future. As for those who had wronged him or insulted him when he was a private citizen (and there were indeed many who had done this, both because they had no respect for him and especially to please Tiberius or Gaius), he did not bring any of them to trial on a fabricated charge. However, if he found them guilty of any other crime, he would also take vengeance for their former conduct towards him.

C.4 RECALL OF EXILES; CLAUDIUS' INTEREST IN JUSTICE
A.D. 41

(60.4.1–4)

4.1 The taxes introduced during Gaius' reign, and any other measures which tended to criticize Gaius' actions, Claudius cancelled – not all at once, but gradually as the opportunity arose. He also brought back those whom Gaius had unjustly sent into exile, including Gaius' sisters Agrip-

4.2 pina and Julia, and restored their property to them. Of those who had been imprisoned (and there was a very large number of them), he released those who had been put there for treason and similar charges, but punished those guilty of criminal offences. For he investigated all these cases with great thoroughness: criminals were not to be released along with the victims of malicious accusations, nor again were the latter to be

4.3 convicted because of the former. Almost every day either alone or together with the full senate he would sit in judgement on a tribunal, usually in the Forum, but sometimes elsewhere. For he renewed the practice, discontinued from the time of Tiberius' withdrawal to the island,

4.4 of having advisers with him on the bench. Often, too, he helped the consuls and praetors and especially those in charge of finance in their inquiries, and he referred only a very small number of cases to the other courts.

C.5 VARIOUS MEASURES OF CLAUDIUS CONCERNING THE CITY OF ROME   A.D. 41

(60.6.1–7.4)

6.1 In all this Claudius' conduct was exemplary. On one occasion in the senate the consuls came down from their seats to speak to him. He got up and walked forward to meet them. Furthermore, when he was in

6.2 Neapolis, he lived just like an ordinary citizen. He and his entourage, for example, dressed in Greek fashion. At the musical contests they wore Greek tunics and boots; while at a gymnastic contest they would wear

6.3 purple cloaks and gold wreaths. Moreover, in financial matters he proved admirable. He refused to accept any gifts of money, a thing which had been usual under Augustus and Gaius. He would not allow anyone who had any relatives still living to nominate him as an heir. And finally all the funds that had been confiscated under Tiberius and Gaius he gave back to the victims themselves, if they were still alive, or otherwise to their children.

6.4 It was the custom at religious festivals that if any detail of the ritual was performed in a way contrary to normal practice, the festival had to be held all over again, as I have already stated. And often it had to be repeated three, four, five or even ten times sometimes because there was a genuine mistake in the ritual, but generally because it was carefully planned by

6.5 those who would benefit from such repetitions. So Claudius decreed that if a second running of the horse-races proved to be necessary, this should only occupy one day. But in practice he did not even allow this to happen. For those who engineered such schemes were not so eager to make mistakes, since they could now derive little profit from it.

6.6 The number of Jews had again increased so much that it would have been difficult to ban them from the city without causing a riot. So Claudius did not expel them, but gave orders that they could continue their traditional way of life, but could not hold any meetings. He also abolished the associations, which had been reintroduced by Gaius.

6.7 Furthermore, he realized that it was pointless to ban the populace from doing something unless it helped to reform their daily habits. Therefore, he closed down the taverns where they were accustomed to meet and drink, and issued an edict to the effect that no meat nor hot water should be sold; and he punished some people who refused to obey this edict.

6.8   He returned to the cities the statues which Gaius had summoned from them; he also returned to the Dioscuri their temple and to the theatre of Pompey its dedicatory inscription. In addition, he inscribed on its stage **6.9** the name of Tiberius, since he had rebuilt it after a fire. He also inscribed his own name on it, but on no other building, not because he had built it, but because he had dedicated it. Furthermore, he did not wear triumphal dress throughout the whole festival, even though he had been voted it, but only wore it to carry out sacrifices. For the other events he wore a purple- **7.1** bordered toga. Any equestrians, women of similar rank or others who had been accustomed to performing on the stage during the reign of Gaius he forced to appear on the stage. He did this not because he took any delight in it, but to censure these people for their past conduct. To be sure, none of them ever appeared on the stage again during the reign of Claudius.

7.2   The boys who had been summoned by Gaius were rehearsing the Pyrrhic dance. Claudius allowed them to perform it once and then sent them home after rewarding them with Roman citizenship. Later some members of his own household were selected to perform the dance.

7.3   This is what happened in the theatre. In the circus various contests were staged, one involving camels, twelve involving horses; in addition, three hundred bears and the same number of Libyan wild beasts were slaughtered. Up to this time, each section of Roman society – the senatorial order, the equestrian order and the plebs – had watched the games sitting together as a group apart from the other two. This had been the practice, but places **7.4** for each group to sit had not yet been assigned. But now Claudius reserved for the senators the section which they still use. Furthermore, he allowed any senator who so desired to sit elsewhere while watching the games and even to wear informal dress. After doing all this, he feasted the senate with their wives, the equestrian order and also the tribes.

C.6 FOREIGN AFFAIRS   A.D. 41–42

(60.8.1–9.1; 9.5)

8.1   Next Claudius restored Commagene to Antiochus (for although Gaius had given it to him, he had then taken it away again); and Mithridates the Iberian, whom Gaius had sent for and put in prison, was sent back home **8.2** to return to power. To another Mithridates, who traced his ancestry back to Mithridates the Great, he granted Bosporus, giving Polemon some land in Cilicia instead. As for Agrippa of Palestine, since he had helped to establish Claudius in power (for he happened to be in Rome), he increased **8.3** his kingdom and granted him consular decorations. And to Agrippa's brother Herod he gave the rank of praetor and a district to govern. He allowed them to appear in the senate and express their thanks to him in Greek.

8.4   These were Claudius' own acts, and they won general approval; but a number of things of quite a different nature were carried out at this time
8.5   by his freedmen and by his wife Valeria Messalina. She was angered by her niece Julia's failure to pay her proper respect or to flatter her. She was also jealous of her because she was extremely beautiful and was often alone with Claudius. She, therefore, had her sent into exile, fabricating various charges including adultery (for which Annaeus Seneca was also exiled),
8.6   and not long afterwards had her murdered. As for the freedmen, they persuaded Claudius to accept triumphal decorations for achievements in Mauretania, even though he had not won any success there and had not
8.7   even come to power when the war there had been completed. However, in this same year Sulpicius Galba conquered the Chatti, while Publius Gabinius, in defeating the Chauci, won particular glory by recovering a legionary eagle, the only one from Varus' disaster that was still in enemy hands. Thanks to these two men Claudius could now be given with some semblance of truth the title of *Imperator*.

A.D. 42

9.1   Next year the same Moors went to war again and were subdued. Suetonius Paulinus, one of the ex-praetors, overran their country as far as Mount Atlas, while after him Gnaeus Hosidius Geta, also of praetorian rank, fought a quick campaign against the Moors' general Salabus, defeating him in two separate battles. ....
9.5   And as a result of this they came willingly to terms and ceased making war. Afterwards Claudius divided the subject Moors into two provinces, one the region around Tingis, the other that around Caesarea. It is from these cities that the provinces of Mauretania Tingitana and Mauretania Caesariensis take their name. He also appointed two equestrians to govern these provinces.

C.7 IMPROVEMENTS TO THE HARBOUR AT OSTIA   A.D. 42

(60.11.1–5)

11.1   A severe famine occurred and Claudius considered the problem of how to ensure an abundant food-supply, not only to cope with that particular
11.2   crisis but for the future as well. Practically all the grain that the Romans used had to be imported, and yet the region near the mouth of the Tiber had no safe landing-places or suitable harbours. As a result, the Romans' control of the Mediterranean was of no practical use to them. For apart from the cargoes brought in during the summer and stored in warehouses, no grain was imported during the winter: anyone risking a voyage then
11.3   was sure to meet with disaster. In view of this Claudius took in hand the construction of a harbour, and would not be put off even when the architects, in answer to an enquiry about the cost of the project, said, "More than you want to pay!" They were sure that the huge expense

would deter him from his carrying out his plan, if he was aware of the cost beforehand. However, he conceived a project worthy of the dignity and
11.4 greatness of Rome, and actually carried it out. First, he excavated an enormous area of land, built retaining walls all around it and then let the sea into it. Right in the open water he constructed huge moles on either side of the entrance, thus enclosing a vast body of water; in the middle of this body of water he constructed an island, on which he sited a
11.5 lighthouse. So "The Harbour", as it is still known locally, was constructed by Claudius at this time. Furthermore, he wanted to drain the Fucine Lake in the territory of the Marsi into the river Liris, to allow the land around it to be farmed and at the same time to ensure that the river became more navigable. But his expensive efforts all came to nothing.

C.8 DEATH OF SILANUS; REBELLION OF SCRIBONIANUS   A.D. 42

(60.14.1–16.4)

14.1   Claudius, now accustomed to having his fill of bloodshed, turned more readily to other forms of murder. For this the imperial freedmen and Messalina were responsible. Whenever they wanted anyone put to death, they would terrify Claudius into letting them do whatever they wanted.
14.2 And it happened frequently that he would suddenly be terrified and in a moment of immediate alarm order that some person be destroyed. He would then come to his senses and, realizing what he had done, would seek him out. And when he learnt what had happened, he would grieve and ask for forgiveness.
14.3   He began this series of murders with Gaius Appius Silanus. Silanus was from a very noble family and was serving at the time as governor of Spain. Claudius sent for him, pretending that he needed his help. He had arranged for him to marry Messalina's mother, and had for some time honoured him as one of his closest friends and relatives. Then suddenly he had him executed. The reason was that Silanus had offended Messalina, who was utterly shameless and licentious, by refusing to have sex with her; and in so doing, he had also offended Narcissus, the emperor's freedman.
14.4 They had no true or even plausible charge to bring against him; so Narcissus invented a dream in which, he said, he had seen Claudius murdered by Silanus' very hand. In the early morning, while the emperor was still in bed, he related the dream, in exaggerated horror; and Messalina took up the tale and emphasized its significance.
15.1   So Silanus met his death merely because of a dream. After that the Romans no longer held any confident hopes in Claudius, but Annius Vinicianus and some others immediately proceeded to form a plot against Claudius. Annius was one of those who had been proposed as a possible emperor after the death of Gaius. Indeed, it was partly because he was
15.2 afraid for his life as a result of this that he launched his rebellion. But he had no military backing, and so sent a message to Furius Camillus Scribonianus, the governor of Dalmatia, who commanded a large body of citizen legionaries and non-citizen auxiliary troops, and gained his sup-

port. Camillus was already making his own plans to revolt, especially
15.3 because he had been thought of as a possible emperor himself. After he
had made his move, many senators and equestrians rallied to Annius' side.
[But it was no use.] For when Camillus offered the troops the prospect of
seeing the republic restored and promised to give them back their ancient
freedom, they suspected that this would only cause troubles and civil wars
once again, and so refused to listen to him any longer. At this he took
fright and fled from them. He got as far as the island of Issa, and there
committed suicide.

15.4   For a while Claudius had been in a state of great terror and ready to
abdicate in Camillus' favour; but now he took fresh heart. First, he
rewarded the soldiers in various ways, in particular by bestowing the titles
"Claudian", "the Loyal" and "the Patriotic" on the Seventh and the
Eleventh Legions, which were composed of citizens, and by having them
so saluted by the senate. He then made a diligent search for those who had
plotted against him and put many to death on this charge, among them a
15.5 praetor, who was first made to resign his office. And many, including
Vinicianus, committed suicide. For Messalina, Narcissus and all Claudius'
freedmen, seizing their opportunity, did not consider any act too terrible.
One of their techniques was to use both slaves and freedmen as informers
15.6 against their masters. These men and others of the highest nobility they
even tortured: not only foreigners, but even Roman citizens, not only
ordinary citizens, but even members of the equestrian and senatorial
orders. And yet Claudius at the very start of his reign had sworn that he
would never torture any freeborn person.

16.1   As a result many men and many women too were executed, some even
being put to death in prison. The women involved, when they were about
to die, were even led in chains, like prisoners-of-war, up onto a platform
and their bodies were hurled down the Steps. As for those who were
executed outside the city, just their heads were brought to Rome and put on
16.2 display. However, some of those who were most guilty managed to escape
through the agency of Messalina and the imperial freedmen in Narcissus'
entourage, by promising them favours or by giving them bribes. At least
the children of those who perished all received immunity, and some even
16.3 received money as well. Their trials took place in the senate-house, in the
presence of Claudius, the prefects and the freedmen. Claudius would read
the charge sitting in between the consuls on a curule chair or even just on a
bench. After reading the charge, he would move to his accustomed seat,
16.4 while curule chairs were put in position for the consuls. This same
procedure was also put into practice on other important occasions.

C.9 LYCIA; EXTENSION OF ROMAN CITIZENSHIP   A.D. 43

(60.17.1–7)

17.1   After this Claudius assumed the consulship for the third time and put
an end to many festivals and days of supplication; for a very large part of

the year was given over to them, much to the detriment of public business.

17.2 He, therefore, cut these festivals and made reductions in as many other areas as possible. On the one hand he demanded back from people things that had been given away by Gaius on grounds that had been neither just nor logical, but on the other hand he returned to the road-commissioners whatever they had been fined during Gaius' reign as a result of Corbulo's activities.

17.3 Furthermore, the provincial governors chosen by lot had become rather slow in setting off from Rome for their provinces and so Claudius issued an edict that they should leave before the middle of April. As for the people of Lycia, because they had revolted and killed some Roman citizens, he reduced them to the condition of slaves and incorporated them

17.4 into the district of Pamphylia. During the investigation of this affair, which he conducted in the senate, he questioned one of the ambassadors in Latin. He had originally been a Lycian, but had been given Roman citizenship. The man failed to understand what was said, and so Claudius took away his citizenship: it was not proper, he said, for a man to be a Roman who had no knowledge of the language of the Romans.

17.5 He deprived many other people of citizenship whom he thought unworthy of it, yet granted it to others quite indiscriminately, sometimes to individuals, sometimes to whole groups. Since those with Roman citizenship had the advantage over foreigners in practically all respects, many sought the franchise directly from the emperor and many bought it

17.6 from Messalina and from the emperor's freedmen. So, though the privilege was at first sold for large sums, it later became so cheapened by the ease with which it could be gained that it came to be proverbial that a man could become a Roman citizen by giving the right person some bits of

17.7 broken glass. As a result, Claudius was ridiculed for this. But for what follows he was praised. Information was being laid against many of these new citizens; some were being accused of not using Claudius' name, others for not leaving him any legacy in their will, on the grounds that it was obligatory for those who had received citizenship from him to do both of these things. Claudius forbade anyone to be brought to trial on these charges.

C.10 CRIMES OF MESSALLINA AND THE IMPERIAL FREEDMEN
A.D. 43

(60.17.8–18.4)

17.8 Messalina and Claudius' freedmen kept offering for sale and peddling not merely citizenship and military commands and procuratorships and provincial governorships, but everything else as well. This caused a scarcity of all commodities. Claudius, therefore, summoned the people into the Campus Martius and there from a raised platform fixed the prices

17.9 of all goods. Claudius also put on a gladiatorial contest in the camp, and he wore a military cloak for the occasion. To celebrate his son's birthday, the praetors on their own initiative put on shows and public banquets. These celebrations were repeated later, at least by those praetors who wanted to do so.

18.1   Meanwhile Messalina kept indulging her own promiscuity and likewise kept forcing other women to engage in various sexual acts. She made many of them commit adultery even in the palace itself in the presence of

18.2   their husbands, who even had to watch. These men she loved and took great pleasure in, bestowing honours and offices upon them. As for those who would not comply with her requests, she bore a grudge against them for this and brought about their destruction in all sorts of ways. However, even though these deeds were so outrageous and carried on so openly,

18.3   Claudius was unaware of them for a very long time. For she used to provide him with slavegirls to have sex with. As for those who could have provided him with any information, she won them over, either by offering them favours, or by inflicting punishments upon them. For instance, it was at this time that she had Catonius Justus, prefect of the Praetorian Guard, killed before he could carry out his intention of providing

18.4   Claudius with information about these goings-on. She also became jealous of Julia, daughter of Drusus son of Tiberius, wife of Nero Germanicus, just as she had been jealous of the other Julia, and so had her murdered as well. And at this time a member of the equestrian order was hurled down from the Capitol by the tribunes and consuls for having plotted against Claudius.

C.11 CLAUDIUS' INVASION AND CONQUEST OF BRITAIN
A.D. 43–44

(60.19.1–22.2; 23.1–6)

19.1   While this was happening in Rome, at just the same time Aulus Plautius, a very distinguished senator, launched a military campaign against Britain. For one Bericus, who had been expelled from the island as a result of a rebellion, had persuaded Claudius to launch an expedition

19.2   against the island. And it was for these reasons that Plautius was leading the expedition. However, he had difficulty in getting his army further than Gaul. For the troops were upset at the prospect of fighting a campaign outside the limits of the known world; they refused to obey his orders until Narcissus, who had been sent out by Claudius, mounted Plautius' tribunal

19.3   and tried to address them. At this they were angrier than ever and refused to let Narcissus say a word. But suddenly they started to chant the well-known cry, "Io! Saturnalia!" (since at the festival of Saturn slaves change into their masters' clothes and revel) and immediately followed Plautius without further question. The delay, however, meant that the invasion started late in the season.

19.4   The men were sent over in three divisions, to prevent their landing being impeded, as might have happened if they had crossed as a single force. On their voyage across the Channel, they were at first discouraged when their

ships were driven back in their course. Then they saw a flash of light appear in the east and shoot across to the west, the direction in which they were trying to sail, and that gave them heart. They landed on the coast of
19.5 Britain, where they met no opposition. Intelligence reports had suggested to the Britons that the Romans were unlikely to make the crossing, and so they had not mobilized their troops in time. And even when they did mobilize, they would not come to close quarters with the Romans, but took cover in the swamps and forests, hoping that they would wear the invaders out in various ways and that, just as when Julius Caesar had invaded, they would sail away without having achieved their objectives.

20.1 Plautius had a great deal of trouble in searching them out, but when at last he found them, he defeated first Caratacus and then Togodumnus, the sons of Cunobelinus, who had now died. (The Britons were not indepen-
20.2 dent, but divided into various groups, each ruled by a king.) After Caratacus and Togodumnus had taken to flight, he accepted the surrender of part of the Bodunni, who were subject to the Catuvellauni. He established a garrison there and then advanced further and came to a river. The barbarians thought the Romans would not be able to cross it without constructing a bridge; and so they had camped without paying much attention to the bank opposite. But Plautius sent across a detachment of Germans, who were accustomed to swimming without difficulty
20.3 in full armour across any river, no matter how strong the current. They took the Britons by surprise, but instead of shooting at any of the men, they kept wounding the horses that drew their chariots, and in the confusion that followed the warriors on board could not survive either. Plautius now sent across Flavius Vespasianus (the future emperor) and his
20.4 brother Sabinus, his second-in-command. They also managed somehow to get across the river and killed many of the barbarians in a surprise attack. The survivors, however, did not withdraw but rallied and fought again next day. The battle was indecisive until Gnaeus Hosidius Geta, after narrowly escaping capture, finally managed to defeat the Britons so thoroughly that he was awarded triumphal decorations, although not of consular rank.
20.5 From there the Britons withdrew to the river Thames, to the point where it flows out into the sea and at flood-tide forms a lake. They crossed easily enough, knowing where the firm ground and the easy crossings
20.6 were. The Romans followed, but were not so successful. However, the Germans again swam across, and some others got over by means of a bridge a little way upstream, and then they attacked the Britons from several sides at once, inflicting heavy casualties. However, they were rather careless in their pursuit of the survivors and found themselves in swamps they could not get out of, and so lost a number of men.

21.1 This setback alarmed Plautius somewhat. And he was even more worried when the Britons, after losing Togodumnus, so far from surrendering, united all the more determinedly to avenge his death. Instead of advancing any further, he consolidated the gains he had made and
21.2 summoned Claudius. He had instructions to do this if he met with any particularly stubborn resistance, and in fact extensive equipment, includ-

ing elephants, had already been assembled for the purpose. When the news reached him, Claudius handed over affairs at home, including command of the troops, to his colleague, Lucius Vitellius, whose consulship, like his own, he had extended to a whole half-year. He himself set out

21.3 for the front. He sailed down river to Ostia, and from there followed the coast to Massilia. From there, advancing partly by land and partly along the rivers, he came to the Ocean and made the crossing to Britain, where

21.4 he joined the legions waiting for him near the Thames. He took over as commander of these legions and crossed the river. He engaged with the barbarians, who had rallied at his approach, and defeated them in battle and captured Camulodunum, Cunobelinus' capital. After that he won over many tribes, some by surrender, others by force, and was hailed

21.5 *Imperator* several times contrary to precedent. For no one general may receive this title more than once during the same campaign. He stripped those whom he had defeated of their arms and handed them over to Plautius, with orders to bring the remaining districts also into submission. Claudius himself now hurried back to Rome, sending his sons-in-law, Magnus and Silanus, on ahead with the news of his victory.

22.1   On learning of his achievements, the senate granted him the title of Britannicus and permission to celebrate a triumph. They voted also that an annual festival should be held to commemorate the event, and that two triumphal arches be erected, one in Rome and the other in Gaul, because

22.2 it was from Gaul that he had set sail and crossed over to Britain. They bestowed upon his son the same honorary name as they had granted him, and in fact Britannicus came in a way to be the boy's regular name. Messalina was granted the right to sit in the front seats at shows (the same honour as Livia had been awarded) and to use a *carpentum*. ....

A.D. 44

23.1   Parts of Britain, then, were conquered at this time as we have described. Later, during the consulship of Gaius Crispus and Titus Statilius (the former holding his second consulship), Claudius arrived back in Rome after an absence of six months, of which he had spent only sixteen days in Britain, and celebrated his triumph. In most respects he followed the customary procedures, even climbing the steps of the Capitolium on his

23.2 knees, with his sons-in-law supporting him on either side. But he did bestow triumphal decorations on all the senators who had taken part with him in the campaign, not only on those who had already held the consulship, [but to the rest as well]. This was something that he did at other times too with great generosity and on the slightest of pretexts. He even granted Rufrius Pollio, the prefect, an image and a seat in the senate-

23.3 house, whenever he went with Claudius to a meeting of the senate. And to prevent his being accused of thus creating a precedent, he declared that even Augustus had done the same thing to honour someone called Valerius Ligur. Laco, formerly prefect of the Night-Watch and at that time procurator of the Gauls, was honoured in the same way and still further by being awarded consular decorations.

23.4   After making these awards, he held his triumphal festival, assuming a

sort of consular power for the occasion. It took place in the two theatres simultaneously. He often retired from the shows, letting others take over
23.5 the presidency in his absence. He announced that there would be as many horse-races as could be fitted into a day, but, as it turned out, there were no more than ten. For there were also bears to be slaughtered in between the races, as well as athletic competitions, and a Pyrrhic dance, performed
23.6 by boys summoned from Asia Minor. Another festival was also held in honour of his victory, consisting of performances by the association of stage artists, who had received authorization from the senate. All these were held to mark his achievements in Britain. And to make it easier for other peoples to come to terms with the Romans, it was decreed that all the agreements worked out by Claudius or even those generals operating on his behalf should be ratified, as if they had been made by the senate and the people of Rome.

C.12 ADMINISTRATIVE ARRANGEMENTS IN ROME AND THE PROVINCES **A.D. 44**

(60.24.1–7)

24.1   Achaea and Macedonia had since the reign of Tiberius been assigned to governors appointed by the emperor. Claudius now made them depend once again upon the lot. He also transferred control of finances from the praetors back to the quaestors, who had formerly been in
24.2 charge. These quaestors, however, were not annual magistrates, as the quaestors who used to be in charge and the praetors after them had been, but the same two quaestors managed the finances for a complete three-year period. Some of these quaestors secured the praetorship immediately after, others drew a salary based upon an evaluation of how they had
24.3 carried out their duties while in office. So Claudius gave these quaestors control of the finances instead of their responsibilities in various parts of Italy outside Rome (for he abolished all these positions). To compensate the praetors, he entrusted them with certain judicial duties which had formerly been carried out by the consuls. And as for the soldiers in the army, since they could not have wives at least in the eyes of the law, he granted them the legal privileges of married men.
24.4   Marcus Julius Cottius received an addition to his ancestral kingdom, which consisted of that part of the Alps that bears his family name; and he was now for the first time given the title of king. The Rhodians were deprived of their independence because they had crucified some Roman
24.5 citizens. In addition, Umbonius Silio, the governor of Baetica, was summoned to Rome and expelled from the senate on the grounds that he had not despatched enough grain to the troops in Mauretania. This was the charge laid against him, but the real reason for his expulsion was
24.6 because he had offended some of the imperial freedmen. It was also this man who took all his furniture to the auction-place (much of it was of very fine quality), as if to put it all up for auction. In the end he sold only his senatorial dress, thereby demonstrating to them that he had not suffered anything terrible and would be able to continue to enjoy a very pleasant

24.7 life as a private citizen. These then were the events of the year. In addition, the market which took place every ninth day was moved to another day because of some sacred rites. This also occurred on many other occasions.

C.13 VALERIUS ASIATICUS RESIGNS HIS CONSULSHIP; DEATH OF VINICIUS; REVOLT OF ASINIUS GALLUS   A.D. 46

(60.27.1–5)

27.1 At the end of that year Valerius Asiaticus and Marcus Silanus took over as consuls, the former for a second time. Silanus held office for the period for which he was elected, but Asiaticus, though appointed to serve for the whole year (as happened in the case of others as well), failed to complete
27.2 his term, but resigned from office voluntarily. It was true that others had also done this, but only through lack of funds. For the expenses connected with the circus games had increased enormously, as there were now usually twenty-four races. But Asiaticus resigned because of his wealth,
27.3 which in fact proved to be the cause of his death. He was very well off. Since he was holding a second consulship, he had aroused the dislike and envy of many people and so he chose, as it were, to bring himself down,
27.4 feeling that by so doing he would incur less danger. Even he was totally deceived.

Vinicius, on the other hand, suffered no harm at the hands of Claudius. He was a distinguished man, and so tried to save his life by keeping quiet and minding his own business. But he was poisoned by Messalina. She suspected that he had killed his wife Julia and was angry because he had refused to have sex with her. And yet he was thought worthy of a public funeral and eulogies; for many people were granted these honours.

27.5 Moreover, Asinius Gallus, the half-brother of Drusus on his mother's side, formed a conspiracy against Claudius. He was not executed, but sent into exile. A possible reason for this was that he had not made careful preparations for it, either by recruiting a military force or by collecting funds in advance. But rather he acted out of sheer folly, since he was convinced that the Romans would support him as their emperor merely because of his ancestry. But the most likely reason was that he was very small and very ugly and as a result was held in contempt; he was the object of ridicule rather than a serious threat.

*C.14 COTYS REPLACES MITHRIDATES AS KING OF BOSPORUS   A.D. 46

(60.28.7: Petrus Patricius)

28.7 Mithridates king of the Iberians revolted and started to make preparations for war against Rome. His mother opposed him. But since she failed to persuade him to lay aside his plans, she decided to go into exile. Mithridates then thought it best to conceal his project. He continued his own preparations, but sent his brother Cotys on an embassy to Claudius with a message of friendship. But Cotys proved a treacherous ambassador and told Claudius everything; and so he was made king of Iberia in place of Mithridates.   **[Petrus Patricius]**

THE REIGN OF NERO

A.D. 66–68:

THE FALL OF NERO

＊ ＊ ＊ ＊ ＊

*D.1 TIRIDATES IS CROWNED KING OF ARMENIA BY NERO
A.D. 66
(63.1.1–7.2: Xiphilinus)

1.1　　In the consulship of Gaius Telesinus and of Suetonius Paulinus, one event took place that much enhanced Nero's prestige, while another brought great shame upon him. For Nero competed in a lyre-playing competition and his lyre-teacher Menecrates arranged a victory ceremony
1.2　for him in the Circus, at which he appeared as a charioteer. And Tiridates arrived in Rome bringing with him not only his own sons, but also the sons of Vologaesus, Pacorus and Monobazus. Their journey all the way from the Euphrates had been like a triumphal procession.

2.1　　Tiridates was in the prime of life, and was quite radiant with his handsome features, his noble birth and his proud bearing. He was accompanied by an entourage of servants and all the trappings of royal power: three thousand Parthian cavalry, and a large number of Romans
2.2　besides, were among his followers. They were welcomed both by cities and by their populations; the cities along the route were decorated in sparkling array and the people shouted out many compliments to them. All their provisions were provided free of charge; it has been reckoned that the cost to the public treasury amounted to 200,000 *denarii* a day; and the same level of expenditure was maintained for all nine months of their journey.

2.3　　Tiridates travelled on horseback as far as Italy, and his wife rode beside him, wearing a golden helmet instead of a veil, to prevent her face being seen, which was against the customs of her country. Once they reached Italy, he travelled in a two-horse carriage, which had been sent to him by Nero. After travelling through Picenum, he met Nero at Neapolis.
2.4　However, he refused to lay down his dagger when he came into Nero's presence, even though he had been ordered to do so. But as a compromise, he nailed it into its scabbard. Yet he did sink to the ground on his knees, cross his arms in front of him, address him as 'master' and prostrate
3.1　himself before him. Nero admired him for this and arranged many entertainments for him, including a gladiatorial show at Puteoli. The show was organized by Patrobius, an imperial freedman, and he brought it off

in such sparkling style and at such expense that in a single day no other type of performers entered the theatre but Ethiopians – men, women and

3.2 children. And since it was appropriate that Patrobius should receive some mark of congratulation for this, Tiridates shot at wild beasts from his seat in the stands and he managed to shoot two bulls with the same arrow, if you can believe it, and kill them.

4.1 After this Nero escorted Tiridates to Rome and placed the diadem on his head. The whole city was decked out with torches and garlands. Great crowds of people were everywhere to be seen. The Forum in particular was

4.2 packed. The citizens stood in middle of the Forum, clothed in white, carrying laurel branches and arranged according to social rank. Around the edge stood the troops in their finest parade armour: their weapons and standards flashed like lightning. The roof-tiles of every single building in the vicinity of the Forum were hidden from view by people who had climbed up on to them.

4.3 This was how everything had been prepared during the night. At daybreak Nero entered the Forum, wearing triumphal dress and accompanied by the senate and Praetorian Guard. He mounted the Rostra and sat down on a curule chair. Then Tiridates and his entourage paraded between two lines of troops marshalled in full armour and came to a halt in front of the Rostra. They then prostrated themselves before Nero just

5.1 as they had done before. At this a great roar went up from all around, which so alarmed Tiridates that he remained speechless for quite some time, as though fearing for his life. Then, a herald called for silence, and he recovered his composure. Swallowing his pride, he subordinated himself to the occasion and his own needs, not caring how obsequiously he spoke in view of what he hoped to gain.

5.2 These were his words: "Master, I am the descendant of Arsaces, the brother of kings Vologaesus and Pacorus; but at the same time I am your slave. I have come to you, my god, to prostrate myself before you, just as I would prostrate myself before Mithras. I shall accept whatever destiny you have spun for me; for you are my Fate and my Fortune."

5.3 Nero replied as follows: "You have done well to come here in person to win my favours face to face. For I am granting you a favour which neither your father bequeathed nor your brothers bestowed and kept in trust for you. I am making you king of Armenia, to ensure that both you and they realize that I have the power not only to take away kingdoms, but also to

5.4 bestow them." At the end of this speech he ordered him to mount the stairs which had been constructed specially for this occasion in front of the Rostra. As soon as Tiridates had taken up his position at Nero's feet, Nero placed the diadem upon his head. At this many shouts went up from all around the Forum.

6.1 A theatrical spectacle took place by special decree. The theatre (not just the stage, but the whole auditorium on every side) had been gilded and all the props that were brought on stage had also been decorated with

6.2 gold. As a result, that day was henceforth known as 'the golden'. The awnings that were stretched across overhead to shade the spectators from the sun were purple in colour, and in the middle of them was

embroidered a picture of Nero driving a chariot; around the edges golden
6.3   stars twinkled all around. This is what happened, and of course they had a
sumptuous banquet. Afterwards Nero played the lyre in public and also
drove a chariot, sporting the colours of the Greens and wearing a
6.4   charioteer's helmet. Tiridates was disgusted with him for this, but praised
Corbulo, only finding fault with him on one point, namely that he
managed to put up with such a master. In no way did he try to conceal
this view even from Nero, but one day said to him, "Master, you have a
6.5   good slave in Corbulo." Nero did not understand the meaning of this
remark.

For the rest of his stay Tiridates flattered Nero and ingratiated himself
very skilfully with him. As a result he received all kinds of gifts, allegedly
worth fifty million *denarii*, as well as permission to rebuild Artaxata.
6.6   Moreover, he took away from Rome with him a large number of
craftsmen, some of whom he obtained from Nero, others he managed to
secure by offering them lucrative contracts. Corbulo, however, did not
allow all of them to enter Armenia, but only those whom Nero had given
him. As a result Tiridates all the more admired Corbulo and despised the
emperor.

7.1   He returned home a different way: not through Illyricum and north
of Ionia, as he had come, but by sailing from Brundisium to Dyrrachium.
He also managed to see the cities of Asia, which impressed upon him
7.2   the strength and beauty of the Roman Empire. Tiridates rebuilt
Artaxata and renamed it Neronia. On the other hand, Vologaesus refused
to come to Nero, even though he was often summoned. In the end he
lost patience with these frequent requests and so wrote a letter to Nero
saying, "It is much easier for you than for me to sail across such a large
expanse of water. Therefore if you come to Asia, we can then arrange
where to meet." Such was the letter that the Parthian eventually sent.

[Xiphilinus]

*D.2 NERO IN GREECE   A.D. 66–67

(63.8.1–10.1; 11.1: Xiphilinus)

8.1   Although Nero was angry with him, he did not sail against him, nor
8.2   against the Ethiopians or to the Caspian Gates, as he had intended. What
he did do, among other things, was to send spies to both areas, but, seeing
that the conquest of these regions would take a long time and a lot of
effort, he kept hoping that they would submit of their own accord.
Instead, he crossed over to Greece, not with the aims of Flamininus or
Mummius, or even of his ancestors Agrippa and Augustus, but for
chariot-racing, lyre-playing, making declamations and acting in tragedies.
8.3   For the city of Rome was no longer big enough for him, neither the theatre
of Pompey nor the Circus Maximus, but he needed some sort of overseas
tour, to become, as he put it, a victor on the festival circuit.

An enormous crowd of people accompanied him, not just the Augus-

tiani, but all sorts of other people. It was big enough, if it had been a military force, to have been used in a campaign against both the Parthians
8.4   and all other nations. But they were true Neronian soldiers: for weapons they carried lyres, plectra, acting masks and high-soled shoes. And Nero won victories that were quite appropriate for such a force. He routed Terpnus, Diodorus and Pammenes, as if they were Philip, Perseus and
8.5   Antiochus. And it was just for this reason, so it seems, that he forced this Pammenes to compete, even though he was now an old man, having been in his prime during the reign of Gaius. Nero wanted to defeat him and then deface his statues.
9.1   Even if this had been the sum total of his actions, he would have incurred ridicule. But how could anyone bear to hear, let alone see, a Roman, a senator, a patrician, a chief priest, a Caesar, an emperor, an Augustus listed among the contestants on the programme, training his voice, practising a repertoire of songs, wearing his hair long and his chin
9.2   clean-shaven, slinging his toga casually over the shoulder at the races, walking around with one or two attendants, looking askance at his opponents, constantly addressing them in a provocative manner and walking in fear of the *agônothetai* and the *mastigophori*, secretly bribing them all in order to avoid being brought to book and whipped? Was he doing all this to win a contest of lyre-players, tragic actors and heralds,
9.3   and yet lose the contest of the Caesars? What proscription list could be harsher than this one, in which it was not Sulla who had listed other people's names, but Nero himself who had put his own name on the list? What more unusual victory was there than this one, in which he won crowns of wild olive, laurel, celery or pine, but lost his civic crown?
9.4   And why should anyone lament only these acts of his, when he raised himself up on to his high-soled stage shoes but fell from power, when he put on the tragic mask but threw off the dignity of leadership, when he begged like a runaway slave, was led around like a blind man, appeared pregnant, gave birth to children, raged like a madman, wandered like an outcast, which he had to do when he was playing his favourite rôles of
9.5   Oedipus, Thyestes, Heracles, Alcmaeon and Orestes? As for his masks that he wore, some of them were made to look like these characters, but others bore a striking resemblance to himself. All the women's masks had been designed to look like Sabina, so that even though she had already
9.6   died, she might still take part in the celebrations. All the dramatic situations he encountered in these plays, he conveyed just like other actors by his words, gestures and sufferings, except that he had to be bound in golden chains. For it was not thought fitting, it seems, for a Roman emperor to be bound with iron ones.
10.1   All these antics were witnessed, endured and applauded not only by the ordinary spectators, but also by the Roman soldiers, who hailed him 'Pythian Victor', 'Olympian Victor', 'Victor in all the great festivals', 'All-conquering Hero' in addition to his customary titles, linking them of course with the titles of his imperial power, so that each one of them had 'Caesar' and 'Augustus' tagged on at the end. ....

11.1   If Nero had gone no further than this, the affair would have been thought disgraceful and ridiculous, but nonetheless harmless. But as it was, he pillaged the whole of Greece as if he had been sent there on a military campaign, even though he did grant all of Greece its freedom, and slaughtered a very large number of men, women and children.

*D.3 HELIUS IN ROME; NERO'S "MARRIAGE" TO SPORUS

A.D. 67

(63.12.1–13.3: Xiphilinus)

12.1   He handed over all the inhabitants of Rome and Italy to the charge of a certain imperial freedman called Helius. He was simply given full authority to confiscate property, or send into exile or execute ordinary people as well as senators and equestrians without even having to inform Nero
12.2 first. And so the Roman Empire was at that time a slave to two masters, Nero and Helius, and I cannot say which of the two was worse. In most respects they behaved in a very similar fashion, with this one difference: the descendant of Augustus was seeking to emulate lyre-players and tragic actors, while the freedman of Claudius was seeking to emulate Caesars.
12.3   As for Tigellinus, I consider him a mere appendage of Nero, since he was always at his side. On the other hand Polycleitus and Calvia Crispinilla independently took, sacked and pillaged everything they could lay their hands on. Polycleitus was with Helius in Rome, while Calvia was
12.4 with Nero and 'Sabina' (who was in fact Sporus). Nero had appointed her guardian of Sporus and keeper of his wardrobe, even though she was a woman and of high rank, and through her activities everyone was stripped.
13.1   Nero called Sporus 'Sabina' not only because he had been made a eunuch as a result of his resemblance to her, but also because 'he' had married Nero in a formal ceremony in Greece, just as Sabina had done. Tigellinus gave the bride away, just as custom demanded. Their wedding was celebrated by all the Greeks, who uttered all the appropriate good wishes and even prayed that legitimate children should be born to them.
13.2 As a result of this Nero now had two people available as sexual partners: Pythagoras to play the part of his husband, Sporus to play the part of a wife. Sporus was addressed in many different ways: for example, lady, queen and mistress. And why should anyone be surprised at this, since Nero would tie young men and girls naked to stakes and then put on the skin of a wild beast and fall upon them, satisfying his lust as though he was
13.3 devouring them? These were the kinds of indecency which Nero practised. He greeted the senators wearing a short, flowered tunic and with a muslin scarf around his neck. For he flouted convention also in matters of dress, even wearing loose-fitting tunics in public. It is also reported that those equestrians on the list for the first time used saddle-cloths at their annual review.

*D.4 THE CORINTH CANAL. DEATH OF THE SCRIBONII AND CORBULO   A.D. 67

(63.16.1–17.6: Xiphilinus)

16.1   He also set himself a subsidiary task to mark his stay in Greece. He desired to dig a canal across the Isthmus of Corinth. He actually began the work in spite of the reluctance of the workforce. For when they first touched the earth, blood spurted up, groans and rumblings were heard,

16.2 and numerous ghosts appeared. He himself grabbed a spade and by turning over the soil, compelled others to follow his example. He also sent for a great number of men from other countries to join in the operation.

17.1   For this and for other projects he required a great deal of money. He was keen on large enterprises and was similarly a great gift-giver. At the same time he feared that the most powerful men would launch an attack

17.2 upon him for doing this, and so destroyed many good men. I shall pass over most of these individuals (for the official charge against them all when they were brought before him was their excellence, their wealth and their family, and all of them either committed suicide or were put to death by others), but I shall mention Corbulo and the two Sulpicii Scribonii,

17.3 Rufus and Proculus. They were brothers of about the same age and had never acted separately, but shared the same preferences and the same amount of property, just as they shared the same family. They had for a long time administered the two German provinces in tandem. They now arrived in Greece, summoned by Nero on the pretext that he had a request

17.4 to make of them. Charges typical of those times were brought against them, but they could neither obtain an audience nor even manage to see Nero. As a result, they were snubbed by all alike and so desired nothing but death. And in fact they committed suicide by slashing their own wrists.

17.5   I mention Corbulo, because Nero summoned him in a very courteous letter, in which he kept calling him among other things 'father' and 'benefactor'. But after he had landed at Cenchreae, Nero ordered his execution before he had even been admitted to his presence. Some explain this on the grounds that the emperor was about to play his lyre and could

17.6 not bear to be seen by Corbulo wearing his long, loose tunic. As soon as Corbulo learned of the emperor's command, he seized his sword, and, stabbing himself vigorously, cried out, "You deserved it!" For only at that moment did he realize that he had made a serious mistake in sparing the lyre-player and in going to him without armed support.

*D.5 NERO'S TRIUMPHANT RETURN TO ROME   A.D. 67–68

(63.19.1–21.1: Xiphilinus)

A.D. 67

19.1   Helius had for some time been sending messages to the emperor urging him to return as soon as possible, but when he did not take any notice,

Helius went in person to Greece. Arriving there on the seventh day, he brought the alarming news that a major conspiracy against him was
19.2 forming in Rome. As a result, Nero immediately set sail for Italy. Some hope arose that he would perish in a storm at sea, but the many celebrations were premature; for he made the crossing quite safely. The fact that some people had prayed and hoped for his death was in fact the cause of their destruction.

A.D. 68

20.1   When Nero drove into Rome, a part of the wall was breached and a section of the gates knocked down, since some claimed that each of these was a customary tribute to those who had received the crown of victory at
20.2 the games. The procession was headed by those carrying the crowns which he had won. They were followed by others holding up placards on spears, on which were inscribed the title of the games, the type of contest involved, and the proclamation that Nero Caesar was the first Roman in
20.3 history to have won it. Next came the victor himself, riding in the triumphal chariot in which Augustus had celebrated his many triumphs. He was wearing a robe of purple embroidered with gold, was crowned with a garland of wild olive, and held before him the Pythian laurel. Diodorus the lyre-player rode alongside him.

20.4   This was how he passed through the Circus Maximus and the Forum, accompanied by the soldiers, the equestrians and the senate. He ascended the Capitol and from there proceeded to the Palatine. The whole city was
20.5 wreathed in garlands, ablaze with torches and redolent with incense. The whole population, not least the senators, shouted out in unison, 'Olympian Victor, hurrah!', 'Pythian Victor, hurrah!', 'Augustus! Augustus!', 'Hail to Nero Heracles!', 'Hail to Nero Apollo!', 'The one Victor in all the great festivals, the only one in history!', 'Augustus! Augustus!', 'Divine
20.6 Voice!', 'Blessed are we that can hear you!'. Why should I use circumlocutions and not reveal the very words that were uttered? For the expressions they used do not disgrace my history; rather, the fact that I have not concealed any of them enhances its dignity.

21.1   When he had performed these rites, he proclaimed a number of horse-races, and brought into the Circus Maximus these crowns and all the others that he had won in chariot races, and laid them around the Egyptian obelisk. There were 1,808 of them. After doing this, he appeared as a charioteer.

*D.6 REVOLTS IN JUDAEA, BRITAIN AND GAUL; REBELLION OF VINDEX   **A.D. 68**

(63.22.1–26.1: Xiphilinus; Zonaras; Valesian Excerpts)

22.1   Such was the nature of Nero's life and reign. I shall now recount how he was overthrown and fell from power.   **[Xiphilinus]**

22.1a While Nero was still in Greece, the Jews embarked on a rebellion which had been clearly coming. He sent Vespasian to deal with them. The inhabitants of Britain and Gaul, burdened by taxation, were also becoming more restive and inflamed.   **[Zonaras]**

22.1²   There was a man from Gaul called Gaius Julius Vindex, an Aquitanian of royal descent, and, by virtue of his father's rank, a Roman senator. He was a man strong in physique and shrewd in intelligence, skilled in warfare and not lacking in courage to meet any big challenge. He also had a passionate love of freedom and boundless ambition. This was

22.2   the man who was the leader of the Gauls. This Vindex summoned the people of Gaul to a meeting. They had suffered a great deal, and were still suffering, from the numerous capital levies imposed upon them by Nero. Vindex mounted a platform and delivered a long attack on Nero, urging

22.3   them to rebel against him and join his revolt. "Because", he said, "he has plundered the whole Roman world, because he has destroyed the full flower of their senate, and because he has committed incest with, and killed, his own mother, and does not even maintain a semblance of being

22.4   in charge. Numerous killings, lootings and other outrages have been committed by a variety of people on a number of occasions. But as for those crimes committed by Nero himself, how could anyone do justice to them in words? I have seen him, my friends and allies, believe me, I have seen that man (if you can call him a man when he has Sporus as a wife and Pythagoras as a husband), in the very heart of the theatre, that is, in the *orchêstra*, sometimes holding a lyre and wearing a loose-fitting tunic and

22.5   buskins, sometimes wearing high-heeled shoes and mask. I have often heard him singing, I have heard him declaiming, I have heard him acting. I have seen him bound in chains, I have seen him dragged along by force, pregnant and, would you believe, even giving birth. In short, by the lines that he speaks and listens to, by the acts that he allows to be done to him and that he does to others, he is experiencing everything in mythology. Is there anyone, then, who will call such a man 'Caesar' and 'Imperator' and

22.6   'Augustus'? Never! No one must ever abuse those sacred titles. These were titles held by Augustus and Claudius; this man deserves to be called Thyestes, Oedipus, Alcmaeon or Orestes. For these are the rôles he acts on stage, and these are the names that he has chosen to take the place of his others. Now, therefore, is the time to rise up against him. Rescue yourselves and rescue the Romans as well! Liberate the entire world!"

23.1   These words of Vindex struck a chord in his entire audience. It was not that he was seeking supreme power for himself, but he preferred to support Servius Sulpicius Galba for the leadership. Galba was a man renowned for his fairness and military experience; he was governor of Spain and had a sizeable military force at his command. And he was the man who was proclaimed emperor by his soldiers.

24.1   Rufus, the governor of Germany, launched an expedition to attack Vindex. When he reached Vesontio, he started to besiege the city on the

24.2   pretext that it had not opened its gates to let him in. Vindex came to the aid of the city in opposition to Rufus and encamped a short distance away. Messages passed between the two leaders until finally they held a private conference with no one else present, at which, it was assumed, they

24.3 came to a mutual agreement to oppose Nero. After this, Vindex set out with his army as though to take control of the town. Rufus' troops saw them approaching and thought that they were advancing directly against them; so on their own initiative they marched out to attack them. They fell upon them when they were least expecting it and were not in any sort of
24.4¹ order. As a result they slaughtered them wholesale. When he saw this,
24.4 Vindex was greatly distressed and committed suicide. This is what actually happened. Many, however, later inflicted wounds on the body and so gave the false impression to some that they had actually killed him.
25.1 Rufus was greatly distressed at Vindex's death, but refused to accept the position as emperor, even though his troops kept urging him to do so, and indeed he might easily have obtained it. For he was an energetic man with a large and enthusiastic force. His soldiers cast down and shattered the
25.2 images of Nero, and hailed their general 'Caesar' and 'Augustus'. When he remained unconvinced by this, one of his soldiers quickly inscribed the words on one of his standards. Rufus, however, erased the words and, after managing with some difficulty to restore order, persuaded them to
25.3 refer the matter to the senate and people. This he did either because he did not think it right for the army to bestow supreme power on anybody (indeed he kept making the point that this was the prerogative of the senate and people), or because he was utterly high-minded and had no personal desire to obtain the position of emperor, for which others were prepared to stop at nothing.   **[Xiphilinus]**

26.1 Nero heard about Vindex's revolt just after lunch as he was watching a gymnastic contest in Neapolis. Far from being disturbed, he leaped down from his seat and eagerly contested a bout with one of the athletes. Nor did he hasten to return to Rome, but simply sent a letter to the senate in which he excused himself for not having come, pleading a sore throat and implying by this that he would have liked – even at such a juncture – to sing to them.   **[Valesian Excerpts]**

*D.7 NERO'S REACTION TO THE REVOLT OF VINDEX AND GALBA
A.D. 68

(63.26.3–27.1a: Xiphilinus; Zonaras)

26.3 In most respects Nero behaved very much as usual and rejoiced in the news, since he was expecting to defeat Vindex and it now seemed that he had a good excuse for levying some fines and ordering some executions. And he continued to live a life of luxury. After the shrine of Sabina had been completed and decorated, he dedicated it in a lavish ceremony, setting up an inscription on the building to the effect that the women had
26.4 built it in honour of Sabina, the goddess Venus. And in this he was telling the truth; for it had been completely built out of the numerous funds that he had confiscated from women.

He also continued to have his little jokes. I shall pass over most of them, but let me recount one. One night all of a sudden he hurriedly summoned

the leading senators and equestrians, as if to consult them about the
current political problems. But he announced to them (and I am quoting
his actual words), "I have discovered how to make the water-organ make

26.5 both a louder and a more musical sound." Such were the jokes that he
made even at this critical moment in his reign. It did not concern him that
the doors both of the Mausoleum of Augustus and of his own bedroom
had opened automatically on that very night, nor that on the Alban
Mount it had rained such a quantity of blood that it flowed like a river,
nor that the sea had retreated a long distance from the coast of Egypt and
submerged a large part of Lycia.

27.1   But when he heard the news that Galba had been proclaimed emperor
by his soldiers and that Rufus had deserted Galba, he became very much
afraid, and not only made preparations himself in Rome, but also sent
Rubrius Gallus and certain others to confront the rebels.   **[Xiphilinus]**

27.1a   But when Nero learned that Petronius, whom he had sent on in advance
against the rebels with the larger part of the army, had joined Galba's side,
he no longer placed any hope in putting down the revolt by force of arms.
                                                                    [Zonaras]

***D.8 THE SENATE TURN AGAINST NERO; NERO'S FLIGHT FROM
    ROME AND DEATH; GALBA DECLARED EMPEROR   A.D. 68**

(63.27.2–29.3: Xiphilinus; Zonaras)

27.2   Now that he had been deserted by all without exception, he made plans
to kill the senators, burn the city to the ground and sail for Alexandria,
giving this clue as to his future: "Even if we fall from power, this little
talent will support us." For he had reached such a point of madness that
he actually believed that he would be able to live as a private citizen and,
what is more, as a lyre-player.   **[Xiphilinus]**

27.2b   Nero was just about to do this, when the senate removed his bodyguard,
and then, entering the camp, declared him a public enemy and appointed
Galba emperor in his place.   **[Zonaras]**

27.3   When he realized that he had been deserted by his bodyguard as well (he
happened to be spending the night in some gardens), he began to plan his
escape. He put on some shabby clothing and mounted a horse of no better
quality. He covered his head and rode to an estate of Phaon, an imperial
freedman, together with the said Phaon, Epaphroditus and Sporus under

28.1 cover of night. While he was doing this, a terrible earthquake occurred,
which gave the impression that the whole ground was being split apart and
the souls of all those who had been put to death on his orders were rising
up together against him. Even though he was in disguise, he was
recognized by one of the people whom he met on the road, so they say,
and addressed as 'emperor'. So he turned off the road and hid in a place
that was covered with reeds.

28.2   And he waited there until daybreak, lying flat on the ground, doing his best to avoid being seen. Every person who walked past he suspected of having come for him. Every voice he trembled at, as though it was seeking him out. And if any little dog barked or any little bird chirped or if any **28.3** bush or branch shook in the breeze, it startled him terribly. And neither was he able to get any rest as a result of these disturbances nor did he dare to chat to any of his companions, in case someone else should hear. But he kept lamenting and bemoaning his fate to himself. For he kept considering among other things how he had once taken great delight in the enormous size of his retinue of attendants, but was now hiding in the dark with just **28.4** three freedmen. For such was the drama that the divine power had prepared for him. He could no longer play the part of other matricides and outcasts; he was now playing himself. Now he was sorry for all the outrages he had committed, as though he were able to undo all the trouble **28.5** he had caused. Such was the tragic rôle that Nero was now playing, and this line kept going through his mind:

> "It is to a cruel death that I am being summoned by my wife and father."

Then later, when no one was apparently searching for him, he crossed over into a cave, and there in his hunger he ate the sort of bread he had never before tasted and in his thirst he drank the sort of water that he had never before drunk. Hardly able to stomach it, he remarked, "So this is my famous boiled drink!"

29.1   Such was the emperor's plight. Meanwhile, the Roman people were offering sacrifices and going mad with delight, some even wearing felt caps as though they had just been freed from slavery. And they voted Galba the prerogatives of imperial power. As for Nero, they organized a thorough search for him. For a while they could not puzzle out where he had taken refuge; but then they discovered his whereabouts and despatched some **29.2** men on horseback against him. He, realizing that they were approaching, ordered his companions to kill him. When they refused, he groaned and said, "I really am alone; I have neither a friend nor a foe." Meanwhile, the men on horseback arrived and so he committed suicide, uttering that famous remark, "Jupiter, what an artist perishes with me!" And as he lingered in the throes of death, Epaphroditus dealt the decisive blow.

29.3   He had lived thirty years and nine months, of which he had been emperor for thirteen years and eight months. He was the last of the descendants of Aeneas and of Augustus, as was clearly signalled when the laurels planted by Livia and her breed of white chickens perished shortly before he died.   **[Xiphilinus]**

HISTORICAL COMMENTARY

A. THE REIGN OF TIBERIUS: A.D. 29 – 31:
THE FALL OF SEJANUS

* * * * *

*A.1 HONOURS FOR SEJANUS. ARREST OF ASINIUS GALLUS
A.D. 29–30
(58.2.7–3.6: Xiphilinus)

2.7 **Sejanus:** L. Aelius Sejanus (hereafter Sej.) (*PIR*² A 255), prefect of the
Praetorian Guard since 14, sharing the command with his father, L. Seius
Strabo, until the latter was appointed prefect of Egypt in 16 or 17 and Sej.
was left in sole command (57.19.5–7). For D.'s view that it was dangerous
for the emperor to have only one Praetorian prefect see 52.24.1–2. Sej. was
from an equestrian family from Volsinii in Etruria (cf. EJ 220 =
LACTOR 8, no. 12), but had built up a sizeable political support among
the senatorial aristocracy. His influence with Tiberius (hereafter Tib.) had
grown steadily since 20 (Tac. *A.* 4.1–5.5; R. Seager, *Tiberius* (1972) 178–
214; B. Levick, *Tiberius the Politician* (1976), 158–71).

public festival to be held to mark his birthday: Such festivals were usually
reserved for members of the imperial family, which vividly illustrates the
dominant position of Sej. at this time. Tib. constantly refused any such
honours for himself (57.8.3–4; 58.12.8), as did Claudius (60.5.3–5). Such
birthday celebrations included prayers, sacrifices, chariot-races, beast-
hunts and public banquets: e.g. 54.8.5; 54.26.2 (Aug.); 59.7.2 (Gaius
Caligula); 60.5.1 (Antonia, mother of Claudius). The priestly college
known as the Arval Brethren (*fratres Arvales*) were responsible for
conducting the prayers and sacrifices on imperial birthdays: the *Acts of the
Arval Brethren* record the sacrifices offered to the emperor Gaius [hence-
forth = G.] in 38 on his birthday, 31 August (*AE* 1983, 95).

statues set up to him: cf. Suet. *T.* 65.1, which reveals that the statues were
of gold (more probably gilded). Tib. had set the precedent by granting Sej.
a bronze statue in 23, an honour immediately imitated by others (57.21.3;
Tac. *A.* 3.72; 4.74; Seneca, *Consolation to Marcia* 22.4 [= Braund 102]).
After describing Sej.'s fall, D. comments that the senate had led Sej. to
destruction by the grant of such honours; as a result, it forbade any similar
grant and the taking of an oath in the name of any living person except the
emperor (58.12.6).

equestrian order: The *equites* (or knights) were the group (or order) in the
Roman citizen body inferior only to the senatorial order in terms of rank
and prestige. For membership free birth and a property qualification of
400,000 sesterces were required. It remains a problem whether this

automatically allowed entry into the order, or whether members had to be enrolled by the emperor; for modern discussion see Bibliography under 'Equestrian Order'. D. here provides a good illustration of the *equites* acting as a corporate group rather like the senate (cf. Suet. *Cl.* 6). For the equestrian order setting up a statue in honour of Nero see 63.18.3. Aug. had given the equestrians a more marked rôle in Roman public life by creating for them various military and administrative posts, from which senators were excluded (53.15.2–5). D. expresses his view on their appropriate rôle in Roman administration in a speech that he puts into the mouth of Maecenas at 52.19.4–6; 52.24.6–25.7.

tribes: D. here refers to the thirty-five voting tribes (*tribus*) into which the Roman citizen body (*populus Romanus*) was divided. Each tribe traditionally had one block vote in the citizen assembly (*comitia tributa*) and at the plebeian assembly (*concilium plebis*). D., therefore, means that the Roman people voted Sej. these honours at a meeting of one of the popular assemblies. The Roman people had lost their power to elect to magistracies and to accept or reject laws under the Principate, but they still met in assembly to ratify laws and to confirm the powers of the emperor and of magistrates now appointed by the senate often on the recommendation of the emperor (F.G.B. Millar, *The Emperor in the Roman World* (1977), 368–69; R.J.A. Talbert, *The Senate of Imperial Rome* (1984), 433–35; B. Levick in *Roman Political Life 90 B.C.–A.D. 69* (ed. T.P. Wiseman, 1985), 50–55). For the "urban plebs of the thirty-five tribes" honouring Drusus son of Tib. and Germanicus see EJ 92 = Braund 111. For other contexts in which the citizen body still functioned in its tribal units cf. 48.4.6 (each tribe bestowing a crown on a triumphant general in 41 B.C.), Tac. *A.* 3.4 (at Germanicus' funeral in 20). Tribes possibly sat together at the theatre (E. Rawson, *PBSR* 42 (1987), 94–97) and at public banquets (60.7.4 + n. [= **C.5**]). On the voting tribes see L.R. Taylor, *Roman Voting Assemblies from the Hannibalic War to the dictatorship of Caesar* (1966).

2.8 **envoys were sent by the senate, equestrian order and people:** Embassies to the emperor were a key aspect of imperial ritual under the Principate. They were frequently sent by the various groups within Roman society, as here (cf. 58.13.2; 59.6.6 [= **B.4**]), or by provincial communities to deliver a speech congratulating him at key moments of his reign, thus emphasizing their loyalty and hoping for favours from him (Millar, *ERW*, 119–22, 217–18, 363–85).

tribunes, plebeian aediles: These magistracies were created by the plebeians at the start of the fifth century B.C. when they were struggling to win protection against the patricians. Like the other plebeian institutions such as their assembly (the *concilium plebis*), they were later integrated into the political organization of the Roman state (A. Drummond, *CAH* VII.2 (2nd ed., 1989), 212–42). For the magistracy under Tib. cf. EJ 207 = Braund 373. The plebeian aediles should be distinguished from curule aediles, originally appointed from among the patricians (7.15.10; 43.51.3).

prayers and sacrifices: Prayers and sacrifices 'for the emperor's welfare' were offered annually on 3 January by the magistrates and priests at Rome and by the Roman governors in the provinces (cf. Plin. *Letters* 10.35, 36, 100, 101). When Tib. found that Germanicus' sons, Nero and Drusus, were being included in these prayers on behalf of the emperor, he asked the senate whether this was proper procedure (Suet. *T.* 54.1). For sacrifices see further 58.8.4n. [= **A.7**].

oaths by their Fortune: There existed under the Principate five main forms of oath/prayer in favour of the emperor and his family: (a) the oath of allegiance sworn throughout the empire on the accession of each new emperor (cf. Smallwood 32, 33 = Braund 562, 563); (b) the oath taken annually by the senate on 1 January to observe all past and future measures of the current emperor and of those emperors deemed worthy of the honour after their death (cf. 57.8.4–5); (c) the prayers offered annually on 1 January (but from 38 onwards on 3 January) for the welfare of the emperor and the imperial family by the magistrates and priests at Rome and by the governor of each province (cf. Plin. *Letters* 10.35, 36, 100, 101); (d) the prayers and sacrifices offered and the oaths taken annually on the emperor's day of accession (*dies imperii*) 'by his Fortune' (cf. 57.8.3; Plin. *Letters* 10.52, 53, 102, 103); and (e) the prayers and sacrifices offered for the welfare of the emperor and members of his family on their birthdays or at other key moments in their life: for example, when they assumed the toga of manhood (*toga virilis*) (cf. 58.2.7n.). It is unclear whether D. here refers to type (a) or type (d); for arguments in favour of the latter see R. Seager, *JRS* 67 (1977), 185. On oaths see H. Mattingly, *Proc. Brit. Acad.* 36 (1950), 155–95; id., 37 (1951), 219–68. The fullest work (in German) remains P. Herrmann, *Der römische Kaisereid* (1968).

3.1 **Gallus:** C. Asinius Gallus (*PIR²* A 1229), consul in 8 B.C., was the son of the famous historian and politician, C. Asinius Pollio, and one of the foremost senators of the early Principate. He had married Vipsania Agrippina, the daughter of M. Agrippa, when Aug. forced Tib. to divorce her and marry his own daughter Julia in 12 B.C. for dynastic reasons (54.35.4; Suet. *T.* 7.2; R. Syme, *The Roman Revolution* (1939), 416). D. here alludes to the part played by Gallus in the senatorial debate in 14 concerning the powers to be granted Tib. on his accession (57.2.5–7; Tac. *A.* 1.12). He had also been outspoken – usually in conflict with Tib. – on many other occasions (Tac. *A.* 1.76, 77; 2.33, 35, 36; 4.20, 30, 71). Gallus' attachment to Sej. became clear in 28, when he replied ambiguously in the senate to Tib.'s letter of thanks at the end of the trial of Titius Sabinus (Tac. *A.* 4.71). For some suggested reasons for his attachment to Sej. see Levick, *Tib.*, 172; D. Shotter, *Historia* 20 (1971), 443–57, esp. 451–57; A.B. Bosworth, *AJAH* 2 (1977), 173–92. D. is always keen to isolate motives for particular events or actions (Introduction, Section 4.1), but his uncertainty in this case is underlined by the presentation of three possibilities.

3.2 **sent a letter to the senate about Gallus:** Tib. also used this method to condemn Titius Sabinus (Tac. *A.* 4.70) and he was to use it again in the toppling of Sej. (58.9–10 [= **A.7**]). The charge recorded here by D. is unconvincing; the real charge is probably cloaked behind the phrase "among other things". For the argument that it was treason, arising out of Gallus' part in the conspiracy of Agrippina, the wife of Germanicus, see R.S. Rogers, *Criminal Trials and Criminal Legislation under Tiberius* (1935), 105–06. Adultery between Gallus and Agrippina was also alleged (Tac. *A.* 6.25). The offence was obviously serious, since all public record of Gallus was eradicated: all statues of him were removed and his name was erased from all public inscriptions: cf. *EJ* 295 = Braund 806 (Rome); *ILS* 97 = Braund 354 (Ephesus).

Syriacus: Vallius Syriacus (*PIR*[1] V 171) was a leading advocate and rhetorician. He had taught Tib. (Suet. *T.* 57) and is frequently mentioned by the elder Seneca (e.g. *Contr.* 1.1.11, 21; 2.1.34; 2.6.13; 7.6.11; 9.4.18). On him see further R. Syme, *Historia* 5 (1956), 207 [= *RP* I, 318].

3.3   **he was banqueted at the house of Tib.:** Tib. had left the city of Rome in 26 (58.1.1; Tac. *A.* 4.57) and was now spending most of the year at his twelve sumptuous villas on the island of Capri (Tac. *A.* 4.67; Suet. *T.* 40–43; G.W. Houston, *G&R* 32 (1985), 176–96; Levick, *Tib.*, 167). For the archaeological remains of some of these villas see F. Sear, *Roman Architecture* (1982), 88–91; J.B. Ward-Perkins, *Roman Imperial Architecture* (1981), 198–201; A.G. McKay, *Cumae and the Phlegraean Fields* (1972), 99–122. Some scholars have found it difficult to accept the intimate dinner on Capri (e.g. Rogers, *Criminal Trials*, 105). But Tib. was similarly ambivalent towards Sej. when it came to condemning him (58.9–10 [= **A.7**]). Alternatively, D.'s rather compressed chronology may be explained by his desire to achieve a dramatic, rhetorical effect.

he was condemned in the senate-house: Under the Principate one of the major functions of the senate was as a judicial court (Talbert, *Senate*, 460–87). That Gallus was ever formally condemned, as D. claims, is put into doubt by Tac. *A.* 6.23, where at the time of his death he is still described as a defendant.

3.4   **Tib. refused to let Gallus die:** Gallus did not die until 33 (58.23.6; Tac. *A.* 6.23). Tib. also found it difficult to put Drusus son of Germanicus to death, keeping him in custody from 30 until 33 (58.3.8 + n. [= **A.2**]; 58.13.1). Whether D. is right to attribute this to Tib.'s cruelty is questionable. He emphasizes Tib.'s cruelty by going on to relate three similar cases (58.3.6–7). Seager (*Tib.* 11–12) defends D. by pointing out that Tib.'s cruelty increased as his reign progressed and as his reason weakened (Suet. *T.* 59–62). However, senatorial sources would have exaggerated his cruelty towards members of the senate, a topic which D., himself a senator, would have been keen to highlight. The frequent persecution of leading members of the senate by successive emperors should not simply be attributed to their evil personalities; rather, emperors constantly needed to demonstrate their ability to outdo senators, since the latter were potential rivals for their position as emperor (K. Hopkins, *Death and Renewal* (1983), 169–70).

3.5   **Gallus kept under guard by the consuls in office:** This is a good illustration that the senior magistrates were responsible for imprisonment and that a magistrate's house was often used for keeping people in custody (cf.

58.10.8 [= **A.7**]; 58.18.4; P.D.A. Garnsey, *Social Status and Legal Privilege in the Roman Empire* (1970), 147–52, esp. 149).

except when Tib. was consul: Tib. was consul for the fifth time in 31, with Sej. as his colleague (58.4.3 + n. [= **A.3**]). The responsibility then passed to the praetors, the highest-ranking magistrates after consuls. Only consuls and praetors possessed *imperium*: that is, the right to command armies and the power to execute legal and administrative decisions.

*A.2 SEJANUS MOVES AGAINST DRUSUS A.D. 30

(58.3.8–9: Valesian Excerpts)

3.8 **Drusus:** Drusus Julius Caesar (*PIR²* J 220), the second son of Germanicus and Agrippina, and elder brother of the future emperor Gaius (Caligula). In 26 he had become a supporter of Sej., allegedly out of a general lust for power and hatred for his elder brother, Nero Julius Caesar, who was at this stage of the reign Tib.'s likely successor (Tac. *A.* 4.60). In 29 Sej. had secured Nero's banishment to the island of Pontia and Agrippina's to Pandateria (Suet. *T.* 53.2; 54.2; 64). As a result, Drusus was now first in line to succeed Tib. For the significance of this whole episode see R.S. Rogers, *Studies in the Reign of Tiberius* (1943), 137–45.
Drusus' wife: Aemilia Lepida (*PIR²* A 421), daughter of M. Aemilius Lepidus, the consul of A.D. 6. For her slanders against Drusus cf. Tac. *A.* 6.40.
by seducing the wives of almost all the men of note: Sej. had secured the condemnation of Nero Caesar through information provided by Nero's wife, Julia (Tac. *A.* 4.60), just as he had earlier had Drusus son of Tib. poisoned through help from his wife, Livilla (Tac. *A.* 4.3). The theme of Sej.'s adultery with, and political use of, the wives of the senatorial aristocracy may have been exaggerated in the hostile senatorial tradition about the equestrian Sej., the 'small-town adulterer' (Tac. *A.* 4.3). Aug. was accused of the same adulterous practice, but his friends justified it on the grounds that he needed to keep abreast of any plots being hatched among the senatorial order (Suet. *Aug.* 69.1).
Tib. sent Drusus to Rome: From this we can infer that members of the imperial family resided with Tib. on Capri; for G.'s presence here from late August, 30 see Suet. *G.* 10.1.
the charge against Drusus: D. is vague about the actual charge, as he had been in the case of Asinius Gallus (cf. 58.3.2 [= **A.1**]). For the supposition that it concerned contumacious speech and ambition for power see Seager 213. D., as summarized by Zonaras, has already hinted at the charge in a 'flash-forward' to the events described here: Agrippina, Nero and Drusus were all accused of being pleased at the death of Tib.'s son, Drusus (57.22.4a). This was a charge frequently used by the emperors (cf. 59.8.1 [= **B.6**]; 59.8.2n. [= **B.6**]; 63.19.2 [= **D.5**]).
Cassius: One of the consuls of 30, but it is unclear whether D. here refers to L. Cassius Longinus (*PIR²* C 503), *consul ordinarius* in 30, or his

brother C. Cassius Longinus (*PIR*² C 501), the great jurist, who was
suffect consul also in 30. The former married Drusus' sister, Drusilla,
in 33 (Tac. *A.* 6.15); on the importance of the latter see Tac. *A.* 12.12;
J.A. Crook, *Consilium Principis* (1955), 157; R. Syme, *The Augustan
Aristocracy* (1986), 306; R.A. Bauman, *Emperors and Lawyers* (1989),
76–118.

persuaded Cassius to take action against him: This excerpt from D. fails to
give precise details; the 'action against Drusus' was presumably that
mentioned by Suet. *T.* 54.2; *G.* 7, viz. that Drusus was attacked by Tib. in
a letter, declared a public enemy in the senate and condemned to a
dungeon under the Palatine. Like Gallus, Drusus was not killed immediately, but kept in custody until his eventual death in 33 (58.22.4; Tac. *A.*
6.23–24; Suet. *T.* 54.2). Tib. allegedly planned to have Drusus declared
emperor if Sej. tried to seize power (58.13.1; Suet. *T.* 65.2), but once Sej.
had been overthrown, there was to be no reprieve for Drusus. Drusus'
imprisonment marked another significant step in Sej.'s removal of possible heirs to Tib. With Drusus son of Tib., Nero and now Drusus son of
Germanicus out of the way, this left only G., Germanicus' youngest son,
and Tiberius Gemellus, the ten-year-old grandson of Tib., as possible
successors; the future emperor Claudius was not at this stage seen as a
serious candidate. On the succession see Levick, *Tib.*, ch. 10; A.A. Barrett,
Caligula: the corruption of power (1989), ch. 2.

3.9   **by betrothing him to Julia, the daughter of Drusus:** Julia (*PIR*² J 636),
the daughter of Drusus son of Tib. and Livia Julia (cf. 58.7.5 [= **A.6**]).
She had been married to Germanicus' son, Nero, from 20 until his exile
in 29 (Tac. *A.* 3.29). For her later career see 60.18.4 + n. [= **C.9**].
However, Seager (*Tib.*, 213, n. 6) argues that D./Zonaras is in error here
and that Sej. was in fact engaged to her mother, Livia Julia (on whom see
58.11.6n. [= **A.7**]), widowed since Drusus' death in 23. This engagement
led to the description of Sej. as Tib.'s 'colleague and son-in-law' (Tac. *A.*
5.6; 6.8). However, Suet. *T.* 65.1 implies that the betrothal never took
place.

*A.3 SEJANUS' POWER INCREASES   **A.D. 30**

(58.4.1–4: Xiphilinus)

4.1   **Tib. was afraid that they might declare Sej. emperor:** Whether Tib. at this
stage feared that Sej. would be declared emperor is questionable, since a
large part of the senatorial order and the Roman plebs were very much
opposed to Sej. (Tac. *A.* 3.29; 4.11). Rather, it serves D.'s artistic purposes
to magnify Sej.'s position to the highest degree, so that his subsequent fall
appears all the more dramatic: see further 58.5.1–4 [= **A.4**]; 58.7.3n. [=
A.6]; 58.11.1 + n. [= **A.7**]. D. structures the episode of the fall of Sej. as
an example of Greek *peripeteia*, the sudden fall of an important public
figure with a fatal flaw: cf. 58.11.1 [= **A.7**] and Introduction, Section 3.4.3.
This was a favourite theme in Greek historiography: e.g. Herodotus'

portrayal of the fall of Croesus and Xerxes, or Thucydides' portrayal of the Athenian Empire. For other examples of this technique in D. see F. Millar, *A Study of Cassius Dio* (1964), 76–77.

4.2   Praetorian Guard: During the later Republic a Roman general on campaign was always protected by a bodyguard of legionary soldiers (known as the "praetorian cohort"). Under Aug. this gradually evolved into an institution for the protection of the emperor in Rome, Italy or when on campaign overseas. Under Tib. the number of cohorts of the Praetorian Guard was increased from three to nine (Millar, *ERW*, 61–62; G. Webster, *The Roman Imperial Army* (3rd ed., 1985), 96–98; L. Keppie, *The Making of the Roman Army* (1982), 187–88). Sej. had been prefect of the Praetorian Guard since 14 (58.2.7n. [= **A.1**]). He had enhanced its (previously negligible) political rôle by stationing all its cohorts in a single camp on the Viminal Hill in 23 (57.19.6; Tac. *A.* 4.2 (more penetrating than D., but the precise date of this crucial change is not clear in either account); Suet. *T.* 37.1).

4.3   Tib. appointed Sej. consul: D. is strictly speaking incorrect to suggest that the emperor could appoint consuls. Tib. had reformed the procedures for electing magistrates in 14 (58.20.3–4; Tac. *A.* 1.15; Vell. Pat. 2.124.3–4; Millar, *ERW*, 302–03): the senate was now responsible for preparing a slate of candidates (usually no more than the number of magistracies available), which the assemblies of the Roman people (*comitia centuriata, comitia tributa*) and of the Roman plebs (*concilium plebis*) merely ratified. This had clearly become the standard practice by the end of the first century A.D. (cf. Pliny, *Letters* 3.20; 4.25; 6.19). The extent to which the emperor recommended certain candidates to the senate remains a controversial problem, but he probably used his influence (as here) to force the issue (B. Levick, *Historia* 16 (1967), 207–30; A.J. Holladay, *Latomus*, 38 (1978), 874–93). From Vespasian onwards it was laid down on the emperor's accession in the formal law outlining his powers that his chosen candidates should be voted on first (EJ 364 = Braund 293, with P.A. Brunt, *JRS* 67 (1977), 95–116).

The appointment of an equestrian to the senior senatorial magistracy, the consulship, was a "startling and flagrant anomaly" (Syme, *AA*, 311). D. fails to make explicit the fact not only that Sej. was to be *consul ordinarius* (more prestigious than just a suffect consulship), but also that he was to hold it together with the emperor (cf. Suet. *T.* 65.1; EJ 50a = Braund 96; EJ 358a = Braund 671). This was Tib.'s fifth consulship (he had already been consul in 13 and 7 B.C., A.D. 18 and 21), but this was the first time that he had held it in absence. Furthermore, he had held his third and his fourth consulship with a chosen successor: with Germanicus in 18, with his own son Drusus in 21. Hence Tib. was (genuinely or with devious irony) marking Sej. out as a potential successor.

A fragmentary and very problematic inscription from Rome (EJ 53 = LACTOR 8, no. 13 = Braund 101 = Sherk 40a) refers to "the improper elections which were held on the Aventine, when Sej. was made consul". R. Syme, *Hermes* 84 (1956), 257–66 [= *RP* I, 305–14] argued that Sej. chose for his election the Aventine with its popularist associations (since it had been the base of the plebeians during their struggles against the patricians during the early Republic) rather than the normal Campus Martius, to win the favour of the plebs.

'Sharer of my Cares': For this soubriquet cf. Tac. *A*. 4.2; Vell. Pat. 2.127.3 [= Braund 95]. For Sej. as Tib.'s "adviser and assistant in all matters" see 57.19.7.

letters addressed to the senate and to the people: Tib.'s absence from Rome first in Campania and now on Capri meant that letters (*epistulae*) between him and the senate became a vital mechanism for the administration of the Empire (Millar, *ERW*, 213–28).

4.4   in inscriptions: Cary in his Loeb edition (vol. VII, p. 197) mistranslates this as 'the records', for which D. uses a different and quite specific term (*ta hypomnêmata*) (57.12.2; 57.21.5; 57.23.2; 60.33.1; 67.11.3). It is more likely, though by no means completely certain, that D. means that Tib.'s and Sej.'s names appeared together in inscriptions (cf. 37.21.2).

gilded chairs in the theatre: The symbolic significance of this honour was purposely ambiguous. Roman curule magistrates (i.e., consuls, praetors and curule aediles) and priests were allowed to use a special kind of seat (the *sella curulis*) as a symbol of their power, and these were occasionally placed in the theatre at festivals as a special honour (e.g. EJ 94a = Braund 115 = Sherk 36b, lines 50–54, with S. Weinstock, *JRS* 47 (1957), 144–54). However, the *sella curulis* was made of ivory, not gilded. The word D./Xiphilinus uses here for 'chair' (*diphros*) was used as the Greek equivalent of the Latin *sella curulis* (e.g. Polybius 6.53.9), but could also be used for a chair for a king or a deity (e.g. *OGIS* 199, line 38). Hellenistic kings (e.g. Alexander the Great) were honoured with gilded chairs, and Julius Caesar had been granted one in the theatre just before his assassination in 44 B.C. (44.6.3). Roman gods had their gilded chairs carried in processions to the theatre during festivals, while images of goddesses were also set on such chairs at cultic banquets (L.R. Taylor, *CPh* 30 (1935), 122–30). This honour could thus be interpreted as a sign that Sej. was not only becoming very closely associated with the imperial family, but also that he was being accorded quasi-divine honours. Theatres were important locations for homage to emperors and their families (S.R.F. Price, *Rituals and Power* (1984), 109, 135–36, 210–11).

they should hold the consulship together every five years: If the senate did vote this honour, this is a clear breaking of the rules for holding magistracies at Rome which Aug. had strongly reinforced (Syme, *RR*, 369). It was very much a symptom of the emperor's power to have these rules waived by the senate in special cases: e.g. for likely heirs to the throne or favourites (Hopkins, *Death*, 149).

sacrifice to the images of Sej. and Tib.: By images (*eikones*) D. could mean portrait busts, paintings or, most likely here, statues. Sacrifice before the statues of the consuls of 38 is attested in the *Acts of the Arval Brethren* (*AE* 1983, 95, lines 31–37). For the symbolic ambiguities of sacrifice offered to statues of living emperors see Price, *Rituals*, 170–88.

*A.4 SEJANUS' POSITION IN A.D. 31   **A.D. 31**

(58.5.1–7: Xiphilinus)

5.1 D.'s hostility to Sej. underlines his senatorial viewpoint. He strongly
disapproved of Sej. because he was the first prefect of the Praetorian Guard to hold the consulship. D. later admits (58.14.1) that
the career of Fulvius Plautianus, the Praetorian prefect destroyed
by Septimius Severus in 205, was highly reminiscent of that of Sej.
(cf. 75.14.1–16.5); this probably coloured his treatment of Sej.
Compare also his comments on Macrinus, the first Praetorian prefect
to become emperor in 217: "he might have been praised above all
men, if he had not set his heart on becoming emperor himself and
chosen instead some senator to head the Roman state .... But he
grasped at monarchy himself, without even having the title of senator"
(78.41.2–4).

5.2 **jostling around his doors:** D. here alludes to the daily morning ritual of the
salutation (*salutatio*), at which a patron was greeted by his clients and
presented them with a handout (*sportula*). Clients were received in strict
order of rank, which underlined visibly their relative social importance
and the importance of hierarchies in Roman society. From D.'s account
here it is clear that clients waited out in the street to be admitted to the
main reception hall (*atrium*) of their patron's house. For senators attending salutations at the houses of both Tib. and Sej. cf. 57.11.1; 57.21.4; Tac.
A. 4.74. Note also how essentially public rituals encroached into the
private sphere of the individual's house: see A. Wallace-Hadrill, *PBSR* 56
(1988), 44–47, 58–77.

5.3–4 Note D.'s moralizing rhetoric here and his implicit hostility to those not
of noble birth: see further Introduction, Section 3.4.3.

5.4 **it is a virtue for emperors to pardon people:** Clemency was the most
publicized of all the imperial virtues (cf. *RG* 34.2; EJ 22 = Braund
13; Sen. *On Clemency*). D. examines the nature of clemency at length
in a supposed dialogue between Aug. and Livia at 55.14–21 and
implicitly praises emperors for showing it (cf. 59.6.3–4 [= **B.4**];
60.3.5–7 [= **C.3**]; 66.19.1; 68.6.4; 69.23.2–3). The emperor displayed
clemency by refraining from punishing citizens as severely as their
guilt demanded and his absolute power allowed (M. Griffin, *Seneca*
(1976), 133–71; A. Wallace-Hadrill, *Suetonius* (1983), 157–60; B. Levick
in *The Ancient Historian and his Materials* (ed. B. Levick, 1975),
123–37).

5.5–7 **omens of impending trouble for Sej.:** D. (as preserved in Xiphilinus)
gives much prominence to the omens foreshadowing the death of Sej.
(cf. 58.7.1–3 [= **A.5**]). He frequently leads up to the death of an
emperor by listing such omens: see Introduction, Section 3.4.1 and
Table 2.

5.5 **on the first day of the month:** D. here probably refers to incidents that took
place on 1st. January, a day of ceremonies on which the new consuls

entered office. The consuls were escorted by a large crowd from their homes to the Capitol, where their inauguration and sacrifices took place. The senate then met to swear to uphold the acts of the current emperor and certain predecessors, and the senior consul made a speech of thanks to the emperor (Talbert, *Senate*, 200–202).

the room in which he was greeting them: The daily ritual at which a patron greeted his clients, the *salutatio*, usually took place in the *atrium* at the front of a Roman house: see 58.5.2n. [= **A.4**].

5.6   This section gives a good impression of the topography at the western end of the Forum (see Map 2). The Capitoline Hill had two peaks: the Capitolium (Capitol) with the temple of Jupiter, Juno and Minerva and the Arx (or Citadel). The normal way down from the Capitolium was by the Clivus Capitolinus, which led into the Forum along the west side of the temple of Saturn. The Gemonian Steps led down from the Arx between the temple of Concord and the prison (or Tullianum). Sej.'s bodyguard had thus been diverted by the crowd towards the north behind the Tabularium and then down the steps. Note also the reference to the practice of hurling the bodies of executed criminals down the Gemonian Steps, where their bodies suffered further maltreatment and dishonour, a fate to be suffered by Sej. later in the year: cf. 58.11.5 + n. [= **A.7**].

the servants who were acting as his bodyguard turned off along the road leading to the prison: The consul as a magistrate with *imperium* was escorted in public by twelve ceremonial attendants known as lictors, who carried bundles of rods and axes (*fasces*). Their presence with the magistrate symbolically emphasized his power. D. here refers, however, to another institution: the bodyguard of a magistrate, privately recruited by the magistrate often from among his household slaves: e.g. M. Antonius as consul in 44 B.C. had a private bodyguard of Ituraean archers (Cic. *Phil.* 2.44.112). See further W. Nippel, *JRS* 74 (1984), 25. The incident is reported because it occurred outside the prison and hence was an omen of Sej.'s imprisonment here later in the year on the night before his execution (58.10.8, 11.4–5 [= **A.7**]).

5.7   **taking the auspices:** This was a type of divination conducted by senior magistrates with the help of the priests known as augurs, to ascertain whether the gods were in favour of a particular course of action being undertaken: e.g. elections, starting a war or battle, or (as here) entering into office. Auspices were taken by scanning the skies for good or bad omens sent by the gods (e.g. thunder and lightning), by observing the flight and cries of birds in the skies (crows and owls were considered ill-omened) and by checking whether the sacred chickens ate in the approved manner (R.M. Ogilvie, *The Romans and their Gods* (London, 1969), 56–59; J.H.W.G. Liebeschuetz, *Continuity and Change in Roman Religion* (1979), 7–29).

flew off towards the prison and perched on top of it: A second omen of Sej.'s impending imprisonment here (cf. 58.5.6n).

*A.5 TIBERIUS PLAYS CAT-AND-MOUSE WITH SEJANUS   A.D. 31

(58.6.1–7.3: Xiphilinus)

6.2   **swore by his Fortune:** See 58.2.8n. [= **A.1**].
Tib. treated both Sej. and the others in a remarkable fashion: Tib.'s
treatment of Sej. is reminiscent of his conduct towards Gallus (cf. 58.3 [=
A.1]). His approach may have been due to his duplicitous nature, on which
see 57.1–6; Tac. *A*. Books 1–6 (passim); but more probably it was because
Tib. could not make up his mind about Sej. (Levick, *Tib.*, 175). D.'s
rhetorical language and heavy use of antithesis underlines Tib.'s ambivalence.
6.3   **kept sending dispatches:** For Tib.'s use of dispatches (*epistulae*) see 58.4.3n.
[= **A.3**].
6.4   **Sej.'s friends:** For discussion on Sej.'s supporters see Levick, *Tib.*, 171–72;
R. Sealey, *Phoenix* 15 (1961), 97–114; G.V. Sumner, *Phoenix* 19 (1965),
134–45.
a revolution: This passage is crucial for the debate whether Sej. formed a
conspiracy against Tib. D. was sceptical about accepting stories of
conspiracies against any emperor (54.15.1–4) and clearly held that Sej. lost
his chance to form a conspiracy by a lack of spirit (58.8.2 = [**A.6**]). Tac.
was also cautious about accepting the idea that Sej. led a conspiracy
against Tib. On the other hand, Josephus *AJ* 18.181 [= Braund 97] and
Suet. *T*. 65.2 both believed that there was a conspiracy, while Josephus
adds that Tib. was warned of it by Antonia, the mother of Claudius, in a
letter. D. refers to this letter, but well out of chronological sequence
(66.14.1–2). Since G. was living with Antonia (Suet. *G*. 10.1), it is more
likely that she had uncovered a plot against G., Sej.'s next potential
victim. The divergencies in the sources have led to much modern discussion: R. Syme, *Tacitus* (1958), 402–6, 752–54; Seager 214–23; Levick, *Tib.*,
158–79.
  Two main reconstructions have been proposed: (a) that Sej. aimed to
succeed Tib. – or at least to act as regent for the young Tiberius Gemellus,
Tib.'s grandson. This view is based on Jos., Suet., possible allusions in
Tac. and an inscription (EJ 51 = Braund 99 = Sherk 40c) which refers to
Sej. as a 'public enemy' (*hostis publicus*) and therefore guilty of treason
against the emperor, but discounts D.'s evidence; or (b) that Sej. rose too
high for Tib.'s (or Tib.'s associates') peace of mind, which forced Tib. to
bring about his downfall. This view seeks to reconcile the sources.
7.1–3   **omens of Sej.'s fall:** cf. 58.5.5–7 + n. [= **A.4**].
7.1   **removed the statue's head:** On statues of Sej. cf. 58.2.7 + n. [= **A.1**]. For
the fate of Sej.'s statues after his death see Juv. *Sat*. 10.58–64. More
generally, the incident provides insight into how Roman statues were
made: the heads were sculpted separately from their bodies and were then
inserted into a deep supporting socket.
7.2   **about to offer sacrifice to himself:** cf. 58.4.4 + n. [= **A.3**]; 58.8.4 + n. [= **A.7**].
a statue of Fortune, which had belonged, so people claim, to Tullius: The cult

of Fortuna was one of the oldest cults at Rome. Servius Tullius (sixth of the supposed seven kings of early Rome, who reigned from c. 578 – c. 534 B.C.) established a joint sanctuary to Fortuna and Mater Matuta in the Forum Boarium, which has now been excavated and can be dated to c. 550 B.C. (R.M. Ogilvie, *Early Rome and the Etruscans* (1976), 62–70; F. Coarelli, *Guida archeologica di Roma* (3rd ed., 1980), 281–84).

7.3 **conducting a sacrifice:** This incident illustrates that sacrifices were carried out inside Roman houses as well as at public altars. Each house had its own shrine (*lararium*) for the household gods (*Lares*), the gods of the storeroom (*Penates*) and the protecting spirit of the father of the house (*Genius*). For domestic religion see Ogilvie, *Gods*, 100–5; J.B. Ward-Perkins and A. Claridge, *Pompeii A.D. 79* (1976), 55–61.

A.6 RELATIONS BETWEEN TIBERIUS AND GAIUS CALIGULA
A.D. 31
(58.7.3–8.3)

7.3 **Tib.'s capricious nature:** This is a leitmotif running throughout D.'s account of Tib.'s reign (e.g. 57.1.1–6; 57.2.3–4; 57.15.4–7). It derives from the hostile senatorial tradition against Tib. (cf. Tac. *A*. 1.11; 6.50).

the instability of human affairs: D. saw the fall of Sej. as an excellent example of the instability of human affairs (cf. 58.4.1n. [= **A.3**]; 58.11.1 [= **A.7**]). This theme recurs throughout D.'s work (see Introduction, Section 3.4.3).

7.4 **Tib. had appointed both Sej. and his son priests along with Gaius:** Sej. had two sons (Strabo and Capito Aelianus) and one daughter (Junilla). D. here presumably refers to Sej.'s elder son, Strabo, often identified as L. Aelius Gallus Strabo (but see Syme, *AA*, 307–8). G. is the future emperor, commonly known as Caligula. He was the youngest and only surviving son of Germanicus not in captivity (58.3.8n. [= **A.2**]). This passage is a good illustration that the emperor had the power to confer priesthoods (51.20.3; 53.17.8). The emperor sometimes asked the senate to confirm his appointments (Tac. *A*. 3.19). The appointment of all new priests had to be formally ratified in the popular assembly (Millar, *ERW*, 355–57; Talbert, *Senate*, 345–46). D. fails to make it clear to which priesthoods Sej., Sej.'s son and G. were appointed. He is also ambiguous on the number of priesthoods bestowed. At 58.7.5 he suggests that Sej. (and, therefore, possibly also G.) received two priesthoods at this time. Suet. *G*. 12.1 reports that G. was first appointed augur (to replace his brother Drusus) and then *pontifex*. For a dedication to G. as *pontifex* see EJ 97 = LACTOR 8, no. 18 = Braund 120. For further discussion see Levick, *Tib.* 175; J.P.V.D. Balsdon, *The Emperor Gaius* (1934), 14; Barrett 27 and 260, n. 43. For further reading on priesthoods see Bibliography under 'Religion'.

they bestowed on him proconsular power: During the Republic the senate had granted proconsular power (*imperium proconsulare*) to ex-consuls either immediately on the expiry of their consulships, to enable them to continue in command of an army on campaign, or after an interval of between two and five years, to empower them to govern a province; these grants were then confirmed by the centuriate assembly of the Roman people (*comitia centuriata*) (Polybius 6.15). Under the Principate the senate and people continued to bestow proconsular power upon those ex-consuls and ex-praetors appointed annually by lot to govern the so-called 'public' provinces (see 59.20.7n. [= **B.15**]), which under Tib. consisted of Asia, Africa, Baetica, Gallia Narbonensis, Macedonia, Achaea, Bithynia-Pontus, Cyprus, Crete-Cyrenaica and Sicily (Talbert, *Senate*, 347–53). But more importantly, *imperium proconsulare* was one of the two main powers granted the emperor (together with tribunician power), giving him control over all Roman territory (Syme, *RR*, 313–15, 336–37). It had also been bestowed on Aug.'s leading assistants in power, M. Agrippa in 23 B.C. and Tib. by A.D. 4 (Syme, *RR*, 337–38, 431–32). This grant was significant in that it appeared to mark Sej. out as the most powerful man in Rome after the emperor. It was probably bestowed on Sej. after he had laid down his consulship on 8 May (58.8.3n.), but D. fails to make this clear. The only higher honour for Tib. to have bestowed was tribunician power (58.9.2 + n. [= **A.7**]).

7.5 **Sej.'s fiancée:** i.e., Julia, the daughter of Drusus son of Tib. and Livia Julia (58.3.9 + n. [= **A.2**]; cf. Suet. *T.* 65.1, who implies that the betrothal never took place).

Tib. did not summon Sej.: D. here again implies that those favoured by Tib. resided with him and his family on Capri: cf. 58.3.8 + n. [= **A.2**].

8.1 **Tib. commended Gaius:** Tib. had summoned G. to Capri after his eighteenth birthday on 31 August 30 (Suet. *G.* 10.1; cf. 8.1). By commendation D. means that Tib. wrote a letter to the senate praising G. and entrusting him to its protection: cf. 56.26.2 (Aug. commends Germanicus in 12); Tac. *A.* 3.29; 57.22.4a (Tib. commends G.'s older brothers, Nero in 20, Drusus in 23). Such commendations were based on traditional rituals of patronage, whereby a patron recommended a client to a friend (cf. Cic. *ad Fam.* Book 13). Politically, they marked the entry into public life of an emerging member of the imperial family.

wanted to make him his successor as emperor: It was not the appointment to the priesthoods that marked G. out as Tib.'s likely successor, as D. suggests here, but rather his early election to the quaestorship and Tib.'s promise to advance him to the other magistracies five years early in 33 (58.23.1–4). In 20 Tib. had allowed G.'s brother Nero to be appointed *pontifex* and, more significantly, to hold the quaestorship five years early (Tac. *A.* 3.29), thus marking him out as a possible successor. On G.'s place in the succession see Barrett 37–41.

8.2 **Sej. would have stirred up a rebellion:** On the 'conspiracy' of Sej. see 58.6.4n. [= **A.5**]. Whether the army would have supported a leader of non-senatorial birth is doubtful. D. may mean the Praetorian Guard, but even its support would have questionable, given its swift transfer of allegiance to Macro on Tib.'s order, backed up with a donative (58.9.5 [= **A.7**]). It is also doubtful whether the urban plebs had ever supported Sej. because of his systematic destruction of the family of Germanicus (Z.

Yavetz, *Plebs and Princeps* (1969), 112–13). For Germanicus' popularity
see 57.6.2; 57.18.6–8; Yavetz, *Plebs*, 17–18, 23, 113–18.

8.3   **Sej. regretted that he had not begun a rebellion when he was consul:** This
comment helps to date these events to the period after 8 May, when Sej.
and Tib. laid down their consulship (*ILS* 6124, correcting Suet. *T.* 26.2,
where 15 May is an error probably due to textual corruption).

A.7 THE FALL OF SEJANUS   **A.D. 31**

(58.8.4–12.1)

8.4   **the death of Nero:** Nero Julius Caesar, the eldest son of Germanicus (*PIR²*
J 223; EJ 95, 96 = Braund 117, 118). In 29 he had been denounced by Tib.
in a letter to the senate and banished to the island of Pontia (Tac. *A.* 5.3–4;
Suet. *T.* 54.2). Tib. claimed in his autobiography that Sej. had caused
Nero's death, which he himself had then used as a pretext for destroying
Sej. (Suet. *T.* 61.1). G. at the start of his reign in 37 personally brought his
brother Nero's bones to Rome and deposited them in the Mausoleum of
Aug. (59.3.5 [= **B.3**]). D. (as preserved by Zonaras) dubiously asserts
(57.22.4b) that Nero was put to death along with his mother Agrippina
and brother Drusus on a charge of being pleased with the destruction of
Tib.'s son, Drusus. Sej.'s removal of Nero might suggest that he sensed
that he was in danger, since there would have been little reason to kill
Nero if he had felt secure. This act may also have convinced Tib. of Sej.'s
guilt: see Levick, *Tib.*, 175–6, who also connects this event with G.'s
summons to Capri and his sudden assumption of the toga of manhood
(*toga virilis*), to which he had been entitled since the year 26.
          sacrifices were being offered to Sej.: There was a clear distinction between
sacrificing "to" an individual and sacrificing "on behalf of" an individual.
The former was equivalent to treating him as a god; the latter, therefore,
was more common (e.g. 58.2.8 [= **A.1**]). Claudius also banned sacrifice to
himself (60.5.4), but G. ordered such sacrifices to be offered to him "as to
a god" (59.4.4 [= **B.3**]). For further discussion see Price, *Rituals*, 207–233,
esp. 209–10.
          Tib. refused to allow any measure that proposed honours for himself:
Emperors frequently refused honours in this way: cf. *RG* 4–6, 10 (Aug.);
57.8.1–4; Vell. Pat. 2.122 (Tib.). The ritual of refusal (*recusatio*) of
honours allowed emperors to advertise their position as being the leading
citizen of the state rather than a true monarch (A. Wallace-Hadrill, *JRS*
72 (1982), 36–37).

9.2   **Tib. circulated the rumour that he was going to give Sej. tribunician power:**
cf. Suet. *T.* 65.1. Tribunician power (*tribunicia potestas*) was the only
major honour yet denied Sej. It formed, along with proconsular *imperium*
(58.7.4n. [= **A.6**]), the most important of the emperor's powers. Aug. had
been granted it in 23 B.C. by a law passed in the people's assembly,
confirming a resolution of the senate (53.32.5; *RG* 10.1). Aug. then
developed it to mark out potential successors: it was first bestowed upon

his son-in-law M. Agrippa in 18 B.C. for a five-year term and renewed in 13 B.C. (54.12.4; 54.28.1), and then upon his stepson and adopted son Tib. in 6 B.C., renewed in A.D. 4 and again in 13 (55.9.4; 55.13.2; 56.28.1). During Tib.'s reign Drusus son of Tib. received it in 22 (Tac. *A*. 3.56–57). It was included among the emperor's full titles: e.g. "Imperator Caesar Augustus, son of the deified (Julius Caesar), father of the fatherland, *pontifex maximus*, holding the tribunician power for the 34th time (i.e., in 11)" (EJ 100 = Braund 125 = Sherk 7C). It is thus useful for historians as a mechanism for dating inscriptions. It gave the holder various important powers: e.g. to propose laws (strictly plebiscites) before the assembly, to summon the senate, to veto proposals of other magistrates and to come to the aid of citizens being oppressed by magistrates. The latter power also gave it a symbolic importance, since it allowed the emperor to pose as the protector of the people. See further Syme, *RR*, 336–37; W.K. Lacey, *JRS* 69 (1979), 28–34.

Naevius Sertorius Macro: *PIR*² N 10. His full name was in fact Q. Naevius Cordus Sutorius Macro (EJ 370 = Smallwood 254 = Braund 458). He was, like Sej., a member of the equestrian order.

Tib. had secretly appointed Macro to command the bodyguard: cf. 58.9.5. By the bodyguard D. here means the Praetorian Guard (on which see 58.4.2n. [= **A.3**]). He had hitherto held the position of prefect of the Night-Watch (*praefectus vigilum*) (see EJ 370 = Smallwood 254 = Braund 458). For his later career see 59.10.6–7 + n. [= **B.8**].

9.3 **Macro entered Rome by night:** On the night of 17 October (Levick, *Tib.*, 177).

Memmius Regulus: P. Memmius Regulus (*PIR*² M 342; cf. EJ 217 = LACTOR 8, no. 14). For his devotion to Tib. see 58.13.3. In 35 Tib. appointed him governor of Upper and Lower Moesia and Macedonia (58.25.5). See further Syme, *AA*, 176–77.

his consular colleague: L. Fulcinius Trio (*PIR*² F 349), a friend of Sej., who was indicted to stand trial in 35 and promptly committed suicide (58.25.2–3; Tac. *A*. 6.38).

Graecinius Laco, prefect of the Night-Watch: P. Graecinius Laco (*PIR*² G 202) succeeded Macro as prefect of the Night-Watch (see EJ 223 = Braund 436). Under Claudius he became procurator in Gaul (60.23.3 [= **C.11**]) and was eventually granted consular decorations (*ornamenta consularia*; i.e., the privileges of an ex-consul) (EJ 222 = Braund 435). The Night-Watch (*vigiles*) was created by Aug. in 6 and consisted of 7000 freedmen, organized into seven cohorts, under the command of an equestrian prefect (55.26.4–5; Suet. *Aug*. 30.1). Each cohort was assigned to two of the fourteen regions of the city of Rome and their main duty was to patrol the streets at night and deal with fires, also burglaries and other crimes (P.K. Baillie-Reynolds, *The Vigiles of Imperial Rome* (1926); J. Rainbird, *PBSR* 41 (1986), 147–69).

9.4 **the session of the senate was to be held in the temple of Apollo:** The senate met in a variety of places, not just in the senate-house (*curia*) in the Forum. The temple of Apollo on the Palatine, adjacent to the house of

Aug., had become a popular meeting-place towards the end of Aug.'s reign (Talbert, *Senate*, 113–20).

9.5 **Macro sent the praetorians who were guarding Sej. and the senate back to their camp:** D. provides an interesting detail here that detachments of the Praetorian Guard guarded the senate, as well as the emperor (Talbert, *Senate*, 159). Their camp was located on the Viminal (E. Nash, *Pictorial Dictionary of Ancient Rome* (1968), I, 221–24; Coarelli, *Guida arch. di Roma*, 228–29). Macro may have been suspicious of the loyalty of the praetorians, whom Sej. had commanded since 14 (58.4.2n. [= **A.3**]), and so preferred to rely on the Night-Watch, which had until very recently been under his own command (58.9.2n.).

Tib. promises rewards for the praetorians: After the fall of Sej. they were granted a donative of 1000 *denarii* (Suet. *T.* 48.2). Donatives came to be increasingly used by the emperor to cement the loyalty of both the regular troops and the praetorians (J.B. Campbell, *The Emperor and the Roman Army* (1984), 186–90). On the praetorians' previous devotion to Sej. see 58.8.2 [= **A.6**]; Jos. *AJ* 18.181.

9.6 **stationing the Night-Watch around the temple to replace the praetorians:** The Night-Watch were called on to perform military functions only in emergencies (cf. Tac. *H.* 3.64).

10.1 **the letter was read out:** For this famous "long and verbose" letter cf. Suet. *T.* 65.1; Juv. *Sat.* 10.71.

two senators who were among his closest friends had to be punished: The identity of these two senators is unclear, but for some speculations see Levick, *Tib.*, 177.

10.2 **Tib. summoned one of the consuls to him:** i.e., the loyal consul, Memmius Regulus (58.13.3).

10.3 **making it clear that they would agree to this grant:** This is a good illustration that the senate formally granted tribunician power on the instructions of the emperor; it was then confirmed by a vote of the plebeian assembly (*concilium plebis*): see 58.9.2n.

10.5 **praetors and tribunes:** Praetors possessed *imperium* and so had the power to take whatever action was necessary against Sej., while tribunes of the plebs had the right to coerce fellow citizens. In 100 B.C. the consuls C. Marius and L. Valerius had similarly called on the praetors and the tribunes to help them put down the insurrection of Saturninus and Glaucia (Cic. *pro Rabirio* 7.20).

10.6 **Laco came back in and stood right alongside him:** Laco, prefect of the Night-Watch (58.9.3n.), was of equestrian rank and so was not entitled to attend meetings of the senate. It seems from D.'s language that he had been waiting outside the temple during the session. For further examples and discussion of when and why non-senators (especially those with military functions) could enter meetings of the senate see Talbert, *Senate*, 159–61.

10.8 **Regulus did not call for a general vote or ask any individual senator to bring up the question of the death penalty:** D. here provides a good illustration of the procedure at meetings of the senate. The senior consul presided and summoned members to speak in a strict order of seniority; he alone was empowered to put an issue to the vote: see Talbert, *Senate*, ch. 7. This section also shows that the magistrates were responsible for carrying out the resolutions of the senate.

the prison: For its location see 58.5.6 + n. [= **A.4**]. The Romans did not use imprisonment as a judicial penalty, but just as a means of keeping watch over those awaiting sentence or punishment (Garnsey, *SSLP*, 147–52).

11.1–3 D.'s rhetoric is full-blown here with its series of emphatic antitheses. Compare his rhetorical treatment of the deaths of G. (59.30.1a [= **B.23**]), Nero (63.28.1–29.2 [= **D.8**]) or Macrinus (78.40.4–5). D. uses the rise and fall of Sej. to make a moral point on the instability of human affairs, as does Juv. *Sat.* 10. 56–107. D. uses very similar language to comment on the fall of Macrinus, who had been the first prefect of the Praetorian Guard to be appointed emperor (78.41.1–4).

11.2 runaway slave: In a large slave-owning society such as Rome runaway slaves were a constant problem. Slave collars have been found with messages to assist masters to recover such runaways: e.g. "Seize me, so that I don't get away, and summon me back to my master Pascasius at the Porphyry Portico in the Forum of Trajan!" (*ILS* 8729). See further K.R. Bradley, *Slaves and Masters in the Roman Empire* (1984), 113–37.

purple-bordered toga: This type of toga (the *toga praetexta*) was worn by curule magistrates (consuls, praetors and curule aediles) during their term of office and thereafter on special ceremonial occasions and by priests when conducting sacred rituals (L.M. Wilson, *The Roman Toga* (1924), 51–56). It was also the type of toga usually worn by emperors in public, although on special occasions they might wear triumphal dress (cf. 59.7.1 + n. [= **B.5**]; 60.6.9 + n. [= **C.5**]).

11.3 the people destroyed all images of Sej.: The people similarly tore down the statues of the emperor G. and of Agrippina wife of Nero after their deaths (59.30.1a [= **B.23**]; 61.16.2a). D. is careful here to distinguish between the three types of images: the people hurled down portrait busts of Sej., cut down images of him painted on wooden plaques and dragged down statues of him. On images see 58.4.4 [= **A.3**]. This popular reaction against Sej. foreshadowed the formal vote by the senate that all public record of him should be obliterated (Levick, *Tib.* 202). Inscriptions and coins survive with Sej.'s name erased (e.g. *ILS* 6124, *Corpus Nummorum Romanorum* X (1976), 8–9, figs. 364.4 and 364.5). However, some traces of his name remained (EJ 358a = Braund 671).

11.4 temple of Concord: At the far west end of the Forum, just below the Tabularium (Nash I, 292–94). It had been restored by Tib. and re-dedicated in 10 (55.8.2; 56.25.1). It housed many works of Greek art (see Plin. *NH* 33.73, 77, 80, 89, 90; 35.66, 131, 144). Meetings of the senate did not regularly take place here; rather, it had special practical and symbolic importance on this particular occasion: practical in that it was located right next to the prison, symbolic in that it was here that the debate on the conspiracy of Catiline had taken place in 63 B.C. (Sall. *Cat.* 49; Talbert, *Senate* 118–19).

11.5–7 Sej.'s death and the destruction of his family: cf. Tac. *A.* 5.9. More precise details are provided by the Fasti from Ostia (EJ p. 42 = Braund 98 = Sherk 28f): Sej. was strangled on 18 October (by the public executioner inside the prison); his elder son, Strabo, was strangled on 24 October; his wife, Apicata, committed suicide on 26 October; and his two younger children, Capito Aelianus and Junilla, were killed sometime in December and had their bodies left out on the Gemonian Steps to be abused by the people (G.V. Sumner, *Phoenix* 19 (1965), 134–45). These dates corroborate Tac. *A*. 5.9, but call into question part of D.'s account. Apicata clearly committed suicide before the death of her two younger children and so the maltreatment of their bodies on the Gemonian Steps cannot have triggered her suicide, as D. claims. This is, therefore, an example of D. perverting the sequence of events to suit his dramatic purposes. Public thanksgivings were held in Italy and the provinces to celebrate the destruction of Sej. (EJ 51 = LACTOR 8, no. 15 = Braund 99 = Sherk 40c; EJ 52 = Braund 100 = Sherk 40b). In 33 the senate passed a resolution to mark the day of Sej.'s death (18 October) with public sacrifices (Tac. *A*. 6.25). On the aftermath of Sej.'s death see Seager 220–23; Levick, *Tib*. 178–79, 201–07.

11.5 **his body was hurled down the Steps, and the mob abused for three days and then thrown into the Tiber:** D. here refers to the Gemonian Steps, which ran down from the Arx (or Citadel, one of the two peaks of the Capitoline Hill) between the prison and the temple of Concord. The executioner used a large hook to drag the bodies of executed criminals from the prison to the steps and thence to the Tiber (60.35.4; Suet. *T*. 61.4). For other examples of bodies being thrown down these Steps for public molestation see 58.1.3; 60.16.1 [= **C.8**]; 65.21.2. Tib. took credit for not having exposed the elder Agrippina's dead body here in 33 (Tac. *A*. 6.25; Suet. *T*. 53.2), which the Roman people threatened to do to Tib. after his death (Suet. *T*. 75.1). Hurling the bodies of executed criminals into the Tiber not only brought further dishonour, but also deprived them of correct burial. The best recent work on Roman public execution is in French (J.-M. David in *Du châtiment dans la cité* (1984), 132–75; F. Hinard in *L'Urbs. Espaçe urbain et histoire* (1987), 111–25).

his daughter who had been engaged to Claudius' son: Sej.'s daughter Aelia Junilla (*PIR*² A 297) had been betrothed in 20 to Claudius Drusus (*PIR*² C 856), son of the future emperor and Plautia Urganilla (Tac. *A*. 3.29). Suet. *Cl*. 27.1 claims that Drusus died very soon after the engagement.

raped by the public executioner: cf. Tac. *A*. 5.9. Roman tradition forbade the strangling of virgins; it would have brought ritual pollution upon the state (Suet. *T*. 61.5). The public executioner, a state-owned slave, was considered a polluted person and so forced to live outside the *pomerium* (sacred boundary) of the city of Rome (Cic. *pro Rabirio* 4.11).

11.6 **the death of Drusus:** Nero Claudius Drusus, the son of Tib. (*PIR*² J 219). He had died in 23, allegedly by poison administered by a eunuch acting on the orders of Sej. and Drusus' wife Livilla (57.22.1–4; Tac. *A*. 4.3). For Sej.'s supposed use of wives to destroy or incriminate their husbands cf. 58.3.8 + n. [= **A.2**].

Livilla: More correctly Livia Julia (*PIR*² L 303), daughter of Tib.'s brother, Nero Claudius Drusus, and hence a sister of Germanicus and the future emperor Claudius. Before her marriage to Drusus, she had been married in 1 B.C. to Gaius Caesar, son of Agrippa and Aug.'s daughter Julia (55.10.18). For her passion for Sej. see 57.22.2; Tac. *A.* 4.3. The truth about Drusus' death was difficult to disentangle from the rumours, which abounded even in Tacitus' day, the early second century A.D. (Tac. *A.* 4.10–11). It would have been even more difficult for D., writing a century later.

11.7 Tib. had Livilla and all the others put to death: D. implies that Tib. tried and condemned Livilla in private (Levick, *Tib.*, 200). For such private trials "inside the bedroom" (*intra cubiculum*) of the emperor see Millar, *ERW*, 516–27; Crook, *CP*, 106.

the note: D. here uses the Greek word for a *libellus*, i.e., a note or petition written on two wax-tablets strung together. *Libelli* were commonly used to pass on information on conspiracies (cf. Plin. *Letters* 7.27; Millar, *ERW*, 240–42).

I have now heard that he pardoned Livilla: This brief section is revealing of D.'s historiographical techniques. First, it suggests that in addition to his written sources, he sometimes derived material from stories still circulating orally about the various emperors. Secondly, it shows that he occasionally included a variant account of a particular event, sometimes (as here) without deciding between the two versions. For further discussion see Introduction, Sections 3.2.1 and 3.3.

Antonia: i.e., the younger daughter of the triumvir M. Antonius, the widow of Tib.'s brother, Nero Claudius Drusus, and the mother of Germanicus, the future emperor Claudius and Livilla (*PIR*[2] A 885; Syme, *AA*, 141, 169; N. Kokkinos, *Antonia Augusta* (forthcoming)). As D. here suggests, she was a very influential figure at the end of Tib.'s reign. For discussion whether she played a rôle in Sej.'s downfall see J. Nicols, *Historia* 24 (1975) 48–58. For the honours granted her by G. at the start of his reign see 59.3.3–4 [= **B.3**].

12.1 this happened later: D. had a penchant for describing events out of strict chronological sequence (Introduction, Section 3.3). Livilla's death is not reported in the surviving parts of Tac. *Annals* and so probably took place late in 31, but before the deaths of Sej.'s younger children in December, since the manuscripts of Tac. resume with the senatorial reaction to her death and then describe the execution of Sej.'s younger children (Tac. *A.* 5.6–9).

B. THE REIGN OF GAIUS (CALIGULA): A.D. 37 – 41

* * * * *

B.1 TIBERIUS' WILL IS SET ASIDE AND GAIUS MADE EMPEROR
A.D. 37
(59.1.1–5)

1.1 **Gaius' names and titles:** G.'s full name was Gaius Caesar Augustus
Germanicus (Smallwood 81 = Braund 175; Smallwood 84, 124, 125 =
Braund 178–80; Smallwood 85, 86 = Braund 187–8); for his nickname
Caligula see 57.5.6; Suet. *G*. 9.
Tib. had bequeathed his position as emperor also to his grandson Tiberius:
Tib.'s grandson was Tiberius Julius Caesar (*PIR*² I 226), the twin son of
Tib.'s son Drusus Caesar and Livia Julia; hence he was known as Tiberius
Gemellus (i.e., 'the twin') (Jos. *AJ* 18.206). He was born during the winter
of 19–20 (Tac. *A*. 2.84). His twin brother, Tiberius Julius Germanicus, had
died in 23 (Tac. *A*. 4.15). For a public dedication to Gemellus from the
reign of Tib. see Braund 184.

Two possibilities exist over D.'s meaning here: "Tib. had *in fact*
bequeathed his position as emperor to his grandson" or "Tib. had
bequeathed his position as emperor *also* to his grandson". The former
would imply that G. had been excluded from the succession and seized
power by challenging Tib.'s will, which would fit with the tradition that
Tib. favoured his own blood-relative Gemellus (Suet. *G*. 19.3). The latter
meaning would suggest that Tib. favoured a joint succession of his
grandson Gemellus and his grandnephew G. (cf. 59.10.6n. [= **B.8**]). Both
are represented on coins of Tib.'s last years (*RIC*, I, 107, no. 28). Tac.'s
view (*A*. 6.46) was that Tib. was uncertain and so preferred to leave the
decision to fate. If Tac. is correct, Tib.'s ambivalence on this matter would
help to explain the uncertainty of the sources. However, G.'s seniority in
age and his popularity with the army and urban plebs as the son of
Germanicus made him a far more likely candidate to succeed Tib. For
further discussion see Levick, *Tib.*, 205–10; Seager 243–44; Barrett 38–40.

D. is being anachronistic in suggesting that emperors could bequeath
their political position as emperor; each new emperor had to be granted
his formal powers by a resolution of the senate, confirmed by a law passed
in the assembly of the Roman people (P.A. Brunt, *JRS* 67 (1977), 95–116).
All an emperor could bequeath by will was his household property, wealth
and slaves. Whoever inherited this was in the most influential position to
be appointed emperor. D. may have been led astray by the practice of his
own period whereby the emperor had his chosen heir appointed joint-
emperor in the latter years of his reign: see Appendix 1; F. Millar, *The*

Roman Empire and its Neighbours (2nd ed., 1981), 33–36; T.E.J. Wiedemann, *The Julio-Claudian Emperors* (1989), 3–8.

1.2–2.3 D. is very cavalier with the exact sequence of events in this opening
section, as a comparison with the Ostian Fasti (Smallwood 31 = Braund
174) reveals. D., as elsewhere, looks ahead to later events (e.g. the death of
Gemellus, on which see 59.8.1 [= **B.6**]) out of chronological sequence: see
further Introduction, Section 3.3. The important events (taken from the
Ostian Fasti unless stated otherwise) took place as follows:

16 March	death of Tib. at Misenum
18 March	G. acclaimed *Imperator* by the army at Mis-enum and by the senate (i.e., his *dies imperii*) (*Acts of the Arval Brethren*)
28–29 March	Tib.'s body reached Rome, escorted by G. and soldiers
30 March	meeting of the senate: Tib.'s will was set aside, but his legacies confirmed (59.1.2–4)
3 April	public funeral of Tib.
21 April (?)	senate formally conferred powers on G. (59.3.1–2)
1 May	death of Antonia
1 June	largesse to people (*congiarium*) of bequests made in Tib.'s will
19 July	second largesse, to make up for the fact that no largesse had taken place when G. had assumed the toga of manhood.

For fuller discussion see Balsdon, *Gaius*, 25–34, Barrett 50–60. It is
instructive to compare the sequence of events on the death of Claudius
[hereafter = Cl.] (Tac. *A.* 12.69).

1.2   **G. sent Macro to the senate with Tib.'s will:** On Macro see further 58.9.2n.
[= **A.7**]. As Praetorian prefect, he had cultivated G.'s favour at the end of
Tib.'s reign (Tac. *A.* 6.45) and was crucial in establishing G.'s position on
Tib.'s death. It was rumoured that he and G. had suffocated Tib. to death
(58.28.3; Tac. *A.* 6.50; Suet. *G.* 12.2–3). He arranged G.'s acclamation by
the troops at Misenum and then set off for Rome. For the occasions on
which a non-senator could enter meetings of the senate see Talbert,
Senate, 159–61.

**Macro had Tib.'s will declared null and void on the grounds that Tib. was
insane:** On Tib.'s will see Philo, *Embassy* 26–28. Aug.'s will had been read
aloud in the senate in 14 (56.3 2; Suet. *Aug.* 101, with direct quotations).
Emperors made private wills in which they bequeathed their private
property; they could not bequeath public funds. However, the precise
relationship between the emperor's private wealth and the public funds
became ever more blurred over time, and is a matter of considerable
scholarly controversy: see F. Millar, *JRS* 53 (1963), 29–42; *ERW*, 189–
201; cf. P.A. Brunt, *JRS* 56 (1966), 75–91 [= *RIT*, 134–62]. Table V of the
Twelve Tables (Rome's earliest code of law, dating to c. 450 B.C.) laid it
down that if a man went insane, he lost all his authority over his property
(LR I, 32); any will that he made was, therefore, invalid.

a mere boy: Gemellus was 17 (59.1.1n.), but unusually had not yet assumed the toga of manhood (*toga virilis*) (Tac. *A*. 6.46; Philo, *Embassy*, 23, 30–31). The sneer is thus legally correct, but more a vestige of rhetoric of those who supported G. Since Gemellus was not strictly an adult, he could not be granted the imperial power.

1.3   G. in spite of having adopted him, put him to death: cf. 59.8.1 + nn. [= **B.6**].

1.4   Tib.'s conduct regarding Livia's will: Livia had died in 29, but Tib. had refused to carry out any of the terms of her will (58.2.3a; Tac. *A*. 5.1; Suet. *T*. 51.2). For G.'s payment of her bequests see 59.2.4 [= **B.2**]. For Livia's importance see N. Purcell, *PCPhS* 32 (1986), 78–105.

Tib.'s bequests were paid to all beneficiaries except his grandson: D. here provides a good illustration that a Roman will was made up of various sections. It listed first the heir(s) to the property of the deceased, then the legacies to be paid to beneficiaries and finally instructions on such matters as manumission of slaves, funeral arrangements etc. (cf. Suet. *Aug*. 101; J.A. Crook, *Law and Life of Rome* (1967), 119–32).

B.2 GAIUS' EARLY EXTRAVAGANCE   A.D. 37

(59.2.1–6)

2.1   distribution to the Praetorian Guard: G. hereby acknowledged the important rôle that the Praetorian Guard under their prefect Macro had played in his accession. A new coin issue was struck for this distribution with the legend 'address to the praetorian cohorts' (*adlocutio cohortium*) (Smallwood 276 = Braund 512 = Barrett pl. 17; C.H.V. Sutherland, *Roman History and Coinage, 44 B.C.–A.D. 69* (1987), 69–70). On the Praetorian Guard see 58.4.2n. [= **A.3**].

2.2   bequest paid to the people: The Ostian Fasti (Smallwood 31 = Braund 174) show that a distribution to the people of 75 *denarii* (= 300 sesterces) per head took place on 1 June, followed by a second of the same amount on 19 July (59.1.2–2.3n. [= **B.1**]). D. clearly puts this largesse too early in his account of the reign. In his will Aug. left ten million *denarii* to the people (56.32.2). In general on G.'s relations with the people see Yavetz, *Plebs*, 113–18.

when G. assumed the toga of manhood: D. always uses the Greek equivalent "enrolled among the ephebes" to express this key Roman rite of passage (cf. 55.9.9; 55.22.4; 56.29.5; 57.18.11; 59.8.1 [= **B.6**]; 60.34.1), an interesting example of his Greek cultural mindset. G. had assumed the *toga virilis* in 31 at the late age of 19 soon after he was summoned by Tib. to Capri (Suet. *G*. 10.1), an event not mentioned in the surviving part of D.'s text. The *toga virilis* was a pure white toga, which a Roman boy normally assumed between the ages of 14 and 16, having set aside his *toga praetexta* (a white toga with a purple stripe around the edge). The assumption of the *toga virilis*, which involved a ceremony around the hearth in the family home and then a procession down into the Forum, symbolically marked a male's entry into adulthood and allowed him to take part in public life (B.

Rawson in *The Family in Ancient Rome* (ed. B. Rawson, 1986), 40–41). D.
here provides good evidence that such key rites of passage (birth, coming-
of-age, marriage, death) in the lives of members of the imperial family
were usually marked by distributions of money (*congiaria*) to the Roman
people, a good way for the emperor to maintain their favour.

2.3 **bequests to the army:** Tib. left exactly the same bequests to the various
types of soldiers as Aug. had done in his will (56.32.2). D. here provides a
neat summary of the different categories of Roman troops under the
Principate (cf. 55.23.2–24.8). The Urban Cohorts had been created by
Aug. to keep order in the city of Rome (55.24.6; T.J. Cadoux, *JRS* 49
(1959), 152–60). For the Night-Watch see 58.9.3n. [= **A.7**]. D. here uses
the same expression for the regular legions (literally "those from the list",
i.e., the list of recruits levied, translating the Latin phrase *ex formula*) as at
52.33.2. For the use of soldiers in smaller garrisons away from the
legionary camps see R.W. Davies, *Service in the Roman Army* (1989), 33–
70, esp. 33–35, 54–66.

2.4 **Livia's will:** Tib. had refused to carry out the terms of his mother's will
(59.1.4n. [= **B.1**]). For Livia's legacies, which were substantial, see Barrett
225. Whether D. is right in assuming that G. was suspicious of the army
and the people is doubtful, given his enormous popularity as the son of the
popular Germanicus (58.8.2 + n. [= **A.6**]).

2.5 **he lavished huge sums on actors, horses and gladiators:** Tib. had banished
actors from the city of Rome in 23 (57.21.3); a senatorial decree in 19 had
attempted to prevent members of senatorial and equestrian families
performing on the stage or in the gladiatorial arena (B. Levick, *JRS* 73
(1983), 97–115 = Sherk 35). G. was hereby distancing himself from the
abstinent, and unpopular, policies of Tib. For G.'s love of chariot-racing
and gladiatorial shows see further 59.5.2 [= **B.3**]; 59.14.1–6 + nn. [=
B.11].

2.5–6 **resources in the treasury:** There is some discrepancy between the sources
about (a) the precise amount of resources in the treasury at the start of
G.'s reign and (b) the time it took for G. to exhaust them. Suet. *G.* 37.3
claims that G. began with 2,700,000 *denarii* (= 675,000,000 sesterces)
and squandered it in less than a year (i.e., by 38). However, Jos. *AJ*
18.256 supports D.'s date of 39. Caution is needed in trusting these
figures since numerals are always prone to errors in the copying of
ancient manuscripts. D. implies here that funds were still kept in
the public treasury (*aerarium Saturni*), but already under G. the
distinction between public funds of the state and the private funds
of the emperor was growing ever more blurred (Millar, *ERW*, 189–201;
P.A. Brunt, *JRS* 56 (1966), 75–91 [= *RIT*, 134–62]). For finances
under Tib. and G. see Levick, *Tib.*, 100–02, 133; Barrett 224–29.
D. fully recognized that army pay and the provision of bounties for
discharged veterans often caused financial problems in the early Principate (cf. 52.6.1). For an estimate of the annual cost of maintaining
Rome's standing army (between 400 million and 500 million sesterces) see
K. Hopkins, *JRS* 70 (1980), 124–25; cf. Campbell, *Emperor & Army*,
161–98.

B.3 GAIUS' CONDUCT AS EMPEROR   **A.D. 37**

(59.3.1–5.5)

3.1–2 G.'s accession: cf. Suet. *G.* 14.1; Barrett 50–63. G.'s accession set the precedent for later procedure. The senate first passed a resolution granting the emperor proconsular *imperium* and tribunician power, which were then confirmed by laws passed in the citizens' assembly (*comitia tributa*): cf. 60.1.4 [= **C.1**]; 60.3.2 [= **C.3**] (for Cl.'s accession); Tac. *A.* 12.69 (for Nero's). In general on emperors' accessions see P.A. Brunt, *JRS* 67 (1977), 95–116. B. Levick in *Roman Political Life* (ed. T.P. Wiseman, 1985), 62–63 ignores this passage when she argues that Cl. was the first emperor to be granted all powers together. D. fails to make explicit here the fact that G. was only a private citizen when he became emperor (unlike Aug. or Tib.) and therefore needed to be granted *imperium*.
G.'s refusal of honours: cf. 58.9.1n. [= **A.7**].

3.2 **the title 'Father of the Fatherland':** i.e., *pater patriae*. Aug. only accepted this title in 2 B.C. (*RG* 35), while Tib. constantly refused it (58.12.8). A fragment of the *Acts of the Arval Brethren* (*AE* 1983, 95, lines 55–63) shows that G. accepted this title "with the approval of the senate" on 21 September 37. The title appears on coins of 37–38 (Smallwood 81 = Braund 175, with Sutherland, *RHC*, 71–72).

3.3 **G.'s sexual relationships with women:** D. first alludes to G.'s abduction of Cornelia Orestilla from C. Calpurnius Piso allegedly on their wedding day (59.8.7; Suet. *G.* 25.1, where she is called Livia Orestilla). The story is no doubt exaggerated (Balsdon, *Gaius*, 40). Piso was co-opted as an Arval Brother on 24 May 37, possibly as compensation for surrendering his wife to G. (so Barrett 77). Later in 37 G. divorced and exiled her on a charge of adultery with Piso (59.8.7–8).
came to hate them all except one: The 'one woman whom G. loved' was Milonia Caesonia, his fourth wife, on whom see Balsdon, *Gaius*, 48; Barrett 95–96 and fig. 31 (coin portrait). In all G. was married four times: (i) to Junia Claudilla (from 35 to 36, died in childbirth), (ii) to Cornelia (or Livia) Orestilla (37, divorced), (iii) to Lollia Paulina (from 38 to 39, divorced) and (iv) to Milonia Caesonia (from 39 until G.'s death in 41; she was put to death shortly after G.: Jos. *AJ* 19.190–200).
G.'s mother: Vipsania Agrippina (Agrippina the Elder), the younger daughter of M. Agrippa and Julia, and wife of Germanicus (*PIR*[1] V 463). She had been exiled in 29 to Pandateria (Suet. *T.* 53.2; Tac. *A.* 5.3–5), where she died on 18 October 33 (Tac. *A.* 6.25). See further 59.3.5n. [= **B.3**].
G.'s sisters: Julia Agrippina (Agrippina the Younger), the mother of Nero and fourth wife of Cl. (*PIR*[2] J 641), Julia Drusilla (*PIR*[2] J 664) and Julia Livilla (*PIR*[2] J 674). They appeared on coins of 37 personified as Security, Concord and Fortune respectively (Smallwood 86 = Braund 188 = Barrett fig. 15, with Sutherland, *RHC*, 72–74).
G.'s grandmother Antonia: See 58.11.7n. [= **A.7**]. The Ostian Fasti reveal that she died on 1 May 37 (Smallwood 31 = Braund 174) at the age of

seventy-three. For the unlikely claim that G. had her poisoned see Suet. *G.* 23.2.

3.4 **honours for Antonia:** cf. Suet. *G.* 15.2; the honours are confirmed on coins of the reign (Smallwood 96 = Braund 206). The title 'Augusta' had previously only been granted to Livia – by the senate carrying out the terms of Aug.'s will (Tac. *A.* 1.8; Suet. *Aug.* 101; cf. 56.46.1). Livia had also been appointed priestess of the deified Aug. by the senate in 14 (56.46.1). The cult of the deified Aug. was supervised by the priestly college known as the *sodales Augustales* (59.7.4n. [= **B.5**]). The privileges of Vestal Virgins included the right to drive through Rome in a two-wheeled carriage known as a *carpentum*, to sit in special seats at the front of the theatre and to be escorted by lictors (ceremonial attendants who escorted curule magistrates and priests). In 23 Livia had been granted the privilege of sitting with the Vestal Virgins at the theatre (Tac. *A.* 4.16). Cl. granted similar rights to his wife Messallina in 44 (60.22.2 + n. [= **C.11**]). On the Vestal Virgins see further J.P.V.D. Balsdon, *Roman Women*, (1962), 235–43; J.F. Gardner, *Women in Roman Law and Society* (1986), 22–26; M. Beard, *JRS* 70 (1980), 12–27.

honours for his sisters: Aug. had allowed his wife, Livia, and his children to sit in the imperial seats at the circus and his family to be included in official prayers (Suet. *Aug.* 45.1; 58.2). All these measures served to enhance the visibility and prestige of G.'s immediate family, an important concern for each new emperor on his accession. D. fails to mention here the honours paid to his dead father Germanicus (59.3.8n. [= **B.3**]). See further Barrett 62–63.

prayers for his welfare and oaths of allegiance: For the inclusion of G.'s sisters in oaths see 59.9.2; Suet. *G.* 15.3. For the various oaths and prayers in favour of the emperor see 58.2.7–8n. [= **A.1**]. G. was the first emperor to have an oath of allegiance sworn every year throughout the Empire (cf. Smallwood 32 = Braund 562 = Sherk 41; Smallwood 33 = Braund 563).

3.5 **brought back the bones of his dead mother and brothers:** His mother, Agrippina, had died on Pandateria on 18 October 33 (Tac. *A.* 6.25), his brother Nero on Pontia in 31 (58.8.4 [= **A.7**]; Suet. *T.* 54.2). D. is slightly inaccurate here, since his other brother Drusus had died at Rome in 33 (58.22.4–5; Tac. *A.* 6.23; Suet. *T.* 54.2). The urns which contained Agrippina's and Nero's ashes still survive (Smallwood 84a, 85 = Braund 178, 187). Coins were issued honouring the memory of Agrippina (Smallwood 84b = Braund 178 = Barrett fig. 19) and of Nero and Drusus, who were depicted on horseback, possibly as "leaders of the youth" (*principes iuventutis*) (Smallwood 85b = Braund 187b = Barrett fig. 20). G.'s ceremonial return to Rome with the ashes of his deceased mother and brothers consciously echoed the famous return of Agrippina from Syria to Rome in the winter of 19–20 with the urn containing Germanicus' ashes. This urn was also deposited in the Mausoleum of Aug. (Tac. *A.* 3.1–5). G.'s mother and brothers were restored to a position of honour throughout the Empire; in a dedication from Mytilene (Asia Minor) they were all associated with Drusilla, the 'new Aphrodite' (Smallwood 128b = Braund 190b).

wearing a purple-bordered toga: i.e., the *toga praetexta*, on which see 58.11.2n. [= **A.7**].

attended by lictors, as if at a triumph: Lictors were the ceremonial attendants of magistrates with *imperium* (consuls and praetors). They carried bundles of rods and axes (*fasces*), symbolic of the magistrate's power, and cleared the way for him when he appeared in public. Emperors were also granted the use of twelve lictors (Millar, *ERW*, 66–68). They took part in triumphal processions with their *fasces* adorned with laurel (Versnel, *Triumphus*, 95). However, they also took part in the funerary processions of the Roman élite, but carried only their rods, not their axes, as a sign of mourning (Versnel 99–100, 126). D.'s comparison of this parade with a triumph is, therefore, unwarranted; it took the standard form of a funeral procession. For further similarities between triumphal and funerary processions see Versnel 98–101, 115–31.

had them laid to rest in the Mausoleum of Augustus: Located in the Campus Martius, it was the largest Roman tomb yet built (R.A. Cordingley and I.A. Richmond, *PBSR* 10 (1927), 23–35; more briefly, Nash, II, 38–43; P. Zanker, *The Power of Images in the Age of Augustus* (1988), 72–77). Urns containing the ashes of various members of the imperial family had been deposited here since 23 B.C., some of which survive (Braund 27, 121; Smallwood 84a, 85a, 87, 88 = Braund 178a, 187a, 191, 185). For the complex, astrologically planned symbolism of the part of the Campus Martius which comprised the Mausoleum, the Altar of Peace (*Ara Pacis*) and Aug.'s sundial see N. Horsfall, *Omnibus* 9 (1985), 5–7; A. Wallace-Hadrill, *JRS* 75 (1985), 246–47.

3.6 **those sent into exile because of some connexion with them:** i.e., those who had been charged with treason (*maiestas*) under Tib. for taking part in the supposed conspiracy of Agrippina in 27–29. For the problems in reconstructing this supposed conspiracy see R.S. Rogers, *TAPA* 62 (1931), 141–168; Seager 209–11; Levick, *Tib.*, 169–70; Barrett 21–24. This action of G. has been seen as part of a supposed general abolition of all charges of treason at the start of his reign, but see 59.4.3n. [= **B.4**].

Antonia's suicide: cf. Suet. *G.* 23.2. It is doubtful that G. forced Antonia to commit suicide. She died on 1 May, too soon for G.'s 'bad' period to have started; and her birthday was still celebrated by the Arval Brethren on 31 January 38 (Smallwood 3), which it scarcely would have been, had she already died in disgrace. This is an example of how the hostile senatorial tradition, which D. followed, sought to blacken G.'s reputation as much as possible.

the exile and death of G.'s sisters: D. again has a 'flash-forward' to events of mid-38. For the death of Drusilla see 59.11 [= **B.9**]; for G.'s incestuous relations with, and banishment of, Agrippina and Julia see 59.22.8 [= **B.17**]; Suet. *G.* 24.3.

3.7 **honours for Tib., his 'grandfather':** Tib. had adopted G.'s father, Germanicus, in 4 (55.13.2) and so the title 'grandfather' was technically correct. By stressing his family connection with, and respect for, Tib., G. enhanced his legitimacy to rule. For further discussion see Barrett 59–60, 68. For the honours paid Aug. on his death (notably deification) see 56.46. The provinces were clearly expecting Tib. to be granted the same honours as Aug., including deification: Lugdunum in Gaul had already minted coins depicting Tib. deified (Smallwood 124 = Braund 179 with Sutherland, *RHC*, 66–68).

public funeral: For Tib.'s funeral see Suet. *G.* 15.1; Jos. *AJ* 18.236. D. unfairly makes the funeral seem hastily arranged. In general on imperial funerals see S. Price in *Rituals of Royalty* (ed. D. Cannadine and S. Price, 1987), 56–105. D. is also wrong to reverse the order of events given by Suet. *G.* 14–15, who rightly puts the senatorial debate concerning honours for Tib. after his public funeral (Balsdon, *Gaius*, 28); for further problems over D.'s chronology see 59.1.2–2.3n. [= **B.1**].

3.8 **reminded the people of Aug. and Germanicus:** For G.'s initial desire to identify himself with Aug. see 59.6.1n. [= **B.4**]; Introduction, Section 4.3. D. also alludes here to the way in which G. played on the memory of his father Germanicus to enhance his popular support. Coins commemorating Germanicus were issued in 37–38 (Smallwood 83 = Braund 177; Barrett figs. 12 and 23), Germanicus' birthday (24 May) was celebrated with sacrifices by the Arval Brethren (Smallwood 3, lines 29–31; Smallwood 10, lines 1–7) and the month of September was renamed 'Germanicus' (Barrett 61).

4.1–6 In this chapter D. lays out in a long series of antitheses one of the main themes of his treatment of G., his extraordinary capriciousness as ruler. He was an emperor of extreme contradictions, and as such caused great problems for those who had to deal with him: his immediate entourage, the senatorial order and even the people (Introduction, Section 4.3). Much of the subject matter mentioned in this chapter is developed at 59.6 [= **B.4**].

4.1 **licentiousness and bloodthirstiness:** D. frequently criticizes G. for these vices (59.10.2–3, 11.1 [= **B.9**], 24.1, 25.5a, 25.7, 28.10–11). They were two of the standard imperial vices commonly found in the biographical tradition (e.g. 58.22.1–3; Suet. *T.* 42–45, 59–62; *G.* 27–33; 60.2.5–6 [= **C.2**]; Suet. *Cl.* 34; 62.24.1; Suet. *N.* 26–29, 33–38).

4.2 **G.'s shifting attitude towards Tib.:** See further 59.6.3 [= **B.4**]; 59.16.1–9 [= **B.12**] and Introduction, Section 4.3.

4.3 **accusations on the charge of treason:** For G.'s shifting attitude towards such charges see further 59.6.2 [= **B.4**], 59.16.2 [= **B.12**]. In general on treason trials under the Julio-Claudians see 59.6.2n. [= **B.4**].

his father, mother and brothers: i.e., Germanicus, Agrippina the elder, Nero Caesar and Drusus Caesar. They had all died during the reign of Tib.: Germanicus in 19 (Tac. *A.* 2.69–75), Nero Caesar in 31 (58.8.4 + n. [= **A.7**]), Agrippina and Drusus Caesar in 33 (Tac. *A.* 6.23–25; cf. 58.3.8 + n. [= **A.2**]).

burned the papers about them: cf. 59.6.3 [= **B.4**]; 59.10.8 [= **B.8**]. D.'s meaning here is not completely clear. He could mean self-incriminating letters written by those accused of treason (hence Cary in the Loeb edition of Dio translates "burned their letters"), but he could just as well be referring to the written depositions (*libelli*) containing evidence that accusers had to present to initiate a trial on this charge (cf. Plin. *Letters* 7.27.14 for a *libellus* incriminating Pliny found in Domitian's archives after the latter's death).

4.4   setting up of images and sacrifices: See 58.2.7–8nn. [= **A.1**], 58.4.4n. [= **A.3**], 58.8.4n. [= **A.7**]. D. in general thought that such honours were dangerous (52.35–36; D. Fishwick, *Phoenix* 44 (1990), 267–75).
temples to G.: For details see 59.28.1 + n. [= **B.22**].

4.5   he would spend money unsparingly and seek out funds in a most sordid fashion: This is another leitmotif of D.'s account of the reign: for expenditure see 59.2.5 [= **B.2**], for extortion 59.14–15 [= **B.11**]. The two themes are often linked by D. and other authors: so the extravagant spectacle at the bridge at Baiae is immediately followed in D.'s account by his attacks on the rich for funds (59.18.1 [= **B.14**]).

4.6   no-one knew how to respond to G.: D. also found this a fault with Tib. (57.1.4).

5.1   the deeds of Tib. were as far superior to those of G. as those of Aug. had been to those of Tib.: For D. comparing one emperor with another see further Introduction, Section 4.3.

5.2   Tib. used others as agents .... G. was controlled by charioteers, gladiators and actors: This is a good summary of D.'s views of Tib. and G., and illustrates his tendency to compare one emperor with another. Tib.'s most famous agents had been Sej. and later Macro. D. was convinced that an emperor should remain at the centre of affairs as much as possible, but when he needed agents, he should be careful to select worthy and reliable men (cf. 52.15.1–4). For G.'s devotion to chariot-racing and gladiatorial shows see 59.14.1–6 + nn. [= **B.11**]; Suet. *G.* 18–20, to actors and the stage 59.2.5 [= **B.2**]. Nero is also criticized by D. for these same pursuits (Introduction, Section 4.3).
Apelles: For this tragic actor from Ascalon in Palestine cf. Suet. *G.* 33; Petr. *Sat.* 64. He was still performing under Vespasian (Suet. *Vesp.* 19). He was one of the most influential members of G.'s body of advisers (*consilium*) and was held particularly responsible for G.'s anti-Jewish policies (Philo, *Embassy* 204–206).

5.3   he and they did everything that men dare whenever they are granted power: D. here moralizes briefly on the dangers of power being bestowed on those unworthy of it: cf. his remarks on Sej. at 58.5.3 [= **A.4**]; see further Introduction, Section 3.4.3.
he forced praetors and consuls to put on games: For the normal rôle of magistrates in putting on, and helping to fund, public games see 60.17.9 [= **C.10**]; 60.27.2 [= **C.13**] + nn.

5.4–5 he started to compete in many events: cf. Suet. *G.* 32.2; 54. For G. as charioteer see 59.14.6 [= **B.11**]; for his impersonations of various deities see 59.26.5–27.2 [= **B.20**]. D. levels the same criticisms against other bad emperors: e.g. Nero (63.9.4–6 [= **D.2**]), Commodus (72.17.1; 72.19.2–21.3).

5.5   **G. summoned the leading senators ... and danced in front of them:** For a
slightly fuller version of the same anecdote see Suet. *G.* 54.2. By "leading
senators" (in Suet. "three consulars") D. means members of the emperor's
advisory board (Crook, *CP*, 29). Almost the same anecdote is told against
Nero, except that he plays the water-organ (63.26.4 [= **D.7**]; cf. Suet. *N.*
41.2). The abuse of advisers was clearly a *topos* told against bad rulers.

B.4 GAIUS' RELATIONS WITH THE SENATE; HE DENOUNCES
TIBERIUS   A.D. 37

(59.6.1–7)

6.1   **G.'s deference to the senate:** G. was at first keen to identify himself with
Aug., his great-grandfather: cf. 59.3.8 [= **B.3**]; Barrett 69–71. This
included co-operation with the senate (M.P. Charlesworth, *CAH* X
(1934), 655). For the people at the games hailing him as "the young Aug."
see 59.13.6. For the view that emperors' apparent deference helped to
boost their prestige see A. Wallace-Hadrill, *JRS* 72 (1982), 37–8.
some members of the equestrian order and the Roman plebs were present at a
meeting of the senate: cf. Jos. *AJ* 19.185; Suet. *G.* 14.1. Strictly speaking,
only senators were allowed to attend meetings of the senate from inside
the senate-house, but others often listened from the threshold (Talbert,
Senate, 154–62, 195–200). Suet. *loc. cit.* claims that the non-senators had
forced their way in, but it is more likely that the equestrian order and plebs
had sent deputations to witness such an important meeting as that which
conferred imperial powers on the new emperor; thus all three orders of
Roman society by their consensus helped to confirm G.'s power. The fact
that D. is keen to establish G.'s precise age suggests that this was the
meeting that formally marked the start of G.'s reign. See further Barrett
56–59.

6.2   **G.'s age:** D. is keen to establish accurate chronology for emperors' reigns
and lives (W.F. Snyder, *Klio* 33 (1940), 39–56). G. was born on 31 August
12 (59.7.2–3; Suet. *G.* 8.1); on D.'s reckoning this would date this meeting
of the senate to 28 March, i.e., the very day that G. arrived in Rome.
Q. Pomponius: D. makes a double error here. First, he confuses Quintus
Pomponius with his brother, P. Pomponius Secundus; and, secondly,
neither of the brothers was consul in 30 (R. Syme, *JRS* 60 (1970), 32 [=
RP, II, 811]). P. Pomponius Secundus, a noted writer of tragedies (Tac. *A.*
11.13; 12.28) and an excellent orator (Tac. *Dialogus* 13.3), had been a
supporter of Sej., after whose fall he has been put on trial and imprisoned
(Tac. *A.* 5.8). Under Cl. he was appointed suffect consul in 44 and won
triumphal decorations (*ornamenta triumphalia*) for military action as
commander of the legions of Upper Germany in 50 (Tac. *A.* 12.28). Q.
Pomponius Secundus was later accused of conspiring against G., but soon
released (59.26.4 [= **B.19**]) and then made suffect consul in 41 (59.29.5n.
[= **B.23**]).

charges of treason: Trials on the charge of treason (*maiestas* or "diminish-ing the majesty of the Roman people") were a keynote of Tib.'s reign, but the exact nature of the crime is difficult to reconstruct. From its inception in 100 B.C. it sought to protect the Roman state against treasonous uprisings or overambitious magistrates, but was extended under Aug. to cover slander, libel and treasonous actions against the emperor and his family (R.A. Bauman, *Impietas in Principem* (1974); Levick, *Tib.* 180–200; J.E. Allison and J.D. Cloud, *Latomus* 21 (1962), 711–31). Cl. and Nero also allegedly abolished such charges at the start of their reigns (60.3.6 [= **C.3**]; 60.4.2 [= **C.4**]; Griffin, *Nero*, 52–53). For the alleged reintroduction of *maiestas* charges by G. in 39 see 59.16.8 [= **B.12**]. Bauman (*Impietas*, 191–223) argues that emperors generally sus-pended all charges of *maiestas* on their accession; but it is extremely doubtful whether there was ever a *total* abolition of such charges (P.A. Brunt in *Sodalitas: scritti in honore A. Guarino* (1984), I, 469–80; J.A. Crook, *PCPhS* 33 (1987), 38–52).

6.3   **he burnt all of Tib.'s papers:** cf. 59.4.3 [= **B.3**]; Suet. *G.* 15.4. By 'papers' D. probably means the records of trials (Millar, *ERW*, 260–61). D. is correct to add that G. was not totally genuine in carrying this out, since he later used Tib.'s papers to convict senators (59.10.8 [= **B.8**]; 59.16.3 [= **B.12**]) and later still Domitian consulted them (Suet. *Dom.* 20). Aug. had had the records of old debts to the treasury burned, since these formed a very profitable means of blackmail (Suet. *Aug.* 32.2).

6.4   **the Saturnalia be celebrated over a period of five days:** This festival was originally held on 17 December, but in the later Republic was extended to four days. G. now extended it still further, but later in his reign abolished this fifth day, which was then restored by Cl. (60.25.8). At the festival masters served their slaves and exchanged clothes and presents with them (Macrobius, *Satires* 1.7.18f; Ogilvie, *Gods*, 98–99; H.H. Scullard, *Festivals and Ceremonies of the Roman Republic* (1981), 205–7).

        collecting just an obol from those who received the grain dole rather than the *denarius* **which they had in the past given the emperor for the manufacture of images:** By 'images' D. refers to the terracotta figurines or dolls (*sigillaria*) which were traditionally given as presents during the Saturnalia (Suet. *Cl.* 5). The Saturnalia was an appropriate time for the emperor, the most important patron in Roman society, to present gifts to his subjects (Suet. *Aug.* 75). D. here provides an interesting insight into how these presents were funded. For similar donations by the people to G. on 1 January cf. 59.24.4. Cl. as emperor put a permanent stop to such donations (60.6.3 + n. [= **C.5**]). On the importance of gifts to and from the emperor see Millar, *ERW* 135–44.

        those who received the grain dole: i.e., the *plebs frumentaria*, who were entitled to a free monthly handout of 5 *modii* of grain (= c. 44 litres, ample for two people, but below the minimum subsistence requirement for a family of three). Aug. had limited this handout to about 200,000 citizens (*RG* 15.4). The *plebs frumentaria* was thus a privileged group within the citizen body; the grain did not necessarily go to those most in need (G.E.

Rickman, *The Corn Supply of Ancient Rome* (1980), 187–97; P. Garnsey, *Famine and Food Supply in the Graeco-Roman World* (1988), 211–17; 236–39).

D., here as elsewhere, uses Greek monetary terms to describe Roman coins (cf. 59.2.1–3, 2.6; [= **B.2**]; 55.12.4). The Roman *denarius* was equivalent to the Athenian drachma. The Greek obol was worth one-sixth of a drachma, the nearest Roman equivalent being the *sestertius*, worth one-quarter of a *denarius*. By using the term 'obol', the smallest denomination of Greek coinage, D. may mean that G. demanded only a very small financial contribution from the *plebs frumentaria* – possibly just a Roman *as*, the smallest denomination of Roman coinage, strictly speaking worth one-sixteenth of a *denarius*. See further J.P.C. Kent, *Roman Coins* (1978).

6.5 **it was voted:** i.e., by a decree of the senate (*senatus consultum*). D. may derive this notice from the published proceedings of the senate (the *acta senatus*), or from a historian of the Julio-Claudian period who used these *acta*; for D.'s use of the *acta senatus* see P.M. Swan, *Phoenix* 41 (1987), 285.

Proculus and Nigrinus: Cn. Acerronius Proculus (*PIR*² A 32) and C. Petronius Pontius Nigrinus (*PIR*¹ P 218), the ordinary consuls of 37 (Smallwood 32 = Braund 562 = Sherk 41; Smallwood 33 = Braund 563). G. and Cl. took up office on 1 July (Suet. *G.* 17.1; *Cl.* 7, confirmed by a fragment of the *Acts of the Arval Brethren* (*AE* 1983, 95, lines 31–37), which records sacrifices on 1 July in front of the consular statues, most probably erected to commemorate G.'s and Cl.'s holding of the consulship). They laid down their office not on 12 September (as D. claims at 59.7.9), but on 1 September (Suet. *G.* 17.1; *Cl.* 7, confirmed by the Ostian Fasti), when A. Caecina Paetus and C. Caninius Rebilus took over. For the full list of consuls during G.'s reign see P.A. Gallivan, *Antichthon* 13 (1979), 66–69.

6.6 **his uncle Claudius:** The future emperor Claudius (*PIR*² C 942) was the son of Drusus Claudius Nero and Antonia, and hence the younger brother of G.'s father, Germanicus. He was born on 1 August 10 B.C. For his early career see Suet. *Cl.* 2–6; A. Momigliano, *Claudius: the emperor and his achievement* (rev. ed., 1961), 1–19; V.M. Scramuzza, *The Emperor Claudius* (1940), 35–41; B. Levick, *Claudius* (1990), 11–25.

sent to G. to represent the equestrian order: For Cl.'s equestrian status cf. Suet. *G.* 15.2. He had also acted as the leader of deputations from the equestrian order in 14, 31 and 37 (Suet. *Cl.* 6.1; Levick, *Cl.*, 26). This is a good illustration that men of senatorial families who had not yet entered the senate were enrolled as members of the equestrian order. For the variety of types of equestrians see P.A. Brunt in *The Crisis of the Roman Republic* (ed. R. Seager, 1969), 83–115. For embassies to the emperor see 58.2.8n. [= **A.1**].

G.'s speech to be read annually in senate: For parallels see Talbert, *Senate*, 318. Cl. suspended the practice in 42, by decreeing that emperors' speeches should just be engraved on tablets (60.10.2). On G.'s oratorical skills see Tac. *A.* 13.3; Suet. *G.* 53; Barrett 48–49.

B.5 GAIUS' CONSULSHIP: THE DEDICATION OF THE TEMPLE OF THE DEIFIED AUGUSTUS IN ROME; MEASURES CONCERNING PUBLIC SHOWS   A.D. 37

(59.7.1–9)

7.1   **shrine of Aug.:** The temple of the deified Aug. had been decreed and started by Tib. and Livia in 14 (56.46.3; Tac. *A.* 1.10; Suet. *G.* 21.1). It was located in the depression between the Palatine and the Capitol, behind the Basilica Iulia (Nash I, 164; D. Fishwick, *Phoenix* 46 (1992) (forthcoming)). The temple of Mars the Avenger in the Forum of Aug. had served as the cult place until the completion of this new shrine (56.46.4). It is unclear whether Tib. finished the temple, leaving G. merely to dedicate it (as 57.10.2; Tac. *A.* 6.45), or whether G. was responsible for its completion as well as dedication (so Suet. *T.* 47; *G.* 21.1). The ceremony of dedication took place on 30–31 August (Balsdon, *Gaius*, 173; Barrett 69–70). The *Acts of the Arval Brethren* (*AE* 1983, 95, lines 39, 51–52, 58) confirm that the "new temple" of the deified Aug. was in full use in 38: sacrifices were conducted there on 1 August and on 21 and 23 September. For a coin depicting G. sacrificing before the new temple see Smallwood 125 = Braund 180 = Barrett fig. 18. In general on the cult of Aug. see D. Fishwick, *The Imperial Cult in the Latin West* I, 1 (1987), 150–68; for it in the Greek East see Price, *Rituals and Power*, esp. 54–57.
triumphal dress: For emperors wearing triumphal dress cf. 56.34.1; 63.4.3 [= **D.1**]. It consisted of a completely purple toga with designs in gold thread (the *toga picta*), worn over a decorated tunic (the *tunica palmata*) (L.M. Wilson, *The Roman Toga* (1924), 84–85; L. Bonfante Warren, *JRS* 60 (1970), 59–61, 64–65; Versnel, *Triumphus*, 56–57, 60–61). There was also an alternative all-white form of triumphal dress: for an imperial freedman in charge of the emperor Nerva's "white triumphal dress" see *ILS* 1763. Emperors only wore triumphal dress on religious and festal occasions and, to do so, needed the formal permission of the senate (60.6.9 [= **C.5**]; 67.4.3). For routine public appearances they wore the *toga praetexta*, on which see 58.11.2n. [= **A.7**]. D. considered it a mark of G.'s megalomania that late in his reign he regularly appeared in public in triumphal dress (59.26.10 [= **B.20**]).
singers of the hymn: The same criteria were used for selecting the twenty-seven boys and twenty-seven girls who sang the hymn at the Secular Games in 17 B.C. (Horace, *Secular Hymn*; EJ 32 = Braund 769 = Sherk 11, lines 147 ff.); see also 59.16.10n. [= **B.12**]; 59.29.6 [= **B.23**].
the senate and people given a public banquet: Public feasting was an integral part of Roman religious festivals and public shows put on by emperors or magistrates. Each separate group (or *ordo*) within Roman society (senators, equestrians, plebs) was clearly differentiated by where they sat and by the quality of the food that they received. For a full study see P. Veyne, *Bread and Circuses* (Engl. tr., 1990), 220–21, 236, 389–90.
spectacles of all sorts were put on: For further details on public spectacles

put on by G. see Suet. *G*. 18, where Suet. clearly distinguishes between the three main types: gladiatorial combats (*munera gladiatoria*), theatre shows (*ludi scaenici*) and chariot races (*ludi circenses*). For further reading see Bibliography under 'Public Entertainments'. Roman emperors were expected to show munificence (*liberalitas*) in putting on public spectacles, which helped to assure the loyalty of the Roman plebs (Suet. *Aug*. 43.1; Veyne, *Bread*, 398–403). But at the same time they had to be careful not to overspend, since this would then require harsh measures to raise revenue (Wallace-Hadrill, *Suet*., 166–71).

7.2   **the number of chariot races:** The exact number of races held on the second day is uncertain. The manuscript reading of 'twenty-four' has sometimes been emended to 'forty', to explain D.'s comment that the number was increased to celebrate G.'s birthday. Twenty-four was the normal number of races under Cl. (60.27.2 [= **C.13**]).

   the emperor's birthday: G. was born on 31 August 12 (Suet. *G*. 8.1).

7.3   **beast-hunts:** i.e., *venationes*. These hunts, held in the amphitheatre or the circus, took on various forms: condemned criminals were forced to fight exotic wild beasts, beasts were forced to fight each other, or trained huntsmen hunted down such beasts (Friedländer II, 62–74; Balsdon, *Life & Leisure*, 302–13).

7.4   **the Trojan Game:** cf. Suet. *G*. 18.3. The Trojan Game (*lusus Troiae*) consisted of ceremonial cavalry drill-exercises for young Romans from patrician families aged between fourteen and seventeen: see Vergil, *Aeneid*, 5.545–603. The ceremony was revived by Julius Caesar, in part to advertise that he traced his ancestry back to the Trojan prince Aeneas (43.23.6). It was regularized by Aug., who used it to introduce youths of noble family into Roman public life (51.22.4; 54.26.1; Suet. *Aug*. 43.2; Z. Yavetz in *Caesar Augustus* (ed. F. Millar and E. Segal, 1984), 16–20). It was often staged as part of the ceremonies marking the dedication of important public buildings: e.g. 51.22.4 (the shrine of the deified Julius in 29 B.C.), 54.26.1 (the theatre of Marcellus in 13 B.C.), 55.10.6 (the temple of Mars the Avenger in 2 B.C.). It was also performed at funerals of members of the imperial family: cf. 59.11.2 [= **B.9**].

   triumphal chariot: It was customary for a triumphal chariot (*quadriga*) to be drawn by four white horses (7.21.3; 52.13.3), as is clearly shown in depictions of triumphs on Roman reliefs: e.g. on the arch of Titus in the Roman Forum (D. Strong, *Roman Art* (rev. ed., 1988), fig. 69) or on Marcus Aurelius' triumphal arch (ibid., fig. 134). See further Versnel, *Triumphus*, 56, 67. For the procession leading up to the chariot-races (the *pompa circensis*) emperors were entitled to wear triumphal dress (59.7.1 + n. above) and to ride in a triumphal chariot. The Julio-Claudian emperors used Aug.'s triumphal chariot (61.16.4; 63.20.3 + n. [= **D.5**]; Versnel, *Triumphus*, 98, 130–31).

   starting signal: The presiding magistrate dropped a napkin (*mappa*) and the bolts were then released from the starting-gates (*carceres*) by a catapult-like mechanism. D. is strictly speaking being anachronistic here, since this method of starting races was not introduced until the reign of

Nero. See J.H. Humphrey, *Roman Circuses* (1986), 19–21 (*carceres*), 24 (starting-signal), 157–74 (bolt-release mechanism).

priests of Aug.: i.e., the *sodales Augustales*, who were first appointed in 14 to supervise the newly established cult of the deified Augustus (56.46.1; Tac. *A.* 1.54). There were 21 regular members of this priestly college, plus co-opted members of the imperial family. For their activities cf. EJ 94a = Braund 115 = Sherk 36b. For further discussion see J. Scheid, *ANRW* II. 16.1 (1979), 610–54, esp. 618, 627, 639, 642, 648–49; S. Price in *Rituals of Royalty* (ed. D. Cannadine and S. Price, 1987), 78–79.

7.5   **he postponed all lawsuits:** It was exceptional, but not impossible, for trials to be held on days of festivals (cf. Cic. *pro Caelio*, 1.1).

periods of mourning: Inscriptions reveal some of the restrictions that applied during periods of mourning (*iustitia*) after the death of a member of the imperial family. After the death of Gaius Caesar in 4, the colony of Pisae in Etruria voted that all the colonists should change into clothes of mourning (i.e., darkened togas), that all temples, public baths and taverns be closed, and that no public sacrifices, banquets, weddings or perform-ances in the theatre or circus take place (EJ 69 = Braund 63 = Sherk 19; for similar restrictions after the death of Germanicus cf. Sherk 36a, fr. II, column A). On mourning in general see S. Price in *Rituals of Royalty* (ed. D. Cannadine and S. Price), 62; J.M.C. Toynbee, *Death and Burial in the Roman World* (1971), 63–64; for the prohibition on remarriage see Gardner, *Women*, 51–56; M. Humbert, *Le remariage à Rome* (1972), 113–31.

7.6   **without having to worry about greeting him in a formal manner:** D. here reveals that a code of ritual had already developed to emphasize the relationship between ruler and ruled. For the greeting 'Hail, Caesar' (*ave, Caesar*) instituted under Aug. see 63.28.1 [= **D.8**]; Friedländer I, 86–92, esp. 86; Price, *Rituals*, 239–48.

7.7   **dress rules at public shows:** Aug. had revived the custom that all Roman citizens should wear the toga in the Forum and at all public shows (Suet. *Aug.* 40.5; Juv. *Sat.* 3. 171–79; E. Rawson, *PBSR* 55 (1987), 94–99).

7.7   **it had been the custom from very early days to try cases in summer barefoot:** D., as elsewhere, likes to trace the origins of customs prevalent in his day (Introduction, Section 3.4.3; Appendix 2). Suet. shared this antiquarian interest (Wallace-Hadrill, *Suet.*, 130 and n. 12). M. Porcius Cato as praetor sat in judgement in the very hot summer of 54 B.C. without his shoes, but also without his tunic (i.e., wearing just a toga) (Plut. *Cato Minor* 44.1; for the heatwave see Cic. *Letters to his brother Quintus* 2.16; 3.1). For another heatwave in 39, when the Forum had to be shaded from the sun with awnings, see 59.23.9.

7.8   **cushions and Thessalian hats:** These privileges for senators further under-lined the social stratification of the Roman citizen body at the public games. Aug. had reinforced segregated seating for the different orders of Roman society (senators separate from equestrians, who in turn were segregated from the various ranks of the Roman plebs) at the theatre (Suet. *Aug.* 44) and also possibly at the amphitheatre (E. Rawson, *PBSR* 55 (1987), 83–114). See further 60.7.3–4 + n. [= **C.5**]. The privilege of cushions was later extended to the equestrian order (Juv. *Sat.* 3.153). Aug. used to wear a wide-brimmed hat to protect him from the sun in summer and even in winter (Suet. *Aug.* 82.1). D. here uses the word for a close-fitting felt cap (*pilos*); the wide-brimmed Thessalian felt hat (more useful for warding off the sun) was strictly called a *petasos*. Canvas awnings to shade spectators were common at the amphitheatre, but seem not to have been used at the circus (Sear, *Architecture*, 142–44; Humphrey, *Circuses*, 101).

Diribitorium: This building stood in the Campus Martius next to the Saepta. The Roman voting assemblies met to vote in the Saepta and the ballots were then sorted in the Diribitorium. By 7 B.C. Aug. had completed Caesar's plan to enlarge and embellish it. It was the largest building yet erected under a single roof and hence was useful for public shows on sunny days. When it was destroyed in 80, its roof was too large to be repaired successfully (55.8.3–4; 66.24.2; Nash II, 291–93; L.R. Taylor, *Roman Voting Assemblies* (1966), 55 and pls. IX, XI).

the theatre: D. (as well as various Latin authors) used the term 'theatre' to refer to a theatre or amphitheatre (43.22.3; 72.17.3–4, 18.1, 20.2, 21.3; Vitruvius 1.7.1). The main amphitheatre at this time was the amphitheatre of Statilius Taurus located near the Tiber next to the Circus Flaminius. D. later reveals that G. often used the Saepta for gladiatorial combats since he despised the 'theatre of Taurus' (59.10.5).

7.9 **duration of G.'s consulship:** D.'s calculation is slightly out: G. and Cl. resigned on G.'s birthday (31 August), i.e., precisely two months after taking up office on 1 July (Suet. *G.* 17.1; *Cl.* 7).

B.6 ILLNESS OF GAIUS; MURDER OF TIBERIUS GEMELLUS A.D. 37

(59.8.1–3)

8.1 **G.'s illness:** Philo, *Embassy* 14 establishes that G.'s illness occurred in October/November 37 and attributes it to intemperance. For discussion of its precise nature (and some doubts on Philo's date) see Barrett 73–74. It caused great consternation throughout the Empire (Suet. *G.* 14.2; Philo, *Embassy* 15–21). D. used it to mark the watershed between G.'s 'good' and 'bad' periods, following earlier sources (e.g. Philo, *Embassy* 22; Jos. *AJ* 18.256), but also to help explain his deterioration as ruler.

Tiberius: i.e., Tiberius Gemellus, on whom see 59.1.1n. [= **B.1**]. For a vivid account of his enforced suicide see Philo, *Embassy* 23–31; cf. Jos. *AJ* 18.223; Suet. *G.* 23.3. His epitaph (probably from the Mausoleum of Aug.) survives (Smallwood 88 = Braund 185). For speculation that he was involved in a plot against G. see Barrett 75–77.

toga of manhood: see 59.2.2n. [= **B.2**].

'Leader of the Youth': i.e., *princeps iuventutis*. Aug. bestowed the title on his grandsons Gaius and Lucius Caesar in 5 and 2 B.C. respectively (*RG* 14.2; EJ 61, 63a, 65–69, 75 = Braund 28, 54, 56–58, 62–63, 71) and later probably on Drusus son of Tib. and on Germanicus, Tib.'s nephew and adopted son. When emperor, Tib. probably conferred the title on Germanicus' sons Nero and Drusus and then on G. (see *RE* 22 (1954) 2299–2302). It marked the recipient out as being a prospective heir, but did not in itself serve to designate the chosen successor (W.K. Lacey, *JRS* 69 (1979), 32).

Gemellus adopted as G.'s son: cf. 59.1.3 [= **B.1**]. D. does not specify when this took place. Suet. *G.* 15.2 and Philo, *Embassy* 26–28 both imply that it occurred at the very start of G.'s reign. Technically under Roman law G.'s adoption of Gemellus was unusual, since it broke the customary rules for adoption, whereby the adopter should be aged sixty or over and eighteen years older than the adopted; G. was only 7 years, 4 months older than Gemellus. But the restriction could be overridden, especially if the chief priests (*pontifices*) gave their approval. Moreover, the restrictions may only have become mandatory in the second century A.D. (W.W. Buck- land, *Textbook of Roman Law* (3rd ed., 1963), 126–27). Levick, *Tib.*, 220 goes too far in asserting that it was a "legal nonsense". D. makes it sound as if these were favours to Gemellus; but in effect they relegated Gemellus to the next generation in the imperial family and so destroyed his claim as heir to Tib., on which see 59.1.1 + n. [= **B.1**].

the charge against Gemellus: D.'s account is more convincing than Suet. *G.* 23.3, who claims that Gemellus was put to death because he had insulted G. by taking an antidote against poison before dining with him. The latter is just a conventional story told against bad rulers (cf. Tac. *A.* 4.54, involving the elder Agrippina and Tib.).

8.2   D.'s historiographical technique is interesting here; he reports these important administrative changes on the eastern frontier of the Empire not as an independent item, but to provide a contrast in a highly rhetorical passage condemning G.'s treatment of Gemellus. This is a good illus- tration of one way in which D. remoulded his source material, to fit it into his own rhetorical framework (Introduction, Section 3.3). The contrast drawn between G.'s disgraceful treatment of Gemellus and his administra- tive changes in the East may imply that D. approved of the latter. By reinstating these allied kings in 37 and others in 38 (59.12.2 [= **B.10**]), he reversed the eastern policy of Aug. and Tib., who had in general abandoned the use of allied kings, preferring to create new provinces ruled directly by Rome (Balsdon, *Gaius*, 196–203; Barrett 222–23).

Antiochus of Commagene: C. Iulius Antiochus IV Epiphanes (*PIR²* I 149; R.D. Sullivan, *ANRW* II.8 (1978), 785–94), whom hostile sources linked with Agrippa of Palestine as G.'s "tutors in tyranny" (59.24.1). Com- magene was a small kingdom on the Euphrates, north of the Roman province of Syria and bordering on the powerful kingdom of Parthia. Tib. had annexed it as a province in 18 after the death of Antiochus' father (Tac. *A.* 2.42, 56; Levick, *Tib.*, 141). It now reverted to being an allied kingdom. Suet. *G.* 16.3 adds that Antiochus was granted a refund of 100,000,000 sesterces from the Roman treasury as compensation for tax revenue lost during the twenty-year period (17–37) that Commagene had been a Roman province. Relations between Antiochus and G. later soured and Antiochus was deposed, to be restored by Cl. in 41 (60.8.1 + n. [=

C.6]). On allied kings in general see D.C. Braund, *Rome and the Friendly King* (1984).

Agrippa: M. Iulius Agrippa (*PIR²* I 131) (commonly but incorrectly known as 'Herod Agrippa') was the grandson of Herod the Great. After his father, Aristobulus, had been executed by Herod the Great, he had spent much of his early life (from c. 7 B.C.–A.D. 23) in Rome in the house of Antonia, G.'s paternal grandmother. After a troubled period back in Judaea, he returned to Italy in 36 and lived with G. in Tib.'s household on Capri until he was imprisoned in September 36 after being found guilty of wishing Tib.'s death. He was thus a close friend of G. (Jos. *AJ* 18.168–69, 179, 185–204; *BJ* 2.179–80; Smallwood, *Jews*, 187–200). For more precise details on the territories that he gained in 37 see Jos. *AJ* 18.237. In 40 he received further territory from G. after the conspiracy of Herod Antipas, tetrarch of Galilee and Peraea (Jos. *AJ* 18.240–252; 19.351). Cl. granted him still more territory in 41 as a reward for helping to establish him as emperor (60.8.2 + n. [= **C.6**]).

without reference to the senate: D. implies that G.'s period of deference to the senate (cf. 59.6.1–3 [= **B.4**]) was now over. However, G. could hardly have brought his adopted son to trial before the senate; it was usual for the emperor to try members of his own family within his own household (cf. Tac. *A.* 11.37; Levick, *Cl.*, 118).

B.7 FINANCES, ELECTIONS AND THE RECRUITMENT OF NEW EQUESTRIANS   A.D. 38

(59.9.4–7)

9.4–7 D. here adopts the biographical technique of grouping together events that occurred at different times to illustrate G.'s general conduct (cf. Wallace-Hadrill, *Suet.*, 142–74). D., here as elsewhere, is keen to emphasize contrasts in G.'s behaviour (Introduction, Section 4.3).

9.4 **published the accounts of public funds, as Aug. had done:** cf. Suet. *G.* 16.1. G. again deliberately associates himself with the actions of Aug. rather than Tib. (cf. 59.2.5n. [= **B.2**]; 59.3.8n. [= **B.3**]; 59.6.1n. [= **B.4**]). Aug. had published accounts in 23 B.C. and A.D. 14 (53.30.2; 56.33.1–2). These had included details of public revenues and expenditure, the disposition of Roman troops and the amount of money in the treasuries (F. Millar, *JRS* 54 (1964), 33–40, esp. 38–39).

Tib.'s absence from the city: Tib. had left Rome in 26 (Tac. *A.* 4.57); he died in 37 without having returned.

he helped the troops put out a fire: The Ostian Fasti refer to a fire that occurred on 21 October 38 in the Aemiliana district to the south of the Campus Martius (Smallwood 31 = Braund 174); for another fire here under Cl. see Suet. *Cl.* 18.1. By troops D. means the Night-Watch (*vigiles*), on whom see 58.9.3n. [= **A.7**]. It was customary for the emperor to provide financial assistance for the victims of such natural disasters: cf. Tac. *A.* 2.47–48; 15.39 see further Millar, *ERW*, 422–25.

9.5   **G. summoned provincial aristocrats to Rome to fill up vacancies in the equestrian order:** G. here acted as censor in reviewing the list of Roman equestrians: cf. 53.17.7 (for the theory); 54.26.3–9; Suet. *Aug.* 38 (for it in practice). Paradoxically, D. soon reports (59.10.2) that G. put twenty-six equestrians to death. For G.'s relations with the equestrian order in general see Barrett 231–34. The recruitment of the provincial élite into the Roman equestrian order was common under the Principate; equestrians were needed for the increasing number of administrative posts and to provide replacements for senators (Hopkins, *Death*, 166–69; P.A. Brunt, *JRS* 73 (1983), 42–75, esp. 64–65). The recruitment of provincials into the central élite also helped to ensure the loyalty of the provinces towards Rome. For provincial equestrians see R.P. Saller, *Personal Patronage under the Early Empire* (1982), 145–204 (on Africa); Syme, *Tacitus*, 585–97; *Colonial Elites* (1958), 1–23; and many articles now collected in *RP* I-V (mostly on Spain, Gaul and the Greek East). D. here also provides good evidence that potential equestrians had to come to Rome to be registered at the official annual review of the equestrians (*recognitio equitum*) (T.P. Wiseman, *Historia* 19 (1970), 68–70).

   the right to wear senatorial dress: Senatorial dress included high red boots laced halfway to the knee (*calcei*), a distinctive ring and a broad vertical purple stripe (*latus clavus*) on the tunic (not, as commonly thought, around the edge of the toga, which was the *toga praetexta*: 58.11.2n. [= **A.7**]). Varro, *Menippean Satires*, 313b satirizes people for wearing transparent togas to show off the broad stripe on their tunics. See further Friedländer I, 132–33; Talbert, *Senate*, 216–20; T.P. Wiseman, *New Men in the Roman Senate* (1971), 68. A young equestrian aspiring to a senatorial career had been entitled to wear senatorial dress, but in 18 B.C. Aug. limited it to senators and their sons (Talbert, *Senate*, 11–16).

   entitle us: D. again refers to his own senatorial rank (Introduction, Sections 1.1–1.2).

9.6   **G. once more put the elections into the hands of the people and plebs:** cf. Suet. *G.* 16.3; Barrett 230–31. Tib.'s reform of electoral procedures in 14 effectively entrusted the appointment of the magistrates to the senate, although the popular assemblies still had to ratify the senate's slate of candidates (58.4.3n. [= **A.3**]). In practical terms this reform of G. made little difference, but its symbolic purpose was to enhance the dignity of the people; for its reversal in 39 see 59.20.3–4 [= **B.15**]. D. is very careful in his terminology to distinguish the Roman people (*populus Romanus*) and the Roman plebs (*plebs Romana*); the former formally confirmed the election of consuls and praetors in the *comitia centuriata* and of curule aediles and quaestors in the *comitia tributa*, the latter confirmed the election of tribunes of the plebs and plebeian aediles in the *concilium plebis*.

   one per cent tax: D. refers to the auction tax (*centesima rerum venalium*) instituted by Aug. at a rate of 1%, over which there were serious civil disturbances in 15 (Tac. *A.* 1.78). These riots caused Tib. to reduce it to 0.5% in 17 (Tac. *A.* 2.42). D. claims that it reverted to 1% in 31 (58.16.2), which this excerpt would confirm. However, Suet. *G.* 16.3 and coins of 39–41 bearing the legend 'the half a per cent tax remitted' (Smallwood 35 =

Braund 183) suggest that D. has failed to record another cut in the tax, made between 31 and 38, before its (temporary) abolition here by G. See further Balsdon, *Gaius*, 186–87; Barrett 226.

he threw tickets into the crowd and distributed gifts to those who successfully scrambled for them: cf. Suet. *G.* 18.2. Emperors often distributed gifts at the games by throwing tickets (*missilia*) for the gifts into the crowd (cf. 61.18.1–2; Suet. *Nero* 11.2; Friedländer II, 15–16). For the games as a major means of the emperor maintaining the support of the people see Veyne, *Bread*, 398–403; Hopkins, *Death*, 14–20.

9.7 **the rabble; the sensible:** These morally-loaded terms reveal very clearly D.'s conservative viewpoint (Introduction, Section 3.4.3). In his language and conservative mind-set D. here closely follows his model historian, Thucydides: cf. Thuc. 3.37.3; 7.77.2; esp. 3.83.3.

B.8 DEATH OF MACRO   A.D. 38

(59.10.6–8)

10.6 **Macro:** Q. Naevius Cordus Sutorius Macro, who had succeeded Sej. as prefect of the Praetorian Guard in 31 (58.9.2n. [= **A.7**]). It is not altogether clear why G. turned against the man who had played a very important rôle in assuring his accession. Philo, *Embassy* 52–61 suggests that he had become suspicious of Macro's increasing influence and saw him as a threat. For speculation that he may have been involved in a conspiracy to push the claims of Gemellus during G.'s illness in 37 see Barrett 78. G. possibly felt restricted by the obligation that he was under to Macro for his earlier support.

Ennia: Macro's wife, Ennia Thrasylla (*PIR*[2] E 65), possibly the granddaughter of Tib.'s astrologer Thrasyllus. She had allegedly had an affair with G. just before his accession (58.28.4; Tac. *A.* 6.45; Suet. *G.* 12.2; Philo, *Embassy* 39–40, 61). For the help given G. by Macro and Ennia at the end of Tib.'s reign see 58.28.4; Philo, *Flaccus*, 11–13; Seager 244; Levick, *Tib.* 174, 215; Barrett 50–55.

to win power for himself alone: D. provides another hint that Tib. had intended a joint-succession of G. and Tiberius Gemellus, and that Macro had assisted in invalidating Gemellus' claim (cf. 59.1.2–3 + n. [= **B.1**]).

prefect of Egypt: D. here implies that the prefecture of Egypt was the senior position to which an equestrian could aspire, superior to the prefectship of the Praetorian Guard. From c. 70 this hierarchy was reversed (P.A. Brunt, *JRS* 65 (1975), 124 [= *RIT*, 215]). It seems that Macro had been appointed to, but had not yet taken up, his post in Egypt at the time of his death. For the later implication of a Greek citizen from Alexandria in Macro's fall see Smallwood 436 = Braund 575 = Sherk 45, with Barrett 79–80.

the charge of acting as a pimp: Macro could have been tried on a charge of *lenocinium* (i.e., acting as a pimp) on the grounds either that he had hired out his wife Ennia as a prostitute (so Barrett 79) or that he had procured sexual partners for G. from among the Roman upper class (cf. Suet. *G.* 36). Technically, Macro was thus encouraging criminal adultery, if married women were involved, or criminal fornication (*stuprum*), if unmarried, high-class women were. The *lex Iulia* on the suppression of adultery, introduced by Aug. and passed in 18 B.C., designated both of these as serious offences to be tried in the criminal (not civil) courts (Braund 698; LR I, 204; Gardner, *Women*, 121–25, 127–31; Crook, *Law & Life*, 101–02; Syme, *RR*, 443–45).

results of Macro's fall: An important result of Macro's fall was that two Praetorian prefects were henceforth appointed as a check on one another, i.e., a return to the system that prevailed before Sej. and of which D. approved (57.19.6; 52.24.1–2; Balsdon, *Gaius*, 39–40). D. includes Macro's conviction in a section on condemnations to gain revenue (cf. 59.10.7); but not all of Macro's funds accrued to the emperor; some went towards the construction of an amphitheatre at Macro's home town, Alba Fucens (EJ 370 = Smallwood 254 = Braund 458).

10.7 **punishing them for wrongs done to his parents and to his brothers:** cf. 59.4.3 [= **B.3**]. They would have been convicted on the charge of treason (*maiestas*) for crimes against Agrippina and G.'s dead brothers, Drusus Caesar and Nero Caesar. For the charge of *maiestas* see 59.6.2n. [= **B.4**]. It was often the charge used by emperors who wished to gain revenue from the Roman upper classes; if they were convicted, their property would strictly speaking fall to the state treasury, but it was often appropriated by the emperor (Millar, *ERW*, 163–74).

exhaustion of the treasury: See further 59.2.5–6 + n. [= **B.2**]; on further measures used by G. to raise cash see 59.14–15 [partly = **B.11**]. Heavy spending and harsh revenue-raising are often associated in the biographical tradition about bad emperors (Wallace-Hadrill, *Suet.*, 166–71).

10.8 **on the basis of those papers which he once claimed to have burnt:** i.e., the papers left behind by Tib.: cf. 59.6.3 + n. [= **B.4**].

people were destroyed as a result of his illness: During G.'s illness in 37 a conspiracy was possibly formed against him to assert the claims of Tiberius Gemellus (59.8.1–3 + nn. [= **B.6**]; Barrett 78). If so, G. was here taking action against those who had supported this conspiracy.

anyone who entertained .... was punished: For the prohibitions which came into force during periods of mourning after the death of a member of the imperial family see 59.7.5n. [= **B.5**].

B.9 DEATH OF DRUSILLA   A.D. 38

(59.11.1–4)

11.1 **Drusilla:** See further 59.3.3–4 + nn. [= **B.3**].

Marcus Lepidus: M. Aemilius Lepidus (*PIR*[2] A 371), a member of one of the leading Roman senatorial families (Syme, *AA*, 130–36; Table IV). His father (consul in 6) had been especially prominent under Tib. (Tac. *A.* 4.20); his sister had been married to Drusus son of Germanicus, but had been forced to commit suicide through the machinations of Sej. (Tac. *A.* 6.40).

marriage of Drusilla and Lepidus: Drusilla had been married to L. Cassius Longinus in 33 (58.21.1; Tac. *A.* 6.15), but G. had later forced her to divorce him and marry his friend Lepidus (Suet. *G.* 24.1; with Syme, *AA*, 136, 179). An inscription from the base of a statue group from Aphrodisias, Caria (Asia Minor) confirms that Lepidus was a member of the imperial family (J. Reynolds, *PCPhS* 26 (1980), 80–81 = Braund 192). He was marked out as a potential successor to G. after Drusilla's death (59.22.6n. [= **B.17**]).

Drusilla and Lepidus as sexual partners of G.: cf. Suet. *G.* 24.1 (Drusilla); 36.1 (Lepidus). The theme of G.'s incest was developed to embrace his two other sisters, Agrippina and Julia (59.22.6 [= **B.17**]; Jos. *AJ* 19.204). Incest was a standard charge levelled against tyrants: cf. Tac. *A.* 14.2 for alleged incest between Nero and his mother Agrippina. Lepidus allegedly also had sexual affairs with Drusilla's sisters, Agrippina and Julia (59.22.6 [= **B.17**]). In general on incest see Gardner, *Women*, 125–27.

Drusilla's death: The Ostian Fasti show that Drusilla died on 10 June (Smallwood 31 = Braund 174). There followed a period of mourning (*iustitium*), during which all public business was suspended (Suet. *G.* 24.2); at Alexandria this extended into August (Philo, *Flaccus* 53–85). See further Barrett 85–86. For public mourning after the death of members of the imperial family see 56.43.1; 59.7.5n. [= **B.5**].

her husband delivered the eulogy over her: A close member of the deceased's family usually delivered the funerary eulogy, as Tib. and his son Drusus did for their adoptive father/grandfather Aug. (56.34.4) and as G. did for his adoptive father Tib. (58.28.5; 59.3.8 [= **B.3**]). Sometimes these eulogies were inscribed and displayed at the family tomb (EJ 357 = Braund 720; *ILS* 8394 = Sherk 184).

her brother gave her the honour of a public funeral: It was traditional for the senate to decide whether to grant a prominent Roman a public funeral; but under the Principate the initiative came from the emperor (as here), although the senate still had to make the formal grant (Tac. *A.* 4.15; Talbert, *Senate*, 370–71). G. was allegedly so overwhelmed with grief that he could not attend Drusilla's funeral in person (Suet. *G.* 24.2; Seneca, *To Polybius* 17.4). The fullest account of a Roman public funeral is provided by Polybius 6.53–54; see further S. Price in *Rituals of Royalty* (ed. D. Cannadine and S. Price, 1987), 62–64; J.M.C. Toynbee, *Death and Burial in the Roman World* (1971), 55–61.

11.2 **the Praetorian Guard under their commander [ran around the pyre]:** D. is wrong to talk of the Praetorian Guard under the command of one man, since following the fall of Macro there were two commanders (59.10.6 + n. [= **B.8**]). Since there is a gap in the manuscripts of D. at this point, the complete sense of the sentence is uncertain. The text translated here is reconstructed from a closely parallel passage where D. describes Aug.'s funeral, at which the Praetorian Guard and the equestrian order ran round his pyre (56.42.2).

Trojan game: A ceremonial cavalry drill-exercise for young members of
the Roman élite: see 59.7.4n. [= **B.5**].

Livia's honours: These included a whole year's mourning, an arch and
eventual deification (58.2.1–3; Tac. *A*. 5.2). D. fails to make it clear that
Livia at this stage had not officially been deified, which only occurred in 41
(60.5.2); but for the view that Livia was already receiving honours as if
deified see N. Purcell, *PCPhS* 32 (1986), 93–94.

deification of Drusilla: The *Acts of the Arval Brethren* reveal that this took
place on 23 September 38 (Smallwood 5 = Braund 189), a good-omened
date since it was the birthday of Aug. (Suet. *Aug*. 5). For surviving
dedications to the deified Drusilla see Smallwood 128 = Braund 190;
IGRR IV 78, 145, 1098, 1721; *ILS* 196–97. See further Barrett 86–89.
Imperial funerals were important ceremonies for the development of the
imperial cult, especially for the deification of new members of the imperial
family (S. Price in *Rituals of Royalty*, 56–105; Talbert, *Senate* 387 and
n. 8).

the temple of Venus in the Forum: i.e., the temple of Venus Genetrix, which
formed the focus of the Forum of Julius Caesar (Nash I, 519–24; Coarelli,
Guida arch. di Roma, 106–07). A statue of Venus Genetrix by the Greek
sculptor Arcesilaos stood in an apsidal niche in the cella of the temple
(Plin. *NH* 35.45.155).

Drusilla and Venus: Drusilla's association (or syncretism) with Venus is
confirmed in various inscriptions from the Greek East: she was honoured
as 'the new Aphrodite' at Mytilene (Smallwood 128b = Braund 190b),
while games were held in honour of the 'divine new Aphrodite Drusilla' at
Cyzicus in 37 (Smallwood 401 = Braund 673). The date of this last
inscription shows that Drusilla was already being worshipped as a goddess
in the Greek East before her death (P. Herz, *Historia* 29 (1980), 324–26).

11.3 a festival to mark her birthday: For subsequent celebrations of her
birthday see 59.13.8–9. Cl. on his accession put a stop to her cult (Balsdon,
Gaius, 45–46).

11.3 the Games of Cybele: i.e., the *Ludi Megalenses* or *Megalesia*, one of the
major Roman state festivals under the Principate, were held annually
from 4 to 10 April in honour of the Magna Mater (Cybele), the Phrygian
goddess brought to Rome in 205–204 B.C. It consisted *inter alia* of six
days of *ludi scaenici* (theatrical performances) and a final day of *ludi
circenses* (chariot-races) (Ovid, *Fasti* 4.179–392; Livy 29.14; T.P. Wiseman, *Catullus and his World* (1985), 200–5). The other major festivals
under the early Principate were the *ludi Cereales* in honour of Ceres (12–
19 April), the *ludi Florales* in honour of Flora (28 April–3 May), the *ludi
Apollinares* in honour of Apollo (6–13 July), the *ludi Veneres* in honour of
Venus Genetrix (20–30 July), the *ludi Romani* (the Roman Games, also
called the *ludi magni*, the Great Games: 4–19 September), the *ludi
Augustales* in honour of Aug. (3–12 October) and the *ludi plebeii* (Plebeian
Games: 4–17 November).

public banquets for the senate and the equestrian order: Public banquets
were traditionally put on for the senate and the equestrian order at the *ludi*

Megalenses (Ovid, *Fasti* 4.353–54). For public banquets in general see 59.7.1n. [= **B.5**].

11.4 Livius Geminius: His name should probably be Livius Geminus (*PIR*² L 206). Such sightings of new divine members of the imperial family ascending to heaven had become a standard part of the ritual of deification (cf. 56.46.2, where exactly the same monetary reward is involved), and became a common motif in official Roman art (Hopkins, *Conquerors*, pls. 1, 2a and 2b); for satirical comment on the deification of emperors from a contemporary witness see Seneca, *Apocolocyntosis* [= *Pumpkinification of Claudius*]. See in general S. Price in *Rituals of Royalty* (ed. D. Cannadine and S. Price), 73–77.

invoking destruction upon himself and his children: Imprecations against oneself and one's family and the summoning of divine witnesses were standard procedures in the taking of oaths in the Greek and Roman world (H. Wagenvoort, *Pietas* (1980), 196–209; W. Burkert, *Greek Religion* (Engl. tr., 1985), 250–54).

B.10 ARRANGEMENTS ABOUT ALLIED KINGS; AEDILESHIP OF VESPASIAN   A.D. 38

(59.12.2–3)

12.2 This passage provides further evidence for G.'s preference for allied kingdoms in the eastern part of the Empire rather than for provinces controlled directly by Rome (cf. 59.8.2 + nn. [= **B.6**]). D. fails to make it explicit that G. staged an elaborate public ceremony in the centre of Rome to hand over their new kingdoms in person to these kings: cf. Nero's coronation of Tiridates as king of Armenia in 66 in Rome at exactly the same location (63.4.3 [= **D.1**]). These incidents reveal the importance of rituals (here to mark a straightforward change in the administration of the Empire) for the consolidation of an emperor's image and political position at Rome.

Sohaemus: Sohaemus was king of Ituraea until his death in 49, when the area east of the Sea of Galilee was incorporated into the province of Syria (Tac. *A*. 12.23). This Sohaemus should not be confused with Sohaemus of Emesa or Sohaemus of Armenia (A.H.M. Jones, *JRS* 21 (1931), 265–75).

Cotys, Rhoemetalces and Polemon: All three were sons of Cotys VIII, king of Thrace under Aug. and Tib., and Antonia Tryphaena (cf. Braund 674). On the death of their father in 18 they as infants had been granted part of the kingdom of Thrace, but had been sent to Rome to be educated while a Roman ex-praetor ruled on their behalf (Tac. *A*. 2.64–67). They had grown up in Rome as companions of G. (Smallwood 401 = Braund 673; Balsdon, *Gaius*, 200–1). All three received considerably more territory in this ceremony than they had inherited from their father. A decree from Cyzicus, Asia Minor (Smallwood 401 = Braund 673), honouring the three sons and their mother, celebrates G.'s grant of the new kingdoms. The decree is dated to 37, but D. places the grant in 38; either D.'s chronology is wrong or the ceremony in Rome took place in 38 after the three had had time to establish themselves in their respective kingdoms. The decree also provides insight into the way contemporary Greeks claimed to perceive G.'s alterations to the allied kingdoms in the East; they saw the changes not in the purely administrative terms of D.'s account, but as the work of a god ('the New Sun Gaius Caesar Augustus Germanicus'): see Price, *Rituals*, 244–45.

Cotys: Cotys IX, the youngest of the three brothers (*PIR*² C 1555; R.D. Sullivan, *ANRW* II.7.1 (1979), 207–09). Lesser Armenia stretched across north-east Asia Minor to the west of the river Euphrates. He was still in power here in 47 (Tac. *A*. 11.9), but died between 47 and 54. It is unclear which parts of Arabia he was granted: possibly the region of Sophene in Upper Mesopotamia, since this area was bequeathed along with Lesser Armenia in 55 following his death (Tac. *A*. 13.7).

Rhoemetalces III: *PIR*¹ R 52; R.D. Sullivan, *ANRW* II.7.1 (1979), 209–11. G. hereby granted him sole control of the kingdom of his father, Cotys VIII: i.e., Thrace. For coins of Rhoemetalces honouring G. see Smallwood 201 = Braund 630. He maintained good diplomatic relations with, and was honoured by, his Greek neighbours (Smallwood 201b). He was murdered by his wife in 46, whereupon after some military action Thrace became a Roman province (Tac. *A*. 12.63).

Polemo, son of Polemo: (C.?) Iulius Polemo, a Roman citizen (*PIR*² J 472; Smallwood 374 = Braund 581b; R.D. Sullivan, *ANRW* II.7.2 (1980), 915–20). D. is in error in calling him the son of Polemo II (*PIR*¹ P 405); he was his grandson; his mother, Antonia Tryphaena, was Polemo II's daughter (cf. EJ 352 = Braund 672; A.A. Barrett, *Historia* 27 (1978), 437–48, esp. 437; Braund, *RFK*, 42).

his ancestral kingdom: i.e., Pontus and Cimmerian Bosporus. The kingdom of Pontus lay along the south-eastern shore of the Black Sea to the north-west of Armenia and to the north-east of Cappadocia. The kingdom of Bosporus on the north side of the Black Sea encompassed the Sea of Azov on its eastern and southern sides and controlled access to the important grain resources of the Crimea. Polemo's grandfather had been set up as king of Pontus by M. Antonius in 37 B.C. (49.25.4) and enrolled among the 'friends and allies of the Roman people' by Aug. in 26 B.C. (53.25.1). He had been granted the kingdom of Bosporus in 14 B.C. by M. Agrippa, after helping Rome put down a revolt here (54.24.4–6). After his assassination later in Aug.'s reign his widow Pythodoris retained control of Pontus, but Bosporus passed into the hands of Aspurgus (Strabo 11.2.10–11; 12.3.29; EJ 172 = Braund 617; Braund 618). Coins bearing regnal years fix the younger Polemo's accession to 38–39 (Smallwood 206 = Braund 634). In 41 Cl. forced him to surrender Bosporus (60.8.2 [= **C.6**]).

on the vote of the senate: The senate continued to play a rôle, even if largely formal, in foreign affairs until the mid-second century (Millar, *ERW*, 343–50; Talbert, *Senate*, 429).

the Rostra: Traditionally the speakers' platform in the Roman Forum, it took its name from the prows or 'beaks' (*rostra*) of six ships which were captured in a naval battle against the fleet of Antium in 338 B.C. and then brought to Rome to decorate this platform (Livy 8.14.12). It was moved from its original site in Caesar's reorganization of the Forum, completed by Aug. in 29 B.C. (Nash II, 272–83; Coarelli, *Guida arch. di Roma*, 62–63, 71).

some add that awnings of silk were used: D. reveals that he used more than one source for this incident as elsewhere (cf. 58.11.7 [= **A.7**]; 59.2.6 [= **B.2**]; 59.25.5 [= **B.18**]; Introduction, Sections 3.2.1 and 3.3). Canvas awnings were used in theatres and amphitheatres to protect spectators from the sun (cf. 63.6.2 [= **D.1**]; Sear, *Architecture*, 37–38, 142–44, 216, 218; they are clearly shown in a wall-painting from Pompeii depicting the riot in the amphitheatre there in 59: M. Grant, *Cities of Vesuvius* (1971), 73; M. Griffin, *Nero: the end of a dynasty* (1984), pl. 6). They were also used to provide shade in the Roman Forum in the heat of the summer (53.31.3; 59.23.9). For D.'s view that the silken awnings used by Julius Caesar were a "device of barbarian luxury" see 43.24.2.

chair: G. and the two consuls would each have sat on a *sella curulis*, a decorated ivory stool, which only magistrates holding *imperium* (consuls and praetors) were allowed to use (O. Wanscher, *Sella curulis* (1980), 121–90).

12.3 Flavius Vespasianus: T. Flavius Vespasianus, the future emperor Vespasian (69–79) (*PIR*² F 398). For the incident cf. Suet. *Vesp.* 5.3. D. is again keen to use anecdotal evidence in the biographical tradition. Vespasian was from a family who had not previously held high senatorial office (Suet. *Vesp.* 1). He and his brother T. Flavius Sabinus, who became urban prefect under Cl., were thus 'new men' (*novi homines*) (Syme, *Tac.*, 43–44). Vespasian had failed in his first attempt on the aedileship (Suet. *Vesp.* 2.3), possibly the result of senatorial rigging: so B. Levick, *Historia* 16 (1967), 224–25; but it is difficult to see why anyone would rig elections to a post for which in some years there was a dearth of candidates largely because of the expense involved in holding the post: cf. 49.16.2 (36 B.C); 53.2.2 (28 B.C.); 55.24.9 (A.D. 5).

duties of the aediles: Their main duties involved the supervision of the city of Rome: the maintenance of streets, public buildings, temples, the water-supply and the markets. Under the Republic they were also expected to put on public shows at the major state festivals, the curule aediles being responsible for the *ludi Romani* and the *ludi Megalenses*, the plebeian aediles for the *ludi Cereales* and the *ludi plebeii*. Under the Principate these responsibilities passed largely to the praetors (54.2.3–4).

the confusion and uproar of civil war: i.e., the wars of 68–69, during which time Galba, Otho, Vitellius and Vespasian were declared emperor (Tac. *H.* (*passim*); K. Wellesley, *The Long Year: A.D. 69* (1975); G.E.F. Chilver, *JRS* 47 (1957), 29–35). D.'s phraseology illustrates his general belief that civil war had to be avoided at all costs as one of the worst evils a state could suffer (Introduction, Section 3.4.3).

omens of Vespasian's rise to power: cf. the sceptical remarks of Tac. *H.* 1.10; 2.78; 4.81. In general on D.'s use of omens see Introduction, Section 3.4.1.

B.11 GAIUS' ATTEMPTS TO RAISE FUNDS; HIS LOVE
OF CHARIOT-RACING   **A.D. 39**

(59.14.1–15.5)

G. held his second consulship during January 39 (cf. Suet. *G.* 17.1). The
year was marked by an increase in the number of trials and condemnations, some being condemned to fight in the arena; G. also lost the
support of the Roman plebs (59.13.3–7; Suet. *G.* 27–32, 35.3; Seneca, *On
Anger* 3.18–19).

14.1–2 For these and other measures to raise revenue cf. Suet. *G.* 38–42. On
finances under G. see Balsdon, *Gaius*, 180–89; Barrett 224–29.

14.2 Circus Games: i.e., *ludi circenses*, a generic term for any games which
included chariot-races, hence Juvenal's famous remark about 'bread and
circuses' being the two major concerns of the Roman plebs (*Sat.* 10.81).
Gladiatorial combats were often put on in the various arenas for chariot-
racing (circuses), especially before the building of permanent amphitheatres at Rome (Friedländer II, 21, 43; Humphrey, *Circuses*, 1, 242).
Chariot-races were staged as the culmination of most major festivals: e.g.
five days of them at the 16-day Roman Games, three days at the 14-day
Plebeian Games (Friedländer II, 19–40; Balsdon, *Life & Leisure*,
314–324).

two praetors be appointed by lot to run the gladiatorial games: Roman
magistrates had traditionally been responsible for putting on public
shows. During the Republic this provided the aediles with a useful means
of winning popular political support (C. Nicolet, *The World of the Citizen
in Republican Rome* (Engl. tr., 1980), 363–73). In 22 B.C. two of the
praetors took over this role (54.2.3–4; 55.31.4; 56.25.8; Tac. *A.* 1.15). An
inscription of 15 (EJ 362 = Braund 783 = Sherk 30) attests the praetors'
putting on races at the Games for Caesar's Victory (*ludi victoriae Caesaris*)
and the consuls' putting on chariot races at the Games of Mars (*ludi
Martiales*). For consuls' putting on games see further 60.27.2 + n. [=
C.13]; Talbert, *Senate*, 59–60.

purchase of gladiators: D. here provides a useful insight into the logistics of
putting on gladiatorial shows. The presiding magistrate had to purchase
the gladiators – usually from the gladiatorial training schools (Friedländer
II, 52–53). This might have been done by letting a contract to the lowest
bidder, as was done to acquire horses for chariot-races (55.10.5). A
surviving extract from a senatorial debate of 177 reveals that the Roman
state collected a tax on such sales (*ILS* 5163, translated by J.H. Oliver and
R.E.A. Palmer, *Hesperia* 24 (1955), 320–49).

14.3 legal restrictions on the number of gladiators: This law was instituted by
Aug. in 22 B.C. (54.2.4) and was reinforced by Tib. (Suet. *T.* 34; Levick,
Tib., 122–3). By such measures the emperor sought (unsuccessfully, it
seems) to control this important means for competitive outlay by senators
(Hopkins, *Death*, 7–14, esp. 7–8).

G. liked to attend gladiatorial shows: cf. Suet. *G.* 18–20; Barrett 44–45.

14.5–6 G.'s passion for chariot-racing: cf. Suet. *G.* 55; Jos. *AJ* 19.257; Barrett

45–6. There were four main teams (*factiones*) involved in chariot-racing: the Greens, the Blues, the Whites and the Reds, each comprising charioteers, trainers, and grooms: see A. Cameron, *Circus Factions* (1976). Charioteers could transfer from one faction to another: in the second century A.D. the immensely successful C. Appuleius Diocles rode successively for the Whites, the Greens and the Reds (*ILS* 5287 = Sherk 167 = LR II, 40; cf. Sherk 168). Nero also favoured the Greens (63.3.3 [= **D.1**]; Suet. *N.* 22.1).

the 'Gaianum': This practice area, located on the right bank of the Tiber near the Vatican, just west of the later Trajan's Naumachia (or arena for naval combats) and north-west of the later Mausoleum of Hadrian (Tac. *A.* 14.14), should not be confused with the Circus of G. and Nero, located partly beneath St. Peter's Basilica in the Gardens of Agrippina to the south-west (Suet. *Cl.* 21.2). The obelisk still to be seen in St. Peter's Square formerly stood in the centre of this Circus (Coarelli, *Guida arch. di Roma*, 318–19 (with plan); Barrett 196).

14.7 Incitatus: or 'Galloper'. Suet. *G.* 55.3 reports the same anecdote with slight variants, but D. draws more humour from the incident by the gradual build-up from the luxurious treatment, to the oaths parodied on those usually associated with the emperor or imperial family, to the offer of the highest political office, the consulship. D. later has G. make one of his horses a priest of the imperial cult (59.28.6 [= **B.22**]). Such malicious stories may have arisen from the Roman élite's scorn for G.'s passion for horse-racing (cf. Pliny, *Letters* 9.6) or from G.'s contempt for ineffectual politicians: he might as well as have had a horse for consul. For other horse-names see *ILS* 5287 = Sherk 167 = LR II, 40; EJ 362 = Braund 783 = Sherk 30; *ILS* 5289 = Sherk 168d. Racehorses are often depicted on Roman mosaics, sometimes along with their names: see K. Dunbabin, *The Mosaics of Roman North Africa* (1978), ch. 6 and Pls. 82, 83, 88, 90; S.J. Keay, *Roman Spain* (1988), 183.

15.1 legacies to the emperor: Legacies were a significant source of imperial wealth (Millar, *ERW*, 153–58). On legacies to G. see Barrett 228.

legal right to accept inheritances: Aug.'s marriage laws (the *lex Iulia de maritandis ordinibus* of 18 B.C. and the *lex Papia Poppaea* of A.D. 9) laid down that if a man or woman of child-producing age remained unmarried, he/she was not legally entitled to receive inheritances; if they married and remained childless, they were entitled to only half their inheritance (Gaius, *Institutes* 2.286; Tac. *A.* 3.28; Crook, *Law & Life*, 121; Gardner, *Women*, 77–78; S. Treggiari, *Roman Marriage* (1991), 60–66; A. Wallace-Hadrill, *PCPhS* 27 (1981), 58–80, esp. 62). Thus technically under these laws G. should have been excluded from receiving inheritances.

G.'s marriages: For details see 59.3.3n. [= **B.3**]. This incident occurred after his divorce of his third wife, Lollia Paullina (59.12.1), and before his marriage to Milonia Caesonia.

had a decree passed: This incident reveals how the emperor still went through the motions of commanding the senate to pass a resolution (*senatus consultum*) supporting the emperor's wishes. Under the Principate senatorial decrees came to have the force of law (Crook, *Law & Life*, 22–23; Talbert, *Senate* 431–59).

15.2 **he took over all the property of those ex-centurions who had bequeathed it to anybody but the emperor:** cf. Suet. *G.* 38.2, who states that this measure covered all property bequeathed after Tib.'s accession in 14 rather than after 17, as D. here claims (see next note for date). It is unclear on what grounds G. reclaimed this property: just possibly he argued that Germanicus had been too generous with his donatives. Tib. had taken back the property bestowed "by the liberality of Aug." on C. Silius, but this was after the latter had committed suicide as he was about to be condemned on charges of extortion and treason (Tac. *A.* 4.20).

after the triumph which G.'s father had celebrated: G.'s father, Germanicus, had celebrated a triumph over the Germans on 26 May 17 (Tac. *A.* 2.41). The event was recalled on coins issued under G. (Smallwood 83 = Braund 177). Troops were traditionally given a donative by their commander at triumphs, centurions receiving proportionally more than soldiers (Hopkins, *Conquerors*, 40).

15.3 **Cn. Domitius Corbulo:** D. here refers to the father (*PIR*² D 141) of the famous general of the same name (*PIR*² D 142), prominent under Cl. and Nero (cf. 63.6.4 [= **D.1**]; 63.17.2–6 [= **D.4**]; Balsdon, *Gaius*, 72). For the elder Corbulo's complaints about the roads and for his prosecution of delinquent road-commissioners in 21 see Tac. *A.* 3.31. However, some scholars have called D.'s account into question and argued that it was the younger Corbulo whom G. used to attack the road-commissioners in 39 (G.B. Townend, *Hermes* 89 (1961), 234–37; R. Syme, *JRS* 60 (1970), 29–31 [= *RP* II, 809–11]; Barrett 97).

the bad state of the roads in Italy: For this problem under Aug. and for the methods that he devised to fund their repair see 53.22.1–2; Suet. *Aug.* 30.1. From 20 B.C. onwards Aug. had appointed a board of senators of praetorian rank (*curatores viarum*) to supervise their upkeep (54.8.4; Suet. *Aug.* 37; Smallwood 227 = Braund 400). Previously the censors had been responsible (P.A. Brunt, *JRS* 70 (1980), 84–88). For details on the road-system in Italy see T.W. Potter, *Roman Italy* (1987), 125–40.

those who had contracted from them the right to do the work: Contracts for all kinds of public works (including the upkeep of roads) were let to the bidder willing to do the job for the smallest sum (E. Badian, *Publicans and Sinners* (1972), 15–25); for such a contractor (*redemptor operum Caesarum et publicorum*) from the reign of Domitian see *ILS* 3512.

15.5 **Corbulo was then appointed consul:** If we accept D.'s version of the incident, this is the only evidence that the elder Corbulo held a suffect consulship. As a result, some scholars have discredited D.'s account and suggested that it was the younger Corbulo who acted for G. against the road-commissioners and was rewarded with a suffect consulship: see 59.15.3n.

Cl.'s repayments of Corbulo's fines: See 60.17.2 [= **C.9**].

B.12 CHANGE IN GAIUS' ATTITUDE TOWARDS TIBERIUS; REINTRODUCTION OF THE CHARGE OF TREASON; HONOURS FOR GAIUS

A.D. 39

(59.16.1–11)

16.1 change in G.'s attitude towards Tib.: G. had begun his reign by distancing himself from Tib.'s policies and even denouncing him (59.2.5n. [= **B.2**]; 59.6.7 [= **B.4**]). But the *Acts of the Arval Brethren* reveal that he had allowed sacrifices to Tib. even before this supposed change in attitude in 39: e.g. on 25 and 26 May 38 (Smallwood 3, lines 38–40) and on 16 November 38 (Smallwood 6, lines 5–7). Thus D. characterizes G.'s attitude towards Tib. in too extreme a way; rather than being totally hostile to him and then suddenly much more sympathetic, G. probably fluctuated between the two positions. On the one hand, G. was Tib.'s adopted grandson and successor, and so needed to emphasize this connexion to legitimate his position as emperor. But on the other hand, as the pious son of Germanicus, he needed to distance himself from Tib., who was held responsible for Germanicus' death. Various factors have been adduced to explain this supposedly sudden change: e.g. that G. needed cash and recognized the possibility of increased revenue that would result from successful prosecutions of the wealthy on treason charges (M.P. Charlesworth, *CAH* X (1934), 657). The fact that D. introduces this in a section concerned with G.'s need to raise funds (cf. 59.14.1; 15.1 [= **B.11**]) lends weight to this hypothesis. Others place more emphasis on G.'s fear of a conspiracy against him – especially from among the senatorial order (Balsdon, *Gaius*, 156; Barrett 92–93). This reversal signalled the end of the period of amnesty towards the supporters of Sej., which explains the suicide of Calvisius Sabinus and his wife (59.18.4 = [**B.14**]; Z. Stewart, *AJP* 74 (1953), 76–77). Furthermore, G. by his change of attitude subordinated any personal grudge against Tib. to his efforts to consolidate the position of the emperor in Roman society; he sought to defend the institution, rather than just one particular emperor. Cl. acted similarly on his accession in 41 in punishing G.'s assassins (60.3.4–5 + n. [= **C.3**]).

16.1–7 G.'s speech in the senate: This is the only speech worked up to any great extent in D.'s account of G.'s reign. As often (cf. 58.19.3–4) D. reports most of the speech in indirect speech and only presents the most dramatic part in G.'s supposed words. It is inserted at a critical point in G.'s reign: his change in attitude towards the senate and the start of a series of senatorial conspiracies, which eventually led to his overthrow. For a full study of the speech see J.-C. Faur, *Klio* 60 (1978), 439–47; cf. Talbert, *Senate*, 325, n. 26). In general on D.'s speeches see Introduction, Section 3.4.2; Millar, *Dio*, 78–83.

16.2 victims of trials on a charge of treason (*maiestas*): For the charge of *maiestas* see 59.6.2n. [= **B.4**]. For these trials, which were conducted in the senate, see Tac. *A*. 5 and 6 (*passim*); R.A. Bauman, *Impietas in*

Principem (1974); Levick, *Tib.*, ch. 11; Talbert, *Senate*, 464–66; 469–70; 477–79.

16.3 those documents that he had claimed to have burned: This reveals that G. had not destroyed all the records of trials conducted during the reign of Tib. as he had earlier claimed (59.6.3 + n. [= **B.4**]). For imperial freedmen assisting the emperor in the senate see Talbert, *Senate*, 167. They were already gaining a prominent rôle in administration under G. (59.26 + n. [= **B.19**]; 60.2.4 + n. [= **C.2**]).

16.4 senatorial flattery of Sej.: cf. 58.2.7–8 [= **A.1**]; 58.4.1–4 [= **A.3**].

16.4–5 he introduced Tib. ..... who spoke: D. here has G. take on the personality of Tib. in mid-speech; for this common rhetorical technique (known as *prosôpopoeia*) cf. Cic. *pro Caelio*, 34–38.

16.6 take thought only for your own pleasure and safety: A succinct summary of the reasons for Tib.'s withdrawal to Capri (cf. 58.3.3n. [= **A.1**]).

16.6–7 The advice which D. here has Tib. give to G. about how to treat his subjects goes directly against that which he has Maecenas give Aug. at 52.34–35. D. thus emphasizes his view that Tib. and G. conducted themselves in a far from ideal manner as emperors (Introduction, Section 4.3). For the doctrine of self-advantage expressed here D. once again owes a considerable debt to Thucydides: cf. Thuc. 5.89; Introduction, Section 3.4.3.

16.8 reintroduced the charge of treason (*maiestas*): For doubts that G. had ever abolished the charge see 59.6.2n. [= **B.4**].

this be inscribed on a bronze plaque: The texts of emperors' speeches in the senate were recorded in the *acta senatus* and occasionally on bronze plaques: e.g. Cl.'s speech on allowing aristocrats from central Gaul into the senate (Smallwood 369 = Braund 570); see Talbert, *Senate*, 318. For the symbolic significance of inscribing decrees and edicts on bronze see C. Williamson, *Classical Antiquity* 6.1 (1987), 160–83.

set out for the suburbs: The suburbs of Rome consisted of a ring of desirable villas or gardens (*horti*) owned by the Roman élite, which were gradually acquired by the imperial family (cf. 60.31.5; Tac. *A.* 11.1). G., and other emperors, made frequent use of such villas as the Gardens of Agrippina, of Lamia, of Sallust, of Maecenas (59.21.2 [= **B.15**]; Philo, *Embassy* 181, 351–67; Millar, *ERW* 22–24). For their archaeological remains see R. Lanciani, *The Ruins and Excavations of Ancient Rome* (1897), 394–427, 544–51 and fig. 150 (plan); P. Grimal, *Les jardins romains* (2nd ed., 1969) 136–59; for discussion N. Purcell in *Ancient Roman Villa Gardens* (ed. E. McDougall, 1987), 185–203.

16.10 clemency: See 58.5.4n. [= **A.4**].

the days belonging to the palace: D. possibly refers to the *ludi Palatini*, for which see 56.46.5; 59.27.4 + n. [= **B.23**]. But the expression that he uses makes his precise meaning unclear.

a golden image of the emperor: Strictly speaking, such an image would have been gilded rather than solid gold. Gilded statues were not granted solely to emperors (Price, *Rituals*, 172–88, esp. 186–87; D. Fishwick, *ZPE* 76 (1989), 175–83).

hymns sung by boys of noble families: At important rituals hymns were usually sung by boys and/or girls from the noblest families and both of whose parents were still alive: e.g. at the Secular Games of 17 B.C. (Horace, *Secular Hymn*; EJ 31 and 32 = Braund 769 = Sherk 11, lines 147ff.); cf. 59.7.1 [= **B.5**]; 59.29.6 [= **B.23**].

16.11 lesser form of triumph: i.e., an ovation (*ovatio*), a less spectacular parade than a triumph. For details see Plut. *Marcellus* 22; Aulus Gellius, *Attic Nights* 5.6.21; Versnel, *Triumphus*, 165–68. Some of differences between the two parades can best be summarized in a table:

ovation	triumph
on foot or horseback	in 4-horse chariot
purple-bordered toga	completely purple toga with gold designs
myrtle wreath	laurel wreath
parade led by equestrian order and plebeians	parade led by senators and troops
flute-players	trumpeters
sacrifice of sheep	sacrifice of bull

The senate had to pass a resolution granting the emperor (or a member of his family) an ovation (48.31.3; 54.8.3; 54.33.4; 54.34.3; 55.2.4). Barrett 278, n. 11 suggests that G. may never have been offered an ovation on this occasion, on the grounds that D. here duplicates the ovation offered G. later in 39 during his German expedition (59.23.2 [= **B.17**]). But there is no firm evidence to contradict D. on this point.

B.13 GAIUS AND THE BRIDGE AT BAIAE   A.D. 39

(59.17.1–11)

17.1–11 For other accounts of this famous incident see Suet. *G.* 19, 32.1; Jos. *AJ* 19.5–6; Seneca, *On the Brevity of Life* 18.5–6. D. works it up into a fine literary passage, part fact, part fiction, full of descriptive and dramatic detail and no little ironic humour. D. is the only source to date the incident, but many small details differ in the various accounts: e.g. the length and exact location of the bridge, the nature of the breastplate. As the story was retold, it gained further elaboration and exaggeration. For D. it serves to underline G.'s extravagance and financial mismanagement, a leitmotif of his account of G. (59.2.5–6 [= **B.2**]; 59.22.1–5 [= **B.16**]). But it also introduces the two major themes of the second part of G.'s reign: (a) his military aspirations and the need to win military glory: e.g. the expedition to Gaul and Germany (59.21–22 [= **B.15** and **B.16**]) and the proposed invasion of Britain (59.25.1–2 [= **B.18**]), and (b) his megalomania and growing madness (cf. 59.28 [= **B.22**]).

From this point on the historian faces a serious problem of how to account for the stories of G.'s eccentric behaviour. If we are to believe them, should we attribute them to mental disorders? Or should they be discounted as merely malicious stories, in part invented to justify the plot to assassinate G.? For further discussion of G.'s madness, which may have been caused by his illness in 37, see 59.8.1 + n. [= **B.6**]; Balsdon, *Gaius*, 212–14; Barrett 214–16.

17.1 G. not impressed with this kind of procession: i.e., the ovation voted G. by the senate (59.16.11 [= **B.12**]). Tib. had shown similar disdain for an ovation in 21 (Tac. *A*. 3.47, where he describes an ovation as "the worthless prize of a suburban peregrination").

Puteoli to Bauli: Puteoli (modern Pozzuoli in the Bay of Naples) was at this date the major seaport on the west coast of Italy (M.W. Frederiksen, *Campania* (1984), 319–58; J.H. d'Arms, *JRS* 64 (1974), 104–24). Ostia, the port at the mouth of the Tiber, was only developed under Cl. and Nero (60.11.2–5 + nn. [= **C.7**]). Bauli lay between ancient Baiae and Misenum. For variations on the exact location of the bridge cf. Suet. *G*. 19.1 (Puteoli to Baiae); Jos. *AJ* 19.5 (Puteoli to Misenum); Barrett 212. D. was personally familiar with the area (Introduction, Section 1.1.1).

three-and-a-half miles: cf. Suet. *G*. 19.1 (just over three Roman miles). D. uses a Greek unit of measurement: 26 stades (1 stade = approximately 200 yards).

17.2 some boats were specially constructed: Two massive "pleasure boats" (one measuring 73m long x 24m wide, the other 71m long x 20m wide) dating from the reign of G. and sumptuously outfitted were discovered at the bottom of Lake Nemi (c. 30 km SE of Rome) in the 15th. century, but unfortunately destroyed during World War II (Barrett 201–02).

severe famine in Rome and Italy: A contemporary witness, Seneca, (*On the Brevity of Life* 18.5) mentions a severe grain shortage under G., but dates it to the winter of 40–41. D. seems to have conflated two separate incidents in his eagerness to connect the requisitioning of merchant ships for the bridge in 39 with the famine of 40–41. Suet. *G*. 19 does not make the causal link, but gives other examples of G.'s cavalier attitude towards the food supply (cf. *G*. 26.5 and 39.1). The parade at the bridge probably took place in high summer, and if so, the ships would have been prevented from sailing to Egypt to bring back the grain harvest. But D. grossly exaggerates in suggesting that all the grain ships were requisitioned for this parade (Garnsey, *Famine*, 222–23). Nevertheless, D.'s account illustrates how heavily Rome and Italy relied on imported grain, especially from Egypt and north Africa (G. Rickman, *The Corn Supply of Ancient Rome* (1981); Garnsey, *Famine*, chs. 12–15).

17.3 G. put on the breastplate of Alexander the Great: cf. Suet. *G*. 52, adding that G. had stolen it from Alexander's tomb at Alexandria. Throughout this ceremony G. consciously modelled himself on Alexander. In addition to the breastplate, his wearing of a silk cloak and jewels from India alluded symbolically to Alexander's subjection of the East. The designation of his entourage as "friends and companions" (59.17.6 + n.) and his personal drunkenness (59.17.9–10 + n.) further emphasized the link with Alexander (Balsdon, *Gaius*, 52–54). For earlier Romans who had modelled themselves on Alexander see Syme, *RR*, 54, 305; Zanker, *Power of Images*, 9–11, 22–24, 36. Cn. Pompeius Magnus had allegedly worn Alexander's cloak at his triumph in 61 B.C. (Appian, *Mithridatic Wars* 117).

cloak of purple silk: A law of 16 had attempted to prevent men from wearing silk (57.15.1; Tac. *A*. 2.33; cf. Suet. *G*. 52); it was considered a sign of Oriental luxury, and hence morally degenerate. For further criticism of G. for using silk cf. 59.12.2 [= **B.10**]; 59.26.10 [= **B.20**].

garland of oak-leaves: i.e., the *corona civica*, the most prestigious Roman military decoration, awarded for saving the life of a Roman citizen in battle (V.A. Maxfield, *The Military Decorations of the Roman Army* (1981), 70–74, 119). By wearing it, G. was seeking to boost his military image. Aug. had turned the oak-garland into an imperial symbol, by accepting the senate's proposal that he set it up over the entrance to his house on the Palatine (53.16.4; *RG* 34.2).

17.4 sacrificed to Envy: D., like many other Greek authors, here personifies the general malignant forces at work in the world as a divine power, Envy (*Phthonos*). The Greeks and the Romans believed that it was necessary to ward off these malignant forces (the "evil eye") by ritual acts of propiation and by wearing protective amulets (cf. Plut. *Moralia* 680c–683b). That Envy constituted one of the chief dangers confronting a monarch was a commonplace of Greek rhetoric (C.P. Jones, *The Roman World of Dio Chrysostom* (1978), 100), and appears as a theme several times in speeches in D.'s account of Aug. (52.2.2; 53.8.6; 55.15.1; cf. 54.31.1).

17.5 Darius, a member of the Arsacid dynasty, as one of the Parthian hostages: Darius had been sent as a hostage to Rome after L. Vitellius' settlement of eastern affairs with Artabanus III of Parthia in 37 (59.27.3 + n. [= **B.21**]; Jos. *AJ* 18.103). The Arsacid dynasty had held power in Parthia since the mid-third century B.C. (63.5.2n. [= **D.1**]). For some suggestions on the militaristic significance of Darius' presence in G.'s triumphal procession see Balsdon, *Gaius*, 52–54.

17.6 friends and companions: These titles had been used to designate Alexander the Great's élite cavalry and closest advisers (N.G.L. Hammond, *The Macedonian State* (1989), 54–58, 140–48; A.B. Bosworth, *Conquest and Empire* (1989), 261–62, 268–70, 274). G. by adopting them enhanced his image as the new Alexander.

dressed in flowered tunics: D. considered such tunics a totally inappropriate form of dress for Romans (cf. 63.13.3 [= **D.3**]).

17.6–8 The address to the troops, the handouts and the celebratory banquet, all here burlesqued, were as much a part of a triumph as the central element, the procession and parade of spoils (43.21.3; Livy 30.45.3; 33.23; Plin. *NH* 37.16).

17.9 fires were lit all around, as if they were in a theatre: D. here provides an interesting insight into how Roman theatres were lit. The simile suggests that the whole semi-circular auditorium (and not just the stage) was illuminated all around by torches. On Roman theatres see Vitruvius 5.3–9; M. Bieber, *A History of the Greek and Roman Theater* (2nd ed., 1961), 190–226.

for he wanted to make the night day, just as he had made the sea land: Such desire to overturn nature was commonly attributed to tyrants in the ancient world: e.g. Xerxes, king of Persia, who bridged the Hellespont, thus making the sea land, during his invasion of Greece in 480–79 (Hdt. 7.33–56).

17.9–10 G.'s drunken behaviour: For violent outbursts at the military banquets of Alexander the Great see Plut. *Alex.* 50–51.

17.11 Darius and Xerxes: Achaemenid kings of Persia; Darius ruled from c. 522–486 B.C., Xerxes from 486–465. Darius had bridged the Bosphorus as a prelude to his unsuccessful invasion of Scythia in c. 512 B.C. (Hdt. 4.83–89), while Xerxes built a bridge of boats across the Hellespont in 480 at the start of his unsuccessful attempt to conquer Greece (Hdt. 7.33–56). The direct comparison between G. and Xerxes had already been made by Seneca, a contemporary witness (Seneca, *On the Brevity of Life* 18.5).

B.14 GAIUS AND TRIALS: DOMITIUS AFER AND SENECA   A.D. 39

(59.18.1–19.8)

18.1 financial exhaustion, persecution of the rich: cf. Suet. *G.* 38. To raise funds, G. had to resort to securing condemnations in the courts, a technique developed by Tib. (Levick, *Tib.*, 101–02). The property of the condemned then accrued to the state (Crook, *Law & Life*, 219, 275–76; Millar, *ERW*, 163–74). The literary sources, putting forth the senatorial viewpoint, exaggerate G.'s rapacity (Millar, *ERW*, 167–68) and play down a much more plausible reason for G.'s persecutions: i.e., that he had to put down serious senatorial opposition to his rule (Barrett 91–113). That emperors' financial extravagance led to extortion of funds from the rich through judicial accusations was a leitmotif of the biographical tradition concerning 'bad' emperors (cf. Suet. *N.* 32.1; Wallace-Hadrill, *Suet.*, 169–74). Cl. in 41 returned the property of those condemned under Tib. and G. (60.6.3 [= **C.5**]).

18.2 trials: For the emperor as judge see Millar, *ERW*, 516–27. For trials presided over by the emperor in the senate see Talbert, *Senate*, 460–87. For appeals to the emperor see Millar, *ERW*, 507–16; A.H.M. Jones, *Studies in Roman Government and Law* (1960), 93–98.

decisions of senate were made public in the usual way: i.e., in the proceedings of the senate (*acta senatus*) (Talbert, *Senate*, 308–23). Aug. had suspended the publication of these *acta* (Suet. *Aug.* 36), a measure rescinded by Tib. (Suet. *T.* 73.1). In what form the *acta* were made public remains problematic. Since it is probable that only senators and emperors could consult these *acta*, G. sought wider publicity by posting lists of the condemned, probably on whitened wooden boards (*alba*) erected in the Forum; for parallels for this method of publication cf. 45.17.1; 47.16.1; 55.3.3; 59.28.11 [= **B.22**]. Both D. and Tac. (or, more likely, their annalistic sources) used the *acta senatus* for source material: for D. see P.M. Swan, *Phoenix* 41 (1987), 272–91, esp. 285; for Tac. R. Syme, *JRS* 72 (1982), 68–82 [= *RP* IV, 199–222].

18.3 hurled down from the Capitol: To be more precise, they were thrown down from the Tarpeian Rock; for this method of execution cf. 57.22.5; 58.15.3; Tac. *A.* 6.19; 60.18.4 [= **C.10**].

there is no need to bore my readers by going into meaningless details: D. frequently admits to this principle of selectivity: cf. 59.11.6; 59.22.5 [= **B.17**]; 60.11.6; 63.26.4 [= **D.7**]; Introduction, Section 3.3.

18.4 C. Calvisius Sabinus: *PIR*[2] C 354; for his earlier career see Tac. *A.* 4.46; 6.9. He had been consul in 26 with Cn. Lentulus Gaetulicus and then governor of Pannonia some time after late 36. On his alleged conspiracy see Barrett 100–01; C.J. Simpson in *Studies in Latin Literature and Roman History. II* (ed. C. Deroux, 1980), 347–66.

was indicted with his wife Cornelia: For Cornelia see *PIR*[2] C 1479. Syme, *AA*, 298 has argued that Calvisius and Cornelia may have been indicted for participating in the conspiracy of Cn. Lentulus Gaetulicus, on which see 59.22.5 + n. [= **B.17**]. This view is based on the possibility that Cornelia may have been a sister of Gaetulicus and the fact that Calvisius had been *consul ordinarius* with Gaetulicus in 26. As governor of Pannonia, Calvisius had command of three legions (A. Mócsy, *Pannonia and Upper Moesia* (1974), 42–48). Gaetulicus at the time of his downfall had been in command of the four legions of Upper Germany since 30. A combination of such forces would have presented a very serious threat to G. However, neither D. nor Suet. *G.* 24.3 suggest that this conspiracy was as serious as some modern scholars suggest. Rather, G. disposed individually of those whom he thought posed a threat. He did not on this occasion need to discover, and taken action against, a "conspiracy".

the charge against Cornelia: Wives were expected to behave with decorum if they accompanied their husbands on provincial commands: Plancina, the wife of Cn. Calpurnius Piso, governor of Syria in 18, went beyond the bounds of feminine decency by attending cavalry and infantry drill exercises (Tac. *A.* 2.55). D.'s words here imply that Cornelia went further; that she was accused of adultery is confirmed by Tac. *H.* 1.48. Adultery was often associated with a charge of treason: cf. 58.24.5; 59.22.6 + n. [= **B.17**]; 59.26.4 [= **B.19**]. For wives accompanying provincial governors to their provinces see A.J. Marshall, *G&R* 22 (1975), 11–18.

18.5 Titius Rufus: otherwise unknown. Barrett 99 suggests that the charge may have been laid by some senators seeking G.'s favour.

Junius Priscus: otherwise unknown.

19.1–6 Domitius Afer: Cn. Domitius Afer (*PIR*[2] D 126), a leading orator of the Julio-Claudian period (Quintilian, *Institutes* 12.11.3; G.A. Kennedy, *The Art of Rhetoric in the Roman World* (1972), 442–46, 487–88). Quintilian published a collection of his witticisms (*Inst.* 6.3.42). Afer had prosecuted Agrippina's cousin, Claudia Pulchra, in 26 (Tac. *A.* 4.52) and Claudia Pulchra's son, Quinctilius Varus, in 28 (Tac. *A.* 4.66). Thus G. was here attacking him for his previous hostility to members of G.'s own family. Afer had been a supporter of Sej. and had, therefore, borne a grudge against the family of Germanicus and Agrippina in the 20s (Z. Stewart, *AJP* 74 (1953), 77). Since G. was now more favourably disposed towards Tib. (59.16.1 [= **B.12**]), it seems strange that he would have let a supposed supporter of Sej. off the hook. See further Barrett 97–98.

19.2 **"it's not you that I hold responsible, but Agamemnon":** Agrippina's retort is adapted from Homer, *Iliad*, 1.335–36, where Achilles responds to Agamemnon's messengers who had come to take his concubine Briseis away to Agamemnon. Agrippina meant that she excused Afer since she realized that he had acted only on the instructions of Tib. ("Agamemnon").

an image of the emperor: By an image D. could mean a bust, a statue or (less likely here) a painting (58.11.3n. [= **A.7**]). The fact that it had an honorific inscription listing G.'s offices and powers might suggest a statue, mounted on an inscribed base.

to the effect that G. was twenty-seven years old and holding the consulship for the second time: G. was born on 31 August 12 (Suet. *G.* 8.1). He held his first consulship in 37 (59.7.9 [= **B.5**]), his second in 39 (59.13.1 [= **B.11**]). The usual age for holding the consulship was 42, although patricians might hold it in their early- to mid-thirties (Talbert, *Senate*, 20).

19.3 **G. always claimed to be the best of all orators:** For his vigorous oratory see Tac. *A.* 13.3; Suet. *G.* 53; Jos. *AJ* 19.208.

19.6 **Callistus:** C. Iulius Callistus, a leading imperial freedman under G. and Cl. (*PIR*² J 229; Jos. *AJ* 19.64–69; Seneca, *Letters* 47.9). For his part in the successful conspiracy against G. in 41 see 59.29.1 [= **B.23**]; for his later career under Cl. see Tac. *A.* 11.29, 38; 12.1–2. D. suggests here that Callistus had become in effect the patron of a leading senator, while his influence on the emperor foreshadows that of later imperial freedmen on Cl. and Nero (cf. 60.2.4 + n. [= **C.2**]; 60.17.5 [= **C.10**]; 63.12 [= **D.3**]).

19.7 **L. Annaeus Seneca:** *PIR*² A 617. Seneca the younger, the writer of tragedies, moral essays and letters on moral philosophy, was born in Corduba, Spain in c. 4 B.C. After holding the quaestorship and entering the senate in c. 32, he was exiled by Cl. in 41 (60.8.5 [= **C.6**]), but recalled in 49 to be the tutor of the future emperor Nero (Tac. *A.* 12.8). He played an influential rôle during Nero's early years as emperor, but was forced to withdraw from public life in 62 (Tac. *A.* 14.52–56) and committed suicide in 65 when accused of complicity in the conspiracy of C. Calpurnius Piso (Tac. *A.* 15.60–64). For a full study see M. Griffin, *Seneca: a philosopher in politics* (1976). Most scholars reject this story as a later invention to explain how Seneca escaped the tyranny of G. (Griffin, *Seneca*, 53–56; Barrett 112–13); cf. Pliny, *Letters* 7.27.14, explaining how he escaped Domitian. D. was generally hostile towards Seneca (61.10; 62.12.1; 62.24.1; 61.25.1; Syme, *Tac.*, 550–51; Griffin, *Seneca*, 427–40). For the suggestion that D. here conflates G.'s known aversion to Seneca's style (Suet. *G.* 53.2) and the incident retold by Seneca, *Letters* 78.6, see Z. Stewart, *AJP* 74 (1953), 80–81.

B.15 ELECTIONS; AFRICA; GAIUS' EXPEDITION TO GAUL   A.D. 39

(59.20.1–21.4)

20.1–3 This section raises considerable problems, but contains vital information on the suffect consuls of 39 and on how they, and other magistrates,

were appointed. The translation of 59.20.3 is based on a textual emendation of the manuscript reading, which helps to resolve some of the
problems, but requires us to revise the standard view on the consular pairs
of the year.

20.1 **he appointed Domitius consul after removing those who were then in office:**
cf. Suet. *G.* 26.3. Two Domitii held suffect consulships in 39: Cn. Domitius
Corbulo (cf. 59.15.3–5 + nn. [= **B.11**]) and Cn. Domitius Afer (cf. 59.19
[= **B.14**]). Since D. has just been discussing Afer at some length, it is more
likely that it was he who was appointed suffect consul after G. had
removed the two incumbents. If this is right, then Corbulo must have been
one of the suffect consuls removed from office; the identity of Corbulo's
colleague who committed suicide remains unknown. It was normal under
the Julio-Claudians for consuls to hold office for six months, although
when the emperor was consul, he often resigned sooner.

they had failed to proclaim a supplication for his birthday: G.'s birthday was
31 August (Suet. *G.* 8.1). From this it follows that G. removed the consuls
early in September. Supplications were held at times of national disaster
or triumph, to allow all Romans to offer appropriate prayers to the gods,
whose statues were placed out-of-doors on sacred couches (*pulvinaria*)
(37.36.3; 39.53.2; 54.3.8; 57.6.4; Liebeschuetz, *CCRR*, 80). They had
become a customary part of celebrations of the emperor's birthday
(51.19.2).

the praetors had put on circus games and had slaughtered wild-beasts: The
praetors had become responsible for such a celebration on Aug.'s birthday
(54.26.2; 54.34.1–2; 55.6.6; cf. 54.8.5, organized by the aediles). Tib. had
not allowed any such celebrations on his birthday (57.8.3; 58.12.8). Aug.'s
birthday was celebrated in the same way even after his death (57.14.4). In
40 G. instituted similar celebrations on Tib.'s and Drusilla's birthdays
(59.24.7).

festival to commemorate the victories of Augustus over Antonius: The *ludi
Actiaci* were held every fifth year on 2–3 September to commemorate
Aug.'s victory at Actium over the forces of M. Antonius and Cleopatra in
31 B.C. (51.19.2; 53.1.4–5). D. here provides evidence that the consuls
were responsible for funding this festival (cf. 60.27.2n. [= **C.13**]).

20.2 **G. poses as the descendant of Antonius rather than of Augustus:** G. was the
great-grandson of both M. Antonius (on his father Germanicus' side) and
Aug. (on his mother Agrippina's side).

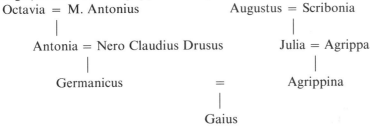

This passage of D. is reminiscent of Tac. *A.* 2.53, where Germanicus
poignantly recalls at the site of the battle of Actium that he traced his
ancestry back to both Aug. and Antonius.

20.3 fasces: These were the bundles of rods and axes carried by the attendants (lictors) of all magistrates with *imperium*; they thus symbolized the magistrate's power to take action (cf. 58.5.6n. [= **A.4**]; 59.3.5n. [= **B.3**]). G. here symbolically terminates the consuls' period in office. For magistrates' *fasces* being broken to pieces as a protest against their intended actions in the violence of the late Republic see 36.39.3; 38.6.3; 38.30.2.

Domitius and his colleague: The manuscripts of D. here read: "Domitius was chosen as his colleague, nominally by the people, but really by Gaius himself." This raises insurmountable problems as to the identity of Domitius and, even more so, his colleague (Syme, *Tac.*, 327–28, 788). My translation is here based on a neat textual emendation of J.W. Humphrey and P.M. Swan, *Phoenix* 37 (1983), 324–27, adding the word 'and', which makes much better sense. Cary's Loeb translation, which has Domitius as the emperor's colleague, is clearly impossible. If D. refers to Domitius Afer (59.20.1n.), then his colleague was A. Didius Gallus, as revealed on a wax tablet, dated to 15 September 39 (*AE* 1973, 138). If the emendation of Humphrey and Swan is accepted, then the conclusions of P.A. Gallivan, *Antichthon* 13 (1979), 66–69 on the consuls of 39 need revision. The pairs of consuls (with their periods in office) can now be shown to have been as follows:

1–30 Jan. (*consules ordinarii*)   G. + L. Apronius Caesianus
31 Jan.–30 June   L. Apronius Caesianus + Q. Sanquinius Maximus
1 Jul.–?2 Sept.   Cn. Domitius Corbulo + unknown colleague
?4 Sept.–31 Dec. Cn. Domitius Afer + A. Didius Gallus

20.4–5 elections under G.: See further 59.9.6n. [= **B.7**].

20.4 the semblance of democracy was maintained, but there was no substance to it: D. here modifies Thucydides' famous remark about democracy in Athens under Perikles: "in theory a democracy, but in fact rule by the first man" (Thuc. 2.65.9). For Thucydides as a major model for D. see Introduction 3.4.2; 3.4.3.

20.5 number of praetors: Praetors were the magistrates next in rank to the consuls. Their number fluctuated until 42, when sixteen became the norm (58.20.5; 60.10.4; Hopkins, *Death*, 157). Some scholars hold that fifteen was the normal number under G. (W.K. Lacey, *Historia* 12 (1963), 175), others that fifteen were only appointed in 39 (P.M. Swan in *Studies in Latin Literature and Roman History* (ed. C. Deroux, 1979), 376–78).

20.6 Carrinas Secundus: *PIR²* C 449; Juv. *Sat.* 7.203–06 alludes to this episode. The orator's fate suggests that freedom of speech, championed by G. at the start of his reign, was now being discouraged (Barrett 99). For a similar incident under Domitian cf. 67.12.5 with R. MacMullen, *Enemies of the Roman Order* (1966), 35–36.

a speech against tyranny: The relative merits of different types of government had always been a common theme in ancient rhetoric (cf. Hdt. 3.80–82) and were discussed at length by D. himself in the debate that he composed between Agrippa and Maecenas, advocating democracy (i.e., a Republican form of government) and monarchy respectively (52.1–40; cf. Millar, *Dio*, 102–18, 194–201). For the nature of Roman rhetorical exercises see G. Kennedy, *The Art of Rhetoric in the Roman World* (1972), 91–94.

20.7 Lucius Piso: L. Calpurnius Piso, consul in 27 (*PIR*² C 293; Syme, *AA*, 59, 369, 379). He was the son of Cn. Calpurnius Piso (consul in 7) and Plancina, the pair suspected of murdering Germanicus in Syria in 19 (Tac. *A*. 2.69–71). In general on the family see Syme, *AA*, chs. 24 and 26.

G. divided the province of Africa into two parts: There were two main types of Roman province: the so-called "imperial" provinces, each governed by a *legatus Augusti pro praetore*, appointed directly by the emperor, and the "public" provinces (often incorrectly termed "senatorial" provinces), each governed by a proconsul chosen by lot in the senate (53.12–15; Strabo 17.3.25 [= Sherk 4]; Millar, *REN*, 54–56; id., *Ancient World* 20 (1989), 93–97). For some strong arguments that in practical terms there was little difference between the two types of province see F. Millar, *JRS* 56 (1966), 156–66.

The province of Africa Proconsularis had hitherto been the only public province in which the governor had command of a legionary garrison, based until the Flavian period at Ammaedara (Haidra) in Numidia. By this reform G. put an end to the anomaly. The emperor henceforth appointed his own legate (i.e., army commander) for Legion III Augusta, while the proconsul of Africa retained civil authority and was chosen by lot in the senate from among the ex-consuls (Barrett 215–23). On the province of Africa in general see P. Garnsey in *Imperialism in the Ancient World* (ed. P. Garnsey and C.R. Whittaker, 1978), 223–54.

D. is anachronistic in talking of the province being divided into two parts, since Numidia was only constituted as a separate province under Septimius Severus (A.R. Birley, *The African Emperor: Septimius Severus* (rev. ed., 1988), 147 + n. 3). The date of the reform given by D. is also disputed, some scholars preferring 37 (Balsdon, *Gaius*, 155; E. Fentress, *Numidia and the Roman Army* (1979), 68–69). As for the motivation for the reform, D. and Tac. concur that it was fear of a senatorially-appointed governor having command of a legion and auxiliaries, but disagree over the identity of the governor. Tac. *H*. 4.48.2 claims that it was M. Iunius Silanus (consul in 19); but since he was proconsul from 29–35 before L. Calpurnius Piso, D.'s version is to be preferred (R. Syme, *Historia* 30 (1981), 189–202, esp. 197 [= *RP* III, 1350–63, esp. 1357–58]). It is typical that D. and Tac., both senators, claim that a sensible administrative reform was brought about by G.'s personal suspicion of senators. Note also the way in which D. likes to trace the origins of customs still prevalent in his own day (Introduction, Section 3.4.3 and Appendix 2).

21.1–4 G.'s Gallic expedition: cf. Suet. *G*. 43–49; Tac. *Agr*. 13; *Germ*. 37; Balsdon, *Gaius*, 58–95; Barrett 125–33. All the sources trivialize this expedition. The reasons given for it by D. are more convincing that those of Suet. *G*. 43 (to collect Batavian recruits for his bodyguard). But D. fails to give a satisfactory account of the German threat, which was real (cf. Tac. *A*. 4.72–74). In addition, G. needed to win both the loyalty of the army and personal military glory by appearing as a leader in battle, since unlike Aug. and Tib. he had had no military experience when he came to power; the same applied to Cl. and Nero (Hopkins, *Conquerors*, 224). For Gaul under G. see D.F. Drinkwater, *Roman Gaul* (1983), 35–36. For a

statue from Lydia of a fighting cavalryman and a female personification of
Germany, commemorating G.'s 'conquest' of the Germans, see Smallwood 34 = Braund 182.

21.2 **the suburbs:** For G.'s use of suburban villas see 59.16.8 + n. [= **B.12**].

21.3 **G.'s abortive invasion of Britain:** For a fuller account see 59.25.1–3 [=
B.18].

he inflicted many cruel injuries on subject peoples, allies and fellow citizens:
Requisitioning by the Roman army was one of the commonest complaints
against Roman misrule in the provinces (Tac. *Agr.* 30–32; McCrum &
Woodhead 466 = Sherk 95; P.A. Brunt, *Historia* 10 (1961), 189–227 [=
RIT, 53–95]. For an edict of the governor of Pisidia, laying down precisely
the services and goods the Pisidians had to provide, see S. Mitchell, *JRS*
66 (1976), 106–31 = Braund 552 = Sherk 29.

subject peoples, allies, fellow citizens: D. here provides a brief summary of
the main status divisions of the population of the Roman Empire. Subject
peoples (or *peregrini*) were the least privileged, since they were forced to
pay annual land and poll taxes to Rome; allies were citizens of communities bound to Rome by a treaty, who might be excused certain, but not all,
tax obligations; by "fellow citizens" D. means Roman citizens, the most
privileged group, which comprised Romans and Italians who went out to
Roman colonies in the provinces and provincial subjects granted Roman
citizenship. See further A.N. Sherwin-White, *The Roman Citizenship* (2nd
ed., 1973), 221–50.

21.4 **individuals and city authorities brought him gifts:** Gift-giving was a
common ritual throughout the ancient world, which helped to define and
reinforce social relationships (M.I. Finley, *The World of Odysseus* (2nd
ed., 1978), 95–98; G. Herman, *Ritualised Friendship and the Greek City*
(1987); Veyne, *Bread*, 5–10). Gifts were given to the Roman emperor not
only to demonstrate an individual's or community's loyalty, but also to
secure, or maintain, his favour and protection. Conversely, the emperor
was also expected on occasion to reciprocate and bestow gifts upon his
subjects (Millar, *ERW*, 139–44).

B.16 FURTHER EXTRAVAGANCE AND ARROGANCE OF GAIUS IN GAUL
A.D. 39

(59.22.1–4)

22.1 **especially on the legions:** The army was the main item of state expenditure
under the Principate (Garnsey and Saller, *RE*, 88–95; K. Hopkins, *JRS* 70
(1980), 227). D.'s criticism of G. on this count is unfair, since military
expenditure was a structural part of the Roman imperial system and not
really a matter of choice for any particular emperor. D. was firmly
opposed to large overseas campaigns, since they were a great drain on
financial resources and brought a small yield in revenue (75.3.2–3).

games at Lugdunum: For more details on these games at modern Lyons,
the capital of Gallia Lugdunensis, see Suet. *G.* 20.

22.2 he was acclaimed *Imperator* seven times: For more details of these battles see Suet. *G*. 45–48. G. here receives a traditional military honour, first paid P. Cornelius Scipio Africanus in Spain in 209 B.C. (Livy 27.19). During the Principate an emperor could be acclaimed *Imperator* on any occasion that a Roman army won a military victory, since technically the emperor was in command of all Roman armies and all Roman generals operated under his auspices (i.e., as representatives of the emperor). The emperor listed the number of such acclamations as part of his official titles (60.8.7 + n. [= **C.6**]). For possible reasons for G.'s acclamations here see Balsdon, *Gaius*, 82. These acclamations should be distinguished from the use of *Imperator* as part of the emperor's name from Aug. onwards (R. Syme, *Historia* 7 (1958), 172–88 [= *RP* I, 361–77]). D. as a conservative senator is mildly critical of G. for subverting a traditional Roman military honour. For further sarcastic attitudes to emperors' sham military achievements cf. 60.21.4–5 [= **C.11**].

22.3–4 These anecdotes all appear in Suet., but in completely different contexts. The bald men incident takes place in the amphitheatre at Rome (Suet. *G*. 27.1); the dice incident also occurs in Rome on the Palatine (id., 41.2); for a man put to death through mistaken identity see id., 30.1. They are derived from the repertoire of traditional stories told against tyrants, and have no value as specific evidence for G.'s acts (R.P. Saller, *G&R* 27 (1980), 69–83). For D.'s inclusion of anecdotes in his history see further Introduction, Section 3.4.1.

22.3 census lists: Provincial censuses were carried out at irregular intervals throughout the Empire from Aug. onwards (P.A. Brunt, *JRS* 71 (1981), 163–72 [= *RIT*, 329–46]). Censuses are known to have been conducted in Gaul in 27 B.C. (53.22.5), 12 B.C. (Livy, *Per*. 138) and A.D. 14–15 (Tac. *A*. 1.31, 33; 2.6). It can be inferred from this anecdote that copies of these census lists were kept in the provinces.

B.17 THE CONSPIRACY OF GAETULICUS AND LEPIDUS; GAIUS' ATTITUDE TOWARDS CLAUDIUS   A.D. 39

(59.22.5–23.2; 23.4–5)

22.5 there is no need to mention them all by name: D. was selective in what he included in his history, to prevent his narrative becoming cluttered with detail (cf. 59.18.3n. [= **B.13**]; Introduction, Section 3.3).
those for whom history demands a mention: D. believed firmly in the dignity of history (cf. 63.20.6 [= **D.5**]; 66.9.4; see further Introduction, Section 3.3).

22.5–23.1 the 'conspiracy' of Gaetulicus: cf. Suet. *G*. 24.5–6. The *Acts of the Arval Brethren* record that sacrifices were conducted on 27 October 39 to commemorate the detection of the 'nefarious plot of Cn. Lentulus Gaetulicus [against Gaius Germani]cus' (Smallwood 9). Both D. and Suet. minimize the seriousness of this 'plot', but some modern scholars have sought to turn it into a major conspiracy, involving G.'s sisters Agrippina and Julia, his brother-in-law Lepidus, Gaetulicus, commander of the four legions in Upper Germany, and even possibly Calvisius Sabinus, governor of Pannonia (cf. 59.18.4n. [= **B.13**]; Balsdon, *Gaius*, 66–76; Barrett 101–06; Z. Stewart, *AJP* 74 (1953), 70–85; Syme, *AA*, 179–81; for more scepticism see C.J. Simpson in *Studies in Latin Literature and Roman History II* (ed. C. Deroux, 1980), 347–66). D. was generally sceptical in his reporting of conspiracies against the emperor (cf. 54.15.1–4).

22.5 **Lentulus Gaetulicus:** Cn. Cornelius Lentulus Gaetulicus, consul in 26 (*PIR*² C 1390; Syme, *AA*, Index, p. 481), proconsular commander of the legions in Upper Germany since 29. D. is here, as elsewhere (cf. 63.17.3 [= **D.4**]; 63.24.1 [= **D.6**]), anachronistic in calling him "governor of Germany" since the provinces of Upper and Lower Germany were only constituted in the 80s (A.C. King, *Roman Gaul and Germany* (1990), 167–68). He was one of the few supporters of Sej. to escape punishment (Tac. *A*. 6.30, also noting his lenient discipline and the fact that he got on well with the forces of Lower Germany, commanded from 28 to 34 by his father-in-law, L. Apronius).

22.6 **Lepidus:** M. Aemilius Lepidus, husband of G.'s sister Drusilla until her death in June 38 (cf. 59.11.1n. [= **B.9**]). D. here suggests that after Drusilla's death G. marked Lepidus out as a potential successor by advancing him to political office five years early, just as Tib. had done with G. in 33 (58.23.1). However, G. was only twenty-seven years old and so was still trying to produce an heir of his own. The charge of adultery was often connected with that of treason under Tib. and G. (cf. 58.24.5; 59.18.4 [= **B.14**]). On his alleged conspiracy see Suet. *G*. 24.3; Barrett 106–112.

the emperor's sisters: Drusilla, Agrippina and Livilla (59.3.3n. [= **B.3**]). Drusilla had died in 38 (59.11.1–4 [= **B.9**]). Agrippina had been married to Cn. Domitius Ahenobarbus (consul in 32) since 28 (Tac. *A*. 4.75; Syme, *AA*, 141), Livilla to M. Vinicius (consul in 30) since 33 (58.21.1; Tac. *A*. 6.15; Syme, *AA*, 172–73 and n. 21). For the charge of adultery cf. Suet. *G*. 24.3, who adds that documents were published, which left little doubt about their adultery or their complicity in the plot. G. had their movable property sold off at an auction at Lugdunum, presumably during his stay there during the winter of 39–40 (Suet. *G*. 39). Agrippina and Livilla were later recalled from exile by Cl. in 41 (60.4.1 [= **C.4**]).

22.7 **G. gave the army a bounty:** Emperors often cemented the loyalty of the army by giving bounties after threats to their rule: e.g. Tib. after the fall of Sej. in 31 (Suet. *T*. 48.2) or Nero after the murder of Agrippina in 59 (61.14.3); see Campbell, *Emperor & Army*, 188–89.

sent three daggers to the temple of Mars the Avenger: cf. Suet. *G*. 24.3. The temple of Mars Ultor had been dedicated in 2 B.C. by Aug. in his new forum, to commemorate his avenging of the assassination of his adoptive father, Julius Caesar (55.10.2–8; *RG* 21.1; Nash I, 401–10; Zanker, *Power of Images*, 105–6).

22.8 **Agrippina forced to return to Rome with the bones of Lepidus:** A cruel parody of Agrippina's mother's return from Syria in the winter of 19–20 with the urn containing ashes of her husband Germanicus (Tac. *A*. 3.1–2).

23.1 G. sent a report to the senate: For this procedure see Talbert, *Senate*, 230–31.

23.2 voted him an ovation: On ovations see 59.16.11 + n. [= **B.12**].

Claudius: G.'s uncle and eventual successor as emperor, he had held the consulship with G. in 37 (59.6.6 [= **B.4**]). For this incident cf. Suet. *Cl.* 9.1. For the procedure of selecting senatorial envoys by lot cf. Tac. *H.* 4.6–8; Talbert, *Senate*, 408–11.

23.4 he was so capricious by nature: G.'s capriciousness is a major theme of D.'s account of his reign; no-one quite knew what he was going to do next (Introduction, Section 4.3). D. also uses this as a characteristic of Tib. (58.7.3 [= **A.6**]; 59.16.4 [= **B.12**]) and Caracalla (77.5.2).

23.5 Claudius gave the impression of great stupidity: cf. Suet. *Cl.* 38.3.

***B.18 GAIUS AND ADDITIONS TO THE ROMAN EMPIRE:
MAURETANIA AND BRITAIN** **A.D. 40**

(59.25.1–5)

25.1 Ptolemy, son of Juba: Aug. had bestowed the kingdom of Mauretania on Juba II in 30 B.C. (51.15.6; Braund, *RFK*, 16–17, 45). His son Ptolemy had taken over as king in 23 (Tac. *A.* 4.23, 26; EJ 163 = LACTOR 8, no. 20 = Braund 605).

How the Mauretanias started to be governed by the Romans: G. annexed Mauretania and divided it into two provinces, Mauretania Caesarensis and Mauretania Tingitana, each under an equestrian governor (Balsdon, *Gaius*, 192–93; Barrett 119–23; D. Fishwick, *Historia* 20 (1971), 467–87). This administrative change caused a revolt against Roman rule among Ptolemy's supporters (60.8–9 [= **C.6**]; Pliny, *NH* 5.11–15). This revolt is a more likely reason for Ptolemy's death than the one given here by D./ Xiph., which bears too many similarities to that given for other deaths in the reign to give it much credibility. Suet. *G.* 35.1 prefers to attribute his death to such trivialities as wearing a purple cloak in G.'s presence at the games. For further discussion see Balsdon, *Gaius*, 192–94; Barrett 116–18; for speculation that Ptolemy was involved in the supposed conspiracy of Gaetulicus see D. Fishwick and B.D. Shaw, *Historia* 25 (1976), 491–94.

25.1–3 G.'s abortive invasion of Britain: D. has already mentioned this invasion briefly at 59.21.3 [= **B.15**]. The repetition of the event is probably due to the fact that we only have Xiphilinus' epitome after the manuscripts of D. break off at 59.25.1. Xiph. may have abbreviated D.'s sequence of events to allow the British invasion to be discussed alongside the reaction in Rome on G.'s return. G.'s invasion was in part spurred by dynastic trouble among the Catuvellauni in 39–40: Rome's client king, Cunobelinus, had expelled his son Adminius, who in turn surrendered to the Roman troops, allowing G. to claim a famous victory (Suet. *G.* 44.2). For the invasion and some suggested reasons for its failure see Tac. *Agr.* 13.4; Barrett 125–29, 135–39; R.W. Davies, *Historia* 15 (1966), 124–28; E.J. Phillips, *Historia* 19 (1970), 369–74.

25.2 the order to gather up sea-shells: cf. Suet. *G.* 46. Various (largely unsuccessful) attempts have been made to rationalize the incident: by sea-shells the sources mean sapper-huts (J.P.V.D. Balsdon, *JRS* 24 (1934), 18); or missiles used in training operations (Davies, art. cit., last note); sea-shells as appropriate spoils for a triumph over the Ocean (M.B. Flory, *Historia* 28 (1988), 500–02; Barrett 136–38) – perhaps in revenge for Ocean's cruel handling of Germanicus in 15–16 (Tac. *A.* 2.23–24). All this reveals that G. had a greater sense of humour (on which see Barrett 216–17) than many modern scholars. On wit in D.'s history see further Introduction, Section 3.4.2. Scipio Aemilianus and C. Laelius liked to collect sea-shells (Cic. *de Oratore* 2.22).

25.3 booty for his triumphal procession: The display of captured booty was a central feature of a Roman triumphal parade (Versnel, *Triumphus*, 95).

he had even managed to enslave the Ocean itself: By Ocean D. here means the English Channel. In Greco-Roman times it was thought that Ocean surrounded the known world and crossing it engendered deep psychological fears, which were a significant drawback to the Roman conquest of Britain (Cic. *Letters to his brother Quintus* 2.16; Tac. *A.* 2.24; E. Rawson, *Intellectual Life in the late Roman Republic* (1985), 265). Cl.'s army in 43 experienced considerable difficulties crossing the Channel; as a result great prominence was given in celebrations of the conquest to his triumph over Ocean (60.19.2–4 + n. [= **C.11**]).

he distributed many rewards among the troops: Another typical feature after a Roman victory (Campbell, *Emperor & Army*, 181–98).

25.4 G. and the senate: Relations with the senate were clearly at a very low ebb. D. goes on (59.25.5b–8) to recount another series of senatorial conspiracies, on which see Barrett 156–58.

25.5 he hurled much silver and gold: Emperors often hurled missiles (*missilia*) containing tickets to be exchanged for gifts at the public games (cf. 59.9.6 + n. [= **B.7**]). For general distributions of money (*congiaria*) to the Roman plebs by the emperor see Millar, *ERW*, 135–39; Yavetz, *Plebs*, ch. 6. For G.'s relationship with the Roman plebs cf. 59.2.2n. [= **B.2**]; 59.13.3–7.

some allege that small pieces of iron were mixed in: D. again reveals that he used more than one source: cf. 59.12.2 + n. [= **B.10**].

*B.19 PROTOGENES, IMPERIAL FREEDMAN, AND THE DEATH OF PROCULUS   A.D. 40

(59.25.9–26.4: Petrus Patricius; Zonaras; Xiphilinus)

25.9 G.'s amnesty towards the senate: i.e., G. put an end to his allegedly indiscriminate persecution of senators, perhaps to ascertain which of them posed the real threats (Barrett 158).

26.1 the senate had failed to condemn certain people: If Zonaras is right, this is one of the few occasions on which the senate openly defied G. by failing to condemn men for supposed crimes against the emperor; but for doubts see Talbert, *Senate*, 479.

Protogenes: An imperial freedman: *PIR*[1] P 757; *RE* 23 (1957), 980. It is uncertain which specific post in the imperial household he was holding at the time. He was renowned for laying charges against people (Juv. *Sat.* 3.120). He was put to death at the start of Cl.'s reign (60.4.5). Imperial freedmen often read out emperors' documents in the senate (cf. 59.16.3 [= **B.12**]; Talbert, *Senate*, 154–62). Philo, *Embassy* provides a vivid picture of freedmen at the court of G.

'Sword' and 'Dagger': cf. Suet. *G.* 49.3, who adds the detail that these books (*Gladius* and *Pugio*) contained the names of those to be executed for treason after the recent conspiracies.

26.2 Scribonius Proculus: (*PIR*[1] S 215), possibly the father of P. Sulpicius Scribonius Proculus and Sulpicius Scribonius Rufus, prominent under Nero (63.17.2–4 + n. [= **D.4**]). It seems unlikely that the senators literally tore him to pieces in the senate-house. The anecdote may have been invented to illustrate how a bad emperor caused severe disunity among senators, with some supporting the emperor sycophantically, while others maintained a distanced distaste. For slight variations see Suet. *G.* 28, making it clear that his body was maltreated, torn apart and dragged through the streets of Rome by the senators after they had stabbed him with their pens (styluses) in the senate-house, and presumably also after he had been executed by the public executioner. For pens as dangerous weapons cf. Suet. *Cl.* 35.2. Suet. *G.* 28 adds the detail that Scribonius had been declared a public enemy (*hostis publicus*). If this is right, it would have been the magistrates' duty to ensure his execution (A.W. Lintott, *Violence in Republican Rome* (1968), 155–74). His death quietened senatorial opposition to G. for the moment; a period of adulation followed (59.26.3–27.6).

26.3 G. allowed to sit on a high podium in the senate-house: A further instance of G.'s growing megalomania. This practice was rescinded on the death of G.; the emperor reverted to sitting on a curule seat (*sella curulis*) between the two consuls (cf. 60.16.3 [= **C.8**]; Talbert, *Senate*, 121–22).

G. allowed a military bodyguard in the senate: For similar grants to emperors cf. 58.17.3–4; Tac. *A.* 6.15; Suet. *Cl.* 12.1; Talbert, *Senate*, 159–61.

26.4 suddenly with youthful eagerness: D. again emphasizes G.'s contrary nature as ruler, which made him very difficult for his subjects to handle (Introduction, Section 4.3b)

Pomponius: Q. Pomponius Secundus, on whom see 59.6.2n. [= **B.4**]. Soon after his release, he was appointed suffect consul for 41 (59.29.5 [= **B.23**]).
since his mistress did not make any statement against him even under torture, G. refused to harm her and even rewarded her with money: A charge of adultery was often laid against those also charged of conspiracy against the emperor (*maiestas*): see 59.18.4n. [= **B.14**]. Under Roman law Roman citizens were theoretically exempt from torture, but, as this story indicates,

it was clearly used even upon citizens in investigating charges of conspiracy; the emperor's will was powerful enough to override legal rights (Garnsey, *SSLP* 141–44). D. also gives the story moral force in sharply contrasting the woman's fierce loyalty towards Pomponius even under torture and her concern for truth with the sycophantic self-interest of the senatorial élite, a major theme of this part of D.'s narrative (e.g. 59.27.2–6 [= **B.21**]).

*B.20 GAIUS' DIVINE PRETENSIONS   A.D. 40

(59.26.5–27.1: Xiphilinus)

This section, in which D. embellishes material found in Suet. *G*. 52, again reveals D.'s wit as a historian. His irony and consistently sardonic tone successfully ridicule G., and the passage reaches a succinct and effective climax with the anecdote of the Gallic cobbler's honest scepticism. G.'s divine pretensions were the subject of contemporary invective against him (cf. Philo, *Embassy* 75–114).

26.5 **he went completely out of his mind:** On the problem of G.'s madness see 59.17.1–11n. [= **B.13**].

having sex with Luna and being crowned by Victory: Luna, the Roman goddess of the Moon; for her temple on the Aventine see Tac. *A*. 15.41; Livy 40.2. The winged goddess Victory is frequently depicted in Roman official art crowning an emperor or member of his family (e.g. Zanker, *Power of Images*, figs. 41, 44d, 81, 180a (Aug.), 178 (?Gaius Caesar), 183b (Tib.); D. Strong, *Roman Art* (1988), fig. 69 (Titus), 88 (Trajan), 134 (Marcus Aurelius)).

Jupiter: In Greco-Roman mythology Zeus/Jupiter was notorious for his seductions/rapes of human and divine females, including his own sisters Hera/Juno and Demeter. With Hera/Juno he fathered Hebe, Ilithyia and Mars; with Demeter, Persephone. For the allegation that G. had sexual relations with his sisters see 59.11.1 + n. [= **B.9**]; 59.22.6 [= **B.17**].

26.6 **he claimed to be Neptune because he had bridged such a large stretch of water:** i.e., at his triumph at the bridge of Baiae (59.17.1–11 [= **B.13**]).

G. appears as female deities: This accusation does not appear in Philo's extensive invective (*Embassy* 75–114), but is mentioned briefly by Suet. *G*. 52.

26.7 **G. in female costume, holding a wine-bowl and thyrsus:** i.e., G. appeared dressed as a Bacchant, a female devotee of Bacchus. A thyrsus was a fennel rod bound with ivy and vine-leaves, and was carried by Bacchus and his followers (cf. Euripides, *Bacchae* 176, 188, 1054–55; J. Boardman, *Athenian Red-Figure Vases: the Archaic period* (1975), figs. 132, 218, 313), hence becoming a central symbol of Bacchic worship. For G.'s appearances as Bacchus cf. Philo, *Embassy*, 78, 79, 82, 88–89.

G. in male costume, carrying a club and lionskin or a helmet and shield: i.e., he appeared as Hercules (cf. Philo, *Embassy*, 78, 79, 81, 90–92) or Mars (cf. Philo, *Embassy*, 111–113).

shaking a trident, brandishing a thunderbolt: i.e., appearing as Neptune or Jupiter.

appeared as a maiden dressed for hunting or for war: i.e, as Diana or Minerva/Roma.

G. appeared as a married woman: cf. Suet. *G.* 52. Roman married women of citizen status (*matronae* or matrons), wore a distinctive dress in public, the stola, which symbolized female virtue and modesty; it was the female equivalent of the toga: see Zanker, *Power of Images*, 165–66 and figs. 131, 253.

26.8–9 the story of the Gallic cobbler: This incident is of dubious historicity, since it was a common rhetorical *topos*, or standard story, used to illustrate that emperors could tolerate freedom of speech, but only in those of low birth; the élite could not get away with such honest scepticism; for other examples see Crook, *CP*, 146–47.

26.8 saw him conducting business from a high platform: D. is ambiguous as to what precisely G. was doing when ridiculed by the Gallic cobbler. Cary's Loeb translation has him "uttering oracles". While D.'s Greek could mean this, it could also mean a great many other things: transacting business (in a financial or non-financial sense), giving an audience to, deciding upon a petition, administering justice. The verb is also used of gods in the sense of listening to (cf. Lucian, *Pseudologist* 8), which would add ironic humour here with G. posing as Jupiter. However, since the context allows little certainty, it is more prudent to leave the sense as general as possible.

26.10 G. appeared in public in silk or in triumphal dress: For Seneca, *On Constancy* 18, G.'s outlandish style of dress was one of the causes of the plot led by Cassius Chaerea to assassinate him. For earlier criticism of G. for wearing silk and for using silken awnings see 59.17.3 [= **B.13**]; 59.12.2 [= **B.10**]; it was considered a mark of Oriental luxury, and hence morally degenerate. N. was similarly criticized for wearing silk in public (Suet. *N.* 51). Emperors usually wore triumphal dress only on special ceremonial occasions; for routine public appearances they wore the *toga praetexta* (59.7.1n. [= **B.5**]).

27.1 G. used to kiss only a very small number of people: G.'s aberrant conduct provides good evidence for the normal rituals involved in greeting the emperor (Friedländer I, 90–92). An emperor was clearly expected to demonstrate his civility by returning the kisses offered by those greeting him at the morning salutation or other meetings: cf. Plin. *Panegyric* 23, 71; A. Wallace-Hadrill, *JRS* 72 (1982), 36, 40–41. For G.'s kissing Mnester, the famous pantomimist, see Suet. *G.* 55.1. For another example of G.'s disregard for the ritual of greeting see 59.7.6 [= **B.5**].

these honours came not just from the masses, but also from people of some esteem in society: D. here once again reveals his conservative socio-political views (Introduction, Section 3.4.3).

*B.21 GAIUS AND LUCIUS VITELLIUS   **A.D. 40**

(59.27.2–6: Xiphilinus)

27.2 L. Vitellius: *PIR*¹ V 500; *RE* Suppl. IX (1962), 1733–41. Father of the later emperor Vitellius, consul in 34, he was appointed governor of Syria in 35 (Tac. *A*. 6.32; Suet. *Vit*. 2.4). This was a post of great military and diplomatic importance, since its holder was responsible for carrying out Roman policy on the eastern frontier of the Empire (Syme, *Tac*., 15–16 and *ZPE* 41 (1981), 125–44 [= *RP* III, 1376–92]). D. uses the cases of Vitellius and Domitius Afer (59.19.1–7 [= **B.14**]) as examples of the depths of adulation to which even the noblest Romans sink when confronting a despot (cf. Tac. *A*. 3.65).

27.3 Vitellius' achievement: This was to settle a dynastic struggle beyond the eastern frontier, involving Parthia, Armenia and the Iberian Caucasus. Three stages were involved:

(a) in 35 Artabanus III (*PIR*² A 1155) had been deposed as king of Parthia by Tib. and replaced by Phraates and then on his sudden death by Tiridates. Tib. acted at the request of some dissident Parthian nobles, but really because he was afraid of Artabanus' expansion into Armenia, where the latter had set his son Arsaces upon the throne (Tac. *A*. 6.31–32). This last act stirred the Iberians of the Caucasus to launch an attack to regain control of Armenia. They engineered the murder of Arsaces, which resulted in Artabanus sending a force to confront the Iberians. But when this force was defeated, Artabanus himself led a second, larger force into Armenia. During this expedition Vitellius by skilful military action forced Artabanus to seek refuge to the north in Scythia and Tiridates was crowned as king of Parthia in an elaborate ceremony on the Euphrates (Tac. *A*. 6.33–37).

(b) in 36 Artabanus was recalled by some Parthian nobles and recovered the throne; Tiridates was expelled to Syria (58.26.3; Tac. *A*. 6.43–44; Jos. *AJ* 18.100).

(c) in 36 (or 37) Artabanus sought to establish friendship with the Romans and so Vitellius summoned Artabanus to the conference on the Euphrates referred to here (Suet. *G*. 14.3; *Vit*. 2.4). There is controversy over the exact date of this ceremony, whether it occurred under Tib. or (more likely) under G. Jos. *AJ* 18.101–104 places the meeting and alliance at the end of Tib.'s reign; but the fact that the episode is not reported in the extant parts of Tac. *A*. supports a date in G.'s reign (Levick, *Tib*., 146–47; cf. Balsdon, *Gaius*, 196–8; Barrett 63–64).

D./Xiph. here conflates two separate events: Vitellius' pursuit of Artabanus in 35 and the conference on the Euphrates in 37. Suet. *G*. 14.3 and Jos. *AJ* 18.101 both state that Artabanus was pleased to accept Rome's offer to discuss terms of peace; he did not have to be coerced by Vitellius.

forced him to sacrifice to the images of Aug. and G.: Provincial subjects and even peoples outside the Roman Empire were forced to take part in the imperial cult: e.g. "the Germans and Gauls and the Gauls who live on this side of the Rhine" were obliged to sacrifice annually after the death of Germanicus in 19–20 at the tomb set up for him and for Drusus, Tib.'s brother, on the Rhine (*ZPE* 55 (1984), 55–100 = Sherk 36a, fragment I, lines 25–35).

took his sons hostage: cf. Jos. *AJ* 18.103, who only mentions one son, Darius, sent to Rome as a hostage. This same Darius took part in G.'s triumph at the bridge at Baiae in 39 (59.17 [= **B.13**]).

27.5 **dressed humbly in a style unworthy of his social standing:** i.e., he chose not to wear his senatorial dress (59.9.5n. [= **B.7**]); as an ex-consul, he would also have been allowed to wear the purple-bordered toga (the *toga praetexta*) on festal occasions (58.11.2n. [= **A.7**]). When Romans were defendants in lawsuits or were in mourning, they usually chose not to wear the dress to which they were entitled: cf. Cic. *pro Plancio* 29 (at a trial); 54.35.5 (at funeral of Octavia); EJ 69 = Braund 63 = Sherk 19, line 22 (in mourning after the death of Gaius Caesar); 56.31.2 (in mourning after the death of Aug.).

fell at the emperor's feet: Self-prostration (in Greek *proskynêsis*) was a ritual closely associated with the Persian/Parthian royal court (Hdt. 1.134; 7.136; J.M. Cook, *The Persian Empire* (1983), 138). Vitellius may well have picked up the idea from the Parthians with whom he had so many dealings (cf. 59.27.3n.). Scholars have used this detail to help prove that G. was seeking to establish an Oriental monarchy at Rome, but for doubts see Barrett 150–51.

27.6 **G. having sexual intercourse with the Moon:** Xiph. has already recounted this anecdote at 59.26.5 [= **B.20**], another example of his including the same material more than once (cf. 59.25.1n. [= **B.18**]).

Vitellius came later to surpass all others in adulation: One of the most polished orators of his day (Tac. *A.* 12.4–6; Syme, *Tac.*, 330–31), Vitellius became a bye-word for sycophancy under G. and Cl. (Tac. *A.* 6.32). He held the consulship again in 43 and 47 (60.21.2 [= **C.11**]; 60.29.1, 6).

*B.22 GAIUS' MEGALOMANIA: IMPERIAL CULT   A.D. 40

(59.28.1–11: Xiphilinus)

28.1–11 In this section D. inexorably builds up the image of G. as omnipotent tyrant, so that his assassination will seem all the more dramatic. Such reversals of fortune constituted a typical story-patterning in Greek and Roman literature: cf. D.'s account of the fall of Sej. (58.4.1 + n. [= **A.3**]; 58.11.1–3 [= **A.7**]). However, these incidents late in G.'s reign also raise the question whether G. was seeking to change the nature of Principate, turning away from the 'citizen-emperor' (*civilis princeps*) style of Aug., Tib. and G. in his earlier years to a more overt, even Oriental, form of monarchy (cf. Suet. *G.* 22.1; Balsdon, *Gaius*, 157–73; Barrett 145–53).

28.1 **G. and the temple of Apollo at Miletus:** The temple was in fact located in Miletus' territory at Didyma, some 16 km. south of Miletus. An inscription (Smallwood 127 = Braund 181 = Sherk 43) confirms the existence of a cult of G. here and provides details on its organization. Suet. *G.* 21 merely reports with approval that G. completed this temple. D.'s version is much more hostile in alleging that G. ordered the cult to be established; it is more likely that the Asians offered it to him. The hostile version may have been developed out of G.'s threat to turn the temple at Jerusalem into a centre for his own worship (Jos. *AJ* 18.261–309; id., *BJ* 2.185). See further Barrett 143–44; Price, *Rituals*, 68, 257.

Artemis had already taken over Ephesus, Aug. Pergamum and Tib. Smyrna: Aug. set a precedent for G. by appropriating a part of the famous sanctuary of Artemis at Ephesus to be used for imperial cult (Strabo 14.1.20–23; Price, *Rituals*, 254). For the temple of Rome and Augustus at Pergamum see 51.20.7; Suet. *Aug.* 52; Price 252; for the temple of Tiberius, Livia and the Roman senate at Smyrna see Tac. *A.* 4.15; 4.55–56; Price, *Rituals*, 258.

28.2–5 G.'s buildings in the centre of Rome: cf. Suet. *G.* 22.2–4. The literary accounts of G.'s building operations in Rome, especially those on the Capitoline and Palatine hills, raise a number of topographical problems (Barrett 203–11; T.P. Wiseman in *L'Urbs: espaçe urbaine et histoire* (1987), 392–413, esp. 406–09). Some of the details may well be invented, or at least embellished, to exaggerate G.'s megalomania and hence justify his assassination.

28.2–4 G.'s alterations on the Capitoline Hill: The major building on the Capitoline Hill had been since c. 509 B.C. the Capitolium, the temple of Jupiter, Juno and Minerva (Sear, *Architecture*, 11–12; A. Boethius, *Etruscan and Early Roman Architecture* (1978), 46–47, 110–14). G. had already revealed his desire to be associated with Jupiter (59.16.10 [= **B.12**]; 59.24.4, where the senate sacrifices en masse to the chair of G. in the temple of Jupiter on the Capitol). For the view that the senatorial sources maliciously overplay the connection between G. and Jupiter merely to emphasize G.'s megalomania see J.R. Fears, *ANRW* II.17.1 (1981), 71–73.

28.2 a temple of his own in Rome: Cary misunderstands D.'s text here when he translates it as "he built two temples of his own, one that had been granted by vote of the senate and another at his own expense on the Palatine". This not only contradicts Suet. *G.* 22.3, who mentions just *one* temple to G.'s *numen* in Rome, but has also forced scholars (unnecessarily) to explain the divergence between Suet. and D. (Balsdon, *Gaius*, 163; Barrett 147).

G.'s lodge on the Capitol: This new part of the palace on the Capitoline was destroyed by fire in 41 (Plin. *NH* 35.36.83; Suet. *G.* 59). G. allegedly constructed a bridge or ramp to connect the Palatine and Capitoline hills (Pliny, *NH* 36.15.111; Suet. *G.* 22.4, who adds that the temple of the deified Aug. was thus integrated into the palace complex). After G.'s assassination the Capitol swiftly returned to a more traditional function, with the consuls convening a meeting of the senate there (60.1.1 [= **C.1**]).

28.3 the statue of Olympian Zeus: This famous gold and ivory statue, sculpted in the fifth century B.C. by Pheidias, stood inside the temple of Zeus at Olympia (Pausanias 5.10.2; M. Robertson, *A Shorter History of Greek Art* (1981), 102–03). On the incident cf. Suet. *G.* 22.2; 57.1; Jos. *AJ* 19.8–9. For the faces of Greek statues being remodelled to resemble Romans see Zanker, *Power of Images*, 30 & fig. 23. D. fails to mention here G.'s attempt to set up statues of himself in the Temple at Jerusalem, which nearly sparked a major Jewish revolt (Jos. *AJ* 18.261–309; Barrett 189–91; Smallwood, *Jews*, 174–86).

28.5 G. cut the temple of Castor and Pollux [= the Dioscuri] in the Roman Forum in two: cf. Suet. *G.* 22.2. For details of the temple see Nash I, 210–13; Coarelli, *Guida arch. di Roma*, 82–83. Recent excavations have revealed traces of a large house of Caligulan date that was built immediately behind the temple and on the same axis. Unfortunately the excavations have not been able to confirm or deny whether this house did cut through the temple; it remained in use as part of the imperial palace until Domitian restructured the area (Barrett 208–10; H. Hurst, *Archeologia Laziale* 9 (1988), 13–17).

Jupiter Latiaris: i.e., Jupiter the protector of Latium (cf. Dion. Hal. 4.49). The manuscript reading ("he appointed himself priest of Jupiter": i.e., *flamen Dialis*) has here been emended, since it duplicates D.'s later report at 59.28.6. The emendation is based on Suet. *G.* 22.2.

entry fees for priesthoods: cf. Suet. *G.* 22.3; *Cl.* 9.2, claiming that the fee was eight million sesterces (= two million *denarii*). Entry fees for priesthoods were a common feature in many cults in the Roman world and are attested on many inscriptions (R. Lane Fox, *Pagans and Christians* (1986), 76–82; R. Gordon in *Pagan Priests* (ed. M. Beard and J.A. North, 1990), 223–31; R.P. Duncan-Jones, *Economy of the Roman Empire* (2nd ed., 1982), 82–88; 151–53). The alleged scale of the entry fee is no doubt grossly exaggerated.

28.6 appointed his horse a fellow-priest: For the allegation that G. had earlier promised his horse Incitatus a consulship and for some possible explanations see 59.14.7 + n. [= **B.11**].

sacrifice of birds to G.: For more specific details on the kinds of birds sacrificed see Suet. *G.* 22.3; 57.

G.'s thunder-machine: Seneca, a contemporary of G., has a different version that is not so malicious: G. uttered the Homeric line in an outburst of temper after a thunderstorm had washed out a play in which he was looking forward to appearing (Sen. *On Anger* 1.20.8; Barrett 214–15).

G. quotes Homer: G. quotes Homer, *Iliad*, 23.724, where Ajax addresses Odysseus during a wrestling-match. Suet. *G.* 22.4 also reports the same quotation, but puts it in a different context; he claims that G. used it to challenge Jupiter during one of their frequent conversations. For another example of Suet. and D. reporting the same quotation, but in different contexts see 63.29.2 + n. [= **D.8**].

28.7 Caesonia: Milonia Caesonia, G.'s fourth wife (59.3.3n. [= **B.3**]). G. had married her in the summer of 39, when she was already pregnant, so that she could bear him a child after just one month (59.23.7; Balsdon, *Gaius*, 48; Barrett 94–95). For possible sacrifices to celebrate her birthday by the Arval Brethren in June 40 see Smallwood 10, lines 20–23. The daughter was named after G.'s dead sister, now deified (59.11.1–2 [= **B.9**]).

28.8 this god, this Jupiter: cf. 72.16.1, where D. describes the emperor Commodus in similarly ironic terms: "this Hercules, this god". For contemporary criticism of G. for exulting in "superhuman" titles see Philo, *Embassy* 354–55. Seneca, *On Tranquility of the Mind* 14.9 ironically describes G. as "our god". An inscription from Cyzicus, Asia honours G. as "the New Sun God" (Smallwood 401 = Braund 673).

one might pass over G.'s various methods for raising revenue: D. here alludes to various taxes introduced by G.: for fuller details see Suet. *G.* 40; Balsdon, *Gaius*, 185–86; Barrett 228. These included taxes on goods sold, services and wages (e.g. on food sold in Rome, on artisans', prostitutes' and porters' fees, on funds gained from the hiring out of slaves and as a result of legal actions). Jos. *AJ* 19.28 adds the details that the taxes were at some stage doubled and that Chaerea, the leader of the plot to assassinate G., had been appointed to enforce these taxes. Cl. abolished these taxes soon after his accession (60.4.1 [= **C.4**]).

28.9 upper-class women and children set up as prostitutes in brothel on the Palatine: cf. Suet. *G.* 41.1, who adds that he even loaned money at interest to interested customers. This was a charge often levelled against evil emperors: cf. Tac. *A.* 15.37 (Nero); 79.13.3 (Elagabalus, emperor from 218–222, whom D. alleges set up a brothel in the palace for himself to act as prostitute).

28.11 G. inscribed severe measures about taxes on white boards in very small letters: cf. Suet. *G.* 41.1. The texts of draft laws, decrees, but most of all lists (of names, sums of money, events) were often painted on whitened boards (*alba*), which were then posted in prominent places in the civic centre, usually the Forum: cf. 47.3.2; 55.3.3; LR I, 131 = Sherk, *RGE* 55 (the so-called Piracy Law of 101 or 100 B.C.), Delphi Copy B, line 25. If the measure was considered of major importance, it might also be inscribed on a bronze plaque and/or stone stele.

the masses rushed into the Circus and protested: For a vivid account of this incident see Jos. *AJ* 19.24–27, revealing that G. had to resort to force to bring the crowd under control. Under the Principate the assemblies of the Roman people no longer had the power to vote down new measures proposed by the magistrates or the emperor; they just met to ratify them formally. As a result, the public games (chariot-races, gladiatorial combats and plays) provided the only opportunity for the people to express their opinion directly to the emperor: cf. 59.13.7; Tac. *A.* 6.13; Hopkins, *Death*, 14–20.

*B.23 THE ASSASSINATION OF GAIUS AND ITS AFTERMATH

A.D. 41

(59.29.1–30.3: Xiphilinus; John of Antioch)

29–30 This final conspiracy against G. was notable in that it was not restricted to senators. By this stage of his reign G. had lost the support of several key members of his own household (e.g. Callistus) and the Praetorian Guard. By far the fullest ancient account of the conspiracy is Jos. *AJ* 19.14–200, probably based on the contemporary senatorial historian, Cluvius Rufus (H.W. Ritter, *Rheinisches Museum* 115 (1972), 85–91). However, Jos. would also have spoken to Agrippa, who was present in Rome at the time of G.'s death and claimed a prominent rôle in establishing Cl. as emperor (cf. 60.1.2n. [= **C.1**]; 60.8.2 + n. [= **C.6**]). On Jos.'s account see T.P. Wiseman, *LCM* 5.10 (December 1980), 231–38 [= *Roman Studies, Literary and Historical* (1988), 167–75]. D. may also have used Cluvius Rufus here as elsewhere (G.B. Townend, *Hermes* 89 (1961), 227–48). For full discussions of the conspiracy see Balsdon, *Gaius*, 101–05; Barrett 159–67; Levick, *Cl.*, 29–39 (accepting Cl.'s complicity in it); Wirszubski, *Libertas*, ch. 5, esp. 126; T.P. Wiseman, *Pegasus*, 31 (1988), 2–9 (for the political slogans used by the conspirators).

29.1 C. Cassius Chaerea: *PIR*² C 488; cf. Tac. *A.* 1.32; Jos. *AJ* 19.18. For G.'s jokes at his expense see Suet. *G.* 56.2.

Cornelius Sabinus: *PIR*² C 1431. Nothing is known of his earlier career. Jos. *AJ* 19.17–23 does not include him among the three leaders of the conspiracy (Cassius Chaerea, Annius Vinicianus and Aemilius Regulus); but Suet. *G.* 56–58 gives him the same prominence as he receives in D.

Callistus: See 59.19.6n. [= **B.14**]. For his leading rôle in the conspiracy see Tac. *A.* 11.29; Jos. *AJ* 19.64–69.

prefect of the Praetorian Guard: M. Arrecinus Clemens (*PIR*² A 1073). For his complicity in the plot see Jos. *AJ* 19.37. His son, though a senator, also held the equestrian post of Praetorian Prefect under Vespasian (Tac. *H.* 4.68). D., as summarized by Zonaras, had earlier intimated that both prefects of the guard were involved in the plot (59.25.7–8). This divergence is possibly an example of D.'s use of variant sources (so Barrett 294, n. 32), but it could also be the result of careless summarizing of D.'s text by either Zonaras or Xiphilinus.

In addition to those already mentioned, the following are attested as conspirators: (a) senators: D. Valerius Asiaticus (Tac. *A.* 11.1), L. Annius Vinicianus (Jos. *AJ* 19.18, 20, 49; cf. 60.15.1–3 [= **C.8**]), P. Nonius Asprenas, consul in 38 (Jos. *AJ* 19.98, 123), Aemilius Regulus from Corduba, Spain (Jos. *AJ* 19.17, 19), Poppaedius, an Epicurean (Jos. *AJ* 19.32), L. Norbanus Balbus (Jos. *AJ* 19.123), Anteius (Jos. *AJ* 19.125), Aquila, who actually killed G. (Jos. *AJ* 19.110: possibly M. Aquila Julianus, consul in 38 with P. Nonius Asprenas); (b) tribunes (i.e., officers) in the Praetorian Guard: Julius Lupus, a relative of Clemens, the Praetorian Prefect (Jos. *AJ* 19.190–91) and Papinius (Jos. *AJ* 19.37).

29.1a those who chose not to join in the conspiracy concealed their knowledge of it: For widespread knowledge of plot cf. Jos. *AJ* 19.62.

29.2 Gaius kept accusing Chaerea of being effeminate and gave him a password such as "Lust" or "Venus": cf. Suet. *G.* 56.2; Seneca, *On the Constancy of the Wise Man* 18.3; Jos. *AJ* 19.28–29, who relates that G. accused Chaerea of effeminacy because he showed too much lenience in exacting taxes for the imperial treasury. The emperor chose a new password for each new detachment of the Praetorian Guard each day as it started its guard duty; the tribune commanding the detachment came into the emperor's presence to receive it (60.16.7; Jos. *AJ* 19.85). "Venus" (like its Greek equivalent "Aphrodite") had a double connotation, hence its offensive nature as a password: for in addition to denoting the goddess of love, it was the standard Latin term for sex.

Gaius Cassius, who was then governor of Asia: C. Cassius Longinus (*PIR*[2] C 501), the pre-eminent jurist. For his earlier career see 58.3.8n. [= **A.2**]. He later became governor of Syria under Cl. (Tac. *A*. 12.11–12), but was exiled by Nero in 66 allegedly for revering a bust of C. Cassius, the assassin of Caesar, among his ancestral busts (Tac. *A*. 16.7–9; Suet. *N*. 37.1). D./Xiph. here accounts for G.'s suspicions of Cassius in exactly the same way as he later explains why Nero exiled him (62.27.2).

that Cassius who had assassinated Julius Caesar: i.e., C. Cassius Longinus (44.14.2). His memory was worshipped not just by members of his own family, but by those who cherished a return to the free Republic. Brutus and the younger Cato were similarly idolized. (Wirszubski, *Libertas*, 126–29; R. MacMullen, *Enemies of the Roman Order*, 1–45).

the divine power: D., here as elsewhere, uses the abstract term "divine power" (*daimonion*) to discuss the supernatural (see Introduction, Section 3.4.3). For other omens foretelling G.'s fall see Suet. *G*. 57; Jos. *AJ* 19.87, 94–95.

29.4–7 date of G.'s assassination: The murder seems to have taken place on the last day of the *ludi Palatini* (Jos. *AJ* 19.77–84, where Chaerea stresses the need to murder G. that day since he was intending to set off for Egypt on the following day). Suet. *G*. 58.1 claims that it took place on 24 January 41 at the seventh hour (i.e., just after midday); cf. Jos. *AJ* 19.99 (at the ninth hour). But for arguments that it took place on 22 January see T.P. Wiseman, *LCM* 5.10 (1980), 231–38 [= *Roman Studies*, 167–75]; Barrett 169–70.

29.4 festival on the Palatine: The *ludi Palatini* (the Palatine Games), consisting of stage plays, were instituted by Livia after the death of Aug. in 14 and were thereafter privately sponsored by the imperial family (56.46.5; Tac. *A*. 1.73; Jos. *AJ* 19.75). They took place annually from 17 to 22 January (T.P. Wiseman, *LCM* 5.10 (1980), 231 [= *Roman Studies*, 167–68]. For further details of the plays and mimes produced on this occasion see Jos. *AJ* 19.94–95; cf. Suet. *G*. 57.4.

29.5 Pomponius Secundus: Q. Pomponius Secundus (*PIR*[1] P 564; *RE* 21.2 (1952), 2349–50), the suffect consul who replaced G. in office from 7 January 41 (P.A. Gallivan, *CQ* 28 (1978), 412, 424). He had been arrested by G., but was released in 40 (59.26.4 [= **B.19**]). He later summoned the senate 'in the name of liberty' (59.30.3 [= **B.23**]; Jos. *AJ* 19.263. For his reputation for servility cf. Tac. *A*. 6.18.

29.6 G. wanted to dance and act in a tragedy: For more details on G.'s skills at dancing and acting see 59.26.5–8; Suet. *G*. 54. For his friendship with actors and especially his homosexual relationship with the comic actor Mnester see 59.27.2; Suet. *G*. 36.1, 55.1.

the choir from Greece and Ionia: For further details see 60.7.2 + n. [= **C.5**]; Suet. *G*. 58.1; Jos. *AJ* 19.104.

they intercepted him in a narrow alley: The precise details of the murder are confused and varied in the tradition, probably as a result of individuals later being keen to associate themselves with, or dissociate themselves from, the event. The fullest account is Jos. *AJ* 19. 99–113; Suet. *G.* 58 gives two versions. No other source discusses the cannibalism imputed by Xiph., no doubt a sensationalist detail invented by those who objected to the murder. Jos. *AJ* 19.237 relates the kind treatment of G.'s corpse by Agrippa, king of Palestine; it was half-cremated and quickly buried, to prevent desecration. It later received full cremation and entombment by his sisters when they returned from exile (Suet. *G.* 59).

his wife and daughter were promptly murdered: For details on the murder of his wife, Milonia Caesonia, and his daughter, Drusilla, see Jos. *AJ* 19.190–200; Suet. *G.* 59.

30.1 **length of G.'s reign:** D.'s computation (as preserved by Xiph.) of the length of G.'s reign is inaccurate, since it is based on an incorrect date for the death of Tib.: 26 March, rather than 16 March 37 (cf. 58.28.5; 59.1.2–2.3n. [= **B.1**]). Jos. *AJ* 19.201 (4 years minus 4 months) is even wider from the mark than D. For the correct length of 3 years, 10 months, 8 days see Suet. *G.* 59. For D.'s interest in the exact computation of emperors' lives and reigns see Introduction 3.4.1 and Table 2. Unusually no figure is given for the exact length of G.'s life, but this may be because D.'s text at this point survives only in the later summaries of Xiphilinus, Zonaras and John of Antioch.

he learned by experience that he was not a god: D.'s comment is sardonically effective in encapsulating his disdain for G.'s increasing megalomania during his final months.

30.1a John of Antioch reproduces here rhetorical antitheses that are very characteristic of D., especially after the death of an important figure (cf. 58.11.1–2 [= **A.7**]).

statues and images of G. were ripped down: For a similarly exultant reaction by the Roman plebs to the death of Nero's mother Agrippina in 59 see 61.16.2a. G., unlike Nero, did not technically suffer the eradication of all memorials to him (*damnatio memoriae*); Cl. prevented the measure from being passed in the senate, but saw to it privately that all G.'s statues were removed (60.4.5–6; Balsdon, *Gaius*, 106; Barrett 177–80). For the few surviving statues and portraits of G. see V. Poulsen, *Acta Archaeologica* 29 (1958), 175–90; F.S. Johanson, *Ancient Portraits in the J. Paul Getty Museum* I (1987), 89–106.

30.1b **G.'s Germanic bodyguard:** A cohort of Batavians served as bodyguard for the emperor, until they were disbanded by Galba in 69 (55.24.7–8; Suet. *G.* 43, 45.1; M. Hassall, *Britannia* 1 (1970), 131–36; M.P. Speidel, *Germania* 62 (1984), 31–45). For the epitaph of a Batavian from Nero's bodyguard see Smallwood 293 = Braund 529 = Sherk 76. For their reaction to G.'s murder cf. Jos. *AJ* 19.119–126; their victims included Asprenas, one of the conspirators. An auctioneer succeeding in quietening them down (ibid., 138–152).

30.1c **"If only you all had one neck!":** For this dictum see 59.13.6; cf. Suet. *G.* 30.2, setting it in a completely different context.

30.2 **Valerius Asiaticus:** D. Valerius Asiaticus, from Vienna (modern Vienne) in Gallia Narbonensis (*PIR*[1] V 25; *RE* 7A[2] (1948), 2341–45). He had been suffect consul in 35. After G.'s death he was one of the candidates for emperor (60.1.1n. [= **C.1**]). For his second consulship in 46 and his eventual destruction in 47 see 60.27.1 + n. [= **C.13**]. Jos. *AJ* 19.159 and Tac. *A*. 11.1 also report this action of Asiaticus, but set it in the context of a meeting of the popular assembly in the Forum. D./Xiph. has probably muddled this incident with the quietening of the German bodyguard by the auctioneer, reported at 59.30.1b.

30.3 **the consuls:** Cn. Sentius Saturninus, the ordinary consul (*PIR*¹ S 296; *RE* 2A² (1923), 1531–37); Q. Pomponius Secundus, suffect consul, on whom see 59.6.2 [= **B.4**]; 59.29.5n. [= **B.23**].

the consuls transferred the public funds from the treasuries to the Capitol: The public funds belonging to the treasury of Saturn were kept in the temple of Saturn in the Forum; the military treasury was located on the Capitol – at least by 65 (Braund 416, controverting the suggestion of M. Corbier, *L'aerarium Saturni et l'aerarium militaire* (1974), 666–67, that it was possibly located in the temple of Concord in the Forum). The funds from the treasury of Saturn were, therefore, transferred either to the military treasury or to one of the other temples on the Capitol, since they were more easily defensible here than in the Forum. The emperors had come to exercise control over these treasuries through their freedmen and slaves (cf. Suet. *Aug*. 101.4), and D. admits (53.22.3) that he found it difficult to differentiate between these public funds and the emperor's private wealth (F. Millar, *JRS* 53 (1963), 29–42; P.A. Brunt, *JRS* 56 (1966), 75–91).

D./John of Antioch here also provides an interesting insight into the mechanics of Roman taxation and financial administration during the early Principate: namely that bullion and coins paid in taxes were physically brought to Rome and stored there.

C. THE REIGN OF CLAUDIUS: A.D. 41 – 46:
THE FIRST YEARS IN POWER

* * * * *

*C.1 CLAUDIUS BECOMES EMPEROR   A.D. 41
(60.1.1–2.3: Xiphilinus)

1.1–4 Cl. became emperor: cf. Suet. *Cl.* 10; Jos. *AJ* 19.212–247; Jos. *BJ* 2.204–17; Levick, *Cl.* 29–39. D./Xiphilinus, Suet. and Jos. all play up Cl.'s passivity in coming to power. Josephus was a leading member of the Judaean aristocracy, writing in the mid- to late-first century A.D. His patron was Agrippa II, king of Palestine, whose father (Agrippa I) had helped to establish Cl. in power (T. Rajak, *Josephus* (1983), 164). He provides more circumstantial detail than Suet. and D., no doubt because Agrippa II gave him a full report, in which he exaggerated his father's rôle in establishing Cl. in power (esp. *AJ* 19.236–245). For arguments that Cl. was actively involved in the plot to overthrow G. see Levick, *Cl.*, 35–39.

1.1   the consuls: Cn. Sentius Saturninus and Q. Pomponius Secundus (59.30.3 + n. [= **B.23**]). Under the Principate it was the consuls' responsibility to carry on the government after the death of an emperor (cf. Tac. *A.* 1.7). **the meeting of the senate on the Capitol:** D./Xiph. seems to conflate two meetings of the senate: the first took place in the Capitolium in the late afternoon of 24 January (Jos. *AJ* 19.158–161; 229–33); the second before dawn on 25 January in the temple of Jupiter Victor on the Capitoline (Jos. *AJ* 19.248–52 [partly = Braund 195]): see Levick, *Cl.*, 31–32. This was the first formal questioning of the system of the Principate since Aug.'s problems in 24–23 B.C., on which see B. Levick, *G&R* 22 (1975), 156–63. It was not a question whether to abolish the Principate, but rather who should be emperor and how the emperor should conduct himself (Wirszubski, *Libertas*, 126); but for arguments that it had been an open question all along see T.P. Wiseman, *Pegasus* 31 (1988), 2–9. At the second meeting there were two main senatorial candidates for emperor: M. Vinicius, ordinary consul in 30 and husband of G.'s sister Livilla, and D. Valerius Asiaticus, suffect consul in 35 (P.M. Swan, *AJP* 91 (1970), 149–64). L. Annius Vinicianus, seen by some as the *éminence grise* of the plot against G. (Scramuzza 51), would have been a serious candidate, but he preferred to support the claims of Vinicius, possibly his uncle (Syme, *AA*, 181, 183). The senate had often met on the Capitol under the Republic, but not under the Principate (Talbert, *Senate*, 116–17). G. had made a mockery of this traditional bastion of Rome (59.28.2–3 + n. [= **B.22**]), and so by meeting here, the senate was symbolically asserting a return not only to normality, but also to traditional Republican values.

1.2–3 some soldiers found Cl. and hailed him as emperor: i.e., some members of the Praetorian Guard; cf. Jos. *AJ* 19.217, who singles out one guardsman, Gratus. The fact that Cl. was the brother of Germanicus was a key factor in his acceptance by the praetorians and the army (Jos. *AJ* 19.217). Cl. soon required the Praetorian Guard and the legions to swear an oath of loyalty in return for a very large donative (Jos. *AJ* 19.247: 5,000 *denarii* per man; cf. Suet. *Cl.* 10.4: 15,000 sesterces = 3,750 *denarii*). Tib. and G. had granted much smaller donatives (56.32.2; 59.2.1 [= **B.2**]). For gold coin issues commemorating the rôle of the praetorians in 41 see Smallwood 36 = Braund 194 = Levick, *Cl.*, pls. 7 and 8; Sutherland, *RHC*, 74–77. The praetorians hereafter received a donative on the anniversary of Cl.'s coming to power (60.12.4). On relations between the Praetorian Guard and the emperor in general see Campbell, *Emperor & Army*, 109–20.

1.3   escorted him to their camp: i.e., the barracks of the Praetorian Guard, on the Viminal Hill just outside the city walls (58.4.2n. [= **A.3**]).

1.3a   Cl. accepted the burden, though with apparent reluctance: D.'s picture of the reluctant emperor probably derives from the official version of events as revised by Cl. once in power; this apparent reluctance enhanced his image as moderate ruler (Levick, *Cl.*, 33–34; A. Wallace-Hadrill, *JRS* 72 (1982), 32–48).

1.4   the consuls sent tribunes and others: Jos. *AJ* 19.234–35 gives the names of the two tribunes of the plebs: Q. Veranius, later consul in 49 on Cl.'s nomination (Smallwood 231 = Braund 404; Braund 587) and the otherwise unattested Brocchus.

the soldiers who had been supporting the consuls: For the supposition that these soldiers consisted of the four Urban Cohorts see Momigliano 20; Levick, *Cl.*, 31–32.

voted all the prerogatives of imperial power: This probably occurred at the meeting of the senate which Cl. summoned on the Palatine on 25 January, Cl.'s *dies imperii* (day of accession) (Jos. *AJ* 19.266). For emperors' accessions cf. 59.3.1–2 + n. [= **B.3**] (G.); Tac. *A.* 12.69 (Nero); 63.29.1 [= **D.8**] (Galba). The "prerogatives of imperial power" are discussed at length by D. at 53.17.3–18.5; they consisted of proconsular *imperium* (58.7.4n. [= **A.6**]) and tribunician power (58.9.2n. [= **A.8**]), the position of *pontifex maximus* (chief priest) and the titles Caesar, Augustus, *Imperator* and *Pater Patriae*. Cl. accepted the senate's offer of all but the last two (60.3.2 + n. [= **C.3**]). The Roman people then passed a series of laws confirming each of these powers, as shown by the surviving law outlining Vespasian's powers (*ILS* 244 = Braund 293 = Sherk 82; P.A. Brunt, *JRS* 67 (1977), 95–116). This passage of D. is used as an argument by those who hold that there was a block vote of all powers: e.g. by B. Levick in *Roman Political Life, 90 B.C. to A.D. 69* (ed. T.P. Wiseman, 1985), 62–63. But since we have only Xiphilinus' summary of D., it should be used with caution; for another case of Xiphilinus' imprecision re emperors' accessions cf. 63.29.1 [= **D.8**].

2.1   Tiberius Claudius Nero Germanicus: cf. Suet. *Cl.* 2.1, where Cl.'s name is given as Tiberius Claudius Drusus. Inscriptions reveal that Cl.'s full title was Tiberius Claudius Caesar Augustus Germanicus (Smallwood 370 = Braund 571 = Sherk 44; Smallwood 368 = Braund 569 = Sherk 52). On Cl.'s names and titles see Levick, *Cl.*, 41–42.

son of Drusus the son of Livia: Ti. Claudius Nero Drusus Germanicus (*PIR*[2] C 857), the younger brother of Tib. (cf. Suet. *Cl.* 1); Cl.'s mother was Antonia (58.11.7n. [= **A.8**]).

Cl. as consul: He had been suffect consul in 37 (59.6.5–6 [= **B.4**]).

in his fiftieth year: This is accurate, since Cl. was born on 1 August 10 B.C. (Suet. *Cl.* 2.1), and hence would celebrate his fiftieth birthday on 1 August 41.

historical treatises: Cl. wrote a history of Rome from the death of Julius Caesar in Latin, histories of the Etruscans and of the Carthaginians in Greek and various other historical works (Suet. *Cl.* 3.1; 41–42; Momigliano, ch. 1; Levick, *Cl.*, 17–20). Cl.'s works are cited by Pliny the Elder (*NH* 5.11.63; 6.10.27; 7.3.35; 12.38.78).

Cl.'s physical disabilities: cf. Suet. *Cl.* 30. They are mercilessly satirized in Seneca, *Apocolocyntosis*. For discussion on their precise nature see Scramuzza 35–36; Levick, *Cl.*, 13–15; J. Mottershead, *Suetonius, Claudius* (1986), 145–47.

2.2   **Cl. in the senate:** He attended meetings regularly (Talbert, *Senate*, 176–77). It was normal for the emperor to use a quaestor to act on his behalf in the senate (ibid., 167). During the Principate two (of the twenty) quaestors were appointed as assistants to the emperor (*quaestores Caesaris*), while four assisted the consuls (ibid., 17). For the exact position of Cl.'s seat in the senate see Suet. *Cl.* 23.2 with Talbert, *Senate*, 122.

2.3   **he was the first of the Romans to use a covered chair:** D. here, as elsewhere, is keen to trace the origins of customs still prevalent in his own day (Introduction, Section 3.4.3; Appendix 2). Cl. created a precedent by using a covered chair (*sella*), which D. here clearly distinguishes from a covered litter (*lectica*). For later emperors using a covered chair cf. 65.20.3. It was only the wives of senators, and occasionally senators when ill, who were allowed to use covered litters within the city of Rome (cf. 57.15.4; 56.43.2). Hence they became marks of social rank, and their use had to be restricted by Julius Caesar (Suet. *DJ* 43.1). For Tib. entering the senate when ill on a covered litter see 57.17.6. Cl. allegedly caused outrage by granting the privilege to one of his freedmen (Suet. *Cl.* 28). See further Balsdon, *Life & Leisure*, 213–15; L. Casson, *Travel in the Ancient World* (1974), 180.

we ex-consuls: D. here refers to his own consular status. He was suffect consul probably in 205 or 206 and then ordinary consul with the emperor Severus Alexander in 229 (Introduction, Sections 1.2.3, 1.2.7).

C.2 CLAUDIUS' WEAKNESSES   A.D. 41

(60.2.4–7)

2.4–5 Claudius' weaknesses: D. presents here, in an emphatic position at the start of his account of the reign, the charges levelled against Cl. in all the literary sources: (a) his domination by women (see Syme, *Tac.*, 437; *AA*, 181–5) and imperial freedmen (see below); (b) his timidity (cf. 60.3.3 [= **C.3**]; Suet. *Cl.* 35–37); (c) his sexual voracity (cf. Suet. *Cl.* 33.2) and (d) his love of food and drink (cf. Suet. *Cl.* 33.1). Tacitus (*A.* 11–12) presents a similar picture, but gives special emphasis to laziness and sloth (cf. *A.* 11.38; E.F. Leon, *TAPA* 79 (1948), 79–86). Despite his alleged enslavement to his wives, he did manage to divorce two of them, have another executed and condemn five of his freedmen (T.F. Carney, *Acta Classica* 3 (1960), 99–104, esp. 104).

Cl. and the imperial freedmen: cf. 60.30.6b; Suet. *Cl.* 28; Levick, *Cl.*, 47, 57, 64–67. The most influential freedmen were those in charge of the Palatine administrative bureaux (on which see P.R.C. Weaver, *Familia Caesaris* (1972); Millar, *ERW*, 69–81): Pallas, *a rationibus* (in charge of financial accounts) (Tac. *A.* 11.29; 12.1–2, 25, 53, 65; Pliny, *Letters* 7.29; 8.6; S.P. Oost, *AJP* 79 (1957), 113–39); Narcissus, *ab epistulis* (i/c letters to and from the emperor) (60.33.5–6; 60.34.4–6; Tac. *A.* 11.29–38; 12.1–2); Callistus, *a libellis* (i/c legal petitions) (60.33.3a; Tac. *A.* 11.29, 38; 12.1–2); and Polybius, *a studiis* (exact function unknown: Millar, *ERW*, 205), later *a libellis* (60.31.2; cf. Seneca, *To Polybius*). They owed their political influence not so much to the actual positions that they held, but to their proximity to, and their ability to channel access to, the emperor (Hopkins, *Death*, 176–84; M.I. Finley, *Aspects of Antiquity* (1967), 127–42) and to their strong personalities. The presence of such freedmen on Cl.'s judicial body of advisers (*consilium*) possibly gave rise to the widespread, if cynical, view that they had Cl. under their thumb (Crook, *CP*, 42). The sources emphasize their power under Cl., but Callistus had been influential under G. (59.19.6 + n. [= **B.14**]), and they continued to be so under Nero (63.12.1–2 [= **D.3**]). D. and other senatorial authors displayed a marked hostility to them (e.g. Tac. *A.* 13.2; Plin. *Letters*, 7.29; 8.6) and held the view that a good emperor kept down the size and influence of the imperial household (52.37.5; Tac. *A.* 4.6; Plin. *Panegyric* 88.1–3). Senators found it difficult to accept the inversion of social norms whereby they now had to seek favours from prominent ex-slaves (Saller, *Patronage*, 45, 66). D.'s hostile picture of Cl.'s freedmen was also coloured by his own experiences under Commodus and Caracalla, when Cleander, Theocritus and Epagathus were especially influential (72.12–13; 77.21.2–4).

2.4 **Cl. had feigned stupidity:** cf. 59.23.5 + n. [= **B.17**].

2.5 **his grandmother Livia:** Cl.'s father, Nero Drusus Germanicus, was the younger son of Livia and Ti. Claudius Nero. For Livia's contempt for Cl. see Suet. *Cl.* 3.2. Nevertheless, soon after his accession Cl. paid her a number of honours, including deification (60.5.2; Suet. *Cl.* 11.2). For further details on Livia cf. 59.1.4 + n. [= **B.1**]; 59.2.4 + n. [= **B.2**]; 63.29.3 + n. [= **D.8**].

his mother Antonia: For biographical details see 58.11.7n. [= **A.7**]; for the honours which Cl. paid her and his father Drusus see 60.5.1; Suet. *Cl.* 11.2. She had been honoured by G. at the start of his reign (59.3.4 [= **B.3**]). Cl. also commemorated his mother, father and other members of his family on the triumphal arch erected after his conquest of Britain

(Smallwood 100 = Braund 218). These honours illustrate how important it was for an emperor on accession to establish his immediate family as the new imperial household (cf. 59.3.4 + n. [= **B.3**].

2.5–6 Cl.'s sexual appetite: Unusually for a Julio-Claudian emperor, Cl.'s sexual tastes seem to have been exclusively heterosexual (Suet. *Cl.* 33.2; cf. Suet. *Aug.* 68; id., *T.* 43; 59.22.6 [= **B.17**]; Suet. *G.* 36; 63.13.1–2 [= **D.3**]; Suet. *N.* 28–29). The reliability of these stories remains uncertain, since lust was one of the canonical vices in the moralistic rhetoric about rulers in the Greco-Roman world (Wallace-Hadrill, *Suet.*, 142–74, esp. 156–58).

2.7 Cl.'s cowardice: cf. 60.3.2–3 [= **C.3**]; Suet. *Cl.* 35–36.

C.3 CLAUDIUS' REACTION TO HIS SUCCESSION A.D. 41

(60.3.1–7)

3.2 accepted all the honours voted to him except the title 'Father of the Fatherland': i.e., accepted the powers and titles voted to him by the senate (60.1.4 + n. [= **C.1**]). Cl. followed Aug., Tib. and G. in initially refusing the title of *Pater Patriae* (59.3.2n. [= **B.3**]), but he had assumed it by January 42 (Smallwood 13 = Braund 199; Smallwood 44 = Braund 214; Levick, *Cl.*, 41; Momigliano 102). He also refused to accept the title *Imperator* as his *praenomen* (first name) (Suet. *Cl.* 12.1; cf. 60.8.7.n. [= **C.6**]). Coins of 41 illustrate these titles (Smallwood 37, 91, 93 = Braund 196–98).

Cl. and the senate: For Cl.'s deference to the senate cf. 60.7.4 [= **C.5**]; Suet. *Cl.* 12. Cl. needed to placate the senators after G.'s conduct towards them at the end of his reign; but the fact that any opposition to his rule was likely to come from within the senate forced him to keep it under close scrutiny (Levick, *Cl.*, 93–103; Momigliano 25–26; D. McAlindon, *AJP* 88 (1957), 279–86). Tib. and G. had also begun their reigns as models of deference towards the senate (57.8–9; 59.3.1 [= **B.3**]).

better candidates for emperor: See 60.1.1n. [= **C.1**].

he exercised great caution in everything: cf. 60.2.6–7 + n. [= **C.2**].

3.3 security measures to protect Cl.'s life: cf. Suet. *Cl.* 35. By soldiers D. means the emperor's German bodyguard (cf. 59.30.1b + n. [= **B.23**]). Aug. had worn a sword and breastplate when attending the senate (Suet. *Aug.* 35.1). During the early Principate emperors were still expected to be accessible to their subjects in the same way as magistrates had been under the Republic (A. Wallace-Hadrill, *JRS* 72 (1982), 32–48). Subjects paid their respects to the emperor in person at his morning reception of clients (*salutatio*) and also at dinner parties. For an example of when Cl.'s searching of guests paid off see Tac. *A.* 11.22. But this visible increase in security measures to protect the emperor was not just a reaction to fears prompted by G.'s assassination; it also represented a further stage in the development of rituals which increasingly separated ruler from ruled (Millar, *ERW*, 61–66, esp. 62). D. again shows interest in the origins of customs still current in his own day (cf. Introduction, Section 3.4.3; Appendix 2).

indiscriminate searching ceased under Vespasian: cf. Suet. *Vesp.* 12; D.'s epitomators do not preserve any specific reference to Vespasian's reversal of this practice, but just note how relaxed he was in his attitude towards palace security (66.10.5).

3.4-5 execution of the conspirators against G.: cf. Suet. *Cl.* 11.1; Jos. *AJ* 19.268–271 [partly = Braund 195]. D. fails to go into the circumstances of the condemnation of the conspirators; Jos. provides a much fuller version, more favourable to Cl., describing how Cl. summoned his body of advisers (*consilium*) and put the issue to the vote. For Josephus' access to an eye-witness account cf. 60.1.2n. [= **C.1**]. Cl.'s swift action clearly demonstrated his faith in the system of the Principate, as D. here emphasizes. However, he also attributes Chaerea's execution to Cl.'s personal fear of a future plot against him. This view may stem from the tradition that grew up concerning Cl.'s timidity.

3.5 Sabinus' suicide: D. again fails to make explicit the fact that Cl. and his *consilium* absolved Sabinus of any guilt and allowed him to remain a tribune in the Praetorian Guard. He, however, decided to commit suicide out of loyalty to Chaerea and the other condemned conspirators (Jos. *AJ* 19.273 [= Braund 195]).

Cl.'s attitude towards the senate's candidates for emperor: Cl.'s magnanimity helped to repair relations between the senate and the emperor. Two of the candidates were especially prominent during Cl.'s reign: M. Vinicius became *consul ordinarius* for the second time in 45 (60.25.1), while D. Valerius Asiaticus held a second consulship in 46 (60.27.1–2 [= **C.12**]; Syme, *AA* 182–84, 279). Both, however, were later forced to commit suicide through the agency of Cl.'s wife, Messallina (60.27.4 [= **C.12**]; Tac. *A.* 11.1–3). Under the Julio-Claudians it was unusual for anyone outside the imperial family to hold more than one consulship (Syme, *AA*, 183); but thereafter the pattern developed whereby senators held a suffect consulship and then a second (ordinary) consulship; the most favoured went on to hold the post of Urban Prefect (*praefectus urbi*) (Syme, *Tac.*, 52–54, 72–73; and *RP* V, 608–21). Excluding members of the imperial family, the following are known to have held more than one consulship under the Julio-Claudians (suff. = suffect consul; cos. = ordinary consul):

Q. Sanquinius Maximus	suff. ?21 or 22		cos. II 39
C. Passienus Crispus	suff. 27		cos. II 44
M. Vinicius	cos. 30		cos. II 45
L. Vitellius	cos. 34	cos. II 43	cos. III 47
D. Valerius Asiaticus	suff. 35		cos. II 46
C. Suetonius Paullinus	suff. ?42 or 43		cos. II 66
C. Antistius Vetus	suff. 46		cos. II 50.

in imitation of the Athenians: D. alludes to the events of 403 B.C., when democracy was restored at Athens after a year of political disorder under the Thirty Tyrants following Athens' capitulation in the Peloponnesian War (431–404 B.C.). The Athenians declared an amnesty and allowed back as full citizens those who had supported the oligarchs (Xenophon, *Hellenika* 2.4.35–43; [Aristotle] *Constitution of the Athenians* 38–40). D.

mentions the same event in a speech put into the mouth of Cicero (44.26.2–4). D. will have known his Xenophon; at 55.12.5 he claims to have read such Greek authors to perfect his Attic style. In general on this interest in Atticism in the later second century A.D. see Introduction, Section 2.1.

3.6 **he abolished the charge of maiestas:** For the charge of *maiestas* see 59.6.2n. [= **B.4**]. D. here makes a clear distinction between *maiestas* charges based on treasonous writings (cf. the case of A. Cremutius Cordus under Tib.: 57.24.2–4; Tac. *A*. 4.34–35) and those based on treasonous acts. Emperors frequently claimed to abolish such charges at the start of their reigns, but it is doubtful whether a total abolition ever took place (59.6.2n. [= **B.4**]). For Cl.'s attitude towards *maiestas* charges see R.A. Bauman, *Impietas in Principem* (1974), 194–204; Levick, *Cl.* 119–20.

C.4 RECALL OF EXILES; CLAUDIUS' INTEREST IN JUSTICE

A.D. 41

(60.4.1–4)

4.1 **taxes introduced by G.:** See 59.28.11 [= **B.22**]; Suet. *G*. 40–41; Balsdon, *Gaius*, 185–86. On finances under Cl. see Levick, *Cl.*, 127–36.
those who had been unjustly sent into exile: G. had exiled his sisters to the Pontian islands in 39 after their alleged implication in the 'conspiracy' of Gaetulicus (59.22.8 [= **B.17**]). D. here provides evidence incidentally for the process whereby the property of those exiled fell into the hands of the emperor, an important source of the emperors' wealth (Millar, *ERW*, 163–74).

4.2 **treason:** For Cl.'s supposed abolition of treason charges see 60.3.6 + n. [= **C.3**]. This passage is revealing of what most likely occurred at the start of each reign: the emperor only allowed those who had clearly committed treasonous acts to be tried on this charge.

4.2–3 **Cl.'s conscientiousness over jurisdiction:** cf. Suet. *Cl*. 14–15, 23. In Suet.'s lives all "good" emperors were shown to be concerned with jurisdiction, but Cl. was exceptionally meticulous (Wallace-Hadrill, *Suet.*, 123–24). For a speech delivered in the senate probably by Cl. outlining a proposal to tighten judicial procedures for prosecutors see Smallwood 367 = Braund 568; M. Griffin, *CQ* 40 (1990), 494–99; cf. Millar, *ERW*, 350, n. 59). In general on jurisdiction under Cl. see Levick, *Cl.*, 115–26.

4.2 **the victims of malicious accusations:** D. here gives a hint of the procedures of criminal law at Rome. It was an accusatorial system, so that all criminal charges had to be brought by an individual accuser (*delator*), who was responsible for his accusation and liable to penalties if he laid a false accusation (Crook, *Law & Life*, 276–78).

4.3 **Cl. as judge either alone or together with the full senate:** For the emperor as judge see Millar, *ERW*, 507–49; for the senate as a court see Talbert, *Senate*, 460–87; for the relationship between imperial and senatorial jurisdiction see A.H.M. Jones, *Studies in Roman Government and Law* (1960), ch. 5.

in the Forum: The large basilicas in the Roman Forum were used for trials, especially the Basilica Iulia, which was the home of the Centumviral court (Pliny, *Letters* 5.9; 6.33).

advisers with him on the bench: cf. Jos. *AJ* 19.268 [= Braund 195]). He did not use this *consilium* to advise him on public business in general, as had been the case with Aug. (Crook, *CP*, 38, 40–45). Cl. himself sat on the advisory body of other magistrates (Suet. *Cl.* 12.2).

since Tib.'s withdrawal to the island: i.e., to Capri in 26 (58.3.3n. [= **A.1**]).

4.4 **those in charge of finance:** Under the Republic the public treasury (the *aerarium Saturni*) had been managed by the quaestors; in 23 B.C. Aug. had put it in the charge of two praetors (the *praetores aerarii*) (53.32.2; cf. Vell. Pat. 2.89.3). For Cl.'s reforms of the treasury later in his reign see 60.10.3; 60.24.3 [= **C.12**]. In general on its administration under the Principate see F. Millar, *JRS* 54 (1964), 33–40.

C.5 VARIOUS MEASURES OF CLAUDIUS CONCERNING THE CITY OF ROME   A.D. 41

(60.6.1–7.4)

6.1–3 This section serves to underline Cl.'s moderation and civility (i.e., respect for other Roman citizens). D. here adopts the biographer's approach of reporting various incidents from different periods to illustrate an aspect of the emperor's character (cf. Wallace-Hadrill, *Suet.*, 142–74). See further Introduction, Section 3.4.1.

6.1 **Cl. in the senate:** See further 60.3.2 + n. [= **C.3**]. D. here provides some insight into seating arrangements inside the senate-house. Cl. did not generally sit on the raised dais in between the two consuls, but rather on the benches occupied by the rest of the senators (cf. 59.26.3 [= **B.19**]; 60.16.3–4 [= **C.8**]; Suet. *Cl.* 23.2; Talbert, *Senate*, 121–28, esp. 122).

Neapolis: modern Naples. In general on Romans going Greek in Naples see 55.10.9; Suet. *Aug.* 98.3; J.H. d'Arms, *Romans on the Bay of Naples* (1970), 83. For the Greek-style musical and gymnastic contests held there see E.N. Gardiner, *Greek Athletic Sports and Festivals* (1910), 169.

6.2 **Greek tunic and boots:** For emperors wearing Greek clothes cf. Suet. *Aug.* 98.3; *Tib.* 13.1; *G.* 52; 63.17.5 + n. [= **D.4**]. For the Greek tunic (*himation*) see E.B. Abrahams, *Greek Dress* (1908), 48–52, 73–96. Scipio Africanus had worn the same kind of Greek calf-length boots (*crêpîdes*) in Sicily in 204 B.C. (Livy 29.19), as had Germanicus in Egypt in 19 (Tac. *A.* 2.59); for *crêpîdes* see Abrahams, *Greek Dress*, 118.

6.3 **he refused any gift of money:** D. here refers to the custom whereby the people offered the emperor good-luck gifts on 1 January. Tib. had refused to accept such gifts (Suet. *Tib.* 34). Cl.'s abolition of this custom seems to have had a permanent effect. See further Millar, *ERW*, 142–43.

the emperor as heir in private wills: For the growing custom whereby the emperor inherited a small part of the property of many Romans on their death see 59.15.1 + n. [= **B.11**]; 60.17.7 [= **C.9**]; Millar, *ERW*, 153–58. In addition, Roman citizens had to pay a five per cent. tax on inheritance. For Roman wills see Crook, *Law & Life*, 119–32.

return of property confiscated under Tib. and G.: Cl. restored the family property of the future emperor Nero, after Nero's father had left part of his estate to G., who then proceeded to take over the whole estate (Suet. *N.* 6.3).

6.4–5 the custom of repeating festivals if any detail was incorrectly carried out: For a Roman religious ritual to be effective, it had to be carried out exactly according to the customary, and extremely precise, rules for each cult; if there were any mistakes made in the utterance of prayers, or if evil-omened birds flew overhead during the ritual, the whole ceremony had to be repeated, a process known as *instauratio* (cf. fr. 51.1; 56.27.4–5; Cic. *On the Response of the Haruspices* 9.23; J.A. North, *PBSR* 44 (1976), 1–3). D. fails to comment on the multifaceted aim of this measure. Its purpose was political (it reduced the number of days on which senators could enhance their popular support by distributing largesse at festivals and on which the people could gather in public, always a potential focus for political disturbance); economic (it reduced the costs involved in repeating festivals); and administrative (it ensured that not too many days for conducting public business were lost: cf. 60.17.1 [= **C.9**]). D. may have been thinking mostly of its value as a security measure, since he goes on immediately to discuss other measures that Cl. took to improve security in the city of Rome.

as I have already stated: D.'s explanation of the process of *instauratio* is preserved only in a fragment (fr. 51.1) possibly from Book 12 of the *Roman History*.

6.6 Jews in Rome: There are problems in reconstructing Cl.'s shifting attitude towards the Jews. No expulsions of Jews from Rome under Cl. are mentioned in the surviving parts of D. or Tac. *A*. The only sources to mention such an expulsion are Suet. *Cl.* 25.4 and *Acts of the Apostles*, 18.2. For further discussion see Momigliano 29–35; Levick, *Cl.*, 87, 121–22, 182–85; E.M. Smallwood, *The Jews under Roman Rule* (1976), 210–16; T. Rajak, *JRS* 74 (1984), 107–23. A slightly modified version of Momigliano's reconstruction seems cogent. Early in 41 at the start of his reign Cl. was conciliatory towards the Jews, as was necessary after the tensions caused by G.'s desire to erect his statue in the temple at Jerusalem: hence the mild tone of Cl.'s edict to the Jews in March 41 (Jos. *AJ* 19.278–291). Later in 41 some violence in Rome caused Cl. to toughen his attitude; the tone of his letter to the Jews in Alexandria dated to 10 November is much more severe (Smallwood 370 = LACTOR 8, no. 27 = Braund 571 = Sherk 44). The Jews in Rome were not expelled, but lost the right to assemble, as D. reports here. That Cl. stopped short of expulsion was probably due to the influence of his friend, Agrippa, rather than for the reason given here by D. In c. 49 further rioting by the Jews in Rome under Chrestus led to the expulsion attested at Suet. *Cl.* 25.4 and *Acts* 18.2. For the date see Smallwood, *Jews*, 211–13. The absence of any reference in D. to an expulsion can possibly be explained on the grounds that his text is for this year preserved only in the abbreviated versions of the Byzantine

epitomators, Xiphilinus and Zonaras; the silence of Tac. is more difficult
to explain.

Cl. abolished the associations: The urban associations (or *collegia*) were
clubs for freedmen, slaves and the poorer members of the Roman urban
populace. Although these clubs often included a trade or occupation in
their titles, they were not trade guilds. For a modest subscription fee, they
provided their members with the occasional communal meal and celebration, while some provided burial services for their members (R.
MacMullen, *Roman Social Relations* (1974), 72–87; J.E. Stambaugh, *The
Ancient Roman City* (1988), 209–12). These associations had often been
the focus of popular disturbances – most dramatically in the late Republic
(A.W. Lintott, *Violence in Republican Rome* (1968), 78–83; R. MacMullen, *Enemies of the Roman Order* (1966), 173–78). Caesar (or just possibly
Aug.) passed a law regulating their activities (Crook, *Law & Life*, 264–68).
For other bans on such associations cf. *Digest* 48.7.4 pr. and ch. 74 of the
Flavian municipal charter from Irni, southern Spain (J. González, *JRS* 76
(1986), 172, 193, 223–24). For Cl.'s concern with public order in general
see Levick, *Cl.*, 121–22.

which had been reintroduced by G.: D. provides the only evidence that Tib.
had abolished clubs altogether and that G. had reinstated them (Yavetz,
Plebs , 114, 119).

**6.7   he closed down the taverns and issued an edict that no meat nor hot water
should be sold:** cf. Suet. *Cl.* 38.2. Two types of establishment frequented by
the Roman poor were involved: taverns (*tabernae*), which just sold drinks,
and cookshops (*popinae*), where the poor could buy a drink and a hot
meal (T. Kléberg, *Hôtels, restaurants et cabarets dans l'antiquité romaine*
(1957); R. MacMullen, *Roman Social Relations*, 86–87; 182, n. 106; J.E.
Stambaugh, *The Ancient Roman City*, 208–09). Many such establishments
have been discovered at Pompeii and Ostia. For the insalubrious nature of
their clientele see Juv. *Sat.* 8.146–78. The sale of hot food and drink was
banned during periods of public mourning as a mark of respect (59.11.6),
but also on other occasions to encourage frugality (Suet. *T.* 34; 62.14.2;
Suet. *N.* 16.2; 66.10.3). It is sometimes held that the poor, who lived in
tenement blocks (*insulae*), did not have the facilities to prepare hot food
and so relied heavily on these *popinae* (so Kléberg, *Hôtels, restaurants*,
105). But Suet. *Cl.* 38.2 reveals that tenants in an apartment block owned
by Cl. could cook, since they were caught selling hot food after Cl.'s ban
recorded here. Furthermore, if they could not cook in their tenement
rooms, Cl.'s action would have been a crippling blow for the poor and
may well have led to serious popular protest. It, therefore, seems more
likely that Cl. closed down those taverns and *popinae* that were known
centres of drunken disorderliness and immorality and/or the meeting-
places of unruly clubs, especially since D. mentions this measure in a
section devoted to Cl.'s measures to stem urban unruliness (cf. Tac. *A.*
13.25; R. MacMullen, *Enemies of the Roman Order* (1966), 167–68).

More generally, the passage is revealing of Roman diet. Wine was often
drunk mixed with hot water, herbs and spices (N. Purcell, *JRS* 75 (1985),
13–15). Although Roman diet was essentially cereal-based, meat was also

consumed as a supplement, as the study of bone remains on archaeological sites is increasingly demonstrating (K. Greene, *The Archaeology of the
Roman Economy* (1986), 76–79). Salted pork joints have even been found
on a Roman shipwreck (G. Charlin, J.-M. Gassend and R. Lequément,
Archaeonautica 2 (1978), 9–93, esp. 16 and fig. 10).

6.8–9 By all these actions Cl. sought to distance himself from the policies of G.
and to advertise his moderation as ruler.

6.8 **he returned to the cities the statues which Gaius had summoned from them:**
cf. 59.28.3 + n. [= **B.22**].

he returned to the Dioscuri their temple: For G.'s alleged alterations to the
temple of Castor and Pollux (= the Dioscuri) in the Roman Forum see
59.28.5 + n. [= **B.22**].

restorations to the theatre of Pompey: This theatre in the Campus Martius
was Rome's first stone-built theatre, dedicated by Cn. Pompeius Magnus
in 55 B.C. (39.38.1–6; Cic. *Letters to his Friends* 7.1; Nash, *Pictorial
Dictionary*, II, 422–28; A. Boethius, *Etruscan and Early Roman Architecture* (1978), 205–06). Tib. had rebuilt the stage of the theatre after a fire in
22 (Tac. *A.* 3.72; 6.45; Suet. *T.* 47), while G. had completed the work
(Suet. *G.* 21), but, as D. here suggests, had allowed Tib. no credit for the
work in the dedicatory inscription that he set up. For further details of the
festival marking its re-dedication by Cl. see Suet. *Cl.* 21.2. Cl. also
completed a marble arch to Tib. near the theatre, a work left unfinished by
G. (Suet. *Cl.* 11.3).

6.9 **he also inscribed his own name on it, but on no other building:** Cl. stressed his
moderation in the same way as Aug. when he boasted that he had rebuilt
the Capitol and theatre of Pompey "without inscribing my own name on
either building" (*RG* 20.1).

he did not wear triumphal dress throughout the whole festival: For triumphal dress and the senate's rôle in voting it to the emperor see 59.7.1n. [=
B.5]. For the purple-bordered toga (*toga praetexta*), which emperors wore
for more routine public appearances, see 58.11.2n. [= **A.7**]. This passage
well illustrates that sacrifice was considered the climax of any Roman
festival.

7.1 **any equestrians, women of similar rank or others who had been accustomed
to performing on the stage during the reign of G.:** G. had forced members of
the equestrian order to fight as gladiators (59.10.4) and even had appeared
on the stage himself (59.5.5). Cl. was thus reverting to the stricter policy of
Aug. and Tib. not to encourage upper-class performers (56.25.7–8; B.
Levick, *JRS* 73 (1983), 97–115 = Braund 724 = Sherk 35). The Digest of
Roman Law (3.1.1.6) reveals that all free men who fought beasts for pay
suffered infamy, while if they fought them purely for sport, they incurred
no penalty.

7.2 **Pyrrhic Dance:** Named after the Hellenistic king Pyrrhus of Epirus (319–
272 B.C.), it was a type of paramilitary display commonly performed by
ephebes (18- to 20-year olds) in the cities of the Greek East (Plin. *NH*
7.55.204). G. had summoned these boys from Asia Minor for a performance at the Palatine Games at which he was assassinated (59.29.6 + n. [=
B.23]). For other occasions on which it was performed in Rome see Suet.

DJ 39.1; 60.23.5 [= **C.11**]; Suet. *N.* 12.1 (where Nero also bestowed Roman citizenship on the performers). For Cl.'s bestowal of Roman citizenship on provincials in general cf. 60.17.4 + n. [= **C.9**].

7.3   **beast-hunts in the circus:** For *venationes* (beast-hunts) see 59.7.3n. [= **B.5**]. Before the opening of the Flavian Amphitheatre (the Colosseum) in 80, beast-hunts often took place in the circus (56.27.4–5; 59.13.8–9; Livy 39.22.2; Humphrey, *Circuses*, 1, 71, 182–86). Bears were still found in central and southern Italy. By 'Libyan' beasts D. means beasts from north Africa. Elephants, lions, panthers, crocodiles, hippopotami, rhinoceros and giraffes are all attested in the Roman arena (G. Jennison, *Animals for Shows and Pleasure in Ancient Rome* (1937), 60–82).

7.3–4 seating arrangements in the circus: The hierarchies in Roman society were visibly reinforced by where people sat at the theatre (see 59.7.8n. [= **B.5**]). Cl. here extends the principle to the circus by reserving a section of seating for senators (cf. Suet. *Cl.* 21.3 with further details on Cl.'s embellishment of the starting-gates and turning-posts), a change that had lasting effect (cf. 61.16.4). It seems that D. was in error when he reported earlier (55.22.4) that Aug. had instituted such segregated seating at the circus in 5. For speculations on where the senatorial seats were located see Humphrey, *Circuses*, 101–2. In 63 Nero created separate seating in the circus for equestrians, who had to date only enjoyed this privilege in the theatre and possibly amphitheatre (Tac. *A.* 15.32). Note again D.'s interest in tracing the origins of customs still prevalent in his day (Introduction, Section 3.4.3; Appendix 2).

informal or ordinary citizens' dress: Aug. had reinforced a strict dress code for the public games (Suet. *Aug.* 44.2). Roman citizens had to wear the pure white toga, while equestrians, senators, curule magistrates, priests and triumphators all wore different types of distinctive dress. Equestrians wore tunics with two narrow purple vertical stripes and a short purple and scarlet toga with a purple border (the *trabea*); senators tunics with a wide purple stripe; priests and those who were holding, or had held, curule magistracies (consul, praetor, curule aedile) wore togas with a purple border (*toga praetexta*), while triumphators wore a purple toga, embroidered with gold (*toga picta*). D.'s meaning here is ambiguous: either Cl. allowed senators to appear in non-senatorial, ordinary citizens' dress, (i.e., in just a plain white toga) or, more drastically, he allowed them to discard the toga altogether and wear informal dress. If the former, it is hard to envisage the point of the privilege. The latter, therefore, is possibly more likely. For the argument that Aug. allowed citizens to attend the theatre and amphitheatre dressed in ordinary cloaks, but restricted them to the very back rows see E. Rawson, *PBSR* 55 (1987), 85. A further complication arises over where senators not attired in senatorial dress sat; it seems unlikely that Cl. would have allowed them to sit with their fellow senators, since it would have created a bad impression for the plebs. Therefore, they either sat with the non-senators, or, more likely, in the very back seats with those members of the plebs who also chose not to dress in togas.

Cl. feasted the senate, the equestrian order and the tribes: For public feasting in general see 59.7.1n. [= **B.5**]; for D.'s use of the term 'tribes' to refer to the Roman citizen body (*populus Romanus*) cf. 58.2.7 + n. [= **A.1**]. The citizens possibly sat in their tribal divisions at the theatre (E. Rawson, *PBSR* 55 (1987), 96–98). If Cl.'s banquet took place in the circus immediately following the beast-shows (as occurred at other times: cf. 67.4.4), this may suggest that the people sat in tribal groups for the games as well.

C.6 FOREIGN AFFAIRS   A.D. 41–42

(60.8.1–9.1; 9.5)

8.1 **Cl. restored Commagene to Antiochus:** cf. Jos. *AJ* 19.276. G. had converted Commagene from being a Roman province back into an allied kingdom in 38 and appointed Antiochus IV king, who was granted extra territory along the Cilician coast (59.8.2 + n. [= **B.6**]). D. here provides the only evidence for Antiochus' later deposition by G. After his return in 41, Antiochus remained king of Commagene until he was deposed by Vespasian in 72 (Jos. *BJ* 7.219–243). For a coin issue of Antiochus, advertising his return as king, see Smallwood 205 = Braund 633. For games established by Antiochus and Polemo of Pontus in honour of Cl. see Smallwood 374 = Braund 581. In general see D. Magie, *Roman Rule in Asia Minor* (1950), 549–50; Levick, *Cl.*, 159, 165–66.

Mithridates the Iberian: *PIR*² M 644, the brother of Pharasmenes king of Iberia in the Caucasus (Tac. *A.* 6.32). With Tib.'s encouragement he had gained control of the kingdom of Armenia in 35 (58.26.4; Tac. *A.* 6.33–36). In 38 G. had summoned him to R., thus leaving Armenia under Parthian control (Tac. *A.* 11.8; Sen. *On Tranquility* 11.12). For Cl.'s reinstatement of Mithridates as king of Armenia cf. Tac. *A.* 11.8–9; Magie, *RRAM*, 551; Braund, *RFK*, 170; Levick, *Cl.*, 159–60. D.'s date of 41 is to be preferred to Tac. who places it in 47 (Magie 1410, n. 33). For Rome's complex relations with Armenia and Parthia under the Julio-Claudians see J.G.C. Anderson, *CAH* X (1934), 747–73; Balsdon, *Gaius*, 198–200; Levick, *Cl.*, 158–61. For Nero's settlement of the area see 63.1–6 [= **D.1**]. Armenia was finally annexed as a Roman province by Trajan (Festus, *Breviarium* 20 = Sherk 136).

8.2 **Mithridates of Bosporus:** *PIR*² M 635. For the Bosporan kingdom see 59.12.2n. [= **B.10**]. D. is incorrect in asserting that Cl. replaced Polemo with Mithridates as king of Cimmerian Bosporus, since a coin of 39–40 (Smallwood 202) clearly shows that Mithridates was already king here under G. (A.A. Barrett, *TAPA* 107 (1977), 1–9). Cl. thus confirmed Mithridates in power (Scramuzza 184–85 *contra* Balsdon, *Gaius*, 201), but later deposed him in 46 (60.28.7 [= **C.14**]).

Mithridates the Great: i.e., Mithridates VI, king of Pontus between c. 112 and 62 B.C. He caused Rome great military problems in the East until his defeat by Cn. Pompeius Magnus in 65 B.C. (Cic. *On the Command of Cn.*

Pompeius; A.N. Sherwin-White, *Roman Foreign Policy in the East* (1984), 102–206).

Polemon: Serious problems exist over the identity of this Polemo. D. may have confused two Polemos who are distinguised by Josephus: Polemo of Pontus (*AJ* 19.338) and Polemo of Cilicia (*AJ* 20.145) (Magie, *RRAM*, 548–49, 1407, n. 26). For arguments that D. here refers to the Cilician Polemo see R.D. Sullivan, *ANRW*, II.7.2 (1980), 926–29; A.A. Barrett, *Historia* 27 (1978), 437–48; but for objections and for the conjecture that D. means a descendant (?son) of the Cilician Polemo see Braund, *RFK*, 42.

Agrippa of Palestine: See further 59.8.2n. [= **B.6**]. Cl.'s grant of extra territory (Judaea, Samaria and Caesarea) to Agrippa in 41 was marked by a treaty celebrated in a ceremony in the Forum at Rome (Jos. *AJ* 19.274–75; Smallwood 209a; Braund 635). Cl. was not just repaying a personal debt for Agrippa's help in establishing him as emperor, but needed Agrippa in Palestine to restore stability after G.'s threat to the temple in Jerusalem (Smallwood, *Jews*, 192–93). On Agrippa's death in 44, Cl. abandoned the use of an allied king in Palestine and re-established the province of Judaea (Jos. *AJ* 19.361–63; Smallwood, *Jews*, 199).

consular decorations: i.e., *ornamenta consularia*, which entitled the recipient to wear a purple-bordered toga (*toga praetexta*) at festivals, to sit in the seats reserved for senators at the theatre and to parade with the ex-consuls at festivals (Talbert, *Senate*, 366–70). Agrippa had already been granted praetorian decorations by G. (Philo, *Flaccus* 40).

8.3 **Agrippa's brother Herod:** Cl. granted him the kingdom of Chalcis at the foot of Mt. Lebanon (Jos. *AJ* 19.338).

Agrippa and Herod make speeches in the senate: Speeches of thanks to the emperor were frequently delivered in the senate, notably by consuls and provincial governors as they entered office, although the latter were forbidden from so doing by an edict of Cl. (60.11.6–7; Pliny, *Panegyric*; E.J. Champlin, *Fronto and Antonine Rome* (1980), 83–86; Talbert, *Senate*, 227–30, citing other occasions). The practice of foreign delegations addressing the senate goes back to the Republic; usually they had to make their speeches in Latin (Talbert, *Senate*, 411–25). In allowing Agrippa and Herod to speak in Greek, Cl. was further honouring them. This passage is also revealing on D.'s source material: *contra* Millar, *Dio* 37, it suggests that he consulted the proceedings of the senate (*acta senatus*), which would have recorded the grant of *ornamenta* and the speeches of thanks by Agrippa and Herod (cf. R. Syme, *JRS* 72 (1982), 75; P.M. Swan, *Phoenix* 41 (1987), 274).

8.4–5 D. recounts these events in chronological order, but also fits them into a topical treatment of Cl.'s domination by women and freedmen, a leitmotif in his account of Cl. (cf. 60.16.2; 60.17.5 [= **C.9**]; 60.17.8–18.4 [= **C.10**]; 60.22.4; 60.27.4 [= **C.13**]; 60.28.2–5; 60.29.6a; 60.30.6b; 60.31; see further 60.2.4–6n. [= **C.2**]).

Valeria Messalina: More correctly in Latin Valeria Messallina, Cl.'s third wife, whom he had married in c. 39 (Syme, *AA*, 147, 178–79, 182–85). His previous wives had been Plautia Urgulanilla and Aelia Paetina (Suet. *Cl.* 26.2).

8.5   **Cl.'s niece Julia:** Julia Livilla (*PIR²* J 674), the youngest daughter of Cl.'s brother Germanicus and Agrippina. G. had exiled her in 39 for her alleged involvement in the 'conspiracy' of Gaetulicus (59.22.6 + n. [= **B.17**]). She had just been recalled by Cl. (60.4.1 [= **C.4**]). As the wife of M. Vinicius, proposed as emperor in the senatorial debate after G.'s death, she posed a potential political threat to Cl. and Messallina and so became the latter's first victim. She was sent to the island of Pandateria and soon murdered by a soldier (Suet. *Cl.* 29.1; Levick, *Cl.*, 56). For another version of her death cf. 60.27.4 + n. [= **C.13**]. For her epitaph (probably from the Mausoleum of Aug.) see Smallwood 87 = Braund 191.

Annaeus Seneca was exiled: For this famous philosopher-statesman see 59.19.7 + n. [= **B.14**]. For his alleged adultery with Livilla and his exile to Corsica between 41 and 49 see 61.10.1; Seneca, *Polybius* 13.2; Tac. *A.* 13.42; Griffin, *Seneca*, 59–63.

8.6   **achievements in Mauretania:** G. had executed Ptolemy, allied king of Mauretania, in 40 and annexed Mauretania as a province (59.25.1 + n. [= **B.18**]). D. is incorrect to suggest that the war was over before Cl. came to power (M.P. Charlesworth, *CAH* X (1934), 675) and is thus unfair in his criticism of Cl. here. The details, and chronology, of these campaigns remain controversial (D. Fishwick, *Historia* 20 (1971), 467–87; Levick, *Cl.*, 149–50; Barrett 117–20).

triumphal decorations: i.e., *ornamenta triumphalia*. These included the grant of a commemorative statue and the right to wear triumphal dress (59.7.1n. [= **B.5**]) at festivals, but crucially did not allow the recipient a triumphal procession through the city of Rome (V.A. Maxfield, *The Military Decorations of the Roman Army* (1981), 101–09). For a list of awards made under the Julio-Claudians see A.E. Gordon, *Quintus Veranius, consul A.D. 49* (1952), Appendix 2; for awards to emperors see Campbell, *Emperor & Army*, 136–39. It was the senate that formally voted such honours (Talbert, *Senate*, 362–63). D. (or his source) has twisted the facts here to exaggerate the power of Cl.'s freedmen: cf. Suet. *Cl.* 17.1, who records that it was the senate who offered Cl. these triumphal decorations, which Cl. turned down. Cl. was particularly generous in awarding such decorations during his British campaign (60.23.2 [= **C.11**]).

8.7   **Sulpicius Galba:** Ser(vius) Sulpicius Galba, the later emperor (*PIR¹* S 723); for his family see Suet. *Galba* 3; Plut. *Galba* 3.1; Syme, *AA*, 75, 435. He had been adopted as a boy by Livia, the wife of Aug., and so changed his name to L. Livius Sulpicius Galba (Suet. *Galba* 4.1; cf. Smallwood 391 = Braund 600 = Sherk 80 = LACTOR 8, no. 50). After being propraetorian legate of Aquitania, he had held the consulship in 33 (58.20.5). He was sent by G. to take over as proconsular commander of the legions of Upper Germany from Lentulus Gaetulicus after the latter's alleged conspiracy (Suet. *Galba* 6.2; cf. 59.22.5 [= **B.17**]).

Chatti: A powerful German tribe, who occupied the basin of the river Main (Tac. *Germ.* 29–32, 35–6, 38). They caused Roman armies further problems in 50 (Tac. *A.* 12.27–28; Levick, *Cl.*, 152–55).

P. Gabinius: P. Gabinius Secundus (*PIR²* G 9). Suet. *Cl.* 24.3 records that

Cl. allowed him to take the extra name (*agnomen*) "Chaucicus" to commemorate the achievement recorded here, i.e., the recovery of one of the legionary standards lost during P. Quinctilius Varus' campaigns in 9 in the Teutoberger forest (56.18–24; Tac. *A*. 1.3, 60–61; Suet. *Aug*. 23; C.M. Wells, *The German Policy of Augustus* (1972), 240–45). Under the Principate it was very rare for anyone outside the imperial family to be granted such an honour; only one other case is known: Cossus Cornelius Lentulus "Gaetulicus", consul in 1 B.C. for his exploits against the Gaetulians in north Africa (55.28.4; Campbell, *Emperor & Army*, 128–33, 362). Gabinius' honour emphasizes the psychological importance to the Romans of expunging the disgrace suffered by Varus.

Chauci: This is an emendation of the manuscript reading ("Maurusii"), to explain the commemorative *cognomen* taken by Gabinius. The Chauci lived along the North Sea between the rivers Ems and Elbe (Tac. *Germ*. 35–36); for further problems with them in 47 see Tac. *A*. 11.18–19; Levick, *Cl.*, 152–55.

Cl. and the title Imperator: Cl. had refused to take the title *Imperator* as his *praenomen* (Suet. *Cl*. 12.1). The use of the title as part of an emperor's name (e.g. Imp. Caesar Augustus) should be differentiated from his salutations as *Imperator* by troops on military campaigns (59.22.2n. [= **B.16**]). D. here refers to the latter. These salutations were counted and recorded along with the emperor's other titles: e.g. Ti. Claudius Caesar Augustus Germanicus, Pontifex Maximus, with tribunician power, *Imperator* for the second time (Smallwood 335 = Braund 832). This was the second of twenty-seven such salutations for Cl. (cf. 60.21.4 [= **C.11**]; Levick, *Cl.*, 137).

9.1   **revolt in Mauretania:** After G.'s annexation of Mauretania as a province in 40, a revolt against Roman rule had broken out under the leadership of Aedemon, a freedman of Ptolemy. Rome subjugated this revolt in 40–41 and gradually regained control over all of Mauretania after more widespread revolts in 41–42 and 42–43, quelled, as D. here reports, by Paullinus and Geta. The precise chronology of these events is by no means certain (D. Fishwick, *Historia* 20 (1971), 467–87; Levick, *Cl.*, 149–50).

C. Suetonius Paulinus: More correctly in Latin Paullinus (*PIR*[1] S 694). For his later career see Tac. *A*. 14.29–39; *Agr*. 14–16; A.R. Birley, *Fasti of Roman Britain* (1981), 54–57. The fact that he campaigned as far as Mt. Atlas makes this a considerable, and no doubt arduous, campaign. He went on to hold a suffect consulship in 42 or 43 (P.A. Gallivan, *CQ* 28 (1978), 418–19) and a second (ordinary) consulship in 66 (63.1.1).

Cn. Hosidius Geta: For his career see *PIR*[2] H 216. He campaigned in 42 against pre-Saharan nomads, a completely separate problem from the revolt quelled by Paullinus (D. Fishwick, *Historia* 20 (1971), 476). The same Geta probably took part in Cl.'s invasion of Britain (60.20.4 + n. [= **C.11**]). D. fails to mention M. Licinius Crassus Frugi, consul in 27, who is commemorated on an inscription as "legate of Tiberius Claudius Caesar Augustus Germanicus in M........." (either Mauretania or Macedonia), for which he received *ornamenta triumphalia* (Smallwood 224 =

Braund 398; Suet. *Cl.* 17.3; Syme, *AA*, 277–78). He may have quelled the first revolt by Aedemon in 40–41 (Levick, *Cl.*, 149).

9.5 **he divided Mauretania into two provinces and appointed two equestrians to govern them:** i.e., Mauretania Tingitana and Mauretania Caesariensis, whose administrative centres were at Tingis (modern Tangiers) and Caesarea (Cherchel) respectively. For an equestrian procurator *pro legato* (i.e., acting-legate) as governor of Mauretania Tingitana under Cl. see Smallwood 407a = Braund 680a. For equestrians as provincial governors of Egypt, Judaea, Cappadocia, Corsica, Sardinia, Raetia, the Graian and Maritime Alps, Noricum, Epirus, Thrace and parts of Dacia see P.A. Brunt, *JRS* 73 (1983), 55–58; Millar, *REN*, 55–57. For Mauretania under Cl. see J. Gascou, *Ktèma* 6 (1981), 227–38. The two Mauretanias were united into a single province by Galba and placed under a senatorial legate (governor) of praetorian rank (Tac. *H*. 2.58).

C.7 IMPROVEMENTS TO THE HARBOUR AT OSTIA   A.D. 42

(60.11.1–5)

11.1 **severe famine:** A series of droughts led to serious grain shortages not in 42, as D. here suggests, but in 40–41 (Seneca, *On the Brevity of Life*, 18.5). D. telescopes the chronology to make a causal link between the grain shortage and the construction of the new harbour at Ostia (for other examples of this technique see Introduction, Section 4.1). Coins were issued in 41 with Ceres (the goddess of grain and symbol of abundance) seated, holding ears of corn and a long torch, to commemorate the resolution of the grain shortage (Smallwood 312a = Braund 815a = Levick, *Cl.*, plate 12). For the suggestion that Cl. probably solved the crisis by persuading merchants to sail during the winter months see Garnsey, *Famine*, 222–23.

11.2 **Rome's grain supply:** Rome in this period had a population of approximately one million; and so ensuring a sufficient supply of food (especially the basic staple, grain) was a major concern for the emperor. Rome could no longer be fed from her surrounding territory nor even from Italy, but relied on grain imported from overseas. Grain shortages in the late Republic and under Aug. had led to serious riots and political instability (e.g. 48.31.1–6; 54.1.1–4). Aug. had provided regular handouts of grain and/or money to the Roman plebs (*RG* 18), a practice which all later emperors followed to ensure their popular support (Garnsey, *Famine*, 218–43). Cl.'s attempts to improve the facilities for importing grain should be seen as an attempt to increase his popular support as emperor; the building works that he commissioned at Ostia also provided much-needed jobs for the urban poor (Levick, *Cl.*, 108–11).

the region near the mouth of the Tiber had no safe landing-places or suitable harbours: Ostia at this stage was just a river port at the mouth of the Tiber, incapable of handling the massive grain ships, for whose size see K. Hopkins in *Trade and Famine in Classical Antiquity* (ed. P. Garnsey and

C.R. Whittaker, 1983), 97–102). Thus Puteoli (modern Pozzuoli, about 200 km. south of Rome) had hitherto been Rome's main grain port (M.W. Frederiksen, *Campania* (1984), 324–28, 331–34). The grain had to be off-loaded onto smaller coastal and then river vessels to transport it to Rome. Even after Ostia became fully operational under Trajan, Puteoli still served as the port for grain from Alexandria (Egypt), while grain from Africa, Sicily, Sardinia and other western provinces was shipped to Ostia (Rickman, *Corn Supply*; Garnsey, *Famine*, 218–43; more briefly Garnsey in *Trade in the Ancient Economy* (ed. P. Garnsey, K. Hopkins and C.R. Whittaker, 1983), 118–30).

no grain was imported during the winter: This passage is revealing of the Roman sailing season, which was essentially restricted to the summer months (i.e. March – October), unless the ships could be protected by a good harbour (L. Casson, *Ships and Seamanship in the Ancient World* (1971), 270–73; cf. F. Braudel, *The Mediterranean and the Mediterranean World in the Age of Philip II* (Engl. tr., 1972), 248–53). A severe grain shortage could dictate winter sailings, as in 51 when Cl. provided substantial incentives for grain shippers to sail during the winter (Tac. *A.* 12.43; Suet. *Cl.* 18.2–19.1; Gaius, *Institutes* 1.32c (= Braund 712); *Digest* 3.6; Garnsey, *Famine*, 233–34; Rickman, *Corn Supply*, 74–76). These incentives included insurance for shippers against the loss of ships carrying grain to Rome, and privileges for those who built especially large merchant ships (of a capacity of over 10,000 *modii* = c. 70 tonnes) and used them for the shipment of grain to Rome for at least six years.

storage of grain in warehouses: The Roman state owned a series of warehouses at Ostia and Rome (G.E. Rickman, *Roman Granaries and Store Buildings* (1971), chs. 1–2). For privately-owned grain from Alexandria being stored in a public warehouse at Puteoli in 37 see J.A. Crook, *ZPE* 29 (1978), 234–36 = Braund 747. Aug. had placed the grain supply under a special prefect (*praefectus annonae*) (55.31.4). Although his precise responsibilities remain uncertain, he seems to have controlled a complex organization of subordinates at Rome, Ostia and in the main grain-producing provinces, to ensure the transfer of sufficient grain from the provincial threshing-floors to the state warehouses at Ostia and Rome (Rickman, *Corn Supply*, 79–93 and Appendix 2). For a full study see H. Pavis d'Escurac, *La préfecture de l'annone* (1976).

11.3 **the architects were sure that the huge expense would deter him:** The same story-pattern is found at Thuc. 6.19–24, where the Athenian general Nikias attempts (also unsuccessfully) to dissuade the Athenians from launching a naval expedition to Sicily by exaggerating its cost.

11.4 **Cl.'s building operations at Ostia:** For the archaeological remains of Cl.'s port installations see R. Meiggs, *Roman Ostia* (2nd ed., 1973), 54–57, 153–59 and 591–92; O. Testaguzza, *Portus* (1970), 129–47; Levick, *Cl.*, 109–10. The building operations took some time: the harbour was not in full regular use until 62 (Tac. *A.* 15.18). Coins commemorating this were issued in 64, one type depicting the new harbour, moles, lighthouse and ships, the other *Annona* (i.e., the Grain Supply) personified with a *cornucopia* and Ceres (Smallwood 313 = Braund 816; Sutherland, *RHC*, 80–83). The harbour was not completely successful until Trajan built a smaller inner harbour (Meiggs, *Ostia*, 54–62). Cl.'s work at Ostia was complemented by work to divert flood-water from the Tiber (Smallwood 312b = Braund 815b).

11.5 "The Harbour", as it is still known locally: Coins reveal that Cl.'s harbour was known officially as "Portus Augusti Ostiensis" (Smallwood 313a = Braund 816a; Meiggs, *Ostia*, 56); the whole area was known simply as "Portus" ("The Harbour") (Meiggs, *Ostia*, 149–71).

he wanted to drain the Fucine Lake: Julius Caesar and Aug. had tried in vain to drain this large lake in the central Apennines, 100 km. east of Rome (Suet. *DJ* 44.3; *Cl.* 20.1). Cl.'s enormous project was completed in 52, but failed disastrously due to engineering shortcomings (60.33.5; Tac. *A.* 12.56–57; Plin. *NH* 36.24.124–25). D., but not Tac., emphasizes that Cl.'s intention was to provide more agricultural land and hence more locally-produced grain for Rome, to lessen (if only marginally) Rome's dependency on overseas grain. The emperors Trajan and Hadrian made further unsuccessful attempts to drain the lake (Scramuzza 173–74; Levick, *Cl.*, 110–11).

C.8 DEATH OF SILANUS; REBELLION OF SCRIBONIANUS

A.D. 42

(60.14.1 –16.4)

14.1 Cl.'s fill of bloodshed: D. has just related Cl.'s love of human bloodshed at the games (60.13); for Cl.'s cruelty as a theme of his reign cf. Suet. *Cl.* 34; for his domination by women and freedmen cf. 60.2.4–6n. [= **C.2**]; 60.8.4–5n. [= **C.6**]; for his timidity cf. 60.2.7 [= **C.2**]; 60.3.3 + n. [= **C.3**]. D. thus interweaves many of the leitmotifs of his treatment of Cl. into this episode.

14.3–4 C. Appius Iunius Silanus: *PIR²* I 822. He had been *consul ordinarius* in 28 and was a member of the priestly college of the Arval Brethren, which marks him out as one of the leading Julio-Claudian senators: see R. Syme, *Some Arval Brethren* (1980). He had been governor of Hispania Tarraconensis since 40 (G. Alföldy, *Fasti Hispanienses* (1969), 15–16). For his family, which was often in conflict with the emperors, see Syme, *AA*, ch. 14. A supporter of Sej., he had escaped from a charge of treason in 32 (Tac. *A.* 6.9). For a similar version of his death, engineered by his stepdaughter Messallina, cf. Suet. *Cl.* 37.2. For arguments that the real reason for his execution was conspiracy (rather than the salacious reasons given by D. and Suet.) see D. McAlindon, *AJP* 77 (1956), 119–23; Levick, *Cl.*, 58–59. D. later uses the same reason to explain the death of M. Vinicius at Messallina's hands (60.27.4 [= **C.13**]).

Messalina's mother: Domitia Lepida (*PIR²* D 180; Syme, *AA*, 164–65).

Narcissus: For further details on this influential imperial freedman see 60.2.4–6n. [= **C.2**]. For his part in the death of Silanus cf. Tac. *A.* 11.29;

Suet. *Cl.* 37.2. He also played a part in the downfall of C. Silius and Messallina herself (Tac. *A.* 11.29–38).

14.4 condemnation of Silanus: For the development of such trials within the private quarters of the emperor under Cl. see Crook, *CP*, 106; Millar, *ERW*, 521–22 (with further examples). For the view that Silanus' execution sparked senatorial revolts against Cl. see Levick, *Cl.*, 59; T.P. Wiseman, *JRS* 72 (1982), 59–63, slightly exaggerating the scale of the "Claudian Civil War", since this is a crucial link in his overall argument that Calpurnius Siculus' poetry be dated to the Neronian period.

15.1 after that the Romans no longer held out any hopes in Cl.: For D., Silanus' execution marked a turning-point in Cl.'s reign. D. liked to establish such turning-points: cf. 57.19.8 (Germanicus' death in Tib.'s reign); 59.10.8 (G.'s illness and Drusilla's death in G.'s); 61.11.1 (Agrippina's death in Nero's).

L. Annius Vinicianus: *PIR*[2] A 701; one of the ringleaders of the successful plot against G. (59.29.1n. [= **B.23**]; 60.1.1n. [= **C.1**]). On his revolt against Cl. see D. McAlindon, *AJP* 77 (1956), 128–29.

15.2 Furius Camillus Scribonianus: L. Arruntius Camillus Scribonianus, consul in 32 (*PIR*[2] A 1140). He was the son of M. Furius Camillus (consul in 8), but was adopted by L. Arruntius (consul in 6) (Syme, *AA*, 259). D. styles him by his original name, as opposed to the name he used after his adoption. As governor of Dalmatia, he commanded just two legions (EJ 257, 258, 265, 266 = Braund 490, 491, 498, 499; J.J. Wilkes, *Roman Dalmatia* (1969), 92, 95). For his rebellion, which only lasted five days, cf. Suet. *Cl.* 13.2 and 35.2; Tac. *H.* 1.89; 2.75; Plin. *Letters* 3.16.4; Levick, *Cl.*, 59–60; Syme, *AA*, 278–79; D. McAlindon, *AJP* 78 (1957), 279–81; T.P. Wiseman, *JRS* 72 (1982), 59–63. But the crucial reason for the failure of the rebellion, not adduced by D., was that Scribonianus could not muster sufficient military support.

15.3 promised to give back to them their ancient freedom: For the continued use of the Republican ideology of liberty under the Principate cf. 60.1.1 + n. [= **C.1**]; Wirszubski, *Libertas*, ch. 5. This incident well illustrates that the army were fully aware that they were better off under a stable imperial system than under a Republic, a view with which D. concurred (53.19.1; 56.43.4; Introduction, Section 3.4.3).

Issa: modern Vis, an island off the Dalmatian coast.

Scribonianus' suicide: For a different version, in which Scribonianus is assassinated, cf. Tac. *H.* 2.75. All public record of him was eradicated, a fate reserved for those declared public enemies; for his name erased on an inscription see EJ 51 = Braund 99 = Sherk 40c.

15.4 Cl. rewarded the soldiers by bestowing the titles "Claudian", "the Loyal" and "the Patriotic" on the Seventh and Eleventh Legions, and by having them so saluted by the senate: Cary's Loeb translation ("by causing the legions ..... to be named Claudian and Loyal and Patriotic by the senate") fails to take account of the word "and" immediately before "by having them so saluted by the senate". This crucially misrepresents what D. wrote and has misled scholars into claiming that this is an unparalleled case of the senate being allowed to grant an honorific title to a legion (Talbert,

Senate, 428). My translation remains more faithful to D.'s text and also removes a supposed anomaly. Legionary titles were bestowed by the emperor, an honour that was then confirmed by the senate. Inscriptions confirm this grant of honorific titles; for Legio VII Pia Fidelis ("Loyal and Patriotic") see Smallwood 291 = Braund 527; *JRS* 60 (1970), 142 = Sherk 117; for Legio XI Claudia Pia Fidelis ("Claudian, Loyal and Patriotic") see *AE* 1934, 176 = Sherk 138. Auxiliary units of cavalry and infantry also assumed "Claudia" as part of their titles (Momigliano 59). For legionary titles in general see Webster, *Army*, 103–07; Campbell, *Emperor & Army*, 88–93.

15.5 using slaves and freedmen as informers against their masters: For Cl.'s detestation of this practice, common during the reigns of Tib. and G., see 60.13.2. For the ways in which the Roman system of criminal justice encouraged informers see Crook, *Law & Life*, 276–77. Freedmen were debarred from laying charges against their patrons – except in the case of treason (Crook 277).

15.6 they even tortured men of the highest nobility: Torture was inflicted not as a penalty, but to elicit evidence; all Roman citizens by definition theoretically had the right of appeal against it, unlike foreigners, i.e., provincial subjects (*peregrini*). But under the Principate Roman citizens were tortured in treason cases (Crook, *Law & Life*, 274–75; Garnsey, *SSLP*, 141–47). D. is annoyed because even very high-ranking Romans were tortured and because it was inflicted at the command of ex-slaves (the imperial freedmen); for his conservative viewpoint see Introduction, Section 3.4.3.

16.1 executions: Different methods of execution were usually applied according to the social status of the person being executed (Garnsey, *SSLP*, 105–111; 122–31). Public executions were normally reserved for prisoners-of-war, who were decapitated at the climax of triumphal processions or forced to fight beasts or other prisoners in the arena. D.'s (or his source's) melodramatic rhetoric here reveals his sympathy especially towards the high-ranking victims.

the Steps: For the location and symbolic functions of the Gemonian Steps cf. 58.11.5n. [= **A.7**].

16.2 the children of those who perished all received immunity: Even Scribonianus' son was spared and possibly even elevated to the priestly college of the Arval Brethren to replace his father (Tac. *A.* 12.52; Smallwood 12; Levick, *Cl.*, 60–61). Such acts helped to advertise the emperor's clemency (cf. 60.12.1; 60.13.4; Syme, *AA*, 299) and show that Cl. was still anxious to win the support of the senate.

16.3 their trials took place in the senate-house in the presence of Cl., the prefects and the freedmen: For trials in the senate see 60.4.3n. [= **C.4**]. By prefects D. means the prefects of the Praetorian Guard. Their presence at trials may be explained on the grounds that it was their duty to keep custody of those on trial in the city (Crook, *Law & Life*, 72); for their presence in the senate see 60.23.2–3 + n. [= **C.11**]; Talbert, *Senate*, 160–61. The two prefects currently in power were Rufrius Pollio (*PIR*[1] R 123), who had been appointed prefect at the very start of Cl.'s reign (Jos. *AJ* 19.267), and probably Catonius Justus (*PIR*[2] C 576), who had been a senior centurion

(*primus pilus*) in the legions in Pannonia in 14 (Tac. *A*. 1.29) and is attested
as prefect in 43 (60.18.3 [= **C.10**]); he was possibly appointed along with
Pollio in January 41 (Barrett 176); for his death see Seneca, *Apocolocyntosis* 13.5.

imperial freedmen in the senate: D. goes on to report (60.16.4–5) an
incident where Narcissus cross-examines a freedman defendant (cf. Talbert, *Senate*, 157, 160, 167).

curule chair: see 59.12.2n. [= **B.10**].

Cl.'s accustomed seat: For Cl. sitting on the benches for ordinary senators
rather than on the dais with the presiding magistrates see 60.6.1 + n. [=
C.5]; cf. 59.26.3 [= **B.19**]. This is a further instance of Cl.'s moderation
and respect for the authority of the senate.

C.9 LYCIA; EXTENSION OF ROMAN CITIZENSHIP   A.D. 43

(60.17.1–7)

17.1 Cl.'s consulship: This was Cl.'s third consulship (Suet. *Cl*. 14; Smallwood
430–31 = Braund 732, 739); his colleague was L. Vitellius (Smallwood
373 = Braund 580), with whom he remained in office for six months
(60.21.2 [= **C.11**] *contra* Suet. *Cl*. 14). He had held his first (suffect)
consulship in 37 (59.6.5–6 [= **B.4**]) and his second (ordinary) consulship
in 42 (60.10.1; Smallwood 405 = Braund 678).

Cl. put an end to many festivals: For Cl.'s concern for not wasting time on
festivals to the detriment of public administration cf. 60.5.7; 60.6.4–5n. [=
C.5]. The surviving inscribed copies of Roman calendars give a vivid
impression of the high number of festivals in the Roman civic year
(*Inscriptiones Italiae* XIII.2, esp. no. 26, which covers part of the reign of
Cl.). For a cynical view of the plethora of religious festivals at Rome cf.
Tac. *A*. 13.41.

days of supplication: See 59.20.1n. [= **B.15**]. But for Cl.'s punctilious
attention to omens, which led him frequently to require ceremonies of
supplication, see Suet. *Cl*. 22.

17.2 the road-commissioners fined under G. by Corbulo: For this incident in 39
see 59.15.3–5 [= **B.11**].

17.3 governors chosen by lot: The governors (*proconsules*) of the public
provinces (on which see 59.20.7n. [= **B.15**]) were appointed annually by
lot from among those ex-consuls and ex-praetors who had held their
consulships or praetorships at least five years previously; the lot was used
to decide who would gain a provincial governorship when the number of
candidates exceeded the number of public provinces and who went to
which province (53.14.2–4). Proconsuls were occasionally selected 'outside
the lot', i.e., were personally appointed by the emperor (Tac. *A*. 3.32; EJ
197 = Braund 360). See further Millar, *REN*, 54–56; Talbert, *Senate*,
397–98.

Cl. issued an edict: This is a good example of the emperor intervening in the running of the public provinces: see G.P. Burton, *ZPE* 21 (1976), 63–68; Millar, *ERW*, 313–28 and *Britannia* 13 (1982), 1–23.

Lycia: in southern Asia Minor; it had enjoyed an anomalous position, remaining a semi-autonomous league rather than being annexed as a Roman province (S.A. Jameson, *ANRW* II.7.2 (1980), 832–855; Magie, *RRAM*, 516–39). For a silver coin issue of the league honouring Cl. see Smallwood 42 = Braund 204; for a dedication to Cl., Messallina and their son Britannicus see Smallwood 136 = Braund 231.

because they had revolted: D. exaggerates in calling it a revolt; rather, fierce inter-city rivalries had led to a series of disturbances, which required that Rome take action (Suet. *Cl.* 25.3; Magie, *RRAM*, 529; G.W. Bowersock in *Opposition et résistances à l'Empire d'Auguste à Trajan* (ed. A. Giovannini and D. van Berchem) (1986), 292–93).

reduced them to the condition of slaves and incorporated them into the district of Pamphylia: i.e., Cl. took away their privileged status and reduced them into the form of a province. D.'s text here has been interpreted to provide the sole evidence for the existence of Pamphylia as a separate province at this date; but for the argument that D. is being anachronistic and means that Lycia was joined to what in his own day constituted the province of Pamphylia see B. Levick, *Roman Colonies in southern Asia Minor* (1967), 30–32. However, this is unneccessary, since D. is careful to refer to Pamphylia as a 'district' (*nomos*) not an independent province (for which D. uses the term *ethnos*). For a vindication of D. see R. Syme, *Klio* 30 (1937), 227–31 [= *RP*, I, 42–46], arguing that Cl. severed Pamphylia from Galatia, which had been a joint-province since Aug., and added it to Lycia, an arrangement that lasted until the reign of Galba. For a decree issued by the first governor of Lycia-Pamphylia, Q. Veranius, see Sherk 48; for his tombstone from Rome see Smallwood 231c = LACTOR 8, no. 30 = Braund 404c.

17.4 **the investigation of the affair in the senate:** cf. Suet. *Cl.* 25.3. This illustrates that the senate still presided over foreign affairs and heard embassies from overseas (Talbert, *Senate*, 392–430).

Cl. deprives a Lycian of Roman citizenship: For Cl.'s desire to seek out those who had usurped Roman citizenship see Suet. *Cl.* 25.3. Inscriptions show that a large number of prominent Lycians had been granted Roman citizenship during Cl.'s reign, since many adopted the name Claudius, while others took the name Veranius, the first governor of the province (60.17.3n.): see Magie, *RRAM*, 535; B. Levick, *Historia* 38 (1989), 114–16. For Cl.'s grants of Roman citizenship cf. Tac. *A.* 11.23–24; Smallwood 369 = LACTOR 8, no. 34 = Braund 570 = Sherk 55 (Cl.'s speech in the senate in 48, advocating the admittance of "long-haired" Gauls to the senate); Smallwood 368 = LACTOR 8, no. 33 = Braund 569 = Sherk 52 (his edict granting citizenship to inhabitants of the Alpine region). In general see Scramuzza 129–44; Levick, *Cl.*, 164–65; Sherwin-White, *Citizenship*, 237–50. This incident also shows that Roman citizenship was one important mechanism whereby the Latin language spread into non-Latin-speaking parts of the Empire.

17.5 Romans had the advantage over foreigners: For the advantages of Roman citizenship over peregrine status see Crook, *Law & Life*, 36–46. D.'s sarcastic comments on the cheapening of citizenship, which he again imputes to his *bêtes noires*, Messallina and the freedmen, may owe something to the fact that during his own lifetime citizenship had been granted to nearly all the free-born inhabitants of the Empire by Caracalla, an emperor whom D. detested (77.9.5; Millar, *Dio*, 150–60).

citizenship by purchase: This seems to have been exceedingly rare throughout the Roman period, but for an example from just this period see *Acts of Apostles* 22.28, where the tribune who rescued Paul in Jerusalem claims without embarrassment that he had paid a lot of money for his Roman citizenship. See further A.N. Sherwin-White, *Roman Society and Roman Law in the New Testament* (1963), 144–62.

17.7 not using Claudius' name: For new citizens taking on the name of the emperor during whose reign they received their citizenship see Sherwin-White, *Citizenship*, 308–09.

legacies to the emperor: Those who had been granted citizenship by Cl. might be considered his clients: see E. Badian, *Foreign Clientelae* (1958); and so it was appropriate for them to leave legacies to their patron in their wills, in the same way that freedmen often left legacies to their former masters (Crook, *Law & Life*, 53). For legacies to the emperor see Millar, *ERW*, 153–58.

C.10 CRIMES OF MESSALLINA AND THE IMPERIAL FREEDMEN
A.D. 43

(60.17.8–18.4)

17.8 procuratorships: Procurators (in legal terms representatives of the emperor) played an important rôle in the administration of the Empire. Appointed from among the equestrians and imperial freedmen, they were responsible for all financial matters in imperial provinces, but in public provinces just for the property of the emperor: see Millar, *REN*, 55–60; R.P. Saller, *JRS* 70 (1980), 44–63; P.A. Brunt, *JRS* 73 (1983), 42–75; A.N. Sherwin-White, *PBSR* 15 (1939), 11–26; for a full study see H.-G. Pflaum, *Les procurateurs équestres sous le Haut-Empire romain* (1950). For the new procuratorships which Cl. introduced see Momigliano 46, 51; cf. Levick, *Cl.*, 48–51; 83–85.

the sale of procuratorships and governorships: cf. Suet. *Cl.* 29.1. D. also alleges that Vespasian's mistress, Caenis, and Cleander, an imperial freedman under Commodus, also sold procuratorships, army commands and priesthoods (66.14.3; 72.12.3). Conversely, Pliny praised the emperor Trajan for not allowing his freedmen to indulge in these very pursuits (*Panegyric* 88). The extreme similarity of these stories raises doubts as to their historicity: they probably derive from the senatorial repertoire of hostile anecdotes told against imperial freedmen and those close to the emperors. However, they do reflect the fact that administrative posts were often bestowed by benefaction of the emperor (Saller, *Patronage*, 41–78). In this particular case, the alleged sales may also have been invented to help explain the enormous wealth of Cl.'s freedman, Pallas (Tac. *A.* 14.65; Plin. *Letters* 8.6).

Cl. fixed the prices of all goods: For financial problems during Cl.'s reign see Scramuzza 118–120, 122–24, 157; Levick, *Cl.*, 127–36. Another attempt to fix maximum prices (also ultimately unsuccessful) took place in 301 under Diocletian; various fragments of his Edict on Maximum Prices survive (S. Lauffer, *Diokletians Preisedikt* (1971) (partially translated at LR II, 123); for additional fragments see K. Erim and J. Reynolds, *JRS* 60 (1970), 120–41; M.H. Crawford and J.M. Reynolds, *ZPE* 26 (1977), 125–51; id., 34 (1979), 163–210; C. Roueché, *Aphrodisias in Late Antiquity* (1989), no. 231.

17.9 gladiatorial combat in the camp: i.e., in the camp of the Praetorian Guard near the Porta Viminalis (58.4.2n. [= **A.3**]). These games were held annually to coincide with Cl.'s handout to the praetorians, to commemorate their rôle in his coming to power and to ensure their continued loyalty (cf. Suet. *Cl.* 21.4; 60.1.2 [= **C.1**]; 60.12.4). In the provinces amphitheatres have been found attached to Roman army camps: e.g. at Caerleon in Wales (R.W. Davies, *Service in the Roman Army* (1989), 82 and pl. 3.9; Webster, *Army*, 207–8). In Rome a military amphitheatre was built in the late Severan age near the Porta Praenestina (Nash I, 13–16; Coarelli, *Guida arch. di Roma*, 189–90).

put on a military cloak for the occasion: Cl. also wore a military cloak (*paludamentum*) for the ceremony to mark the draining of the Fucine Lake in 52 (Tac. *A.* 12.56). His wearing of military attire helped to boost his military image. The emperor's cloak, however, was purple, which marked him out from senatorial generals, whose *paludamenta* were red (Griffin, *Nero*, 222–24).

the praetors on their own initiative celebrated his son's birthday: D. here suggests that Cl. did not force magistrates to fund celebrations connected with the imperial family (cf. 60.17.1 [= **C.9**]), another example of his moderation. For magistrates putting on public shows see further 60.27.2n. [= **C.13**]. Cl.'s son was Ti. Claudius Caesar Germanicus (*PIR*² C 820), who was given the commemorative extra-name "Britannicus" after the conquest of Britain in 43 (60.12.5; 60.22.2 + n. [= **C.11**]; Smallwood 108, 112, 134, 136, 138 = Braund 241, 271, 229, 231, 233). He was born on 12 February 41 (Tac. *A.* 13.15 *contra* Suet. *Cl.* 27.2). For a coin issue from Alexandria alluding to his birth see Smallwood 98a = Braund 209a; for another from Cappadocia commemorating him and his sisters, Octavia and Antonia, see Smallwood 99b = Braund 217b = Levick, *Cl.*, pl. 18 (by mistake transposed with pl. 6).

18.1 Messallina's sexual exploits: For further escapades see Tac. *A.* 11.13–38.
she made many of them commit adultery even in the palace itself: This was clearly a standard charge levelled against tyrants: cf. 59.28.9 + n. [= **B.22**].

18.3 she used to provide him with slavegirls to have sex with: Livia was similarly accused of providing Aug. with young virgins for sexual purposes (Suet. *Aug.* 71.1).

214 Cassius Dio: Roman History

Catonius Justus: see 60.16.3n. [= **C.8**].

18.4 death of Julia, daughter of Drusus, wife of Nero Germanicus: cf. Suet. *Cl.*
29.1; Tac. *A.* 13.32, 43, emphasizing the rôle of P. Suillius Rufus, but
leaving it unclear whether he was operating as Messallina's agent or
independently of her. This Julia (*PIR²* J 636) was the daughter of Drusus
son of Tib. and Cl.'s sister, Livia Julia, and hence niece of Cl. (Syme, *AA*,
170–71, 182). She had been married to Nero Iulius Caesar, the eldest son
of Germanicus, from 20 until he was exiled in 29 (Tac. *A.* 3.29; 58.8.4n. [=
A.7]). For her earlier career see 58.7.5n. [= **A.6**]. Since 33 she had been
married to C. Rubellius Blandus, suffect consul in 18, from a family new
to high political office (58.21.1; Tac. *A.* 6.27; R. Syme, *AJP* 103 (1982), 62–
85 [= *RP* IV, 177–98]). By removing both Julias, Messallina was seeking
to ensure the claims of her own children (especially Britannicus) to inherit
Cl.'s property. See further Levick, *Cl.*, 56–57, 118–19.

just as she had been jealous of the other Julia: Julia Livilla (*PIR²* J 674), the
youngest daughter of Germanicus and Agrippina (and hence another
niece of Cl.), had aroused Messallina's jealousy in 41, and as a result been
exiled and then murdered (60.8.5 + n. [= **C.6**]; cf. 60.27.4 [= **C.13**]).

a member of the equestrian order was hurled down from the Capitol: For this
method of execution (i.e., being hurled from the Tarpeian Rock on the
Capitol) under Tib. and G. cf. Tac. *A.* 6.19; 57.22.5; 58.15.3; 59.18.3 [=
B.14]. For the charge (no doubt exaggerated, but containing a kernel of
truth) that Cl. had 321 equestrians put to death during his reign see
Seneca, *Apocolocyntosis* 14.1; Levick, *Cl.* 102–3.

C.11 CLAUDIUS' INVASION AND CONQUEST OF BRITAIN
A.D. 43–44

(60.19.1–22.2; 23.1–6)

D. provides the only extended account of Cl.'s conquest of Britain in 43–
44, which resulted in the annexation of the southern part of the island as
the province of Britain. Suet. *Cl.* 17 is very brief and hostile to Cl. D. has
much credible circumstantial detail, but problems remain over his chronology of the invasion (A.A. Barrett, *Britannia* 11 (1980), 31–33) and over
some topographical details. For clear syntheses of the literary and
archaeological evidence for the invasion see Webster, *Invasion*; Dudley
and Webster, *Conquest*; Peddie, *Invasion*; Frere, *Britannia*, 48–80; Salway,
Britain, 65–99; more briefly Levick, *Cl.*, 138–48.

D. gained some military experience as governor of Dalmatia and Upper
Pannonia in the 220s, but this was probably after he had composed this
section of the *Roman History* (Introduction, Sections 1.2.6; 2.1.2). For his
qualities as a military historian see D. Harrington, *Acta Classica* 20
(1977), 159–65; but for the persuasive view that his accounts of battles owe
more to rhetoric than to fact see G.B. Townend, *Hermes* 92 (1964), 467–
81. D. discusses the geography of Britain at 39.50 (in the context of Julius
Caesar's invasion in 55 B.C.); it may have in part derived from inform-

ation gained from those who went on Septimius Severus' expedition to Britain in 208–211. D., although one of Severus' advisers, probably did not accompany him on this campaign (Millar, *Dio*, 148–150; Birley, *African Emperor*, ch. 16).

19.1   reasons for the invasion of Britain: D. is content merely to present the immediate occasion for the invasion, i.e., the expulsion of Bericus; cf. 40.1.2, where when dealing with Caesar's invasion in 54 B.C., he gives not only the alleged reason, but also what he saw as the real reason. For more long-term causes and objectives of Cl.'s invasion see Momigliano 54–57, Levick, *Cl.*, 140–41 (more balanced than Scramuzza ch. 11). The invasion also provided Cl. with the chance to win military glory in person, to help consolidate his position as emperor after the senatorial conspiracies (Campbell, *Emperor & Army*, 140); in general on emperors' need for military glory see Hopkins, *Conquerors*, 224.

Aulus Plautius: *PIR*[1] P 344; suffect consul in 29. As provincial governor of Pannonia in command of three legions from 41 to 43, he had remained loyal to Cl. during the rebellion of Scribonianus (60.15.1–4 [= **C.8**]). He was to be the first governor of the province of Britain from 43–47 (A.R. Birley, *The Fasti of Roman Britain* (1981), 37–40).

Bericus: Probably to be associated with Verica, a pro-Roman leader of the Atrebates, portrayed on surviving coins. Their territory (in modern Sussex) had been overrun by Cunobelinus and his sons in 42; Verica was driven out by an anti-Roman party (possibly with the aid of Caratacus) and fled to Rome (R. Dunnett, *The Trinovantes* (1975), 31; Salway, *Britain*, 69–70; Levick, *Cl.*, 139–40).

19.2   Plautius' army: The invasion force, numbering about 40,000, consisted of the following legions: II Augusta, IX Hispana, XIV Gemina and XX Valeria Victrix, all removed from the Rhine-Danube frontier for the invasion, plus unknown auxiliary infantry and cavalry units (Frere, *Britannia*, 48; 77–78, n. 1; Peddie, *Invasion*, 23–46; 180–95). For inscriptions commemorating officers and men who served on the expedition see Smallwood 281–284 = Braund 516–520; Sherk 49.

upset at the prospect of fighting a campaign outside the known world: For the psychological fear that crossing the English Channel engendered cf. 59.25.3n. [= **B.18**]. D. works out this theme more fully in a speech put into the mouth of Boudica, as she leads the Britons in revolt in 61 (62.4.2). The idea of triumphing over the Ocean is given prominence in inscriptions and poems commemorating the conquest (Smallwood 43b = LACTOR 8, no. 29 = Braund 210b; Braund 212).

Narcissus: For this imperial freedman, who at this time held the post of *ab epistulis*, see 60.2.4–6n. [= **C.2**].

19.3   "Io! Saturnalia!": This was the cry associated with the banquet at the festival of the Saturnalia, on which see 59.6.4 + n. [= **B.4**]. At this festival a reversal of rôles took place whereby masters served their slaves. Thus the Roman troops by their jibe sought to draw attention to Narcissus' servile origins and the incongruity of an ex-slave attempting to give orders to the Roman army, composed mainly of freeborn Roman citizens: it was conduct only appropriate at the Saturnalia. The incident is interesting in that it reveals that it was not just the senators who bore a grudge against influential imperial freedmen.

late in the season: The traditional campaigning season ran from February/ March to October (Y. Garlan, *War in the Ancient World* (1975), 41–43).

19.4 **sent over in three divisions:** This has been interpreted to mean that the army landed at three separate places; but for arguments that the entire force landed at Richborough (Kent) see Webster, *Invasion*, 94–95; Frere, *Britannia*, 48–49; Peddie, *Invasion*, 47–65.

a flash of light in the east: For D.'s interest in celestial phenomena cf. his long digression on the eclipse of the sun at 60.26; for his inclusion of omens see Introduction, Section 3.4.1.

19.5 **the Britons had not mobilized in time:** For the suggestion that the Britons were misled by news of the supposed mutiny on the Gallic side of the Channel see Frere, *Britannia*, 49.

when Julius Caesar invaded: For full details of Caesar's invasions in 55 and 54 B.C. see Frere, *Britannia*, 16–26; Webster, *Invasion*, 34–40.

20.1 **Plautius had a great deal of trouble in searching them out:** For doubts on this see Webster, *Invasion*, 97.

he defeated first Caratacus and then Togodumnus: For these first two skirmishes see Webster, *Invasion*, 97; cf. Frere, *Britannia*, 49. Cunobelinus and his sons Caratacus and Togodumnus controlled the powerful Catuvellauni tribe. Cunobelinus was king from 5 to 42 and after conquering the pro-Roman Trinovantes, moved his capital to Camulodunum (Colchester). His power was such that he styled himself "king of the Britons" (Suet. *G.* 44.2). Similarly Caratacus "ruled over several peoples" (Tac. *A.* 12.37). On Caratacus' later capture and imprisonment in Rome see 60.33.3c and (especially) Tac. *A.* 12.33–40. For a full account see G. Webster, *Rome against Caratacus* (1981).

the Britons were not independent: On the social and political condition of the various ethnic groups in Britain at this time, and especially their fragmentation, see B. Cunliffe, *Iron Age Communities in Britain* (1974), 75–106.

Dobunni: This is Hübner's emendation of the manuscript reading "Bodunni", an otherwise unattested tribe. The Dobunni controlled part of modern Gloucestershire, and their coinage suggests that they were split into two kingdoms. The northern half had an alliance with Cunobelinus, and so could be said to have been "subject to the Catuvellauni"; on the death of Cunobelinus, they did not approve of his sons' anti-Roman stance and so surrendered to the Romans without a fight (C.F.C. Hawkes in *Bagendon: a Belgic oppidum* (ed. E.M. Clifford, 1961), 56–67).

20.2 **came to a river:** The river Medway in Kent. On the battle see Peddie, *Invasion*, 66–88; A.R. Burn, *History* 38 (1953), 105–115, arguing that D.'s account, though brief, has enough circumstantial detail to give it credibility; he suggests that it may ultimately be based on an official Roman despatch or the reports of eye-witnesses. The battle was unusual for ancient battles in that it was fought over two days.

Germans: i.e., auxiliary cohorts of Batavians; for their service on Cl.'s expedition see Tac. *H.* 4.12; for their expertise in swimming across rivers fully-armed see 69.9.6; Tac. *A*. 2.8; *H*. 2.17; *ILS* 2558; see further M.W.C. Hassall, *Britannia* 1 (1970), 131–36.

20.3 T. Flavius Vespasianus: *PIR²* F 398; the future emperor (69–79). For his earlier career see 59.12.3 + n. [= **B.10**]. He was commander of Legion II Augusta in Upper Germany at the time of its transfer to the British invasion force (Suet. *Vesp*. 4.1). For his actions in Britain see Tac. *H*. 3.44. The length of his stay in Britain and the date of his award of triumphal decorations (60.20.4) are both disputed: see D.E. Eichholz, *Britannia* 3 (1972), 149–163.

T. Flavius Sabinus: *PIR²* F 352; Vespasian's older brother (Tac. *H*. 1.46). For his rôle in the invasion see Webster, *Invasion*, 91.

20.4 Cn. (or C.) Hosidius Geta: His identity is disputed. Most editors emend the manuscript reading, which gives his *praenomen* as Gaius, to "Gnaeus", to associate him with the Roman commander in Mauretania in 42 (60.9.1–4 + n. [= **C.6**]). For the family and the problems of identification see R. Syme, *AJP* 77 (1956), 264–273, esp. 270 [= *RP* I, 292–99, esp. 297]. Cn. Hosidius Geta went on to hold a suffect consulship (Smallwood 365 = LACTOR 8, no. 31 = Braund 711); wax-tablets from Puteoli show clearly that this took place in the latter months of 47 (*Puteoli* 6 (1982), 10; id. 7–8 (1983–84), 40–41; id. 9–10 (1985–86), 18), disproving the date for his suffect consulship suggested by P.A. Gallivan, *CQ* 28 (1978), 420.

20.4 triumphal decorations: i.e., *ornamenta triumphalia*, on which see 60.8.6 [= **C.6**]. For further awards during this expedition see 60.23.2 + n. [= **C.11**]. D.'s remark here shows that these honours were usually granted only to those of consular rank.

20.5–6 The Britons withdrew to the Thames: For discussion of the topographical problems of D.'s account here see Frere, *Britannia*, 51; Webster, *Invasion*, 101–2. The Thames was narrower in Roman times than it is now; the Britons probably crossed near Tilbury; the bridge upstream may have been near Westminster.

21.1 death of Togodumnus: For some suggestions as to the context of his death see Frere, *Britannia*, 51.

summoned Cl.: i.e., sent an official despatch. For doubts that Cl. would have come to Plautius' aid in a real emergency and the suggestion that it was rather part of a propaganda campaign to give Cl. the credit for the victory in Britain see A.A. Barrett, *Britannia* 11 (1980), 31.

21.2 he had instructions to do this: This is a good illustration that the emperor would lay down initial, general guidelines (*mandata*) for commanders on how to conduct their military campaigns (F. Millar, *Britannia* 13 (1982), 4–15; Campbell, *Emperor & Army*, 59–69).

equipment, including elephants: Presumably siege equipment (for the siege of Colchester). Cl. also brought with him a detachment of the Praetorian Guard, probably under their prefect Rufrius Pollio (60.23.2n. [= **C.11**]; cf. Smallwood 283 = Braund 518), and vexillations from other legions (Frere, *Britannia*, 52; Peddie, *Invasion*, 90–92). Elephants had been used in Roman armies under the Republic, but very infrequently during the Principate, when they were mainly reserved for imperial parades and shows (H.H. Scullard, *The Elephant in the Greek and Roman World* (1974),

178–200; for an imperial freedman as "procurator at Laurentum of the elephants" see *ILS* 1578 = Sherk 181). Their use in Cl.'s campaigns seems extremely unlikely. Possibly D. – or D.'s source – garbled a report that elephants were used in Cl.'s triumphal procession at Rome and erroneously transposed the elephants to the war-zone. For a similarly unlikely report that Julius Caesar brought an elephant to Britain during his invasion see Polyaenus, *Stratagems* 8.23.5.

he handed over affairs at home, including command of the troops, to L. Vitellius: For Vitellius see 59.27.2–3nn. [= **B.21**]. Consuls held *imperium* and so by definition had the right to command troops. By leaving the consul in charge at home, Cl. was acting according to Republican precedent. Vitellius was also possibly granted the powers of Prefect of the City (*praefectus urbi*) during Cl.'s absence; on the post see 60.3.5n. [= **C.3**].

whose consulship he had extended to a whole half-year: cf. Suet. *Cl.* 14, who claims that Cl.'s consulships in 42 and 43 lasted only two months. See further A.A. Barrett, *Britannia* 11 (1980), 31; P.A. Gallivan, *CQ* 28 (1978), 408, 412, 424.

21.3 Cl.'s route to Britain: cf. Suet. *Cl.* 17.2. Cl.'s route illustrates the importance of the river network of Gaul for communication between the Mediterranean and the north-western provinces (cf. Strabo 4.1.2).

Massilia: modern Marseilles.

21.4 D.'s series of short sentences emphasizes the speed of Cl.'s military actions in Britain. He, however, fails to mention that part of the campaign in which Vespasian led Legion II Augusta into the south-west, where he fought thirty battles, overcame two tribes (the Durotriges and either the Belgae or the Dobunni), captured twenty hill-forts (supported by archaeological evidence from Maiden Castle and Hod Hill) and subjugated the Isle of Wight (Suet. *Vesp.* 4.1; Webster, *Invasion*, 103–4; 107–110; Peddie, *Invasion*, 130–62).

Camulodunum: Colchester, the main urban centre of Britain at this date (J. Wacher, *The Towns of Roman Britain* (1975), 104–20).

was hailed Imperator several times: For salutations as *Imperator* see 59.22.2n. [= **B.16**]. Cl. received five salutations as *Imperator* on this occasion, twenty-seven in all during his reign (60.8.7n. [= **C.6**]), the most received by any emperor until Constantine (emperor 306–337). This is another good indication that Cl. felt the need to emphasize military achievements during his reign (cf. 60.17.9 + n. [= **C.10**]).

contrary to precedent: But if the victories were gained by different Roman commanders fighting under his auspices, Cl. was perfectly entitled to such acclamations (cf. 59.22.2n. [= **B.16**]).

21.5 sending his sons-in-law, Magnus and Silanus, on ahead with news of his victory: His sons-in-law were Cn. Pompeius Magnus (*PIR*[1] P 477) and L. Iunius Silanus Torquatus (*PIR*[2] J 829). Pompeius Magnus had married Claudia Antonia, daughter of Cl. and Aelia Paetina, in 41 (60.5.9; Smallwood 235 = Braund 408; Syme, *AA*, 277–79). For his divorce and death at some time before 47, since his death is not recorded in the surviving parts of Tac., see Suet. *Cl.* 27.2, 29.1–2; Syme, *AA*, 183. Silanus had married Octavia, daughter of Cl. and Messallina, also in 41 (Small-wood 236 = Braund 410; Syme, *AA*, 174, 181). For his divorce and suicide in 49 after being falsely accused by Agrippina see 60.31.8; Tac. *A.* 12.4, 6; 13.1. For emperors sending military and diplomatic news back to the senate see F. Millar, *Britannia* 13 (1982), 4 and n. 26.

22.1 the senate granted him the title "Britannicus" and permission to celebrate a triumph: On honorific names to commemorate military victories see 60.8.7n. [= **C.6**]. Cl. did not use this title, but chose to confer it on his young son (60.22.2 [= **C.11**]). D. provides a good illustration of how the senate had to vote emperors triumphs and other honours (Talbert, *Senate*, 354–71). For Cl.'s triumph in 44 see 60.23.4–6 [= **C.11**].

an annual festival to commemorate the event: The senate hereby voted to establish a festival modelled on the *ludi Actiaci*, which were held every fifth year to celebrate Aug.'s victory at Actium (cf. 59.20.1 + n. [= **B.15**]). For the celebration of this festival later in Cl.'s reign see Suet. *Cl.* 21.6. There is no hint in our sources that it continued to be celebrated after Cl.'s death.

two triumphal arches: The arch in Rome, on the Via Lata in the Campus Martius, was eventually dedicated in 52; for its commemorative inscription see Smallwood 43b = LACTOR 8, no. 29 = Braund 210b; it was also represented on gold coins (*aurei*) of 46–47 (Smallwood 43a = LACTOR 8, no. 28 = Braund 210a = Levick, *Cl.*, pl. 15). The arch in Gaul was erected at Gesoriacum (Boulogne), the terminus of the road network, where Cl. also developed the harbour, making it the most important port on the North Sea (Dudley and Webster, *Conquest*, 84). Another overseas triumphal arch to commemorate the conquest of Britain was set up at Cyzicus, Asia Minor (Smallwood 45 = Braund 216). The victory was also celebrated in contemporary poetry (Braund 212) and art: a relief from the Sebasteion (sanctuary for imperial cult) at Aphrodisias, Asia Minor, depicts Cl. trampling on a personified Britannia (K.T. Erim, *Britannia* 13 (1982), 277–81; R.R.R. Smith, *JRS* 77 (1987), 115–17 and pls. XIV–XV; Levick, *Cl.*, pl. 20). For vows paid to the gods 'for the safety and return and victory in Britain of Claudius' see *ZPE* 39 (1980), 229, no. 24 = Braund 211 = Sherk 51.

22.2 his son: Ti. Claudius Caesar Germanicus, who came to be known by the honorific name Britannicus (60.12.5; 60.17.9 + n. [= **C.10**]).

the right to sit in the front seats: The right to sit in the front seats at the theatre was a special honour in the cities of the Greek and Roman world. Livia had been granted the privilege of sitting in the front seats with the Vestal Virgins in 23 (Tac. *A.* 4.16), while G. had bestowed the same honour upon his sisters in 37 (59.3.4 [= **B.3**]).

the right to use a carpentum: cf. Suet. *Cl.* 17.3. A *carpentum* was a two-wheeled, covered vehicle used at special parades and ceremonials. Coins of 22–23 suggest that Livia was also granted this privilege (EJ 87 = Braund 106), although this is not attested in any literary source. Cl. later bestowed the honour on his next wife Agrippina (Tac. *A.* 12.42; Smallwood 102b = Braund 220b). Other female members of the imperial house were granted this as a posthumous honour, their images being paraded in such vehicles on ceremonial occasions: e.g. the elder Agrippina in 37 (Suet. *G.* 15.1; cf. Smallwood 84b = Braund 178b = Barrett pl. 19), or Antonia in 41 (Suet. *Cl.* 11.2).

Since both of these honours were customarily awarded to the Vestal Virgins, female members of the imperial house like Messallina were being closely assimilated to these priestesses; just as the Vestals were responsible for maintaining the hearth (i.e., the continued prosperity) of the city of Rome, so the female members of the imperial family were responsible for maintaining the hearth/prosperity of the imperial house (N. Purcell, *PCPhS* 32 (1986), 85–87).

23.1 results of Cl.'s victory: It ensured Roman control of the whole lowland region of southern Britain stretching from the river Trent to the Severn, which was turned into a tribute-paying province (Frere, *Britannia*, 55–59). **Gaius Crispus:** C. Sallustius Passienus Crispus (*PIR*¹ P 109), suffect consul in 27 and now consul for the second time in 44 (this time ordinary consul). The grand-nephew of the historian Sallust, he was extremely wealthy and famed for his skills as an orator and barrister in the Centumviral Court. He had married Agrippina, the daughter of Germanicus, early in Cl.'s reign (Suet. *N.* 6.3; Syme, *AA*, 159–60). He died at some stage between 44 and 47; for arguments that he died while in office in 44 see P.A. Gallivan, *CQ* 28 (1978), 408; for more caution ("before early 47") Syme, *AA*, 160. For second consulships see further 60.3.5n. [= **C.3**]. **T. Statilius Taurus:** *PIR*¹ S 618; he was also noted for his wealth and later perished at the hands of Agrippina (Tac. *A.* 12.59). **after an absence of six months:** cf. Suet. *Cl.* 17.2; but for doubts, and an alternative hypothesis, see A.A. Barrett, *Britannia* 11 (1980), 32–33. For the suggestion that Cl. used the return trip from Britain to boost his support in Gaul and the Alpine regions see Levick, *Cl.*, 143, 177. **celebrated his triumph:** For further incidental details, including that all provincial governors and exiles were summoned to Rome for the occasion, see Suet. *Cl.* 17.3. **climbing the steps of the Capitolium on his knees:** All triumphs culminated at the Capitolium, i.e., the temple of Jupiter, Juno and Minerva (59.28.2–4n. [= **B.22**]). For a triumphant general climbing the steps of the temple on his knees cf. 43.21.2 (Julius Caesar) and D.'s general description of a triumph in Book 6, preserved in an excerpt by the 12th.-century writer Ioannes Tzetzes (see Loeb ed. of Dio, vol. I, 200–201).

23.2 triumphal decorations: i.e., *ornamenta triumphalia*, on which see 60.8.6n. [= **C.6**]). For Cl.'s generosity in awarding them cf. 60.20.4 [= **C.11**]; Suet. *Cl.* 17.3; id., *Vesp.* 4.2; Smallwood 226a = Braund 399. D. again stresses that they were usually awarded only to those of consular rank (cf. 60.20.4 + n.). For awards made to men of lower rank see Sherk 49. **Cl. granted Rufrius Pollio an image and a seat in the senate-house:** For Rufrius Pollio, prefect of the Praetorian Guard since 41, see 60.16.3n. [= **C.8**]. Honorific busts (*imagines*) of illustrious men were erected, for example, in the temple of Apollo on the Palatine, a common meeting-place for the senate under the Principate (EJ 94a = Braund 115 = Sherk 36B, lines 1–4; Talbert, *Senate*, 117–18). The Praetorian Prefect often accompanied the emperor into the senate (cf. 60.16.3 [= **C.8**]), but granting him a special seat was a considerable innovation. This probably did not allow him to attend the senate in his own right, but just gave him a special seat when he accompanied the emperor (Talbert, *Senate*, 160–61).

23.3 Valerius Ligur: *PIR*¹ V 68. 'Ligur' should be taken as Valerius' *cognomen*, rather than as an ethnic ("the Ligurian") (*contra* Cary in his Loeb translation and Talbert, *Senate*, 160). Valerius was no more a Ligurian than P. Graecinius (next note) was a Spartan. D. is the only source to mention this Praetorian Prefect under Aug. (A. Passerini, *Le coorti pretorie* (1939), 275–76).

P. Graecinius Laco: For his position as Prefect of the Night-Watch (*praefectus vigilum*) and his rôle in the downfall of Sej. in 31 see 58.9.3 + n., 9.6, 10.8 [= **A.7**]. He had turned down the offer of quaestorian decorations (*ornamenta quaestoria*) after the fall of Sej. (58.12.7).

procurator of the Gauls: i.e., the equestrian official responsible for tax collection and other economic matters in the Gallic provinces (i.e., Belgica, Aquitania and Lugdunensis). On procurators in general see 60.17.8n. [= **C.10**]. There is no firm evidence for a procurator being in charge of all three provinces (although *ILS* 1341 has been restored by many editors to attest this). It was more common for one procurator to be in charge of Aquitania and Lugdunensis (*ILS* 1330, 1339, 1342, 1385, 1389, 1454), while another looked after Belgica and the two Germanies (*ILS* 1326, 1340, 1362). See J.F. Drinkwater, *Roman Gaul* (1983), 97–98; E.M. Wightman, *Gallia Belgica* (1985), 61–62.

consular decorations: i.e., *ornamenta consularia*, on which see 60.8.2n. [= **C.6**]. For epigraphic confirmation of Laco's award see EJ 222 = Braund 435.

23.4 triumphal festival: It was customary for a triumphant general to provide largesse for the people after his triumph by sponsoring public feasts and/or games, and/or by funding new public buildings (Veyne, *Bread*, 235–36; Versnel, *Triumphus*, 111). For triumphal games cf. 48.19.1; 56.1.1; 67.8.1–4 (Domitian); 68.10.2; 68.15.1 (Trajan); 76.1.3–5 (Septimius Severus).

assuming a kind of consular power for the occasion: D. here implies that emperors did not have permanent consular *imperium*, but received *ad hoc* grants when the occasion demanded (e.g. to celebrate a triumph). They did have permanent proconsular *imperium*, which by tradition had no force within the sacred boundary (*pomerium*) of Rome (53.17.4). For the controversial nature of the emperor's formal powers see A.H.M. Jones, *Studies in Roman Government and Law* (1960), ch. 1; P.A. Brunt and J.M. Moore (ed.), *Res Gestae Divi Augusti* (1967), 8–16. For ultimately unconvincing arguments that Cl. never dispensed with consular *imperium* see Levick, *Cl.* 43.

the two theatres: It is difficult to be sure exactly which theatres D. means: possibly the theatre of Pompey (60.6.8n. [= **C.5**]) and the theatre of Marcellus in the Circus Flaminius (53.30.5–6; 54.26.1; *RG* 21.1; Nash II, 418–22; J.B. Ward-Perkins, *Roman Imperial Architecture* (1981), 26–28). But D. often also describes amphitheatres as 'theatres': so the amphi-

theatre of Statilius Taurus might also have been used (59.10.5; 59.7.8n. [=
B.5]). Temporary wooden stages could also be erected for festivals, as for
the Secular Games of 17 B.C. (EJ 32 = Braund 769 = Sherk 11, lines 108,
161–62).

23.5 the number of chariot-races: Ten had been the usual number of races in a
day until G.'s reign (59.7.2–3 + n. [= **B.5**]). Levick, *Cl.*, 133 argues that
Cl. reduced the number of chariot-races and increased the number of
beast-hunts as an economy measure.

bears slaughtered between the races: For beast hunts (*venationes*) held on
the same programme as chariot-races cf. 60.7.3 + n. [= **C.5**]; 61.17.3.
athletic competitions: For details see Balsdon, *Life & Leisure*, 324–26.
Pyrrhic dance: See 60.7.2n. [= **C.5**].

23.6 association of stage actors: The so-called *parasiti Apollinis*; for actors, and
their organization into associations, see Balsdon, *Life & Leisure*, 270–88;
A. Müller, *Philologus* 63 (1904), 342–61. D. here provides evidence that
the senate was responsible for authorizing the performances of such
associations, a point not noted by Talbert, *Senate*.

**23.6 all agreements worked out by Cl. and his generals to be ratified as if they had
been made by the senate and people of Rome:** Under the Republic only the
senate and Roman people had the power to declare war and make binding
peace treaties. The law granting Vespasian his imperial powers (EJ 364 =
Braund 293 = Sherk 82, lines 1–2) authorized him to make binding
settlements after war, a right which it claims Aug., Tib. and Cl. had all
possessed. D. claims at 53.17.5 that Aug. and all emperors had the power
to make war and peace. D.'s remarks here, however, imply that Cl. had
not received this power at the start of his reign, and hence contradict
53.17.5 and the law on Vespasian's powers. Therefore, either Vespasian
invented false precedents for this power to make settlements or (more
plausibly) this passage must be interpreted to mean that Cl. already
possessed the power, but chose to seek confirmation for his settlements
after wars, another instance of his respect for the traditional rôle of the
senate and people (so P.A. Brunt, *JRS* 67 (1977), 103 and n. 41). See
further Levick, *Cl.*, 42–43; Talbert, *Senate*, 425–30, esp. 428 (citing
instances of emperors consulting the senate before making treaties).

those generals operating on his behalf: This well illustrates that the emperor
was strictly speaking commander of all Roman troops and, therefore, all
generals operated under his auspices as his representatives (*legati Augusti*):
see 59.22.2n. [= **B.16**].

C.12 ADMINISTRATIVE ARRANGEMENTS IN ROME AND THE
PROVINCES   A.D. 44

(60.24.1–7)

24.1 Cl. made Achaea and Macedonia once again depend on the lot: D. means
that Cl. converted Achaea and Macedonia from an imperial province
under a governor appointed directly by the emperor (*legatus Augusti pro*

praetore) to a public province, governed by a proconsul appointed by lot: cf. Suet. *Cl.* 25.3. For the two types of province see 59.20.7n. [= **B.15**]; 60.17.3n. [= **C.9**]. In 27 B.C. Aug. had separated Achaea from Macedonia and made both public provinces. Tib. had reunited them in 15 and converted them into a single imperial province under the control of the governor (*legatus*) of Moesia (58.25.5; Tac. *A.* 1.76 (the crucial sentence is omitted in Grant's Penguin translation); 1.80; Levick, *Tib.*, 129. This gave the governor of Moesia an enormous area to supervise. Cl.'s reform allowed him once again to concentrate his efforts on the Danube frontier zone in Moesia (Levick, *Cl.*, 157). An inscription, attesting a proconsul of Achaea chosen 'outside the lot' during Cl.'s reign (Smallwood 232 = Braund 405), confirms Cl.'s reform, even if Cl. decided on this occasion not to leave the appointment to chance. For Nero's later liberation of Achaea, which made it once again independent of Macedonia, see 63.11.1 + n. [= **D.2**].

24.1–2 he transferred control of finances from the praetors back to the quaestors: Under the Republic the public treasury (*aerarium Saturni*) had been managed by the quaestors, elected annually; but from 23 B.C. Aug. had appointed two praetors (*praetores aerarii*) annually to run the treasury (53.32.2; cf. 60.4.4 + n. [= **C.4**]). Cl. here creates a new kind of official: styled quaestor (to recall the Republican system of administration), but specially appointed by the emperor. An inscription commemorates the 'first quaestor in charge of the treasury for a three-year period outside the lot' (Smallwood 233 = Braund 406; cf. Smallwood 234 = Braund 407). Cl.'s system remained in place until 56, whenceforth two 'prefects of the treasury' (*praefecti aerarii*) were selected by the emperor from among the ex-praetors (Tac. *A.* 13.28–29). See further F. Millar, *JRS* 54 (1964), 33–40, esp. 33–34.

some of these quaestors secured the praetorship immediately: i.e., they did not have to hold an aedileship or tribunate of the plebs, but were allowed to stand for the praetorship early. For this career pattern see Smallwood 233 = Braund 406.

others drew a salary based upon an evaluation of how they had performed while in office: D.'s meaning here is unclear. For the argument that those not advanced to praetorships were appointed to salaried imperial posts (often as legionary commanders, who were usually appointed from among the ex-praetors) see Levick, *Cl.*, 85, 97. But if this is what D. meant, it is odd that he did not express it more explicitly. In Maecenas' speech advising Aug. D. recommends (52.25.2) that the treasury be run by equestrians, whose salary was to be determined according to their dignity and the importance of their positions.

24.3 instead of their responsibilities in various parts of Italy: cf. Suet. *Cl.* 24.2. Under the Republic four quaestors (*quaestores classici*) had been assigned to posts in Italy (Livy, *Epitome* 15; Tac. *A.* 11.22), the best attested of which was the quaestor with responsibility for Ostia (Cic. *pro Sestio* 17.39; *pro Murena* 8.18). D. is, therefore, wrong to claim (55.4.4) that Aug. created these posts. For further discussion see Levick, *Cl.* 84–85, 97; W.V. Harris, *CQ* 26 (1976), 92–106.

he entrusted the praetors with judicial duties formerly carried out by the consuls: The only well-documented type of consular jurisdiction is that over inheritance trusts (*fideicommissa*) (D. Johnston, *The Roman Law of Trusts* (1988), 222). D. may here refer to the creation by Cl. of a special fideicommissary praetor, who could judge these cases in addition to the consuls (Crook, *Law & Life*, 125–26).

soldiers in the army could not have wives in the eyes of the law: This is the earliest reference to the fact that soldiers could not contract a marriage that was recognized under Roman law, but this legal restriction had probably been established by Aug. It was lifted in D.'s lifetime by Septimius Severus. Soldiers on demobilization were granted the right to marry. For some relevant texts see LR II, 149–50; for discussion J.B. Campbell, *JRS* 68 (1978), 153–66, esp. 153–54; Crook, *Law & Life*, 99–100.

the legal privileges of married men: Aug.'s marriage laws of 18 B.C. and A.D. 9, which were still in force, prevented bachelors from receiving inheritances and legacies from anyone except close relatives and from attending public festivals (54.16.1; LR I, 204; P.A. Brunt, *Italian Manpower* (1971), 558–66; S. Treggiari, *Roman Marriage* (1991), 60–80). The privileges of parents with three children (*ius trium liberorum*) could be granted as a special favour by the senate or (more usually) the emperor (55.2.6). Cl.'s action thus enabled soldiers to receive inheritances and legacies from anyone. Cl. had also granted these same privileges to those who equipped large merchant ships to import grain for Rome (Suet. *Cl.* 19.2).

24.4 M. Iulius Cottius: *PIR²* I 275. His father (of the same name) had supported Aug.'s campaigns in the Cottian (i.e., western) Alps and been appointed prefect of several tribes in the region (EJ 166 = Braund 611; R. Syme, *CAH* X (1934), 347–51). When the younger Cottius died in c. 65, Nero annexed the kingdom as a province under an equestrian governor (Suet. *N.* 18).

Cottius for the first time given the title of king: For an inscription confirming Cottius' title "king" (*rex*) see *ILS* 848. The same title was held by Cogidubnus, allied king in Britain (J.E. Bogaers, *Britannia* 10 (1979), 244–245 = Braund 627 = Sherk 56, improving the text of Smallwood 197). Cl. possibly bestowed this title as he was returning from Britain in 44 (Levick, *Cl.* 143).

the Rhodians were deprived of their independence: Rhodes was deprived of its special status as an autonomous allied state (*civitas foederata et libera*) and incorporated into the province of Asia (Levick, *Cl.*, 167). Compare Cl.'s treatment of Lycia in 43 (60.17.3–4 [= **C.9**]) or Tib.'s of Cyzicus in 25 for using violence against Roman citizens (Tac. *A.* 4.36). In 53 Cl. restored the Rhodians to their former freedom after an effective speech from their patron, the young Nero (Tac. *A.* 12.58; Suet. *Cl.* 25.3; id., *N.* 7.2, dating the speech incorrectly to 51). In general on Rhodes under the Principate see Magie, *RRAM*, 548 and 1406, n. 24; Jones, *Dio Chrysostom*, 26–35. More generally the incident reveals that the Roman emperor did take steps to protect the position of Roman citizens in the provinces and that any special privileges granted to provincials could easily and quickly be revoked.

by crucifying them: Crucifixion was the standard means of executing low-status *peregrini* (subject peoples) and slaves (Garnsey, *SSLP*, 126–29).

24.5 Umbonius Silio expelled from the senate: *PIR*¹ U 590. For his term as proconsul of Baetica, which lasted possibly from 43 to 44, see G. Alföldy, *Fasti Hispanienses* (1969), 153–54. Cl. here uses the emperor's censorial power to have a member expelled from the senate. Again D. chooses to castigate the imperial freedmen for a senator's downfall, when the *prima facie* charge against him seems quite plausible.

grain supplies for the army in Mauretania: Legionary detachments were stationed in Mauretania near Caesarea (modern Cherchel) and during 44 were still engaged in mopping up after the military campaigns of 40–43 (60.8.6n. [= **C.6**]; Levick, *Cl.*, 149–50). D. here provides an interesting insight into how the legionary garrisons in the provinces were supplied with food: essentially through taxation of the provinces. This consisted not just of money taxes (as stressed by K. Hopkins, *JRS* 70 (1980), 101–25), but also of taxes raised in kind in those provinces in, and near, which the legions were stationed (Garnsey and Saller, *RE*, 88–95; R.P. Duncan-Jones, *Structure and Scale in the Roman Economy* (1990), 187–98).

24.6 he sold his senatorial dress: For senatorial dress see 59.9.5n. [= **B.7**]. Those senators who were holding curule office (curule aediles, praetors, consuls) were entitled to wear the purple-bordered toga (*toga praetexta*) during their period in office and thereafter on ceremonial occasions: see 58.11.2n. [= **A.7**]. For magistrates resigning their office and disposing of their purple-bordered togas cf. 57.21.2; Plut. *Cic.* 19.

the market which took place every ninth day: D. here provides good evidence for the close, centralized control of markets in the Roman Empire. That a market was held in a given town only every ninth day is suggested by the Latin term for market, *nundinae* (= "ninth day"), and confirmed by an inscription from Pompeii (*CIL* IV 8863 = Sherk 198), which shows that Rome was linked with seven other towns in Latium and Campania to form a market-circuit. Permission was needed of the emperor to establish a new market: see further Balsdon, *Life & Leisure*, 59–65; B.D. Shaw, *Antiquités Africaines* 17 (1981), 37–83.

C.13 VALERIUS ASIATICUS RESIGNS HIS CONSULSHIP; DEATH OF VINICIUS; REVOLT OF ASINIUS GALLUS   A.D. 46

(60.27.1–5)

27.1 Valerius Asiaticus and Marcus Silanus took over as consuls: D. marks the start of a new year in traditional annalistic fashion by including the names of the new ordinary consuls: see Introduction, Section 3.4.1.

D. Valerius Asiaticus: See further 59.30.2n. [= **B.23**]. His enormous wealth aroused Messallina's cupidity and led to his destruction at her hands in 47 on a charge of treason and adultery (Tac. *A.* 11.1–3; Levick, *Cl.*, 61–63).

M. Iunius Silanus: *PIR²*J 833. He was the elder brother of Cl.'s son-in-law, on whom see 60.21.5n. [= **C.11**]. His obsequiousness towards G. had resulted in him being nicknamed "the Golden Sheep" (Tac. *A.* 13.1 *contra* 59.8.5, where D. wrongly attributes the nickname to a kinsman whose daughter, Junia Claudilla, was G.'s first wife: see Syme, *AA*, ch. 14, esp. 192 and n. 39 and Tables 12 and 13). He was put to death at the very start of Nero's reign at the instigation of Agrippina (Tac. *A.* 13.1).

resignation of Asiaticus: An edict of Cl., dated by the inclusion of the consuls' names (Smallwood 368 = Braund 569 = Sherk 52), shows that Asiaticus had been replaced by Q. Sulpicius Camerinus as Silanus' colleague as consul by 15 March.

length of tenure of the consulship: It was rare under the Julio-Claudians for the ordinary consuls to hold office for the whole year, but not unprecedented under Cl.: e.g. C. Caecina Largus in 42, L. Vipstanus Poplicola Messalla in 48, Cl. himself in 51 (despite Suet. *Cl.* 14) and Faustus Cornelius Sulla Felix in 52 (P.A. Gallivan, *CQ* 28 (1978), 424–25).

27.2   circus games: See 59.14.2n. [= **B.11**].

consuls funding games: The consuls were expected to help fund several sets of public games: e.g. the Games of Mars (EJ 362 = Braund 783 = Sherk 30), the Actian Games (59.20.1–2 [= **B.15**]), the games commemorating Aug.'s birthday (56.46.4), as well as games to celebrate the present emperor's birthday (Tac. *H.* 2.95; Pliny, *Panegyric* 92.4–5). The ordinary consuls also marked their entry into office by putting on circus games on 7 January (Fronto, *Letters* 2.1.1; *Inscriptiones Italiae*, XIII.2, p. 392). See further Talbert, *Senate*, 58–64.

the number of races at circus games: cf. 59.7.2 + n. [= **B.5**]. Circus games were the most expensive kind of games to put on, since the magistrates involved had to negotiate a contract with the managers of the four charioteering factions, to cover the cost of the horses, chariots, drivers and prize money (Balsdon, *Life & Leisure*, 261–3, 316, 318). The Calendar from Antium (*Inscriptiones Italiae*, XIII.2, p. 206) reveals that at the very end of G.'s reign a state subvention was instituted to help out the magistrates putting on various public games.

27.3   consul for the second time: This was a rare honour up until the reign of Cl., but became increasingly frequent thereafter (60.3.5n. [= **C.3**]).

27.4   M. Vinicius: *PIR¹* V 445. An elegant orator, he had been ordinary consul in 30 and was one of the main candidates to become emperor after G.'s assassination in 41 (60.1.1n. [= **C.1**]; Tac. *A.* 6.15; Syme, *AA*, 172–73). The reasons that D. adduces here for his death are hardly credible, but the real causes are impossible to ascertain (Syme, *AA*, 276; Levick, *Cl.*, 61).

Julia: i.e., Julia Livilla (*PIR²* J 674), the youngest daughter of Germanicus and hence sister of G. She had married Vinicius in 33 (58.21.1; Tac. *A.* 6.15; Syme, *AA*, 172–73 and n. 21), but was exiled by G. in 39 (59.22.6 + n. [= **B.17**]). She was recalled by Cl. in 41 (60.4.1 [= **C.4**]), but promptly

exiled once again and soon killed at the instigation of Messallina (60.8.5
+ n. [= **C.6**]; 60.18.4 [= **C.10**]). D.'s earlier account of her death (60.8.5,
confirmed by Suet. *Cl.* 29.1) contradicts the suggestion made here by D.
that Messallina took action against Vinicius because he had killed Julia.
D. is so anxious to paint Messallina in a bad light that he has her not only
murdering people, but also destroying those who by murdering her
intended victims, deprived her of the satisfaction.

refused to have sex with her: Messallina's sexual promiscuity was legendary
(cf. 60.14.3 [= **C.8**]; 60.18.1–2 [= **C.10**]; 60.22.3–5; 60.31.1.5; Tac. *A.*
11.12; 11.26–27; 11.31; 11.36; Suet. *Cl.* 26.2; 29.3). D. here uses the same
reason to explain Vinicius' death as he had used to explain the death of C.
Appius Iunius Silanus in 42 (60.14.3 [= **C.8**]), which reduces its credibility; it appears to be a standard rhetorical *topos*.

public funeral and eulogies: See further 59.11.1n. [= **B.9**].

27.5 **C.(?) Asinius Gallus:** *PIR*² A 1228; the youngest son of C. Asinius Gallus
(58.3.1 + n. [= **A.1**]) and Vipsania Agrippina, the daughter of M.
Agrippa. Gallus was a half-brother of Drusus son of Tib. on his mother's
side, since Vipsania had been married to Tib. from c. 20–12 B.C. (54.31.2;
Suet. *T.* 7.2). For his supposed conspiracy against Cl., in which Taurus
Statilius Corvinus, ordinary consul in 45, was also implicated, see Suet. *Cl.*
13.2; Levick, *Cl.* 57; but for doubts as to its seriousness and even its
authenticity see Syme, *AA*, 183, 240.

*C.14   COTYS REPLACES MITHRIDATES AS KING OF BOSPORUS
A.D. 46

(60.28.7: Petrus Patricius)

28.7 **Mithridates king of the Iberians revolted:** D. is in error here: he means
Mithridates king of Cimmerian Bosporus (*PIR*² M 635), the brother of
Mithridates of Iberia. For the latter see 60.8.1 + n. [= **C.6**]. Cl. had
confirmed Mithridates in power in Bosporus in 41 (60.8.2 + n. [= **C.6**]).
His revolt was serious for Rome, since this was from where grain from the
Crimea was despatched to Rome. Cl. sent A. Didius Gallus, probably then
governor of Moesia, to quell the revolt (Tac. *A.* 12.15; Smallwood 226 =
Braund 399; cf. *ILS* 9197); as a result of his military actions Cl. received
further salutations as *Imperator* (Levick, *Cl.* 157–58). Mithridates was
eventually captured in 49 and brought as a prisoner to Rome (Tac. *A.*
12.15–21), where he remained until his execution by Galba in 68 after
taking part in the conspiracy of Nymphidius Sabinus (Plut. *Galba* 13.4;
15.1).

his mother: probably Gepaepyris (*PIR*² G 168); it is not entirely clear if she
was his mother or his stepmother. She is depicted on Bosporan coins of 39
(*CAH. Plates IV*, 208 h and i).

his brother Cotys: i.e., Cotys I of Bosporus (*PIR*² C 1556). He was set up in
power in Bosporus (again not Iberia, as D. claims) by A. Didius Gallus

(Tac. *A*. 12.15) and ruled from 45/6 to 67/8; he was the first king of Bosporus to be honoured with Roman citizenship (Braund, *RFK*, 41). For a gold coin issue of Cotys dated to 45–46 commemorating his debt to Cl. see Smallwood 203a.

D. THE REIGN OF NERO: A.D. 66 – 68:
THE FALL OF NERO

* * * * *

*D.1 TIRIDATES IS CROWNED KING OF ARMENIA BY NERO
A.D. 66

(63.1.1–7.1, 2: Xiphilinus)

1.1   **In the consulship of C. Telesinus and Suetonius Paulinus:** D. starts his account of the year 66 in traditional annalistic fashion by giving the names of the ordinary consuls (see Introduction, Section 3.4.1). C. Luccius Telesinus (*PIR*² L 366), who had a keen interest in philosophy, was later exiled by Domitian (Philostratus, *Life of Apollonius of Tyana* 4.40; 4.43; 7.11; 8.7.14; 8.12); for C. Suetonius Paullinus see 60.9.1n. [= **C.6**].

one event took place that much enhanced Nero's [hereafter N.] prestige: D. emphasizes right at the start of his account of the year 66 that the coronation of Tiridates as king of Armenia was an important piece of diplomacy by N. Armenia had been causing Rome problems for years. Formerly a kingdom allied to Rome, Armenia had been controlled by Parthia since 54. Under N. Rome had unsuccessfully made various military and diplomatic attempts to recover control until N.'s general, Cn. Domitius Corbulo, made a truce and effected a diplomatic settlement in 63 (63.1.2n.) N.'s solution was to give up practical Roman influence in Armenia, while making it appear to the Roman people that Armenia was a Roman vassal. This solution lasted longer than those of his predecessors, while the coronation of Tiridates in Rome fitted in perfectly with N.'s flamboyant style of rule. See further Warmington 85–98; Griffin, *Nero*, 226–27; J.G.C. Anderson, *CAH* X (1934), 754–72; M. Hammond, *HSCPh* 45 (1934), 81–104; M.-L. Chaumont, *ANRW* II.9.1 (1976), 101–23.

N.'s settlement of Armenia was commemorated by a series of coin issues emphasizing Victory and Peace (Smallwood 50–55 = Braund 244–249) and in official art in the Roman provinces: a relief from the Sebasteion at Aphrodisias (Caria) depicts a heroically naked, helmeted N., picking up from the ground a slumping female personification of Armenia (R.R.R. Smith, *JRS* 77 (1987), 88–138, esp. 117–20 and pls. XVI–XVII; Braund 251: inscription only).

N. competed in a lyre-playing competition: For his musical training and talents cf. Suet. *N.* 20. For a coin issue with Apollo as lyre-player see Smallwood 144 = LACTOR 8, no. 40 = Braund 280 = Griffin, *Nero*, pl. 31 = Warmington, pl. III; cf. Suet. *N.* 25.2; Sutherland, *RHC*, 91–95.

his lyre-teacher Menecrates: He was one of the foremost lyre-players (*citharoedi*) of his day, whom N. rewarded with houses and estates (Suet. *N.* 30.2).

victory ceremony in the Circus: This ceremony was held to celebrate N.'s victory in the Neronia, quinquennial Greek games with contests in oratory, poetry, singing and lyre-playing, inaugurated by N. in 60, on which see 61.21; Tac. *A.* 14.20–21; Smallwood 57 = Braund 254. On Greek games at Rome see Balsdon, *Life & Leisure*, 324–26. N. held a still more elaborate triumph after his victories in Greece in 67 (63.20–21.1 [= **D.5**]).

N. appeared as a charioteer: cf. 61.6.1; 62.15.1; Tac. *A.* 14.14; Suet. *N.* 22.1–2. He favoured the Greens, like his predecessor G. (62.6.3 [= **D.1**]; cf. 59.14.6 [= **B.11**]). Suet. *N.* 20–25 groups N.'s musical and charioteering exploits into one combined section.

1.2 **Tiridates:** A Parthian, he had been set up as king of Armenia in 54 by his brother Vologaesus, king of Parthia (Tac. *A.* 12.50). In 60 N.'s general, Cn. Domitius Corbulo, had expelled and established Tigranes V as king in his place (Tac. *A.* 14.23–26). But when Tigranes started to attack neighbouring territory, Vologaesus of Parthia invaded Armenia in 62, trapped Tigranes inside Tigranocerta and forced the Roman forces under L. Caesennius Paetus to withdraw from Armenia (62.20.2–21.4; Tac. *A.* 15.1–17). As a result in 63 Corbulo agreed at a conference with Parthian delegates at Rhandeia in Armenia to the reinstatement of Tiridates as king, as long as he laid down his royal diadem and came to Rome to receive it back from N. Soon after this conference Tiridates met Corbulo in front of the Roman and Parthian armies and laid down his diadem before a statue of N. (62.22.1–23.4; Tac. *A.* 15.24–31; cf. Sherk 65).

Vologaesus: Vologaesus I, king of Parthia from 51 – c. 80. For coins issued by him see Smallwood 213 = Braund 639. He later supported Rome in the Jewish War (Suet. *Vesp.* 6.4; Jos. *BJ* 7.105ff.)

Pacorus: King of Media since c. 54, he was also an older brother of Tiridates (Tac. *A.* 15.2; 15.14; 15.31). His sons were Exedares and Parthamasiris (68.17.2–3).

Monobazus: King of Adiabene since 60. When his kingdom was devastated by Tigranes, he appealed to Volagaesus to take action; he himself played a leading rôle in besieging Tigranes inside Tigranocerta and re-establishing Tiridates as king (62.20.2; Tac. *A.* 15.1; 15.14).

like a triumphal procession: For details on Roman triumphs see 59.3.5n. [= **B.3**].

2.1 **proud bearing:** Cary in the Loeb edition translates this as "intelligence", but D. is here stressing Tiridates' outward appearance, which makes pride or haughtiness more appropriate in this context.

2.2 **they were welcomed by the cities decorated in sparkling array:** When members of the Roman imperial family toured the Empire, provincial cities were expected to provide hospitality for them and their entourage; for the reception given Germanicus when he visited Egypt in 18–19 see EJ 320 = Braund 558–559 = Sherk 34. For the financial burdens that such tours placed upon provincials see Millar, *ERW*, 28–40; T.D. Barnes, *JRA* 2 (1989), 247–61. For cities in festal array cf. 63.4.1 + n. [= **D.1**].

all their provisions were provided free of charge, the cost to the public treasury amounted to 200,000 denarii a day: D. is slightly misleading when he suggests that the Roman treasury provided all the funds for these ceremonies; provincial communities also had to contribute (Pliny *NH* 30.6.16). However, it was still a considerable drain on Rome's resources: Suet. *N.* 30.2 gives the same figure (800,000 *nummi* (= sesterces) = 200,000 *denarii* per day). Over a period of nine months this would have amounted to c. 54 million *denarii*, about one-quarter of the estimated annual total tax income from the provinces of the Empire (824 million sesterces = 206 million *denarii*: see K. Hopkins, *JRS* 70 (1980), 119). On financial problems under N. see Griffin, *Nero*, 197–207; Warmington 63–70.

2.3   **his wife wore a helmet instead of a veil, to prevent her face being seen, which was against the customs of her country:** D. here illustrates the secluded position of women in Parthian society (*Cambridge History of Iran* (1985), 226–27), but fails to explain why she wore a golden helmet instead of a veil.

two-horse carriage: For the various types of Roman wheeled vehicles see L. Casson, *Travel in the Ancient World* (1974), 179–82.

Tiridates' route: He travelled through Illyricum and then into Italy via Aquileia; he then proceeded down the east coast through the region of Picenum, crossing the central Apennines south of Rome, hence to Naples (63.7.1 [= **D.1**]). Other sources stress that he avoided travelling by sea, since he was a Magus (Pliny, *NH* 30.6.16; Tac. *A.* 15.24) and these Zoroastrian priests were not allowed to defile water, a sacred element in the Zoroastrian faith (Griffin, *Nero*, 216). This, however, did not stop him returning by sea (63.7.1 = **D.1**).

Neapolis: modern Naples, still very much a Greek city and a frequent haunt of N., where he could freely indulge his Hellenized tastes (cf. Tac. *A.* 14.10; 15.33; 16.10; Suet. *N.* 20.2; Griffin, *Nero*, 208–220; Warmington 108–22); see further 60.6.1n. [= **C.5**]).

prostrated himself: For the Parthian/Persian ritual of prostration before social superiors (*proskynêsis*) see 59.27.5n. [= **B.21**].

3.1   **Puteoli:** modern Pozzuoli, an important port city on the Bay of Naples, on which see further 59.17.1n. [= **B.13**].

Patrobius, imperial freedman: One of the most hated of N.'s freedmen (cf. Tac. *H.* 2.95). D. here provides an interesting insight into the organization of shows put on by the emperor: it was left in the hands of the imperial freedmen; for a freedman of N. putting on gladiatorial shows at Antium see Pliny, *NH* 35.33.52; for freedman procurators of the games (*procuratores munerum*) see *ILS* 1567, 1738; G. Boulvert, *Esclaves et affranchis impériaux sous le Haut-Empire romain* (1970), 160–62.

no other performers but Ethiopians: The Greeks and Romans commonly used "Ethiopians" to refer to blacks; they did not necessarily all come from Ethiopia (L.A. Thompson, *Romans and Blacks* (1989)). During the Principate gladiatorial shows became ever more elaborate; the use of exclusively black fighters is a good illustration of the increasing specialization of the shows, as novel effects were sought to impress the crowds (Thompson, *Romans and Blacks*, 53, 119).

women and children as gladiators: Another example of increasing specialization (see last note). For women as gladiators cf. 61.17; 75.16.1; Tac. *A.* 15.32; Balsdon, *Life & Leisure*, 290–91. A relief from Halicarnassus (Asia Minor) shows two female gladiators (*British Museum, Catalogue of Sculpture*, no. 1117; I. Jenkins, *Greek and Roman Life* (1986), pl. 75). For fights involving women and dwarfs under Domitian see Statius, *Silvae* 1.6.51–64.

3.2 Tiridates shoots at bulls: Tiridates here demonstrates the traditional Persian prowess in archery. Persian gold coins ('Darics') and cylinder seals show King Darius shooting at wild animals from a chariot (*Cambridge History of Iran* (1985), pls. 12.3 and 47b). The personification of Armenia on the relief from Aphrodisias (see 63.1.2n.) is depicted with a bow and quiver. This anecdote also implies that beast-hunts (*venationes*) were part of this show; they were often combined with gladiatorial combats (Friedländer II, 62–73). For beast-hunts with bulls and gladiators on the same programme at Pompeii see *ILS* 5053 = Sherk 170c.

if you can believe it: D. here adds a small note of scepticism to the version he found in his source(s). For his handling of his sources see Introduction, Sections 3.2–3.3.

4.1–7.1 Tiridates' coronation at Rome: cf. Suet. *N.* 13, who includes it among the commendable acts of N. and adds the detail that after the celebrations in the theatre N. was hailed as *Imperator* (for the eleventh time) by the people, dedicated a laurel wreath in the Capitoline temple of Jupiter, Juno and Minerva and closed the doors of the temple of Janus, an event also commemorated on a coin issue (Smallwood 53 = Braund 247), which symbolically declared that all wars (especially those against Parthia) were at an end. The coronation was one of the major spectacles of N.'s reign and served to boost N.'s military prestige in front of the Roman people. It was also suffused with Oriental/Mithraic imagery, which has led some scholars to argue that N. wanted himself to be seen as an incarnation of the Indo-Iranian god Mithras; for doubts and further discussion see Griffin, *Nero*, 216–17.

4.1 torches and garlands: i.e., Rome was decked out as on any festal or cultic occasion with garlands, torches and burning incense (cf. 63.20.4 [= **D.5**]; 74.1.4). Torches (or especially candelabra) and garlands are often represented as symbols of piety on Roman religious iconography (e.g. on the *Ara Pacis*: see Zanker, *Power of Images*, 114–18, 276 and figs. 96, 99, 220).

4.2 clothed in white: i.e., clad in white togas, the traditional dress that visibly differentiated Roman citizens from non-citizens.

carrying laurel branches: The Roman symbol of victory *par excellence*, a theme that ran through this ceremonial. A triumphant general held a laurel branch in his right hand during his triumphal procession, as is clearly depicted on one of the Boscoreale silver cups (F. Barratte, *Le trésor d'orfèvrerie romaine de Boscoreale* (1986), 74; Zanker, *Power of Images*, fig. 181). Garlands of laurel were granted as special honours to victorious generals (43.43.1; 49.14.4; 49.15.1; Suet. *T.* 17.2; Versnel, *Triumphus*, 57).

arranged according to social rank: Distinctions of social rank were constantly reinforced in visible terms; rank determined where one sat at the theatre, amphitheatre or even at a private dinner-party (Garnsey & Saller, *RE*, ch. 6; see further 59.7.8n. [= **B.5**]; 60.7.3–4nn. [= **C.5**]).

troops in their finest parade armour: On the various types of armour of Roman soldiers (including parade armour) see Webster, *Army*, 121–27 (legionaries), 151–56 (auxiliaries). The auxiliary cavalry had special, elaborately decorated parade armour (ibid., 155–56; R.W. Davies, *Service in the Roman Army* (1989), 92, 100–01, pls. 4.1 and 4.4).

standards: For further details on these important legionary emblems see 63.25.1–2n. [= **D.6**].

4.3 **triumphal dress:** See 59.3.5n. [= **B.3**].
Rostra: See 59.12.2n. [= **B.10**].
curule chair: See 59.12.2n. [= **B.10**].

5.1 **herald:** Heralds (*praecones*) played an important rôle in controlling Roman public ceremonials; they were recruited from among leading members of the *plebs romana*, i.e., those just below the equestrians in rank (N. Purcell, *PBSR* 51 (1983), 125–73).

5.2 **Arsaces:** The first king of Parthia, who ruled from c. 238–218 and gave his name to the Arsacid royal dynasty, which held power in Parthia from the mid-second century B.C. to the mid-second A.D. (Justin 41.4.6–8).
Mithras: An ancient Indo-Iranian god, whose cult became very popular among the Romans from the end of the first century A.D. See J. Ferguson, *The Religions of the Roman Empire* (1970), 47–49; 111–22; R.L. Gordon, *Religion* 2 (1972), 92–121; R. Beck, *ANRW* II.17.4 (1984), 2002–2115; for Mithraic iconography see M. Vermaseren, *Corpus inscriptionum et monumentorum religionis Mithriacae* (2 vols., 1960); for the worship of Mithras in Armenia see R. Merkelbach, *Mithras* (1984), 46–49 (in German).
whatever destiny you have spun for me: Tiridates here alludes to the Greco-Roman mythic imagery of the Fates (or *Parcae*) as three old women who spun out, measured and cut off the thread of life (cf. Petr. *Sat.* 29). The allusion had added point at this ceremony, since it was being played out directly alongside the statues of the Three Fates, which stood on the Rostra in the Forum (Coarelli, *Guida arch. di Roma*, 65). It is unlikely that Tiridates was familiar with such allusions, which suggests that D./Xiph. (or his source) invented this short speech.

5.4 **diadem:** A thin band worn around the head was a symbol of royalty used by Hellenistic kings, and can be seen depicted on sculpted and coin portraits of them (R.R.R. Smith, *Hellenistic Royal Portraits* (1988), 34–38; pls. 10.2, 14.4, 16.2, 18.2, 20.2 etc.).

6.1 **by special decree:** D. means by a special decree of the senate (*senatus consultum*). The senate still had to give its permission for all special celebrations (triumphs, ovations and celebratory games and festivals): cf. 43.14.3; 54.31.4; 55.10.3; 59.23.2 [= **B.17**]; 60.22.1 [= **C.11**]; 60.23.6 [= **C.11**]; 63.20.4 [= **D.5**]; Talbert, *Senate*, 362–64.

6.1 **the theatre:** Pliny, *NH* 33.16.54 reveals that these celebrations took place in the theatre of Pompey, which was often referred to as just 'the theatre': see 60.6.8n. [= **C.5**].
decorated with gold: cf. Plin. *NH* 33.16.54. N.'s new palace was also notable for its lavish gold decoration (his 'Golden House') (A. Boethius,

The Golden House of Nero (1960); Griffin, *Nero*, 133–42, adding details of more recent excavations). On another occasion N. decorated the amphitheatre with amber (Plin. *NH* 37.11.45 [= LR II, 30]).

6.2 awnings: See 59.12.2n. [= **B.10**]. The imagery on this awning had possible Mithraic significance (cf. Griffin, *Nero*, 216–17).

6.3 banquet: Public banquets were often given by the emperors after special celebrations (see 59.7.1n. [= **B.5**]) and were sometimes served to the crowd still sitting in their seats in the Circus, theatre or amphitheatre (67.4.4). It is unclear where this particular banquet took place.

N. as lyre-player and charioteer: A leitmotif of D.'s account of N. (cf. 62.1.1nn. [= **D.1**]; Introduction, Section 4.3d).

6.4 Corbulo: Cn. Domitius Corbulo (*PIR*² D 142), N.'s general in the east since 54 (Tac. *A.* 13.8). For further biographical details see 62.19.2; 59.15.3n [= **B.11**]; 59.20.3n. [= **B.15**]; for a surviving portrait see Griffin, *Nero*, pl. 5. He was soon to fall from grace and commit suicide (62.17.2–6 [= **D.3**]).

6.5 Artaxata: The capital city of Armenia on the river Araxes, north of Mt. Ararat. It had been razed to the ground by Corbulo during his campaigns of 58 (62.19.4; Tac. *A.* 13.41).

6.6 artisans: N. needed a good supply of artisans in Rome to complete the rebuilding of the city after the fire of 64 (Tac. *A.* 15.42–43; Suet. *N.* 16.1; 31; Griffin, *Nero*, 125–42. N. had not thought through the consequences of releasing so many, but fortunately for him Corbulo did. For another shortage of skilled labour at Rome in 111 cf. Pliny, *Letters* 10.40. In general on the organization of building work at Rome see D.E. Strong, *BICS* 15 (1968), 97–109; P.A. Brunt, *JRS* 70 (1980), 81–100.

7.2 Neronia: It was common for allied kings to name their cities after Roman generals or emperors: e.g. Pompeiopolis in Bithynia, Caesarea in Mauretania and in Palestine and Sebastopolis (named after Augustus – 'Sebastos' in Greek) in Iberian Colchis (Braund *RFK*, 107–8). Caesarea in Palestine was renamed Neronias during N.'s reign (Smallwood 211a = Braund 637a). Artaxata, however, soon reverted to its original name (cf. Juv. *Sat.* 2.170).

Vologaesus: See 63.1.2n. [= **D.1**].

*D.2 NERO IN GREECE   A.D. 66–67

(63.8.1–10.1; 11.1: Xiphilinus)

8.1–11.1 N.'s tour of Greece: For further details see 63.14.1–17.6 [partly = **D.4**]; Suet. *N.* 22.3–24.2; Philostratus, *Life of Apollonius of Tyana* 4.24 [= Braund 264]. The trip had been planned for 64, but was postponed because of the burning of Rome in July (cf. Tac. *A.* 15.36, deriving from hostile anti-Neronian propaganda). N.'s trip probably lasted from August 66 to December 67 (K.R. Bradley, *Latomus* 37 (1978), 61–72; Warmington 116–122; Griffin, *Nero*, 211; B. Levy in *Ancient Coins of the Graeco-Roman world: the Nickle Numismatic Papers* (ed. W. Heckel and

R.D. Sullivan, 1984), 165–85). D.'s account of it, though lively, is generally hostile to N. and may derive from the senatorial historian, Cluvius Rufus, suffect consul in 39 or 40, who was made to act as N.'s herald on the trip, socially demeaning for an ex-consul (63.14.3). In general on D.'s use of Cluvius Rufus see G.B. Townend, *Hermes* 89 (1961), 227–48.

8.1 expeditions to Ethiopia and the Caspian Gates: For the possibility that N. was planning an Ethiopian expedition see Pliny, *NH* 6.35.181, 184; Seneca, *Natural Questions* 6.8.3; Warmington 99–100, but for doubts see Griffin, *Nero*, 229. N. certainly was planning a campaign to the Causasus (Tac. *H.* 1.6; Suet. *N.* 19.2), although not strictly to the Caspian Gates, as Plin. *NH* 6.15.40 is at pains to point out. The purpose of the expedition was to take action against the Rhoxolani (a group of Sarmatian tribesmen on the move) and to establish Roman control of the two main passes through the Caucasus (Warmington 98–99; Griffin, *Nero*, 228–29; J. Kolendo in *Neronia 1977* (ed. J.-M. Croisille and P.-M. Fauchère, 1982), 23–30).

8.2 Flamininus: C. Quinctius Flamininus, consul in 198 B.C. and the victorious Roman general in the Second Macedonian War (198–196 B.C.) against Philip V (Livy 32.8–33.35; Plut. *Flamininus*; R.M. Errington, *CAH²* VIII (1989), 261–73).

Mummius: L. Mummius, consul in 146 B.C., finished off the Achaean war in 146 and was responsible for the ruthless sacking of Corinth (Pausanias 7.15–16; Zonaras 9.31; Livy, *Periochae* 52; P.S. Derow, *CAH²* VIII (1989) 319–23).

his ancestors Agrippa and Aug.: N. was related to Agrippa and Aug. on his mother's side: his mother (the younger Agrippina) was the granddaughter of M. Vipsanius Agrippa and Aug.'s daughter, Julia. D. here alludes to the campaigns of Aug. and Agrippa in Greece against M. Antonius and Cleopatra in 31 B.C., culminating in the decisive battle of Actium in September (50.11–51.4; Syme, *RR*, 294–98; J.M. Carter, *The Battle of Actium* (1970), 200–27).

making declamations: For N.'s skills cf. Suet. *N.* 10.2. Such eminent Romans as Cicero, Pompey, M. Antonius and Aug. were all keen devotees (Suet. *On Rhetoricians* 1); see further S.F. Bonner, *Roman Declamation in the late Republic and early Empire* (1949).

acting in tragedies: See further 63.9.4 + n. [= **D.2**]; 63.22.6 [= **D.6**].

8.3 theatre of Pompey: See further 60.6.8n. [= **C.5**].

Circus Maximus: The largest of the arenas for chariot-racing in Rome, alleged to have been first constructed during the reign of Tarquinius Priscus (Livy 1.35.8). See further Humphrey, *Circuses*, 56–294.

8.3 'victor on the festival circuit': This title (in Greek *periodonikês*) was bestowed on those athletes who had won victories at the four major Greek athletic festivals (the 'festival circuit' or *periodos*): the Olympic Games at Olympia, the Pythian Games at Delphi, the Isthmian Games at Corinth and the Nemean Games at Nemea (L. Moretti, *Iscrizioni agonistiche greci* (1953), 34–35). For an inscription from a statue base from N.'s reign found on the outskirts of Rome commemorating just such a victor see

Moretti, no. 65. For further details on Greek athletics in the Roman period see H.A. Harris, *Sport in Ancient Greece and Rome* (1972), ch. 2.

To achieve his purpose, N. had to order the rescheduling of the Nemean and Olympic Games (due to be held in 68 and 69 respectively) and force the organizers to introduce musical competitions into the festivals which normally consisted merely of athletic events (Suet. *N.* 22.3; 23.1; Warmington 116–17; Griffin, *Nero*, 162–63; K.R. Bradley, *Suetonius' Life of Nero* (1978), 140–41; N.M. Kennel, *AJP* 109 (1988), 239–51). At the Olympics N. fell from his chariot, but was still crowned victor (63.14.1; Suet. *N.* 24.2). His proclamation after each victory was "Nero Caesar wins this contest and crowns the Roman people and his whole world" (63.14.4).

Augustiani: These were a group of about 5000 Romans who led the applause whenever N. appeared on the stage or at festivals. D. claims that they were made up of soldiers (61.20.4); but for variants cf. Tac. *A.* 14.15 (young Roman equestrians); Suet. *N.* 20.3 (youths from the equestrian order and the plebs, divided into three groups, trained in various Alexandrian methods of applause and known as 'The Bees', 'The Roof-tiles' and 'The Bricks').

8.4 **acting masks:** All Greek and Roman actors wore masks, which made physical gesture all-important, since facial expression was denied them (O. Taplin, *Greek Tragedy in Action* (1978), 14–15; Bieber, *Theater*, 243–47 with figs. 562–78 and 799–806).

high-soled shoes: D. here refers to *embatae*, high clogs which tragic actors started to wear in the Hellenistic period (Bieber, *Theater*, 239, 242 and fig. 591). They were very different from the calf-length, soft-leather boots, flexible tragic buskins (*cothurni*), worn by tragic actors since the fifth century B.C. (Taplin, *Greek Tragedy in Action*, 14; Bieber, *Theater*, 26–27, 163–64 and figs. 85–95, 772–73, 799).

Terpnus, Diodorus, Pammenes: All three were leading lyre-players; Terpnus had been summoned to teach N. at the start of his reign (Suet. *N.* 20.1; Philostratus, *Life of Apollonius of Tyana* 5.7); Diodorus was present alongside N. at N.'s triumphal procession on his return from Greece (63.20.3 [= **D.5**]); this Pammenes should not be confused with the astrologer who had been exiled by N. (Tac. *A.* 16.14). For Terpnus' and Diodorus' later careers see Suet. *Vesp.* 19.1.

Philip: Philip V of Macedon, defeated by C. Quinctius Flamininus in the Second Macedonian War in 196 B.C. (cf. 63.8.2n. [= **D.2**]).

Perseus: King of Macedon during the Third Macedonian War, defeated by L. Aemilius Paullus in 167 B.C. (Livy 45; Plut. *Aemilius Paullus*; P.S. Derow, *CAH²* VIII (1989), 303–19).

Antiochus: Antiochus III = Antiochus the Great, Seleucid king of Syria, defeated by Rome in 190 B.C. (Livy 34.57–37.45; R.M. Errington, *CAH²* VIII (1989), 274–89).

8.5 **deface his statues:** Some of the most famous classical Greek sculptures were made for victors in the Olympic, and other major Greek, Games (Plin. *NH* 34.9.16): e.g. the famous 'Youth tying victory-band round his head' ('Diadumenos') by Polykleitos (M. Robertson, *Shorter History of Greek Art* (1981), 112–115 and fig. 156). The bases of statues of victors often bore commemorative inscriptions (H.A. Harris, *Greek Athletes and Athletics* (1964), 125–28).

9.1–6 D./Xiph. works up a highly rhetorical passage here to emphasize his moral outrage at N.'s undignified behaviour in Greece. For D.'s love of rhetoric see Introduction, Section 3.4.2. Much of the same rhetoric is also found in a later speech of Vindex (cf. 63.22.3–6 + nn. [= **D.6**]). The material may derive from rhetorical exercises criticizing the tyrannical behaviour of N. (so S.F. Bonner, *Roman Declamation* (1949), 34, 43) and/ or from the propaganda put out to subvert Romans from their loyalty to N. (so P.A. Brunt, *Latomus* 18 (1959), 531–39 at 533–34 [= *RIT*, 9–32 at 11]).

9.1 wearing his hair long: For N.'s Greek hairstyle see Suet. *N.* 51.1, with Bradley, *Nero*, 284–85.

9.2 *agônothetai* **and** *mastigophori*: These were official titles of officials at the ancient Olympic Games, which literally translate as 'those in charge of the games' and 'the whip-carriers'. The *mastigophori* carried whips which they used on the competitors if they broke the rules (e.g. in the *pancration*) or if they made a false start in a race. These whips are visible on depictions of athletics on Greek painted vases (Harris, *Greek Athletes and Athletics*, 106–7 and plates 13a, 14a, 15, 16, 18 etc.). For the organization of the games see M.I. Finley and H.W. Pleket, *The Ancient Olympic Games* (1976), 59–67.

9.3 proscription list of Sulla: L. Cornelius Sulla Felix, as dictator in 80 B.C., had published a list of supporters of his political rivals and authorized anyone to go out and kill those on the list; their property then accrued to the state (Appian, *Civil Wars* 1.95; P.A. Brunt, *Italian Manpower* (1971), 301–05). The young Octavian and Antony repeated the procedure in 43 B.C. against the supporters of those who had murdered Julius Caesar (Syme, *RR*, 187–201).

crowns of wild olive, laurel, celery or pine: The victors' wreaths were made out of different sacred plants: of wild celery at the Nemean Games, laurel at the Pythian Games, wild olive at the Olympics, celery (but later pine) at the Isthmian Games. On coins of Aug. and N. commemorating the Isthmian Games celery crowns are depicted, while pine crowns appear on coins of the mid- to late-second century (E.H. Gardiner, *Greek Athletic Sports and Festivals* (1910), 222). D. is thus being anachronistic here in the highly rhetorical passage. The Olympiad in which N. was victorious was later expunged from the record (Pausanias 10.36.9). For coins minted in Alexandria commemorating N.'s victories at the four Panhellenic Games and at the Games of Actian Apollo see Smallwood 63 = Braund 263.

lost his civic crown: Cary in his Loeb edition translates this less specifically as "lost his political crown"; but D. uses the term for a specific Roman military decoration, the *corona civica*, a wreath of oak-leaves awarded for rescuing a Roman citizen in battle (59.17.3n. [= **B.13**]). Aug. had been awarded the *corona civica* in 27 B.C. (*RG* 34.2; EJ 19 = Braund 12) and been allowed to mount it over the entrance to his house on the Palatine; it thereafter became a symbol of the Augustan ruling family (Zanker, *Power of Images*, 93–98).

9.4   high-soled stage shoes: see 63.8.4n. [= **D.2**].

runaway slave: Another incidental remark that reinforces the view that runaway slaves were a common feature of Roman life: cf. 58.11.2 + n. [= **A.7**].

N.'s tragic rôles: cf. Suet. *N.* 21.3. The characters from Greek tragedy that D. here lists do not quite cover the rôles alluded to. A possible resolution would be:

character	rôle	tragedy
beggar	Thyestes	Euripides, *Thyestes*
blind man	Oedipus	Sophocles, *Oedipus at Colonus*
pregnant woman giving birth	Canace	Euripides, *Aeolus*
raging madman	Heracles	Euripides, *Hercules Furens*
or	Alcmaeon	Euripides, *Alcmaeon*
outcast	Orestes	Euripides, *Orestes*
or	Alcmaeon	Euripides, *Alcmaeon.*

For N. playing Canace in childbirth cf. 63.10.2; Suet. *N.* 21.3. Of these plays, Soph. *Oed. Col.* and Eur. *Herc. Fur.* and *Orestes* survive in full, but only fragments of the others, for which see A. Nauck, *Tragicorum Graecorum Fragmenta* (2nd ed., 1964), 480–82 (Eur. *Thyestes*), 365–73 (Eur. *Aeolus*), 379–85 (Eur. *Alcmaeon*). For further rôles of N. cf. Juv. *Sat.* 8.228ff. (Antigone and Melanippe), Philostratus, *Life of Apollonius of Tyana* 5.8 (Creon). It remains controversial whether complete tragedies were put on in Roman times, or whether the actor gave renditions of the most dramatic scenes: see further Bieber, *Theater*, ch. 15.

9.5   tragic masks: See 63.8.4n. [= **D.2**].

Sabina: i.e., Poppaea Sabina, N.'s second wife, whom he had married in 62 after divorcing Octavia, Cl.'s daughter (Tac. *A.* 14. 59–64; 13.45; Suet. *N.* 35.1; Griffin, *Nero*, 100–03; Warmington 50–51). She had died in 65 (62.28.1). For N.'s determination to keep alive the memory of her facial features cf. 63.13.1 [= **D.3**]; for her deification cf. 63.26.3 + n. [= **D.7**].

9.6   not thought fitting for a Roman emperor to be bound in iron chains: D. uses this same idea to explain why M. Antonius used silver chains to bind the Armenian king Artaxes in 34 B.C. (49.39.6). This is a good example of D.'s dry, ironic wit, on which see further P. Plass, *Wit and the Writing of History* (1988).

10.1   they hailed him 'Pythian Victor' etc.: D./Xiph. reports that N. was saluted in much the same terms at his victory ceremony in Rome on his return from Greece: see further 63.20.5 + n. [= **D.5**].

he pillaged the whole of Greece as if on a military campaign: D./Xiph. here compares the expenses incurred by the cities of Greece in entertaining the emperor and his entourage with the burdens imposed by an invading army, which expected to be supplied with food and equipment and given winter quarters. This had been a standard complaint against Roman armies under the Republic (e.g. LR I, 141; cf. *ILS* 38 = Sherk, *RGE*, 72 = LR I, 134). For the expenditure incurred by cities in entertaining an emperor while on tour in the provinces see 63.2.1n. [= **D.1**]. For N.'s particular rapacity in Greece see Bradley, *Nero*, 189.

11.1 granted all of Greece its freedom: N. granted this privilege in an impressive ceremony at the Isthmian Games at Corinth in 67 (cf. Suet. *N.* 24.2; Pliny, *NH* 4.6.22; Pausanias 7.17.2; Bradley, *Nero*, 145–47; P.A. Gallivan, *Hermes* 101 (1973), 230–34). This freedom meant that Greece (strictly speaking, Achaea) was now liberated from the control of the Roman governor of Macedonia, thus reversing the changes brought in by Cl. (60.24.1 [= **C.12**]), and so was no longer subject to Roman law or Roman taxes: see Sherwin-White, *Citizenship*, 174–89. The emperor Vespasian reversed this measure (Suet. *Vesp.* 8.4; Pausanias 7.17.4). For his political rhetoric N. owed a considerable debt to C. Quinctius Flamininus, who "liberated" Greece in 196 B.C. also at a well-staged ritual at the Isthmian Games at Corinth after the Roman victory in the Second Macedonian War (Livy 33.32; Plut. *Flamininus* 12.13). Part of the text of N.'s speech granting this privilege has been preserved in an honorific decree from Akraiphia in Boeotia (Smallwood 64 = LACTOR 8, no. 46 = Braund 261 = Sherk 71). Another inscription honoured the secretary of the Panachaean League for 'having established firmly the conditions of freedom' (Smallwood 65 = Braund 265 = Sherk 73).

*D.3 HELIUS IN ROME; NERO'S "MARRIAGE" TO SPORUS

A.D. 67

(63.12.1–13.3: Xiphilinus)

12.1–2 Helius: *PIR*[2] H 55; a freedman of Cl., who was on the staff of the procurator of Asia at the very start of N.'s reign (Tac. *A.* 13.1; P.R.C. Weaver, *Familia Caesaris* (1972), 279). After N.'s death, Helius and other unpopular imperial freedmen were paraded through the streets of Rome by his successor Galba and then executed (64.3.4; Plut. *Galba* 17). In general on imperial freedmen under the Julio-Claudians see 60.2.4n. [= **C.2**].

confiscations, exile and executions: D. again concentrates on detrimental actions against the propertied upper class, to which he himself belonged, but here also mentions ordinary people, who were not usually at risk. For details on those who suffered during N.'s reign see Bradley, *Nero*, 185–90. Such acts are common leitmotifs in accounts of 'bad' emperors and are often associated with the emperor's need to raise revenue to sustain his extravagant expenditure: see further 59.18.1n. [= **B.14**].

12.3 Tigellinus: (?) Ofonius Tigellinus (*PIR*[2] O 91), one of the two Praetorian prefects since 62 and a close companion of N. (62.13.3; Tac. *A.* 14.57; 15.37). When an emperor left Rome, he was always accompanied by a detachment of the Praetorian Guard; Tigellinus went with N. to Greece (Suet. *N.* 19.2), while the other prefect, Nymphidius Sabinus, remained in Rome. In general on emperors' bodyguards see Millar, *ERW*, 61–66.

Polycleitus: An imperial freedman (*PIR*[1] P 430), sent by N. to Britain in 60 to mediate between the Roman governor of the province and the equestrian procurator (Tac. *A.* 14.39). One of the most unpopular of N.'s freedmen, he became a proverbially hated figure (cf. Tac. *H.* 2.95; Pliny, *Letters* 6.31.9; Millar, *ERW*, 77).

12.3–4 Calvia Crispinilla: *PIR²* C 363; for her presence among N.'s retinue in Greece see K.R. Bradley, *Illinois Classical Studies* 4 (1979), 152–57. She later helped to organize the revolt of L. Clodius Macer, legate of the legion in Africa, against N. (Plut. *Galba* 6; Tac. *H.* 1.73). For her own estates cf. Braund 750–51.

12.4 keeper of his wardrobe: The wardrobe of all members (male and female) of the imperial family was usually in the charge of male, imperial freedmen rather than females of senatorial rank: cf. *ILS* 1755–1766; Smallwood 186 = Braund 336; G. Boulvert, *Esclaves et affranchis impériaux* (1970), 176–77; S. Treggiari, *PBSR* 43 (1975), 52–53.

13.1 Sporus/'Sabina': N. named Sporus 'Sabina' after his second wife, Poppaea Sabina, on whom see 63.9.5n. [= **D.2**]. After her death N. allegedly castrated and 'married' Sporus, the son of one of his freedmen, even providing Sporus with a dowry (62.28.2–3; Suet. *N.* 28). For an unconvincing attempt to rationalize this marriage as a type of Mithraic initiation rite see Bradley, *Nero*, 161–62. D. fails to make it explicit that N. had by now married a third genuine wife, Statilia Messallina (Suet. *N.* 35.1). She was probably part of N.'s entourage in Greece (Griffin, *Nero*, 285, n. 83). For honours paid to her during the tour of Greece see Smallwood 64 = Braund 261 = Sherk 71.

marriage: For the details of the Roman marriage ceremony see J.P.V.D. Baldson, *Roman Women* (1962), 181–86; S. Treggiari, *Roman Marriage* (1991); for Greek weddings 'Hans Licht', *Sexual Life in Ancient Greece* (1932), 42–56.

13.2 Pythagoras: For N.'s supposed marriage to the freedman Pythagoras at a public banquet in 64 see 62.15.2f; 62.28.3; Tac. *A.* 15.37; Martial 11.6.10. Suet. *N.* 29 erroneously reports that N. 'married' another imperial freedman Doryphorus. The variation in the names of N.'s freedman mate (Sporus, Pythagoras, Doryphorus) and the conflation of the two incidents of the marriage and the bestial rapes suggest that the stories derive not from fact, but from malicious anecdotes: see R.P. Saller, *G&R* 27 (1980), 75–76.

N.'s sexual abuse of young boys and girls: The theme of his sexual enormities continues with the story of N.'s quasi-bestiality (cf. Suet. *N.* 29). His conduct is reminiscent of that part of a *venatio* where condemned criminals were tied to stakes and devoured by wild-beasts (*damnatio ad bestias*): cf. Tac. *A.* 15.44; Garnsey, *SSLP*, 129–31; K.M. Coleman, *JRS* 80 (1990), 44–73.

13.3 he greeted the senators: D./Xiph. here refers to the emperor's morning reception (or *salutatio*), which took place even when the emperor was on tour (Millar, *ERW*, 21–22, 37–38, 209–10).

he flouted convention also in matters of dress: This illustrates that N.'s outrages were social as well as sexual; he failed to behave in the dignified manner of a Roman emperor, and in particular showed little respect for the senators or the people of Rome. For emperors' customary dress in public cf. 59.7.1n. [= **B.5**]; 60.6.9n. [= **C.5**]. G.'s entourage at his procession at the bridge at Baiae also wore flowered tunics, a point noted with disdain by D. (59.17.6 [= **B.13**]). D.'s hostile comments on such improper dress may derive from his own personal experience of, and exasperation at, the undignified and un-Roman dress worn by Caracalla (cf. 78.3.2–3).

those equestrians on the list: D./Xiph. probably uses the expression "on the list" to distinguish those equestrians "with the public horse" (*equites equo publico*) from the rest of the equestrian order (cf. 56.46.2; 61.9.1). The precise distinction between these two groups is a matter of considerable controversy: see T.P. Wiseman, *Historia* 19 (1970), 67–83; cf. Millar, *ERW*, 280–82.

for the first time used saddle-cloths at their annual review: D./ Xiph. is again keen to point out when social customs first came into operation (Introduction, Section 3.4.3; Appendix 2). Aug. had revived the *transvectio equitum*, an annual parade of the equestrian order in Rome (Suet. *Aug.* 38; T.P. Wiseman, *Historia* 19 (1970), 68–70).

*D.4 THE CORINTH CANAL. DEATH OF THE SCRIBONII AND CORBULO   A.D. 67

(63.16.1–17.6: Xiphilinus)

16.1 **Corinth Canal:** cf. Suet. *N.* 19.2; 23.1; 37.3; Philostratus, *Life of Apollonius of Tyana* 4.24 [= Braund 264]; Warmington 133. Without the canal ships had to be dragged across the narrow isthmus of land along a slipway (the *diolkos*) (J.B. Salmon, *Wealthy Corinth* (1984), 136–39; B.R. MacDonald, *JHS* 106 (1986), 191–95). Julius Caesar and G. had both planned to construct a canal across the isthmus (Suet. *DJ* 44.3; id., *G.* 21). For archaeological traces of N.'s canal, obliterated by the construction of the modern canal in 1881–82, see B. Gerster, *BCH* 8 (1884), 225–32, esp. 228.
N. sent for a great number of men from other countries: Jos. *BJ* 3.10.10 confirms that forced labour was used when he reports that 6,000 captives from the Jewish War were brought to work on this project. Work on the canal was abandoned at the end of N.'s reign.

17.2 **Corbulo:** On N.'s famous general see further 59.15.3 + n. [= **B.11**]; 59.20.1–3 + nn. [= **B.15**]; 63.1.2n. [= **D.1**]; 63.6.3n. [= **D.1**]. For the suggestion that Corbulo and the Scribonii, all prominent generals, were put to death for their involvement in the 'conspiracy' of Annius Vinicianus see Griffin, *Nero*, 177–79; Warmington 156–57.
the Sulpicii Scribonii: P. Sulpicius Scribonius Rufus (*PIR*[1] S 219) and P. Sulpicius Scribonius Proculus (*PIR*[1] S 217). Both of these brothers from a very prominent, aristocratic family had held suffect consulships by 56. The former was now commander of the legions in Upper Germany, while the latter commanded the legions in Lower Germany (cf. Smallwood 160 = LACTOR 8, no. 45 = Braund 780; Braund 416). In 58 N. had appointed them both to deal with local problems at Puteoli (Tac. *A.* 13.48) and in 59 or soon afterwards to their legionary commands in Germany (Griffin,

Nero, 116). They had thus been in command in Germany for almost eight years. The emperor's legates held office for much longer spells than the provincial proconsuls who were appointed in the senate for one-year terms (Millar, *REN*, 54–69).

17.3 administered the German provinces: D. is anachronistic in talking about Upper and Lower Germany as provinces; the areas were only constituted as provinces in the 80s: see 59.22.5 + n. [= **B.17**].

17.5 Cenchreae: The port of Corinth on the Saronic Gulf, used by ships approaching from the east: i.e., from the Aegean. Lechaion was Corinth's port on the Corinthian Gulf, used by ships coming from the west. See further J.B. Salmon, *Wealthy Corinth* (1984), 133–47.

long, loose tunic: the *orthostadion*, a Greek loose-fitting gown usually worn by women (cf. Aristophanes, *Lysistrata* 45). It thus reinforces the jibes made about N.'s effeminacy (cf. 62.6.5; 63.13.2 [= **D.3**]), but also underlines N.'s disregard for social conventions (cf. 63.13.3 + n. [= **D.3**]). For N.'s tendency to dress in Greek clothes cf. 63.22.4 [= **D.6**]; Suet. *N.* 51.1. However, a long tunic was the traditional attire for lyre-players: Apollo is often thus attired in sculpture (Bieber, *Theater*, fig. 781) and on coins (Smallwood 144 = Braund 280 = Griffin, *Nero*, pl. 31 = Warmington, pl. III).

*D.5 NERO'S TRIUMPHANT RETURN TO ROME   **A.D. 67–68**

(63.19.1–21.1: Xiphilinus)

19.1 Helius' lightning trip to Greece: For discussion on the speed of sea travel in Roman times see L. Casson, *Ships and Seamanship in the Ancient World* (1971), 292–96; R.P. Duncan-Jones, *Structure and Scale in the Roman Economy* (1990), 7–29.

a major conspiracy was forming against N. in Rome: This is the only reference in our ancient sources to this particular conspiracy in Rome. The two major conspiracies against N. to date, led by Piso and Annius Vinicianus respectively, had already been crushed (Griffin, *Nero* 166–80; Warmington 135–41, 156–57). For speculation that Helius may have invented it because he was alarmed by the first signs of revolt in Gaul (on which see 63.22 [= **D.6**]), see Griffin, *Nero*, 180.

19.2 the fact that some people had prayed for his death was the cause of their destruction: The emperors frequently used this as a charge to dispose of potential threats to their rule (cf. 57.22.4a; 59.8.1 [= **B.6**]; Jos. *AJ* 18.187.

20.1–5 N.'s triumphal procession: cf. Suet. *N.* 25, with further details, especially that N. held similar processions at Naples (scene of his début as a performer: cf. 63.2.3n. [= **D.1**]), Antium (his birth-place: Suet. *N.* 6.1) and Alba Longa (a favourite rural retreat: M.E. Blake, *Roman Construction in Italy* (1959), 134–38). The ceremony in Rome was clearly modelled on, and came close to parodying, the traditional Roman triumph in terms of its route, the parade of the spoils of victory, the placards announcing the scenes of the victories, N.'s triumphal dress (cf. 59.3.5n. [= **B.3**]), the soldiers, members of the equestrian order and senators accompanying the victor and the participation of the entire citizen body in the ceremony. But there were some clear differences to emphasize that it was an artistic, not a military, triumph: it imitated the processions of victorious Greek athletes through their home towns (on which see E.N. Gardiner, *Greek Athletic Sports and Festivals* (1910), 76–78) and ended appropriately not at the temple of Jupiter on the Capitol, but at the temple of Apollo on the Palatine (Griffin, *Nero*, 163 and n. 130).

20.1 **a part of the wall was breached and a section of the gates knocked down:** For 'iselastic' triumphs, at which Greek victors entered their home cities in triumph by breaching a hole in the city wall, see Plut. *Convivial Questions* 2.5.2.

20.3 **Aug.'s triumphal chariot:** This shows that a repository of equipment for imperial ceremonials had already developed; such equipment was kept in the *aedes tensarium* on the Capitol along with the wagons (*tensae*) for parading the sacred images of gods (cf. Smallwood 296 = Braund 532); for an imperial freedman in charge of the elephants used for imperial processions cf. *ILS* 1578 = Sherk 181.

wearing a robe of purple embroidered with gold: i.e., wearing the traditional *toga picta* of a triumphant Roman general (cf. 59.7.1n. [= **B.5**]).

crowned with a garland of wild olive: i.e., the crown of an Olympic victor (cf. 63.9.3n. [= **D.2**]).

the Pythian laurel: i.e., the crown awarded to victors in the Pythian Games at Delphi (cf. 63.9.3n. [= **D.2**]).

Diodorus the lyre-player: cf. 63.8.4n. [= **D.2**].

20.4 **the city was wreathed in garlands etc.:** cf. 63.4.1 + n. [= **D.1**].

20.5 **the whole population shouted out in unison, 'Olympic victor, hurrah!' etc.:** It had become customary for crowds to acclaim the Roman emperor or members of his family whenever they appeared in public with short laudatory chants, or acclamations (C. Roueché, *JRS* 74 (1984), 181–89). A papyrus (EJ 379 = Braund 557) records the same cry of "hurrah", used by a crowd at Alexandria watching Germanicus receive ambassadors from the city.

"Nero Heracles", "Nero Apollo": N. was often associated with these particular gods. At his birth he was allegedly touched by the sun's (i.e., Apollo's) rays (Suet. *N.* 6.1); for a dedication from Athens to 'Imperator Caesar Augustus Nero, the new Apollo' see Smallwood 145 = LACTOR 8, no. 41 = Braund 281. During N.'s childhood the skin of a snake had been found in his bed, which he wore enclosed in a golden bracelet (Suet. *N.* 6.4); this story probably grew out of N.'s association with Hercules, who was famous for strangling snakes as a boy, as depicted on a wall-painting from the House of the Vettii, Pompeii (R. Brilliant, *Pompeii A.D. 79* (1979), 210). These associations are best seen not as indicators that N. was trying to establish for himself divine cult, but rather as extravagant compliments to his prowess at athletics (Heracles) and lyre-playing (Apollo) (Griffin, *Nero*, 215–20; Bradley, *Nero*, 288–90).

"victor in all the great festivals": see further 63.8.3n. [= **D.2**].

20.6 **the expressions they used:** D. is keen to point out that he is here relying on an eyewitness account, perhaps Cluvius Rufus, the senatorial historian, on whom see 63.8.1n. [= **D.2**].

do not disgrace my history, but enhance its dignity: D. believed firmly in the dignity of his history, for which dignified language was fundamental: see Introduction, Sections 3.3 and 3.4.2.

21.1 Egyptian obelisk: Aug. had brought the obelisk from Heliopolis in Egypt and set it up on the central reservation (*spina*) of the circus arena in 10 B.C. (Humphrey, *Circuses*, 269–72). On the Circus Maximus in general see 63.8.2n. [= **D.2**].

N. as charioteer: A leitmotif of D.'s account of N.: see further 63.1.1n. [= **D.1**].

*D.6 REVOLTS IN JUDAEA, BRITAIN AND GAUL; REBELLION OF VINDEX   A.D. 68

(63.22.1–26.1: Xiphilinus; Zonaras; Valesian Excerpts)

22.1 a rebellion of the Jews: On this revolt and for N.'s reaction to it see Josephus, *BJ* 2.499–558; 3.1–8; Tac. *H.* 5.1–13, esp. 10; Suet. *Vesp.* 4.5–6; 5.6; Warmington 100–7; Smallwood, *Jews*, 293–312; M. Goodman, *The Ruling Class of Judaea* (1987), 152–75. The revolt was not fully put down until the fall of Masada in 73. For coins struck by the rebels with Hebrew legends see Smallwood 68 = Braund 267. For the suggestion that it was caused by Cl.'s re-annexation of Judaea as a Roman province and by a succession of unsuccessful governors see Griffin, *Nero*, 101, 233.

he sent Vespasian to deal with them: For the future emperor Vespasian's command in Judaea see Tac. *H.* 5.10; Suet. *Vesp.* 4–5.

the inhabitants of Britain and Gaul, burdened by taxation, were becoming restive: If this is correct, it is the only evidence for trouble in 68 in Britain, one of the provinces that remained loyal to N. D./Zonaras may have telescoped the chronology here, and be referring to the outbreak of dynastic trouble among the Brigantes in 69, which required the intervention of the Roman governor M. Vettius Bolanus (Tac. *H.* 3.45; Frere, *Britannia*, 82–83). In general on Roman taxation of the provinces see A.H.M. Jones, *The Roman Economy* (1974), 164–85; K. Hopkins, *JRS* 70 (1980), 101–25, esp. 116–24; P.A. Brunt, *JRS* 71 (1981), 161–72 [= *RIT*, 324–46].

22.1[2] C. Iulius Vindex: *PIR*[2] I 628, a Romanized Gaul from a leading Aquitanian family, which had obtained Roman citizenship from Julius Caesar. His father had probably been admitted to the Roman senate by Cl. in 48 along with other members of the aristocracy of central Gaul (Tac. *A.* 11.23–25; Smallwood 369 = Braund 570 = Sherk 55; M. Griffin, *CQ* 32 (1982), 404–18). Vindex, himself a senator, was at the time of his revolt governor of one of the Gallic provinces (Plut. *Galba* 4.2; Tac. *H.* 1.16) – probably Gallia Lugdunensis (Bradley, *Nero*, 245–46). For his revolt see Tac. *H.* 1.51; Suet. *N.* 40–44; id., *Galba* 9.2; 11; Plut. *Galba* 4.2–6.4; P.A. Brunt, *Latomus* 18 (1959), 531–59 [= *RIT*, 9–32]; Warmington 158–62;

Griffin, *Nero*, 180–82. Vindex revolted in mid-March 68, since N. received news of it on the anniversary of his mother Agrippina's death (i.e., sometime between 19–23 March) (Suet. *N.* 40.4). The revolt was not a Gallic nationalist movement, as D./Xiph. claims. D./Xiph. may have been influenced towards such an interpretation by the Gallo-Germanic uprising led by Julius Civilis in 69 (Tac. *H.* 4.12ff.), which Tacitus (*H.* 4.59) describes as a 'Empire of the Gauls' (*imperium Galliarum*). Rather, it was a revolt led by a Roman senator against an emperor who had increasingly exasperated the senatorial order (so Brunt, art. cit.). For coins struck by Vindex with anti-Neronian themes see Smallwood 70 = LACTOR 8, no. 47 = Braund 288; Smallwood 72 = Braund 290; Sutherland, *RHC*, 103–06; C.M. Kraay, *Num. Chron.* series vi, 9 (1949), 129–49.

22.3–6 D./Xiph. emphasizes the importance of Vindex's revolt by incorporating a full speech, a rare event in the Julio-Claudian section of his narrative (see Introduction, Section 3.4.2). The speech reflects the major themes of Vindex's propaganda against N., many of which recur on the coinage issued by Vindex (Brunt, art. cit., 533–34; Kraay, art. cit.). It also draws together in one place many of the criticisms implicitly levelled by D. against N. earlier in his account of the reign, most of all those points raised in his lengthy rhetorical critique of N. at 63.9.1–6 [= **D.2**]. This repetition of material could be the result of careless summarizing of D. by Xiph., but was more likely designed by D. to underline the strength and nature of the opposition to N. at this stage of his reign.

22.3 committed incest with, and killed, his own mother: N. had allegedly arranged Agrippina's murder in 59 (61.12–14; Tac. *A.* 14.1–13; Suet. *N.* 34.1–4). For their supposed incest cf. Tac. *A.* 14.2; Suet. *N.* 28.2.

22.4 Sporus and Pythagoras: For these 'spouses' of N. see 63.13.2 + n. [= **D.3**].

22.4–5 N.'s stage costume and rôles: For his footwear and his various rôles in Greek tragedies see 63.9.4 + n. [= **D.2**]; for his fondness for the *orthostadion*, a Greek loose-fitting tunic, see 63.17.5 + n. [= **D.4**].

22.5 N.'s life as a mirror of Greek myth: For attempts, not wholly successful, to substantiate this assertion see B. Baldwin, *Mnemosyne* 32 (1979), 380–81; R.M. Frazer Jr., *Classical Journal* 62 (1966), 17–20.

22.6 titles held by Aug. and Cl.: D./Xiph. here implicitly praises these two emperors, in contrast to Tib., G. and N. (see further Introduction, Section 4.3). Aug.'s full title was Imperator Caesar Divi f. Augustus (e.g. EJ 40, 61 = Braund 43, 28); Cl.'s was Ti. Claudius Caesar Augustus Germanicus (e.g. Smallwood 99, 43b = Braund 217, 210b). Cl., unlike Aug., spurned the use of *Imperator* as part of his name, but was content to list the number of his salutations as *Imperator* among his titles: see 60.8.7n. [= **C.6**].

23.1 these words of Vindex struck a chord: Zonaras in his summary of D. adds the detail that Vindex made the soldiers swear to do everything in the name of the senate and people of Rome, but he may have merely duplicated the action of Verginius Rufus, as reported by Xiph. at 63.25.2–3 [= **D.6**]. The authority of the senate and people of Rome was widely proclaimed on the coins issued by Vindex and Galba (Smallwood 70, 72 = Braund 288, 290; R. Talbert, *AJAH* 2 (1977), 69–85).

Ser. Sulpicius Galba: The future emperor, who assumed power after the fall of N. For his earlier career see 60.8.7n. [= **C.6**]. Following his period as commander of the legions in Upper Germany, he had taken part in the invasion of Britain and was then proconsul of Africa "outside the lot" under Cl., who also granted him triumphal decorations (*ornamenta triumphalia*) and various priesthoods (Suet. *Galba* 7–8; Plut. *Galba* 3).

he was governor of Spain: He had been legate of Hispania Tarraconensis for eight years (i.e., since 60) when Vindex's rebellion broke out (Suet. *Galba* 8–9). As governor of Tarraconensis, he had command of the only legion in the Iberian peninsula, *Legio VI Victrix*, stationed at modern León. But he proceeded to recruit another legion (*VII Galbiana*, later renamed *VII Gemina*) from among the numerous Roman citizens in Spain (Suet. *Galba* 10.2). D./Xiph. fails to mention that Galba's revolt also had the support of Otho, the governor of neighbouring Lusitania (Tac. *H.* 1.13.4; Suet. *Otho* 4.1), and Caecina Alienus, quaestor of the third Spanish province, Baetica (Tac. *H.* 1.53).

24.1 **Rufus:** L. Verginius Rufus, consul in 63 and later suffect consul in 69 and consul for a third time in 97 (*RE* 8A² (1958), 1536–43; cf. Plin. *Letters* 2.1; 6.10; 9.19). He had only taken over as commander of the four legions in Upper Germany in 67. This incident illustrates the rôle of the legate of Upper Germany in maintaining order in the Gallic provinces, which had no legionary garrison (Griffin, *Nero*, 181). D. is anachronistic in calling him the "governor of Germany" (59.22.5n. [= **B.17**]; 63.17.3n. [= **D.6**]). **Vesontio:** modern Besançon.

24.2–4 **a conference at which, it was assumed, they came to an agreement:** For this alleged alliance see Plut. *Galba* 6.3; but D./Xiph. here adds a note of scepticism. Tac. *H.* 4.69.2 and Plin. *Letters* 9.19.1 both suggest that Rufus willingly led his army against Vindex and fail to mention any agreement between the two. However, neither Tac. nor Pliny attribute the attack on Vindex to a spontaneous decision on the part of Rufus' troops, as D./Xiph. does here; for arguments in favour of Tacitus' and Pliny's version see Griffin, *Nero*, 286–87, n. 94; but for a partial vindication of D. see P.A. Brunt, *Latomus* 18 (1959), 537–38 [= *RIT*, 14–15]. For further discussion see Syme, *Tac.*, 179; J.B. Hainsworth, *Historia* 11 (1962), 86–96; D.C.A. Shotter, *CQ* 17 (1967), 370–81.

25.1 **Rufus refused to accept the position of emperor:** cf. Pliny, *Letters* 9.19.1; Plut. *Galba* 6 (who has Rufus offered the position both before and after the battle) and the modern works cited in 63.24.2–4n. For a vow in return for the 'safety and victory' of Rufus see Smallwood 71 = Braund 289 = Sherk 79a.

25.1–2 **cast down the images of N.; .... inscribed the words on one of his standards:** An image (*imago*) of the emperor was carried by the image-bearer (*imaginifer*) at the front of each legion; it bore a portrait of the emperor, with a plaque beneath listing his various titles. In addition, the standard-bearers (*signiferi*) carried the various legionary standards: the silver or gilded-silver eagle, which all legions carried, and the additional distinctive standards peculiar to each legion. The image of the emperor and the other standards were an important focus for the loyalty of the troops and were paid quasi-divine honours: see further Webster, *Army*, 133–39 and pl. X.

25.3 this he did either because he did not think it right for the army to bestow supreme power ..... or because he was utterly high-minded: This is another example of how D. is keen to speculate on motivations (see further Introduction, Section 4.1). He himself believed that it was a travesty for power to be bestowed upon an emperor by the army or praetorian guard: see 73.11.3–6, where D. comments on the accession of Didius Julianus in 193.

26.1 N.'s reaction to Vindex's revolt: See further 63.26.3 + n. [= **D.7**]. N. paid frequent visits to Naples (63.2.3n. [= **D.1**]); for his interest in athletic competitions see Suet. *N.* 12.3. For other occasions on which he sent letters to spare his voice see Suet. *N.* 25.3; for his weak voice and his elaborate voice training see Suet. *N.* 20.1; Plin. *NH* 34.50.166.

*D.7 NERO'S REACTION TO THE REVOLT OF VINDEX AND GALBA
A.D. 68

(63.26.3–27.1a: Xiphilinus; Zonaras)

26.3 N. was expecting to defeat Vindex: Vindex, as governor of a Gallic province without a legionary garrison (Tac. *H.* 1.16), had no Roman troops to support his revolt and N. had no reason to doubt the loyalty of the urban cohorts stationed at Lugdunum (Lyons) or of Verginius Rufus, the recently appointed commander of the legions of Upper Germany (Griffin, *Nero*, 181).

he had a good excuse for levying fines and ordering some executions: N. could gain much-needed revenue by fining or condemning to death those Gauls who had supported the revolt, hence gaining their property (cf. Suet. *N.* 40.4).

26.3 he dedicated the shrine of Sabina, the goddess Venus: N.'s second wife, Poppaea Sabina, on whom see 63.9.5n. [= **D.2**], had died in 65 and then been embalmed and buried in the Mausoleum of Aug. (62.28.1; Tac. *A.* 16.6). Dedications were made to her as a goddess (Smallwood 149 = Braund 287) and her deification was commemorated on coins minted in Greece (Smallwood 148 = Braund 285). Members of the imperial family were often worshipped in association with Olympian divinities (i.e., Sabina-Venus): cf. Drusilla-Venus (59.11.2 + n. [= **B.9**]), Nero-Apollo, Nero-Hercules (63.20.5 + n. [= **D.5**]). The exact site of the shrine of Sabina in Rome is unknown.

26.4 the funds confiscated from women: D./Xiph. may be referring to the activities of Calvia Crispinilla and Helius reported at 63.12.4 [= **D.3**]. This hostile anti-Neronian version may cloak the fact that women might well have contributed funds voluntarily towards the cult of a female member of the divine imperial family; the cult of Livia was an important focus for Roman matrons (N. Purcell, *PCPhS* 32 (1986), 78–105, esp. 93).

N.'s little jokes: For more of these see Suet. *N.* 26.1–27.1.

I shall pass over most of them, but I shall recount one: D. is again selective in the material that he discusses: see Introduction, Section 3.3.

he summoned the leading senators and equestrians and discussed the water-organ: For this anecdote cf. Suet. *N.* 41.2, where N. hastily discusses the situation in Gaul before expatiating on the water-organ. This episode took place before the emperor's advisers (or *consilium*), a body which comprised both senators and equestrians and even imperial freedmen (Crook, *CP*, 46, comparing it to Tac. *A.* 15.25, where N. summons his *consilium* to discuss the Armenian problem in 63). A very similar anecdote was told against G. (59.5.5 + n. [= **B.3**]). For N.'s proficiency on the water-organ cf. Suet. *N.* 54; for further details on this instrument see Vitruvius 10.8; J.E. Scott in *New Oxford History of Music* I (1957), 408–10 and pl. XI (b); G. Wille, *Musica romana* (1967), 203–10 (in German).

26.5 D. here as usual includes a group of omens just before the downfall of a major figure: see Introduction, Section 3.4.1 and Table 2.

on the Alban Mount: The Alban Mount was the main peak of the Alban hills, thirteen miles south-east of Rome, on which was located the sanctuary of Jupiter Latiaris (= the protector of Latium) where the annual Latin Festival was put on by the Roman consuls (39.30.4; 54.29.7). D. reports a number of omens that allegedly took place here (fr. 12.6; 39.15.1; 39.20.1; 47.40.4; 50.8.6; 54.29.7). An imperial villa, much redeveloped by Domitian, lay at the foot of the mountain (67.1.2; M.E. Blake, *Roman Construction in Italy* (1959), 134–38).

Lycia: On the south coast of Asia Minor (modern Turkey); see 60.17.3n. [= **C.9**].

27.1 **Galba proclaimed emperor:** cf. Tac. *H.* 1.4; Suet. *Galba* 11; Plut. *Galba* 7.2. The exact sequence of events between N.'s return to Italy in mid-March and his death on 9 June is problematic: for plausible reconstructions see Griffin, *Nero*, 181–82; Warmington 159–60. For Galba's supporters see R. Syme, *Historia* 31 (1982), 460–83 [= *RP* IV, 115–39].

Rufus had deserted him: Whether Verginius Rufus remained loyal to N. is extremely problematic: see further 63.24.2–4n. [= **D.6**].

made preparations: N. suddenly assumed the consulship (Suet. *N.* 43.2), had Galba declared a public enemy by the senate (Plut. *Galba* 5.4), summoned troops from Illyricum, Germany and Britain to northern Italy and recruited a new legion (*I Adiutrix*) (Tac. *H.* 1.6). For further details on his military preparations see Griffin, *Nero*, 181; G.E.F. Chilver, *Historical Commentary on Tacitus' Histories I–II* (1979), 6–7.

Rubrius Gallus: C. Rubrius Gallus, suffect consul before 68 (*PIR*[1] R 94). He led a second force to north Italy against the rebels (Chilver, *Commentary on Tacitus' Histories*, 11–12).

27.1a **Petronius:** P. Petronius Turpilianus, consul in 61 (*PIR*[1] P 233). N. had sent him to Britain in 61 to mop up after the revolt of Boudica, for which he was rewarded with a triumphal decorations (*ornamenta triumphalia*) (Tac. *A.* 14.39; 15.72). D.'s claim here that Turpilianus joined Galba is inconsistent with the fact that Galba, after becoming emperor, had him executed (Tac. *H.* 1.6; Plut. *Galba* 15.2; 17.3). For a possible compromise see Griffin, *Nero*, 182.

*D.8 THE SENATE TURN AGAINST NERO; NERO'S FLIGHT FROM ROME AND DEATH; GALBA DECLARED EMPEROR   A.D. 68

(63.27.2–29.3: Xiphilinus; Zonaras)

27.2 N.'s plan to sail to Alexandria: cf. Plut. *Galba* 2.1; Suet. *N.* 47.2, adding that N. wondered whether to ask Galba to make him prefect of Egypt; Griffin, *Nero*, 182 and 287, n. 97.

27.2b the senate removes N.'s guard: Zonaras is unclear whether the senate removed the emperor's Praetorian Guard or his German bodyguard, and also seems to have garbled D.'s text, since the senate had no power to remove an emperor's bodyguard; rather, the senators must have persuaded the Praetorian Guard to abandon N. On the emperor's bodyguard in general see Millar, *ERW*, 61–66. For N.'s final attempt to persuade some officers of the Praetorian Guard to accompany him on his escape see Suet. *N.* 47.1. The Guard was now effectively under the sole control of Nymphidius Sabinus, who was instrumental in getting Galba proclaimed emperor (Plut. *Galba* 2.1); the other prefect, Ofonius Tigellinus (63.12.3n. [= **D.3**]), had supported N., but was now in hiding (Plut. *Galba* 2.2; 14.2).

the senate entered the camp: i.e., the camp of the Praetorian Guard, located on the Viminal on the north-east fringes of the city (58.4.2n. [= **A.3**]). If this report is correct, it was an astonishing site for a meeting of the senate (Talbert, *Senate*, 120).

and declared him a public enemy: cf. Suet. *N.* 49.2; for the senate's right to declare public enemies see Talbert, *Senate*, 356 (with further examples).

appointed Galba emperor: cf. Suet. *Galba* 11; Tac. *H.* 1.4. Galba had previously only allowed his legions to salute him as 'legate of the senate and people of Rome' (Suet. *Galba* 10.1, 11).

27.3–29.2 N.'s escape from Rome: cf. Suet. *N.* 48–49 (with slight variations). D.'s version is fuller in circumstantial detail, pathos and rhetorical flourish than Suet.'s. For other examples of D.'s narrative skills cf. 58.9–12 [= **A.7**] (the fall of Sej.); 59.17 [= **B.13**] (G.'s 'triumph' at the bridge at Baiae). Xiph. here probably gives more or less D.'s full text, as he does elsewhere for climactic episodes (e.g. Sej.'s fall and G.'s triumph at Baiae).

27.3 sleeping in some gardens: D./Xiph. means that he was spending the night at one of the suburban villas (or *horti* = gardens) on the outskirts of Rome, on which see 59.21.2n. [= **B.15**]: possibly the Horti Serviliani (the Servilian Gardens), since this was where N. had gone to try to persuade some officers of the Praetorian Guard to flee with him (Suet. *N.* 47.1).

Phaon: Phaon was one of N.'s leading imperial freedmen and probably the head of the Palatine bureau dealing with financial accounts (*a rationibus*) (P.R.C. Weaver, *Familia Caesaris* (1972), 259, 289; Millar, *ERW*, 77). His estate lay four miles north-east of Rome between the Via Nomentana and the Via Salaria (Suet. *N.* 48.1). The incident provides good evidence for imperial freedmen owning substantial estates: cf. the property of Pallas, freedman under Cl. (Plin. *Letters* 7.29; 8.6).

Epaphroditus: *PIR²* E 69; another imperial freedman and the head of the Palatine bureau dealing with written legal petitions to the emperor (*a* *libellis*) (Tac. *A*. 15.55; Epictetus 1.1.20; 1.26.11–12; Weaver, *Familia Caesaris*, 261; Millar, *ERW*, 77–78). He remained prominent until his exile and eventual execution under Domitian on the grounds that he had not defended N. (67.14.4; Suet. *Dom*. 14.4). For the posts *a rationibus* and *a libellis* see 60.2.4–5n. [= **C.2**]

Sporus: See 63.13.1–2 + n. [= **D.3**].

he was recognized and addressed as emperor: Further incidental evidence for the customary greeting that citizens formally made whenever they met the emperor: cf. 59.7.6 [= **B.5**]. Suet. *N*. 48.2 adds the detail that the traveller who recognized him was a retired member of the Praetorian Guard.

28.3 **he had once taken great delight in the enormous size of his retinue of attendants, but was now hiding with just three freedmen:** D. here, as elsewhere, resorts to ironic antithesis to highlight the dramatic fall of a once powerful figure: cf. 58.11.1–2 [= **A.8**]; 59.30.1a [= **B.23**]; Introduction, Section 3.4.2. For N.'s massive retinue on his tour of Greece see 63.8.3–4 [= **D.2**].

28.4 **such was the drama that the divine power had prepared for him:** For D.'s interest in divine power (*daimonion*) see Introduction, Section 3.4.3.

matricides and outcasts: For N. playing such rôles from Greek tragedy cf. 63.9.4 + n. [= **D.2**].

28.5 **"It is to a cruel death that I am being summoned by my wife and father":** D./ Xiph. has N. quote a line from a lost Greek tragedy (A. Nauck, *Tragicorum Graecorum Fragmenta* (2nd ed., 1964), 839); the speaker is clearly Oedipus, referring to Jocasta, his wife and mother, and Laius, his father. The same line is quoted in a slightly different version by Suet. *N*. 46.3.

28.5 **N.'s famous boiled drink:** "Boiled" is a translation of an emendation of the manuscript reading. It makes D./Xiph.'s text tally with the same remark reported at Suet. *N*. 48.3. N. invented the drink called *decocta*, i.e., water that had been boiled and then cooled by plunging it into snow (Pliny, *NH* 31.23.40; Martial 14.116–118). For the use of snow by the wealthy to cool drinks in later periods see F. Braudel, *The Structures of Everyday Life* (Engl. tr., 1981), 231.

29.1 **some even wearing felt caps as though they had just been freed:** cf. Suet. *N*. 57.1. Such egg-shaped caps (called *pilei*) were worn by manumitted slaves, to signify that they had recently won their freedom (S. Treggiari, *Roman Freedmen in the late Republic* (1969), 14; T. Wiedemann, *Slavery* (G&R New Surveys in the Classics, 19; 1987), fig. 7). For further details on the manumission of slaves see Crook, *Law & Life*, 43–44, 50–55. By this symbolic gesture the Roman people articulated their joy at being liberated from the tyranny of N.'s last years; for the rhetoric of liberty in the early Principate see Wirszubski, *Libertas*, 124–71.

the Roman people voted Galba the prerogatives of imperial power: Zonaras in his summary of this same section (see Loeb. ed. of Dio, VIII, 190–91) and again at 63.29.6 has the senate vote Galba these prerogatives. The normal pattern was that the senate first decreed these privileges, which were then confirmed by laws passed by the Roman people in the assembly. On emperors' accessions see further 60.1.4n. [= **C.1**].

29.2 **"I really am alone; I have neither a friend nor a foe"**: cf. Suet. *N.* 47.3, where N. utters it just before leaving Rome.

"what an artist perishes with me!": For N.'s famous last remark (in Latin *Qualis artifex pereo!*) cf. Suet. *N.* 49.1.

29.3 **length of N.'s life and reign**: For D.'s interest in computing the length of emperors' lives and reigns see further 59.30.1n. [= **B.23**] and Introduction, Section 3.4.1. Zonaras' summary of D. gives different figures from those of Xiph.: 30 years, 5 months and 20 days for N.'s life, 13 years and 8 months minus 2 days for his reign. N. was born on 15 December 37 (Suet. *N.* 6.1), became emperor on 13 October 54 (see the *Acts of the Arval Brethren* for 58: Smallwood 21, lines 9ff.) and died probably on 9 June 68 (P.A. Gallivan, *Historia* 23 (1974), 318). These dates confirm Zonaras' figures for his reign, but not for his life: the correct length of his life should be 30 years, 5 months and 25 days. Suet. *N.* 57.1 is also incorrect in asserting that N. died in his thirty-second year.

descendant of Aeneas and Aug.: N. was the last of the Julio-Claudian dynasty of emperors. Julius Caesar claimed divine ancestry, tracing his family back to Venus, mother of Aeneas (S. Weinstock, *Divus Julius* (1970), 80–87). Aug. also advertised his descent from Aeneas and Venus (Syme, *RR* 462–63; Zanker, *Power of Images*, 201–210, 195–201). For D.'s tendency to compare emperors see further Introduction, Section 4.3.

the laurels planted by Livia and her breed of white chickens: In 37 B.C. an eagle had allegedly dropped a white hen carrying a laurel branch into the lap of Aug.'s wife, Livia, at her villa at Prima Porta. As a result, the area around this villa on the outskirts of Rome came to be known as "White Hens" (*ad Gallinas Albas*). Livia planted the laurel sprig, which flourished and provided sufficient laurel for all the triumphal wreaths worn by the imperial family on ceremonial occasions until it withered in 68. The hen gave birth to a brood of chickens, which also flourished until 68 (48.52.3; Plin. *NH* 15.40.136–37; Suet. *Galba* 1; N. Purcell, *PCPhS* 32 (1986), 90; M.B. Flory, *Classical Journal* 84 (1989), 343–56). White hens were symbolically associated with those favoured by Fortune (Juv. *Sat.* 13.141). Just as their appearance was seen in 37 B.C. as an omen of the future greatness of Aug.'s family, so their demise in 68 heralded the end of the Julio-Claudian family as the ruling dynasty of Rome. For D.'s interest in Fortune see further Introduction, Section 3.4.3.

APPENDICES

APPENDIX 1. EMPERORS DURING DIO'S LIFETIME

Marcus Aurelius + Lucius Verus, joint emperors	7 Mar. 161 – Jan. 169
Marcus Aurelius, sole emperor	Jan. 169 – 31 Dec. 176
Marcus Aurelius + Commodus, joint emperors	1 Jan. 177 – 17 Mar. 180
Commodus, sole emperor	17 Mar. 180 – 31 Dec. 192
Pertinax	1 Jan. – 28 Mar. 193
Didius Julianus	28 Mar. – 1 June 193
Septimius Severus	1 June 193 – 28 Jan. 198
Septimius Severus + Caracalla, joint emperors	28 Jan. 198 – Dec. 210
Septimius Severus + Caracalla + Geta, joint emperors	Dec. 210 – 4 Feb. 211
Caracalla + Geta, joint emperors	4 Feb. – 26 Dec. 211
Caracalla, sole emperor	26 Dec. 211 – 8 Apr 217
Macrinus	8 Apr. 217 – 8 June 218
Elagabalus	8 June 218 – 12 Feb. 222
Severus Alexander	12 Feb. 222 – 21 Mar. 235

N.B. It is unclear whether Dio outlived Severus Alexander; for the view that he did see M. Eisman, *Latomus* 36 (1977), 657–73.

APPENDIX 2. DIO ON THE ORIGIN OF ROMAN INSTITUTIONS AND CUSTOMS: BOOKS 57–63

(This is intended to supplement the incomplete list in Millar, *Dio*, Appendix IV).

A. CUSTOMS STILL IN FORCE

57.8.4	oath sworn on 1 Jan. to uphold all acts of past and present emperors
57.15.4	wives of senators accustomed to use covered litters (point repeated at 60.2.3)
57.17.6	senators when ill allowed into the senate-house on a litter
57.22.5	those debarred from fire and water unable to make will
58.20.4	formal election of magistrates before assemblies of Roman people just as is done today
59.7.8	first use of cushions and Thessalian hats by senators at games
59.8.6	G. abolished the custom of the presiding consul being able to determine which senior senator should vote first; G. established that

all senators should vote in strict order of seniority based on the order in which they had held office.

59.9.1   Tib. not included in oath to support acts of past and present emperors sworn by senators on 1 Jan.

59.9.5   change in rules as to who was entitled to wear the *latus clavus*

59.14.6   area of Rome still known as Gaianum since this was where G. practised his chariot-driving

59.20.7   division of Africa into 2 commands: the proconsul of Africa now separate from the legionary legate

60.2.3   the first use of covered chair by the emperor, a custom by D.'s time extended to ex-consuls

60.2.3   Aug., Tib. had been carried in litters just as women are carried today

60.3.2–3   Cl. institutes that soldiers be present at the emperor's banquets

60.4.6   Cl. in 41 removed G.'s name from the list of emperors mentioned in oaths and prayers

60.7.3–4   separate seating instituted for senators in Circus

60.11.5   Ostia harbour still called Portus

60.19.3   custom of masters exchanging dress with slaves at Saturnalia still prevalent

60.25.8   Cl. restored fifth day of Saturnalia, which had been designated but later abolished by G.

?60.31.8   senatorial decree passed in 49 permitting Romans to marry their nieces, previously impossible (D. does not specify if this was still in force or not.)

61.17.1–2   the gymnasia which N. built on estates inherited from his (poisoned) aunt at Baiae and Ravenna still flourishing in D.'s day

63.13.3   equestrians first used saddle-cloths at their annual review (*transvectio*)

B. CUSTOMS NO LONGER PREVALENT

57.23.5   restricted rôle of procurators in administration of provinces under Tib.; now their powers very much enhanced

59.7.7   (?temporary) return to custom of allowing spectators to turn up to games barefoot: G. returns to the practice prevalent under Aug., but which had been abolished by Tib.

59.13.1   oath-taking on 1 Jan. differed in D.'s day from G.'s reign

59.14.2   (temporary) return to former custom of 2 praetors chosen by lot being in charge of *ludi circenses*

59.24.4   senators (temporarily) return to custom prevalent under Aug. of leaving money at chair of G. on Capitol

60.3.2–3   indiscriminate searching of banquet guests, instituted by Cl., ended by Vespasian

60.6.3   Cl. (temporarily) abolished custom (prevalent under Aug. and G.) of people bringing gifts to the emperor and naming him as heir in will if sons still alive

60.10.2   Cl. stopped practice of having speeches of Aug. and Tib. read out in the senate on 1 Jan.

60.25.1–2 Cl. (temporarily) returned to earlier practice of just one member of each magisterial college swearing the oath on 1 Jan. Followed for several years.

60.25.4–5 Cl. in an attempt to stop senators' escaping from charges of extortion returns to earlier custom of magistrates' not being allowed to hold a second political office immediately on retirement from a first. Now in disuse.

SUGGESTIONS FOR FURTHER READING

A. CASSIUS DIO

F.G.B. Millar, *A Study of Cassius Dio* (1964) (with review by G.W. Bowersock, *Gnomon* 37 (1965), 469–74)

T.D. Barnes, 'The composition of Cassius Dio's *Roman History*', *Phoenix* 38 (1984), 240–55

J.W. Rich, 'Dio on Augustus' in *History as Text. The Writing of Ancient History* (ed. Averil Cameron, 1989), 86–110

J.C. Edmondson, 'Dio on the Principate: Tiberius to Nero' (forthcoming)

For the period in which Dio lived see also A.R. Birley, *The African Emperor: Septimius Severus* (rev. ed., 1988); for the literary culture of his age see G.W. Bowersock, *Greek Sophists in the Roman Empire* (1969); B.P. Reardon, *Courants littéraires grecs des IIe. et IIIe. siècles après J.-C.* (1971).

B. THE JULIO-CLAUDIAN PERIOD (A.D. 14–68)

GENERAL

Cambridge Ancient History. X. The Early Principate (1934) (A completely new edition is in preparation.)

C.M. Wells, *The Roman Empire* (1984)

A. Garzetti, *From Tiberius to the Antonines* (1974)

H.H. Scullard, *From the Gracchi to Nero* (5th ed., 1982)

P. Garnsey and R. Saller, *The Early Principate: Augustus to Trajan* (*Greece & Rome, New Surveys* 15) (1982)

T.E.J. Wiedemann, *The Julio-Claudian Emperors: A.D. 14–70* (1989)

C.H.V. Sutherland, *Roman History and Coinage, 44 B.C.–A.D. 69* (1987)

There is also much useful discussion of the period in R. Syme, *Tacitus* (2 vols., 1958) and M.T. Griffin, *Seneca: a philosopher in politics* (1976).

DETAILED STUDIES OF INDIVIDUAL REIGNS

R. Seager, *Tiberius* (1972)

B. Levick, *Tiberius the Politician* (1976)

A.A. Barrett, *Caligula: the corruption of power* (1989)

J.P.D.V. Balsdon, *The Emperor Gaius (Caligula)* (1934)

A. Ferrill, *Caligula: emperor of Rome* (1991) (This work appeared too late for use here.)

B. Levick, *Claudius* (1990)

V.M. Scramuzza, *The Emperor Claudius* (1940)

A. Momigliano, *Claudius: the emperor and his achievement* (rev. ed., 1961)

M.T. Griffin, *Nero: the end of a dynasty* (1984)

B.H. Warmington, *Nero: reality and legend* (1969)
K. Wellesley, *The Long Year A.D. 69* (2nd ed., 1989)
P.A.L. Greenhalgh, *The Year of the Four Emperors* (1975)

SEJANUS

D. Hennig, *L. Aelius Seianus* (1975, in German)
R. Seager, *Tiberius*, 178–223
B. Levick, *Tiberius the Politician*, 158–79
H.W. Bird, 'L. Aelius Sejanus and his political significance', *Latomus* 28 (1969),
    61–98
A. Boddington, 'Sejanus. Whose conspiracy?', *AJP* 84 (1963), 1–16
For Sejanus' supporters see R. Syme, *Tacitus* (1958), 402–06, 752–54; R. Syme,
    The Augustan Aristocracy (1986), ch. 22; R. Sealey, 'The political attachments
    of L. Aelius Sejanus', *Phoenix* 15 (1961), 97–114; G.V. Sumner, 'The family
    connections of L. Aelius Sejanus', *Phoenix* 19 (1965), 134–45.

C. ROMAN SOCIETY

GENERAL

P. Garnsey and R. Saller, *The Roman Empire: Economy, Society and Culture*
    (1987)
J.A. Crook, *Law and Life of Rome, 90 B.C.–A.D. 212* (1967)

SOCIAL RELATIONS

R. MacMullen, *Roman Social Relations* (1974)
R.P. Saller, *Personal Patronage under the Early Empire* (1982)
Patronage in Ancient Society (ed. A. Wallace-Hadrill, 1989)

THE FAMILY

J.A. Crook, *Law and Life*, 98–138
The Family in Ancient Rome: new perspectives (ed. B. Rawson, 1986), esp. ch. 1
S. Dixon, *The Roman Mother* (1987)
J.F. Gardner, *Women in Roman Law and Society* (1986)
S. Treggiari, *Roman Marriage: Iusti Coniuges from the time of Cicero to the time
    of Ulpian* (1991)
T.E.J. Wiedemann, *Adults and Children in the Roman Empire* (1989)

SLAVERY

K.R. Bradley, *Slaves and Masters in the Roman Empire: a study in social control*
    (rev. ed., 1987)
M.I. Finley, *Ancient Slavery and Modern Ideology* (1980)
K. Hopkins, *Conquerors and Slaves* (1978), ch. 1–2
S. Treggiari, *Roman Freedmen during the late Republic* (1969)
A.M. Duff, *Freedmen in the early Roman Empire* (1928)

ECONOMY

M.I. Finley, *The Ancient Economy* (rev. ed., 1985)

M. Rostovtzeff, *The Social and Economic History of the Roman Empire* (2nd ed., 1957)

A.H.M. Jones, *The Roman Economy* (ed. P.A. Brunt, 1974)

Trade in the Ancient Economy (ed. P. Garnsey, K. Hopkins, C.R. Whittaker, 1983)

K.D. White, *Roman Farming* (1970)

K. Greene, *The Archaeology of the Roman Economy* (1986)

DAILY LIFE

J.P.V.D. Balsdon, *Life and Leisure in Ancient Rome* (1969)

J. Carcopino, *Daily Life in Ancient Rome* (1940)

P. Veyne (ed.), *A History of Private Life. I. From Pagan Rome to Byzantium* (1987)

J.E. Stambaugh, *The Ancient Roman City* (1988), ch. 6–14

EDUCATION AND LITERACY

W.V. Harris, *Ancient Literacy* (1989)

S.F. Bonner, *Education in Ancient Rome* (1977)

M.L. Clarke, *Higher Education in the Ancient World* (1971)

H.I. Marrou, *A History of Education in Antiquity* (1956)

G. Kennedy, *The Art of Rhetoric in the Roman World* (1972)

ART AND ARCHITECTURE

R. Bianchi Bandinelli, *Rome. The centre of power: Roman art to A.D. 200* (1970)

D. Strong, *Roman Art* (rev. ed., 1988)

F. Sear, *Roman Architecture* (1982)

J.B. Ward-Perkins, *Roman Imperial Architecture* (rev. ed., 1981)

For the buildings of the city of Rome see E. Nash, *Pictorial Dictionary of Ancient Rome* (rev. ed., 2 vols., 1968); F. Coarelli, *Guida archeologica di Roma* (3rd ed., 1980).

RELIGION

R.M. Ogilvie, *The Romans and their Gods in the Age of Augustus* (1969)

J.H.W.G. Liebeschuetz, *Continuity and Change in Roman Religion* (1979)

Pagan Priests: Religion and Power in the ancient world (ed. M. Beard and J.A. North) (1990), esp. chs 6–9

S.R.F. Price, *Rituals and Power: the Roman imperial cult in Asia Minor* (1984)

D. Fishwick, *The Imperial Cult in the Latin West* (2 vols., 1987)

PUBLIC ENTERTAINMENTS (LUDI)

L. Friedländer, *Roman Life and Manners* (7th ed., Engl. tr., 1908), II, 1–130

J.P.V.D. Balsdon, *Life and Leisure in Ancient Rome*, 244–339

P. Veyne, *Bread and Circuses* (Engl. tr., 1990), 292–419

For gladiators see K. Hopkins, *Death and Renewal* (1983), 3–30; on chariot racing Alan Cameron, *Circus Factions* (1976), which, although focused on the late Empire, is more concerned with the social context of chariot-racing than J.H. Humphrey, *Roman Circuses: arenas for chariot racing* (1986), which concentrates on the physical remains and technology of racing; for drama in the early Empire see M. Bieber, *The History of the Greek and Roman Theater* (2nd ed., 1961), ch. 15.

THE EMPEROR

F. Millar, *The Emperor in the Roman World* (1977)
A. Wallace-Hadrill, 'Civilis Princeps: between citizen and king', *JRS* 72 (1982), 32–48
J.A. Crook, *Consilium Principis* (1955) (for his advisers)
P.R.C. Weaver, *Familia Caesaris* (1972) (on his household)
Z. Yavetz, *Plebs and Princeps* (1969)
J.B. Campbell, *The Emperor and the Roman Army* (1984)
A. Wallace-Hadrill, *Suetonius: the scholar and his Caesars* (1983)

THE SENATE

R.J.A. Talbert, *The Senate of Imperial Rome* (1984)
K. Hopkins and G. Burton, *Death and Renewal* (1983), 120–200 (on the changing social composition of the senatorial order)
F. Millar, *The Emperor in the Roman World*, 290–313, 341–55

THE EQUESTRIAN ORDER

S. Demougin, *L'ordre équestre sous les Julio-Claudiens* (1988)
T.P. Wiseman, 'The definition of "eques Romanus" in the late Republic and early Empire', *Historia* 19 (1970), 67–83
F. Millar, *The Emperor in the Roman World*, 83–101, 279–90
P.A. Brunt, 'Princeps and equites', *JRS* 73 (1983), 42–75
R.P. Saller, 'Patronage and promotion in equestrian careers', *JRS* 70 (1980), 44–63

POLITICS

R. Syme, *The Roman Revolution* (1939) and *Tacitus* (2 vols., 1958)
Roman Political Life 90 B.C.–A.D. 69 (ed. T.P. Wiseman, 1985), 45–68
R. MacMullen, *Enemies of the Roman Order* (1966), ch. 1 (on political opposition towards the emperor)
C. Wirszubski, *Libertas as a Political Idea at Rome during the late Republic and early Principate* (rev. ed., 1968)

THE ROMAN ARMY

L.J.F. Keppie, *The Making of the Roman Army* (1984) (on its development from Republic to Empire)
G.R. Webster, *The Roman Imperial Army* (3rd ed., 1985)

On conditions of service see G.R. Watson, *The Roman Soldier* (1969); R.W. Davies, *Service in the Roman Army* (ed. D. Breeze and V. Maxfield, 1989).

THE ROMAN EMPIRE: PROVINCES AND ADMINISTRATION

F. Millar, *The Roman Empire and its Neighbours* (2nd ed., 1981)

E.N. Luttwak, *The Grand Strategy of the Roman Empire* (1976)

J.S. Richardson, *Roman Provincial Administration* (1976)

The Administration of the Roman Empire: 241 B.C.–A.D. 193 (ed. D. Braund, 1988)

A.N. Sherwin-White, *The Roman Citizenship* (2nd ed., 1973)

A.N. Sherwin-White, *Roman Society and Roman Law in the New Testament* (1963)

On allied kings see D. Braund, *Rome and the Friendly King: the character of client kingship* (London, 1984); Luttwak, *Grand Strategy*, 30–40.

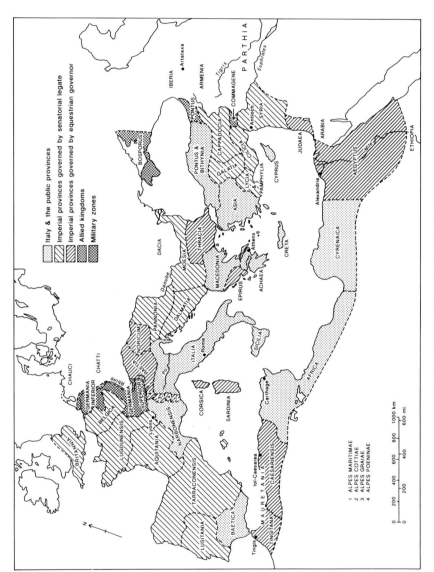

The Roman Empire in A.D. 46.

Italy & the public provinces

Imperial provinces governed by senatorial legate

Imperial provinces governed by equestrian governor

Allied kingdoms

Military zones

1 ALPES MARITIMAE
2 ALPES COTTIAE
3 ALPES GRAIAE
4 ALPES POENINAE

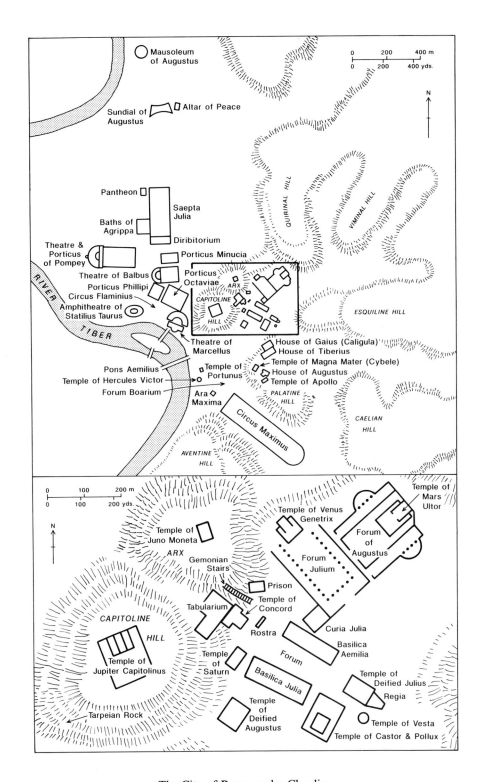

The City of Rome under Claudius.

INDICES

I. INDEX OF PERSONS
II. INDEX OF PLACES
III. INDEX OF SUBJECTS

Material from Dio's text is indexed by book, chapter and section numbers (e.g. "60.23.3"); material from the Historical Commentary is indexed in the form "60.23.3n." If material is found in both Dio's text and the commentary, it is indexed in the form "60.23.3 + n." Numbers in italics refer to page numbers of this edition.

I. INDEX OF PERSONS

(a) Roman emperors

Augustus 58.2.7n.; 58.3.1n.; 58.3.8n.;
   58.4.2n; 58.4.4n.; 58.7.4n.; 58.9.2–
   3nn.; 59.1.2n.; 59.2.2–3nn.;
   59.3.2n.; 59.3.4–5 + nn.; 59.3.7–
   8 + n.; 59.5.1; 59.7.1 + n.;
   59.7.4 + n.; 59.7.7–8 + n.; 59.9.4 + n;
   59.9.6n.; 59.12.2nn.; 59.17.3n.;
   59.20.1–2 + nn.; 59.22.7n.;
   59.25.1n.; 59.27.3 + n.; 59.28.1 + n.;
   60.1.1n.; 60.2.3; 60.3.3n.; 60.4.4n.;
   60.6.3; 60.7.3–4n.; 60.11.2n.;
   60.17.3n.; 60.18.3n.; 60.22.1n.;
   60.23.3; 60.23.6n.; 60.24.1–4nn.;
   63.8.2; 63.9.3n.; 63.13.3n.; 63.20.3;
   63.21.1n.; 63.22.6; 63.29.3 + n.
Caracalla 20; 27; 252; 60.17.5n.
Claudius 38; 52–53; 58.2.7n.; 58.3.8n.;
   58.11.5 + n.; 59.6.5–6 + n.; 59.15.5;
   59.23.2–5 + n.; 59.28.5; 60.1–28
   (passim); 63.12.2; 63.22.6 + n.
Commodus 252
Elagabalus 21; 28; 252
Gaius Caligula 52; 58.2.7n.; 58.7.4 + n.;
   58.8.1–2 + n.; 59.1–30 (passim);
   60.1.1–2; 60.3.2; 60.3.7; 60.4.1;
   60.6.3; 60.6.6 + n.;60.6.8 + n.;
   60.7.1 + n.; 60.8.1–2 + n.; 60.8.5–
   6nn.; 60.15.1; 60.17.2; 60.27.1n.;
   63.16.1n.
Galba 60.8.7 + n.; 63.23.1 + n.; 63.27.1–
   1a; 63.27.2b; 63.29.1
Macrinus 20–21; 28; 252; 58.5.1n.
Marcus Aurelius 24; 252
Nero 53–54; 58.2.7n; 60.6.3n.; 63.1–29
   (passim)

Pertinax 19; 252
Septimius Severus 19–20; 26–28; 252;
   58.5.1n.
Severus Alexander 21–22; 27; 252
Tiberius 37–38; 51; 58.2.7–12.1
   (passim); 59.1; 59.2.3n.; 59.2.5n.;
   59.3.2n.; 59.3.6n.; 59.3.7–8 + nn.;
   59.4.1–2; 59.4.6n.; 59.5.1–2 + nn.;
   59.6.2–3 + n.; 59.6.7; 59.7.1n.;
   59.7.7; 59.8.1–2 + nn.; 59.9.4;
   59.9.6 + n.; 59.11.1n.; 59.12.2nn.;
   59.14.3n.; 59.15.1; 59.15.2n.;
   59.15.3; 59.16.1–7 + nn.; 59.17.1n.;
   59.18.1–2nn.; 59.19.1; 59.20.1n.;
   59.20.5; 59.22.6–7nn.; 59.23.4n.;
   59.27.3n.; 59.28.1 + n.; 60.1.2–3n.;
   60.2.3 + n.; 60.3.2n.; 60.3.6n.;
   60.3.7; 60.4.3; 60.6.3 + n.; 60.6.6n.;
   60.6.8 + n.; 60.23.6n.; 60.24.1n.;
   60.24.4n.; 60.27.5n.
Vespasian 59.12.3 + n.; 60.3.3 + n.;
   60.20.3 + n.; 63.11.1n.; 63.22.1a

(b) Other members of the Imperial family

Aelia Paetina, wife of Claudius 60.8.4–
   5n.; 60.21.5n.
M. Agrippa: see M. Vipsanius Agrippa
Agrippina, wife of Germanicus: see
   Vipsania Agrippina
Antonia, mother of Claudius 58.2.7n.;
   58.6.4n.; 58.11.7 + n.; 59.3.3–
   6 + nn.; 59.8.2n.; 59.20.2n.;
   60.2.5 + n.
Britannicus, son of Claudius 60.17.3n.;
   60.17.9 + n.; 60.22.2 + n.

(c) Other Persons

(d) Gods and Goddesses

II. INDEX OF PLACES

III. INDEX OF SUBJECTS

NOTES

NOTES

NOTES

NOTES

NOTES